CONTEMPORARY
PERSONNEL
MANAGEMENT

a reader on human resources

MICHAEL T. MATTESON
ROGER N. BLAKENEY
DONALD R. DOMM

CANFIELD PRESS SAN FRANCISCO

A Department of Harper & Row, Publishers, Inc.

New York • Evanston • London

CONTEMPORARY PERSONNEL MANAGEMENT:
A READER ON HUMAN RESOURCES

Standard Book Number: 06-385386-8

Library of Congress Catalog Card Number: 71-172166

72   73   74 75   10   9   8 7 6 5 4 3 2 1

46640

CONTENTS

PART ONE: The Personnel Management System   1

The Personnel Job in a Changing Business Environment, HENRY E. THIEL   3
A Systems Approach to Personnel Management, THOMAS W. GILL   14
Interface Between Personnel and Organizational Psychology,
    BERNARD M. BASS   17

PART TWO: Acquiring Human Resources   27

MANPOWER PLANNING

Manpower—Today's Frontier, FRANK H. CASSELL   29
The Nature of Long Range Manpower Planning, ERIC W. VETTER   36
The Growing Role of Manpower Forecasting in Organizations,
    RICHARD B. PETERSON   48
Planning for a Personnel Reduction, THOMAS H. SEBRING   56
Job Analysis: National Survey Findings, JEAN J. JONES, JR.,
    and THOMAS A. DE COTHS   62

MANPOWER PROCUREMENT

A Behavioral Science Approach to Personnel Selection, EVERETT G. DILLMAN 67
Decision Models for Personnel Selection and Assignment, LAWRENCE J. CLARKE 78
A Case Study in Effective Recruitment, STEPHEN GOULD   87
Uses and Misuses of Tests in Selecting Key Personnel, HERBERT H. MEYER
    and JOSEPH M. BERTOTTI   92
What Does the Selection Interview Accomplish? CALVIN W. DOWNS   99

PART THREE: Developing Human Resources   105

A Systems Approach to Orientation, OTIS LIPSTREU   106
The Application of Behavioral Science Theory to Professional Development,
    GEORGE P. HUBER   113
Management Development: A Systems View, PAUL S. GREENLAW   122
Guidelines for the Design of New Careers, SIDNEY FINE   128
SET: A Skill-Element Approach to Job Training Under Uncertainty,
    RAYMOND C. HELWIG   143

PART FOUR: Performance Monitoring Processes   151

*A Study of Factors Relating to the Effectiveness of a Performance
    Appraisal Program*, HERBERT H. MEYER, and WILLIAM B. WALKER   153

Assessing the Performance of Key Managers, CHARLES L. HUGHES   158

The Dollar Criterion—Applying the Cost Accounting Concept to Criterion Construction, H. E. BROGDEN and E. K. TAYLOR   162

PART FIVE: Rewards   175

Toward a Behavioral Science Theory of Wages, DAVID W. BELCHER   177

Wage Inequities, Productivity and Work Quality, J. STACY ADAMS   190

Perceptions Regarding Management Compensation, EDWARD LAWLER III and LYMAN W. PORTER   196

Career Mobility and Organizational Commitment, OSCAR GRUSKY   202

PART SIX: Feedback Processes   213

Validity of Exit Interviews, JOEL LEFKOWITZ and MYRON L. KATZ   214

Union-Management Relations: From Conflict to Collaboration, ROBERT R. BLAKE and JANE S. MOUTON   231

Handling Grievances Where There Is No Union, ROBERT E. SIBSON   231

PART SEVEN: Special Topics   235

EDP APPLICATIONS

How EDP Is Improving the Personnel Function, RICHARD T. BUESCHEL   237

EDP: A Management Recruiting Tool, R.H. HAWK and G.A. BASSETT   242

CIVIL RIGHTS AND EMPLOYMENT

The Impact of the Civil Rights Act on Employment Policies and Programs, FRED LUTHANS   245

Building Groundwork for Affirmative Action EEO Program, DEAN B. PESKIN   250

A Hidden Issue in Minority Employment, RICHARD ALAN GOODMAN   260

Paycheck and Apron—Revolution in Womanpower, ELI GINZBERG   265

ENVIRONMENTAL QUALITY

The Office Landscape: A "Systems" Concept, HANS J. LORENZEN and DIETER JAEGER   275

Industry's Role in Mental Health, PAT GREATHOUSE   283

COUNTER-PRODUCTIVE BEHAVIORS

The Unsatisfactory Performer: Salvage or Discharge? LAWRENCE L. STEINMETZ   289

Industry's $2-Billion Headache—The Problem Drinker, RICHARD E. DUTTON   295

Managing the Drug User, ROBERT J. FIRENZE and STEVEN K. KLEIN   299

Young Drug Users and the "Value Gap," PAUL W. PRETZEL   307

PART EIGHT: A Look at the Future   311

The Personnel Function in Tomorrow's Company, FRANK E. FISCHER   312

Reorganize the Personnel Department? STANLEY L. SOKOLIK   318

PREFACE

The personnel function in today's organizations is changing. This change is taking place on at least two fronts. One involves the application of new techniques, theories and approaches to the classical areas within personnel's domain (hiring, firing, wage and salary administration, training, etc). The other involves a thrust in new directions, made necessary by changes in the larger environment of the organization (civil rights, affirmative action, drug abuse, etc).

This book, edited for students as well as professionals, contains selections relevant to both types of changes. From the widely scattered literature on personnel management, we have attempted to bring together those articles which address themselves to redefinitions of traditional functions and to emerging areas or problems. For this reason, most of the articles are recent. Two-thirds were written in the last five years; only five were written prior to 1960.

The personnel function is a *process*. In recent years, much attention has been directed toward the *systems approach* as one meaningful way of looking at processes. Many of the selections in this book reflect this emphasis. But in the final analysis, the personnel function is about *people*. Thus, the reader will find most of the selections have a definite behavioral orientation. Basically, then, our approach in selecting articles for this book has been to recognize the important traditional functions, borrow heavily from the behavioral approach and utilize the systems concept to provide a framework for the personnel process. Our goal has been to assemble a coherent and relevant selection of readings.

The book is arranged in sections which will reasonably parallel most texts in personnel management. The rigor of the articles is such that third- and fourth-year college students will experience little difficulty in following and understanding the content. While previous exposure to management courses is desirable, the readings do not require such experience.

Our deepest appreciation goes to our friends and colleagues who offered us many valuable suggestions. We are particularly grateful for the cooperation of the publishers and authors who have granted us permission to use their materials.

MTM
RNB
DRD

PART ONE

THE PERSONNEL
MANAGEMENT SYSTEM

The purpose of this section is to provide the reader with an overview of the scope and direction of personnel management activities, as well as the relationship of these activities to other organizational endeavors.

We have referred to the personnel management function as a "system." A system may be defined as a set of objects or components together with the relationships between these objects or components. One important characteristic of a system, then, is an organized integration of parts into some whole. This type of systematic perspective is critical to personnel management. Too often, attention of personnel departments has been directed toward performance of various important but non-integrated functions in a process largely responding to pressure. If this "disintegrated" approach is to be replaced, it will occur only through new perspectives and systems, not through projections of the old. The human resource function of personnel management must be perceived as an integrated effort with numerous interrelated activities and outcomes.

The articles in this section have been selected with the view in mind of not only delineating personnel functions, but of demonstrating the interrelationships of these functions with each other and with other organizational activities.

The first article, "The Personnel Job in a Changing Business Environment," explores the various activities of personnel and discusses how the nature of these activities have both affected, and been affected by, societal and technological changes taking place in the business environment. The need for greater flexibility and receptivity to change on the part of personnel administrators is stressed.

The second article, "A Systems Approach to Personnel Management," describes personnel as being at the crossroads between chaos and the systems approach. As machines take over the routine clerical work of the personnel department, the personnel administrator must perform more sophisticated tasks, such as preparing job descriptions and making forecasts, and in so doing may well help determine the organization of the future.

The final article in this section, "Interface Between Personnel and Organizational Psychology," provides a behavioral perspective for viewing the organization of the personnel function. The first part of the article delineates the importance of organizational considerations to personnel in the areas of recruiting, selection, training, and job design. The second part deals with the converse: the importance of personnel considerations to the organization in dealing with problems of morale, supervision, teamwork, organizational design, and conflict resolution.

THE PERSONNEL JOB
IN A CHANGING
BUSINESS ENVIRONMENT

Henry E. Thiel

Not long ago I heard a fellow remark, "The Personnel Department's job is to look after the employees' problems, isn't it? Well, it can't be too tough nowadays—because the only problems employees have are how to keep from getting fat, and where to park their Cadillacs!" Even noted management consultants think personnel types are fair game. Peter Drucker has been quoted as saying that personnel men are "partly file clerks, partly housekeepers, partly social workers, and partly fire fighters heading off union trouble." Others have characterized personnel executives as hail fellows well met, trying to keep everybody happy by administering a variety of employee benefits and handouts.

I may be asked to turn in my Personnel Association badge for saying so, but I believe that opinions such as Drucker's *were founded* on more truth than fiction. However, I'd like to qualify that confession by pointing out that I use the past tense "were founded" purposely, for I believe that there has been a tremendous change in the attitude and character of personnel administrators in recent years. We are beginning to confront our problems head-on and are beginning to get away from fixed positions and static thinking.

Personnel administrators will have to admit that they have been jarred out of the comfort of their previous postures by the technological typhoon that has descended upon the business world. The havoc created in our environment by the accelerating pace of information technology and automation

From Henry Thiel, "The Personnel Job," AMS Professional Management Bulletin 7, 1–15 (July 1966). Reprinted by permission.

has battered us out of our complacency into full realization that there is a challenging and rewarding job to be done.

The business world we are in today is a new world. A world where young engineers, still wet behind the ears, are experts in fields that were the subject of Buck Rogers stories ten years ago. A world where computer technology is being applied to everyday business problems and solving in a matter of minutes what previously took days or weeks or months.

In our business we've found that interviewing techniques designed for stenos and clerks don't work too well for Ph.D.'s. We've found that the old benefit plans don't satisfy employees who feel that automation is threatening their security. We've found that our bargaining table approach isn't as effective when there are white collar workers on the other side of the table instead of blue collar workers. We've found that the old concepts of supervision and management just don't work any more. We've found that it's imperative to get into the swim of things or drown—and we've remodelled, and rebuilt, and a new breed of personnel administrators is emerging.

The purpose of this presentation is to examine the various aspects of the personnel function in the light of the business setting as it now exists, to see if we can detect what progress has been made, and to analyze our previous interpretations of the personnel department's contribution. Although this may be a dangerous game I'm playing, I address myself to it with enthusiasm because I'm convinced that a periodic appraisal by every profession is necessary to ensure that it is making a maximum contribution to the organization it serves.

As we review the specific items in the personnel "grab-bag," I will try to present an overview of trends and practices rather than present my own ideas, the ideas of my company, or any particular industry or region.

EMPLOYMENT

One of the traditional roles of the personnel department has been that of employment. In fact, I suspect that this task may have been the one that originated personnel departments as such. I can hear the harried manager saying, "Let's get some one to talk to these blankety blank people who are coming around looking for jobs. My time's too valuable to waste on things like this!" And so they assigned the job to some purchasing agent or accountant and the personnel department was born.

The early concept of employment was a rather crude one. The person who did the job was usually chosen because he liked people. Because of his heartfelt sympathy, he felt he was a good judge of people. His technique was rather simple—he sat the applicant down and they had a real heart-to-heart talk—then the judgment was made by instinct. I'd think it would be accurate to say that it wasn't much more than a "seat of the pants" judgment.

Compare that type of approach with the one we know today. First of all we substitute the purchasing agent for a man who invariably has a degree, (probably in some field of business or in psychology) and who is given considerable training in interviewing techniques. In his bag of tricks he has such things as:

1. Aptitude and ability tests.
2. Intelligence tests.
3. Personality and attitude tests.
4. Reference checking systems.
5. Performance appraisal reports.
6. Manpower planning forecasts.
7. Assistance from Employee Appraisal Consultants where necessary.

In prior years the employment officer's report to the supervisor was usually not much more than a few words stating "This looks like a good bet, Joe." Compare that with the following analysis you might receive.

"We have administered personnel classification tests Alpha and Beta to the above named subject, including sub-tests in both verbal and numerical categories. His standard score based on the Stanine ratings indicates abnormal intelligence. Moreover, a computation of his percentiles shows his scores considerably above the arithmetical mean based on norms comprising applicants applying for similar work, with comparable education, and in the same age group. It should of course be recognized that this is an objective evaluation, applying only to the subject's aptitude or capacity for work and not to his personality or motivational factors, which are not measured by this type of test."

Need For More Highly Skilled People

If we analyze this dramatic revolution in the employment area to determine what has caused the change we will undoubtedly come to the conclusion that it has been brought about by technological change. Our businesses are more complex—so we need more highly educated, more highly skilled people. Whereas we previously established educational prerequisites of Grade 10 or Grade 11, we are now demanding R.I.A.'s, C.A.'s and university graduates. In fact it's not uncommon for the personnel administrator to have Ph.D.'s waiting in the reception room.

And it's no longer a case of taking the load off the supervisor's back and shooing away bothersome applicants. It's now a question of hunting for prospective candidates for certain jobs. As a consequence the employment man has had to get his feet off the desk and hit the road. By that I mean he now doubles-in-brass as a university recruitment expert.

University recruitment has become big business. The competition for the technically trained university graduate is such that companies have developed elaborate programs to lure good men from universities all over North America. There are companies in

Canada and United States who regularly recruit in the United Kingdom and Europe.

There has been a material change in the employment function. The changing manpower needs in business have brought about startling conversion—from an odd job filled by a fellow with not much more than sympathy for people—to a responsible position requiring technical knowledge, analytical ability, and an appreciation for good public relations.

WAGE AND SALARY ADMINISTRATION

How about the area of wage and salary administration? What developments have occurred in this area?

Until recently wage and salary administrators have concerned themselves mainly with techniques and with policy. It was assumed that the function of the wage and salary administrator was to relate (a) individual performance to (b) job worth to (c) market forces, and then juggling these three balls, arrive at a proper wage or salary. To assist in this juggling process and to keep things neat and orderly, techniques were developed such as the factor comparison system which evaluated job worth by awarding points for each factor associated with any job position. This enabled the wage and salary administrator to coordinate and co-relate compensation throughout the various operations of the company.

In this role the wage and salary administrator tended to become a policeman. Instead of viewing his function as one of helping the manager to accomplish the purposes of the organization, he saw himself as a man with his back to the wall of the corporate treasury with a single weapon to protect it—a baseball bat. Instead of perceiving himself as a trainer and innovator, he acquired police power and exercised control by approval. In this role he was looked upon as a bureaucrat in the worst sense of the word.

Recently there has been a move by wage and salary administrators to focus less attention to policing and more attention on devising new compensation plans that will produce stimulus for greater productivity. This trend may have been prompted, to some degree, by the research work of behavioral scientists such as Herzberg, Maslow, and others. These men have questioned the motivating power of the salary scheme as presently in effect.

Herzberg formulated a theory of motivation based on a dissatisfiers evaluation concept. He postulates that dissatisfiers are factors that, if lacking or deficient, can reduce employee motivation; on the other hand, regardless of how much they are improved, they don't seem to improve job performance beyond the neutral point. Along with pay, such factors are supervision, interpersonal relations, working conditions, company policy, benefits, and job security were found to fall into this group.

Herzberg believes that satisfiers or achievement factors, as he calls them, are related to success in work and industrial growth and will continuously motivate people to better performance. In this category he includes improvements in the nature of the work itself, increased responsibility and advancement. If pay is geared to achievement and serves as recognition of achievement it would seem to be an achievement factor and thus motivator. It is when pay is unrelated to performance that it serves purely as a maintenance factor.

In the past, I believe, to a great extent we used compensation as a maintenance factor in that we did not adequately tie it to performance. We paid lip service to the merit increase philosophy which provides for increases based on performance. But all too often that was a facade and our employees knew it. We were granting merit increases which closely resembled the amount of an industry wage pattern, and the employee who received the increase, with the customary letter of congratulations, recognized it for what it was—his share of the cost of living increase package being dealt out to the greater proportion of his fellow workers. It had very little, if anything, to do with his performance.

Merit Allotment Divided With Staff

Many supervisors take their merit allotment and divide it amongst their staff because they know that these are the only funds to be apportioned and nearly everyone should get some of it; not necessarily because of performance but for a variety of compassionate reasons—because Joe has a very large family, or Pete is badly in debt, or Mike's wife just had an operation, or because Dick was bothering him about money and this should serve to shut him up.

We are slowly recognizing that no value is derived from this method of granting salary increases and we are now shifting away from long established practices. Where economic increases are granted, the trend is to grant them to the majority of employees and to present them as such. Merit increases, on the other hand, are and should be limited to those who have performed well. In this concept at least, the dollars spent on merit become satisfiers or achievement factors in Herzberg's concept and do motivate people to perform for reward.

To assist management in the proper administration of salaries and wages, new techniques and devices are being developed. One device being used to some extent is graphic projection of the salaries of various calibre employees. If properly related to job evaluation it can become a most useful tool.

There is also some honest research being applied now in the area of remuneration for hourly paid personnel. The question here is can hourly paid people be motivated to better effort and be given greater dignity by putting them on salary? The mere conversion of hourly wage rates to the salaried equivalent, although sometimes beneficial, is only a tiny step in the direction some people are contemplating. There are those who are seriously considering a wholesale move whereby employees traditionally paid on an hourly basis will be converted to a full scale salary plan with accompanying provision for merit consideration, abolition of overtime pay, abolition of shift differential, etc.

BENEFITS

There was a time not many years ago, when an employee's compensation consisted solely and entirely of wages or salaries and the employee benefits package amounted to little more than a life insurance scheme. Today, however, the benefits package may include: Pension Plan, Medical Plan, Self-Improvement Plan, Savings Plan, Sick Leave Plan, Scholarship Plan, Hospital Plan, Life Insurance Plan, Travel Insurance Plan, etc.

These benefits may cost the average corporation something in the neighborhood of 20% of the total salary budget and the administration of the benefits package has become a complex and time-consuming proposition. This assignment, invariably, has been given to the personnel department and has resulted in the creation of another personnel speciality and, I guess, is the reason why we have been accused of molly-coddling employees and giving the company away.

There is no doubt in my mind that this addition to the personnel department's assortment of odd jobs is the most significant change in many years. Our society has become more and more security conscious and it is not at all unusual to find an applicant for employment more interested in the benefits a company provides than in the salary it is willing to pay.

The most recent development in corporate benefits coverage is the introduction of a group insurance plan called a "salary continuance plan." Under a salary continuance plan protection is provided to any employee who becomes totally disabled and unable to provide for himself and his family. In group plans now in existence, an employee can collect, as long as he is unable to work, a payment approximately equivalent to one-half of his salary. This payment usually commences after the company's sick leave pay runs out and terminates at retirement age when retirement benefits take over. It is not expensive coverage which, in part, accounts for its rapidly growing acceptance by firms on a voluntary basis.

Automation is making its presence felt in the benefits area as it is in most other areas, and one result is the gradual evolvement of "early retirement provisions." These provisions usually apply to employees who have reached a minimum age of 50 or 55 and who have 15 or more years of service. Some firms use a numbers game approach whereby any combination of age and years' service which adds up to, let's say, 80 is eligible for retirement. (Example: 50 years of age and 30 years' service). Those that qualify are then given pension benefits commencing immediately at income levels that they normally would not be entitled to until regular retirement age.

There are many variations and innovations in this area covering voluntary retirement at employee option, voluntary retirement with company approval, retirement due to ill health, retirement at company option because the employee is surplus, and so on. The employees are keen to see developments in this area as they stand to gain and corporations benefit as it allows them to prune the corporate tree in such a way that older members can be removed rather than remove or stunt the growth of the young and vigorous buds.

The entry of government into the benefits area has made the personnel administrator's task a more complex one, and has caused a few grey hairs in some quarters. At the present time in Canada we are faced with the complex problem of integrating our Company Pension Plan with the Canadian Pension Plan which went into effect January, 1966. It is a matter that will not be resolved easily and it will be even more difficult in provinces such as Ontario where there is a provincial plan to contend with as well.

To add to the disarray, it is quite apparent that trade unions have noted with some degree of satisfaction the extent of employee interest in benefit plans. They are exerting more and more pressure in this area as they know that gains in benefits are as good as direct wage increases and will win them much favour with their constituents. They are not unmindful, either, of government's sympathy in these areas and there is a continual lobbying by pro-labour members to win benefits gains through legislation.

As a result of these factors, personnel administrators, through their benefits specialists, must be alert to determine the pro's and con's of any extension to the benefits package. They need the combined talents of an actuary, insurance specialist, financial wizard, and politician to examine the whys and wherefores, to weigh possible future changes in costs, to anticipate pitfalls etc., in order to ensure the wisest use of a corporation's benefits dollar.

LABOUR RELATIONS

In the field of labour relations, it is absolutely essential that management be well informed and fully cognizant of the goals, objectives, and probable strategies of all those involved in the bargaining process. This is one of the assignments which falls to the lot of the personnel administrator and his staff.

Unfortunately it is not all that simple to analyze the collective bargaining climate. First of all, who is involved in the bargaining process? I posed this question to a group that I was addressing not too long ago. To them the answer was simple: management and the union were the two participants. They agreed, after some discussion, however, that perhaps employees as such should be considered separately, as they did not always react exactly as their union wanted them to, even though the union was their spokesman. They agreed that basically an employee's motivation was "self-preservation" while the union was motivated by the need for "self-perpetuation." They also agreed that the demands that would flow from these two different motivations could be vastly different.

The forces involved in collective bargaining have materially changed in recent years and a new party to collective bargaining has emerged, namely government. In my view, a diagram of the active labour relations participants would show a triangle with the employee as one corner of the triangle, the union as another corner of the triangle, and government as the third corner of the triangle. In the centre of the triangle would be a circle which would represent the company or corporation. The three corners of the triangle would all be shown to be exerting pressure inward on the corporate circle.

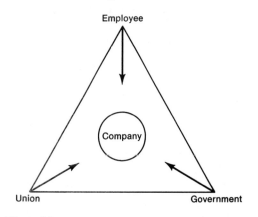

Figure 1.1

This emergence of various governments as major factors in the negotiating process is one of the most significant developments in the field of labour relations in recent years. Examples of the influence that can be and has been exercised by governmental bodies is illustrated by:

(1) Recent labour legislation in both United States and Canada and the growing power of quasi-judicial bodies such as the National Labour Relations Board and the Boards of Industrial Relations.

(2) The active participation by Labour Ministers Goldberg and Wirtz in the U.S. steel strike and the Dock Workers' strike.

(3) The recent decision by the Federal and Provincial Governments to legislate Statutory Holidays.

There are any number of examples of a similar type which testify to the increased government involvement in matters previously reserved to direct negotiation between the company and employees or between the company and a union.

You might ask—what's the matter with the government taking a hand to protect the public interest? For one thing, labour unions are now using a whipsaw approach to bargaining by winning some gains from companies at the bargaining table and by lobbying for the remainder through government legislation. Companies must, therefore, be continually on guard to ensure that demands granted to the bargaining table may not become monstrously expensive when coupled with future government legislation.

Let's take for example a company who makes a trade with a union in which it agrees to a sizeable wage increase in exchange for a union's promise not to demand statutory holiday pay—only to find that it is forced to pay holiday pay as well, because its union, in conjunction with other unions, has successfully lobbied for statutory holiday legislation.

Fear Of Job Loss To Automation

Another development that has affected considerable impact in the collective bargaining arena is the fear of job loss due to automation. I am not at all convinced that this fear is justified, but that's beside the point. As long as employees consider it a threat to their employment, automation will engender the type of bargaining demands we are receiving today. Among these are demands for guaranteed employment for life, job retraining, restrictions on lay-off, longer vacations, etc.

Aside from the effect on the nature of bargaining demands, there is the effect it has had on white collar workers. For the first time in history there is a genuine fear that white collar workers are sufficiently concerned about job security that they will seek the protection of collective bargaining. The number of certifications of office workers is not as large as some people believe, but nonetheless there is a discernible growth. Should it mushroom, it will pose many additional problems for both personnel people and administrators.

To counteract some of these new influences, new approaches to collective bargaining have been developed. The most significant development, perhaps, is the establishment and utilization of Human Rights Committees. These committees consist of high level representation from both management and labour who meet year around in an attempt to iron out their problems. They were conceived out of the belief that it is better to negotiate in an atmosphere where no contract deadline or strike deadline is hanging over the head of the participants. It is a device to avoid crisis bargaining. It has also been prompted by the realization that if management and labour commence bargaining one to two months before contract termination, invariably a crisis situation will develop, government intervention will ensue, and after conciliation, arbitration, etc., compromise solutions will be inflicted on the parties with little benefit to either.

From these Human Rights Committees have come such developments as profit sharing schemes (such as at Kaiser Steel in the U.S.) sabbatical vacation plans, early retirement plans, etc. They have been particularly effective in solving problems of great complexity where long periods of time and discussion are required in order to fully acquaint all with the ramifications and implications.

There are many other labour relations trends; some negative, some positive, some important, some not important, but all adding their small part to that thing called growth. In this particular area, nothing remains static. Some people would like to cling to fixed positions and maintain the status quo but this can cost you dearly at the bargaining table. Procrastination and inflexibility have a high price tag in the area of collective bargaining.

MANAGEMENT DEVELOPMENT

There are many other areas which fall into the personnel administrator's field of interest which I have not mentioned which have also seen interesting developments in recent years. For instance, there is the matter of university recruitment, which I touched on briefly.

There is also the subject of accident prevention which has seen revolutionary change in basic philosophy. No longer is it considered a necessary evil to be dropped in the lap of the fall guy known as the "safety man." It is a piece of business worthy of top management attention and line responsibility supplemented by an accident prevention staff specialist.

There is the matter of performance appraisal which has come under close scrutiny and now is more related to review of future objectives and employee-supervisor planning to meet needs, rather than a supervisor's denunciation of past faults rendered from on high.

These and other areas could be discussed in some detail; however, I'm going to sidestep them in favour of a subject in the personnel administrator's area of interest that I feel is of major importance today and one that has become tremendously exciting. It could pay wonderful dividends to a corporation that can reap its benefits. It is variously referred to as management development, management theory, management training, etc.

In the era of technological revolution in which we find ourselves today, the greatest challenge to profit conscious executives is "How to turn managers into a team—a group of men who work well and enthusiastically with one another, who pull for the company and not merely each for himself? How can they be led to understand their point, as well as their individual, functions in the enterprise so that responsibility is best met and authority most effectively exercised? And how, finally, can this be done in terms of managerial control in the carrying out of company plans and policies?"

The concern shown by management today regarding these questions indicates a growing awareness that the authority—obedience concept that was so effectively utilized by entrepreneurs in the past is no longer an effective stimulant to greater efficiency, profit, and growth. Today's manager, whether the head of a huge corporation or the supervisor of eight delivery men, is learning that the power of coercion eventually causes conflict, apathy, and resistance. As a result the customary methods of training supervisors and management personnel has come under careful scrutiny and many of the basic assumptions about employee behavior and interests have been seriously questioned.

The late Douglas McGregor, former professor at the School of Industrial Management at M.I.T., recognizing that behind every management decision or action are assumptions about human nature and human behavior, set out to examine these assumptions in the light of current social science knowledge.

Theory X. He reviewed the assumptions upon which the traditional organizations are based and which appear inadequate for the full utilization of human potentialities. He called this Theory X. Behind this theory he found a deep-rooted belief that:

(1) The average human being has an inherent dislike of work.

(2) Most people must be coerced, con-
trolled, directed, threatened with punishment to get them to put forth adequate effort.

(3) The average human being prefers to be directed, wishes to avoid responsibility, has relatively little ambition, wants security above all.

Theory Y. McGregor then developed a new theory called Theory Y which embodied assumptions consistent with current research knowledge which could lead to higher motivation and greater realization of both individual and organizational goals. The basic assumptions that he sets out for Theory Y are:

(1) The expenditure of physical and mental effort in work is as natural as in play or rest.

(2) External control and the threat of punishment are not the only means for bringing about effort toward organizational objectives. Man will exercise self-direction and self-control in the service of objectives to which he is committed.

(3) Commitment to objectives is a function of the rewards associated with their achievement.

(4) The average human being learns, under proper conditions, not only to accept but to seek responsibility.

(5) The capacity to exercise a relatively high degree of imagination, ingenuity, and creativity in the solution of organizational problems is widely, not narrowly, distributed in the population.

(6) Under the conditions of modern industrial life, the intellectual potentialities of the average human being are only partially utilized.

Non-Linear Systems Experiment

One particular experiment conducted in California does add validity to theories such as McGregor's. The particular experiment was conducted at Non-Linear Systems Inc. in San

Diego, California. Non-Linear Systems was a typical manufacturing plant producing digital volt meters. It had the traditional, highly regimented assembly line process, time clocks, and myriad of rules and regulations for employee control. However, management was talked into doing away with assembly lines, time clocks, and tight employee control in favour of small production teams. Each team was allowed to run its own business in its own way. Each employee, instead of monotonously installing one small part to every unit when it went past on the assembly line, assembled the entire complex instrument. If the unit was faulty in any way it was returned to its original builder for repair.

The results achieved from this somewhat idealistic experiment were astounding. The man hours of production per unit were cut in half. Sales were doubled in the first three years. Efficiency was greatly improved. Morale became excellent. Turnover was reduced to one-quarter the national average. Customer complaints dropped off by 90%. Employee skills were developed tremendously.

Practical experiments of this type have resulted in a wholesale re-examination of long held assumptions about human behavior. The Non-Linear Systems experiment illustrates the results that can flow from creating job satisfaction for employees.

Dr. Robert Blake and Dr. Jane Mouton, both from The University of Texas, have developed significant innovations in regard to a slightly different problem—the question of team effort in industry. They have developed training labs designed to illustrate that managers should and can use a team approach effectively in business effort. The overall philosophy is based on the proposition that a modern manager really has two principal concerns in operating his enterprise. One is the concern for production and its many facets and the other is the concern for people with all its complications.

Blake and Mouton believe that any manager's style can be assessed by examining the degree of concern he has for production and the degree of concern he has for people. To accomplish this they have developed a graph.[1] The horizontal axis represents concern for production and is graduated numerically from 1 to 9. The vertical axis of the graph represents concern for people and is also marked 1 to 9. If you have a maximum concern for people and a maximum concern for production, Blake and Mouton state that you have a 9-9 managerial style. If you have a low concern for people and a high concern for production, then you will be what they term a 9-1 managerial style, and so on.

At Blake's Management Grid Seminars, groups of eight or nine men are formed. Usually there will be eight or ten of these groups and each will be assigned a task each morning which requires numerous group decisions. Each evening, at a joint session, all groups come together and the effectiveness of each group answer is analyzed and charted against the effectiveness of the various individuals in each group and also as against the effectiveness of other groups who are handling the identical problem. Day by day the same problem solving action is undertaken and effectiveness is charted and analyzed.

The three basic objectives of this group exercise are:

(1) To develop an awareness that group action can result in better decisions than that of any individual member of the group.

(2) To develop methods of gaining group participation and effort through actual experience.

(3) To give each participant a better appreciation of his managerial style and how he really projects to his employees or fellow

[1]For complete exposition of the Managerial Grid, see *Advanced Management-Office Executive,* p. 12 (September 1962).

THE MANAGERIAL GRID

CONCERN FOR PEOPLE

9	Country Club Management—(1,9)					Team Management—(9,9)		
8	Production is incidental to lack of conflict and "good fellowship."					Production is from integration of task and human requirements.		
7								
6				Dampened Pendulum—(5,5)				
5	Impoverished Management—(1,1)			(Middle of the Road) Push for production but don't go "all out." Give some, but not all. "Be fair but firm."				
4	Effective production is unobtainable because people are lazy, apathetic							
3	and indifferent. Sound and mature relationships					Task Management—(9,1)		
2	are difficult to achieve because human					Men are a commodity just as machines. A manager's responsibility is to plan,		
1	nature's being what it is, conflict is inevitable.					direct and control the work of those subordinate to him.		
	1	2	3	4	5	6	7	8	9

CONCERN FOR PRODUCTION

managers as opposed to how he thought he projected.

Acquire an Understanding of Human Behavior

The significance of all of this adult game playing is that it shows up the weakness inherent in the autocratic, authority-obedience concept, and develops growing recognition that many of the programs of management training that we utilized in the past have limited value. Further, it develops recognition for the fact that it is better to first acquire an understanding of the behavior of people and how to communicate with them and to develop managerial styles that will have the most productive effect.

Although I have cited only two approaches in the management theory, there are many, many others. In fact, Lindall F. Urwick recently wrote an interesting article which he entitled "Have We Lost Our Way in the Jungle of Management Theory?" In this article he suggests that the many alternatives in management theory must be carefully analyzed. This is the task in which personnel administrators are involved. If they can judiciously examine all new theories of management in the light of their own environment, and gain acceptance for the program that will provide maximum benefit for their firm, they will have performed a valuable function.

CONCLUSION

I have tried to present to you a rough outline of the changes that have taken place in the area of personnel administration as a result of the changing business environment. I have mentioned:

The new techniques in employment and recruitment prompted by changing personnel needs;

the shift in wage and salary administration from a policing and auditing function to the development of ways and means of increasing the motivational effect of salary expenditures;

the growing complexity in benefits planning and administration and the influence of employee, unions, government and automation;

the altered approach to collective bargaining resulting from government involvement, employee fears regarding job security, and the potential emergence of white collar unions;

the personnel administrator's role in developing sound management concepts and training plans.

A recent study completed by the American Management Association entitled "A Look at Personnel Through the Presidents' Eyes," drew the following conclusions:

1. The personnel department will become more and more important to the corporation as executives begin to realize that in the final analysis most of their problems are human problems.

2. Personnel department budgets will grow.

3. The personnel department will be brought organizationally closer to such departments as data processing and systems.

I sincerely hope I have been successful in giving you a better picture of the personnel executive in today's business world, and, if you were not previously a believer, you will at least be more tolerant of characters like myself.

A SYSTEMS APPROACH TO PERSONNEL MANAGEMENT

Thomas W. Gill

Personnel people and the personnel "profession" stand today where barber-surgeons stood in Henry VIII's England. A barber-surgeon cut hair and performed surgery, the latter because he had razors and other sharp instruments. During Henry's reign, and presumably between wives, he found time to issue an edict which forever separated the two. Barbers were only to cut hair and surgeons were only to cut people, although barbers continued to extract teeth and do blood letting.

The barbers retained the ancient symbol of the barber-surgeon: the spiral-striped red, white and blue pole. The striped pole, some say, is a descendant of the post in front of the barber-surgeon's shop where the barber-surgeon threw his bloody apron to dry after an operation. Another school says the striped pole represents the bandages which were wrapped around a patient's limbs after blood letting. At any rate, today's barber has the striped pole and a middling reputation in the community.

Surgeons, who were forced to drop the nickel and dime business of cutting hair and barbering, adopted the Caduceus as their symbol, and now have a towering reputation in the community. The Caduceus, the staff of Hermes, the Greek God of science and invention, is now a universally accepted emblem of excellence.

Today, personnel people stand on the threshhold of professionalism. There has been an exploding technology in the personnel field and in the behavioral sciences, and the personnel man, to become truly professional, must fill the gap between the behavioral scientists who write on management and the managers who manage. They must separate themselves from the nickel and dime business of preparing forms and making records and reports and become manpower managers with a systems approach to personnel management. In short, they must adopt the fire-symbol of Prometheus, who was the original Forethinker and symbolic of all that is daringly original and creative.

Machines are doing what Henry did with an edict. They will soon take over all the routine clerical work, acting as clerical steamshovels; and eventually they will be doing much more sophisticated things, such as preparing position descriptions and making forecasts. Record keeping will be done once. Personnel information will be recorded and stored in machines and print-outs from the machines will satisfy all reporting needs.

Personnel people working with behavioral scientists can help determine the organizations of the future, just as management engineers helped determine organizations of the present.

"The first step towards the goal we all aspire to—the betterment of the individual—is to realize that the future is only partially fixed by the nature of the universe and by the character of the human species. Part of what will happen in the future is for us to determine and arrange the way we want that future to be. To do this, we must first believe that we have a choice and then we must decide to make it our business to understand the relationship between science and society so we can exercise our choice. These two steps are vital; if they are taken, the third step—the achievement of our goal—is inevitable."[1]

The traditional organization pyramid emerged out of the demands of the industrial

From Thomas Gill, "A Systems Approach to Personnel Management," Personnel Journal 47 (5), 336–337 (1968). Reprinted by permission.

[1]Simon Ramo, "A Critical Imbalance," *Engineering Opportunities,* College Edition, p. 52 (November 1967).

revolution and was suited to its times. Now new organizational concepts are emerging which will, hopefully, replace our present mechanistic systems. Traditional management has tried to motivate people through control and fear. "The management engineering system works not only against the odds of what we know about people today but also against the long-term good of people. If people are treated as though they are of limited capacity rather than capable, lazy rather than conscientious, hostile rather than cooperative, disinterested rather than curious, and security-seeking rather than creative, they will tend to become so—or to rebel against the system by turning to power seeking."[2] Or to paraphrase Eric Hoffer, we should be more concerned about people wasting their lives than wasting their time.

Personnel people will, of course, continue to service management, but the personnel manager will become a member of the management team and will assist in the formulation of policy. He will spend less and less time on operational personnel matters.

The biggest contribution thus far of the behavioral sciences to management is the questioning attitude that now exists among managers. Managers now *want* to know what workers want, for they recognize, generally, that individuals in high productivity groups feel they can talk to their supervisors. Organizations must have feedback and people who are actively involved in planning major organizational changes will adapt to the changes much better than those who are not. Personnel people can encourage and facilitate this feedback.

There must be continuing dialogue between the manager and the behavioral scientist, and it is there that the personnel manager can make his biggest contribution. He must begin, of course, with himself. He must look deep within himself and re-examine his own needs and values. With increased insight into himself, he will find himself looking into the insights of others.

"Much of the criticism of laboratory training, by such people as George Odiorne of the University of Michigan, centers on the kind of emotional experience which occurs in the T-groups as participants learn to 'level' with each other and perhaps realize for the first time how their behavior is perceived by others in the group. But surely, as Schein and Bennis point out, increased awareness of his own feelings and the feelings of others is a vital necessity for the adaptation of the individual to the organization. The manager who is insensitive to the impact of his behavior on others is the cause of resentment, withheld effort, and often lack of initiative in his associates and subordinates; the consequence is reduced organizational effectiveness. Every thoughtful manager can recall many examples of this from his own experience in organizations."[3]

Another factor that hinders organizational effectiveness is the gap between the policy maker and the implementer. The personnel man should foster a closer relationship between people who make policy and those who carry it out. "Individual creativity is always lessened by ignorance of what is wanted, by lack of knowledge of organizational needs and problems, by the feeling that there is little understanding or appreciation by superiors of the contribution the individual is making, and by lack of status."[4] In short, the personnel man must help create a new work climate in which individual employees will have a strong commitment to the organization; and the organization, in turn, will foster and encourage creativity in all its members.

This kind of organization is a functional necessity in an age of rapid and often bewil-

[2]Robert C. Sampson, *Managing the Managers* (New York: McGraw-Hill Book Company, 1965), p. 247.

[3]Charles A. Myers, "Behavioral Science for Personnel Managers," *Harvard Business Review,* reprint (July-August 1966).

[4]David S. Brown, "The High Cost of Hierarchy," *Civil Service Journal,* p. 19 (January-March 1967).

dering change. A new democratic system of management is imperative if we are to survive, and the personnel manager can be an effective instrument in bringing it about. He must make the decision now to cast his lot with the barbers or the surgeons.

INTERFACE BETWEEN PERSONNEL AND ORGANIZATIONAL PSYCHOLOGY

Bernard M. Bass

Among the Inca farmers, work was regarded as an end in itself, a ritualistic form of religious worship. But work that was not ceremonial lacked sense and meaning. Work and worship were inseparable.[1] Nevertheless, more often in non-industrialized societies, work was done merely to subsist. Better yet, it was delegated to women or slaves. The Tibetan concentrated on his prayer wheel; the Talmudist on studying the Law; the Balinese on art; the Athenian on citizenship; and the Iroquois on military honors. Success, well-being, security, and prestige depended not on one's job but on contemplative zeal, scholarship, artistic efforts, oratory, or bravery in battle.

On the other hand, in modern industrialized society, as among the Incas, work is becoming the center of life. Twenty years may be spent preparing to enter the world of work. As much as half of each working day will be spent at work or commuting to and from it. Success in life, sense of well-being, sense of accomplishment, security, and prestige all will be tied to what work is done. Likewise, work will determine one's standard of living and economic well-being. Therefore it should come as no surprise to find that in our "work-intoxicated" society there are

few considerations about employment recruiting, testing, hiring, training, job design, and other personnel problems that can be divorced from their setting within a larger context of social forces, organization, and society.

More generally, as Porter noted in his recent annual review chapter on personnel management,[2] few issues in personnel psychology can be completely examined without attention to what usually are thought to be problems of organizational psychology. It may be profitable at this time to look at some of the more lively issues that lie at the interface between the two fields. Let us examine some organizational questions that appear when dealing with what usually are the concern of technicians in personnel psychology. To do this, I will focus briefly on recruiting, the application blank, testing, interviewing, training, and job design. Following this I will reverse the examination and look briefly at some significant personnel questions, questions of individual differences, which usually are the concern of organizational technicians.

PERSONNEL ISSUES INVOLVING ORGANIZATIONAL QUESTIONS

Recruiting

In one large sales organization, approximately 3% of those applicants for jobs as salesmen were hired if they had been attracted to apply for the jobs through newspaper ads. On the other hand, 14% of those who had made application because of friends' suggestions or who had been recommended to the sales agency by friends were hired. Unfortunately, analyses of the merit ratings a year afterwards of those hired found that those who had been recruited through newspaper ads were in the fiftieth percentile in merit while those who had been introduced

From Bernard M. Bass, "Interface between Personnel and Organizational Psychology," Journal of Applied Psychology 52 (1), 81–88 (1968). Reprinted by permission of the American Psychological Association.

[1]V. W. von Hagen, *Realm of the Incas* (New York: Mentor, 1957).

[2]L. W. Porter, "Personnel Management," *Annual Review of Psychology* 17, 395-422 (1966).

to the organization through friends were likely to be found below the twentieth percentile in merit. What had been revealed was quite simple to a technician. Different selection ratios were operating.

Those recruited by newspaper advertisements were screened more carefully; proportionately fewer were hired. Those recommended by friends were screened less thoroughly; proportionately more were hired. The same phenomenon was seen quite differently by the social psychologist. For him, interviewers were showing too much acceptance of applicants simply because they had been sent for consideration for employment by friends.

There has been surprisingly little research on the social psychology of applicant sources. Yet, personnel technicians are aware of the overriding importance to the utility of a selection program of the selection ratio as well as the importance of the quality and quantity of recruits who apply for testing. There is little systematic evidence of the many biases involved in decisions about where to recruit and whom to recruit for testing. For example, in academia, we seldom try for a low selection ratio. Rather, we solicit applications for academic jobs from only the most prestigeful sources, neglecting the utilities of uncovering a larger number of recruits. The problem is complicated further when the recruits gravitate toward or away from certain occupations and organizations because of extraneous factors. Consider how difficult it is to hire Negro engineers when the problem is compounded by the difficulties in encouraging Negroes to prepare for careers in engineering, since traditionally it has been so difficult for them to enter such a career.

Application Blank

In a sales selection program, serendipity revealed two *dynamic items* on an application blank (dynamic application questions concern the interplay between applicant and organization). When combined, these two items yielded a phenomenal validity of .70 against subsequent merit ratings. Hindsight made it relatively easy to understand why these two items were such powerful predictors of subsequent job performance. These items were: "Is it all right to contact your boss?" and "How soon can you start work?" Applicants who subsequently were meritorious on the job gave an unqualified "yes" in answer to the first question. It was perfectly all right to contact their boss. Applicants who did not turn out well on the job either said "no" or "yes, but. . . ." Those who turned into poor performers were ready to start work immediately, while those who insisted on at least 2-weeks notice were likely to be better salesmen, subsequently. Probably, what was being assessed by these dynamic items was the sense of responsibility and sense of security of applicants.

The increasing attention we are giving to biographical information blanks points to a likelihood of focusing more fully on the social and organizational history of the applicant, for so much of what is contained in biographical information is of this form. Consider some of the factors which emerged in Cassens' factor analyses of biographical information blank items in three cultures:[3] upward mobility, family attitudes, achievement by conforming, interpersonal relations, etc.

Testing

There has been a merger of interest of social and personnel psychologists concerning attitudes toward work. There seems to be no simple response to the question "Why men work?" Much research suggests quite strongly that what may be rewarding for the task-oriented worker may be punishing to the interaction-oriented worker.[4] Non-cognitive

[3]F. W. Cassens, "Cross-cultural Dimensions of Executive Life History Antecedents," (Unpublished dissertation, Louisiana State University, 1966).

[4]B. M. Bass, "Social Behavior and the Orientation Inventory: A Review," *Psychological Bulletin* **68**, 290-292 (1967).

dimensions of particular importance for selection and placement testing lie close to work itself or to organizational considerations. Heretofore, to a considerable degree, personality and motivation assessment have developed within counseling and clinical psychology and have been lifted bodily for application to industry. There has been more concern about neuroticism than there has been for need for achievement, yet there is likely to be more payoff from concentrating on the latter. Even in the case of hospitalized mental patients, it seems more prognostic in vocational rehabilitation efforts for them to know about how task oriented they are than how neurotic they are.[5]

There has been little further exploration so far of some intriguing evidence that ability and aptitude tests tend to be more predictive of early success in organizations while interest and personality factors tend only to become useful for prediction of criteria where the criteria are measured much later in the applicant's subsequent career. This proposition as well as others which are being generated about the dynamic nature of criteria cannot help but result in a more sophisticated approach to forecasting using psychometric measurements.

Early in the history of industrial psychology, the miniature test was devised for selection purposes. Replicas of the real-life job were constructed and performance evaluated in these simulated situations. Now we see much more use of such simulations of organizations for assessment purposes. Such simulations can be accomplished through the "in-basket" technique, leaderless discussions, business games, organizational design problems, and the like. To date, there has been relatively little exploration of the possibilities of creating for assessment purposes relatively simple games, each representing important

organizational dilemmas with which to confront applicants who are seeking careers in those organizations.

Culture fair testing is still another critical issue lying between personnel and social psychology. Is culture fair testing even theoretically possible if past behavior is the best predictor of future behavior? Is it possible to rule out cultural influences in testing without eliminating the validity of the tests? To what extent does previous organizational history play a role in test responses? How different is the applicant of today who grows up in a school system where the administration of objective tests is an almost weekly routine from the applicant of the last generation for whom objective testing was more of a novelty?

As long as there is a basic mistrust between the applicant and the organization, we will live in a situation where the sensible applicant attempts to distort and fake his results on noncognitive tests. In what ways could sufficient trust be promoted between applicant and organization to increase the applicant's desire to give honest responses rather than socially desirable ones, or responses which he judges to be ideal or like those of his boss or like those that would land him the job?

Still another issue in testing which may involve public and organizational policy questions deals with the selection ratio and how it is set.

In one northeastern state, the Human Relations Commission suggests that cut-off scores should be no higher than necessary to screen out unqualified applicants. The company which exploits the selection ratio by recruiting more applicants and setting higher cut-off scores does so at the expense of discouraging applicants who score reasonably well on the tests in question. Which is more important: more efficient use of screening devices by the company or avoiding the discouragement of average applicants?

[5]M. K. Distefano, Jr., and M. W. Pryer, "Task-orientation, Persistence, and Anxiety of Mental Hospital Patients with High and Low Motivation," *Psychological Reports* **14**, 18 (1964).

Interviewing

Studies of the bases upon which interviewers make their decisions are beginning to appear more frequently. They may point ultimately to an interview which is a situational test, a replica of an organizational problem where performance can be evaluated completely objectively, primarily by attention to the process by which the interviewee copes with the interviewer. This most promising approach to interviewing treats it primarily as "the social psychology of two-person interaction." Thus Yonge permitted the interviewer considerable latitude as far as the content of the interview was concerned, but had him rate the interview process itself, specifically to assess the social skill and motivation demonstrated during this process by the interviewee.[6]

The interview presents a particular challenge to the personnel and social psychologist, for no matter what can or cannot be demonstrated about its utility as an assessment device, it is almost universal in use for selection purposes. Above and beyond consideration of the interview as needed for transmittal of information about the job and organization to the interviewee and for helping the interviewee develop realistic expectations about the job for which he is applying, the typical employer still feels the need for face-to-face contact with the applicant before making the employment decision. Yet, it may be that even where the interviewer has been found to add validity to the assessment predictions above and beyond what could be done by statistical integration alone, such results may be handled more adequately in the future by better statistics. For instance, more attention to modifier variables may be required. Actually, modifiers may be merely symptoms of curvilinearity in the predictors. Under such circumstances, a Bayesian solution will always yield more accurate decisions, and in the last analysis will match the regression decisions when the data is linear.[7] At best, Sawyer's comprehensive review of research on methods for combining assessments strongly indicates that predictive efficiency is increased when interviewer judgments are mechanically combined or synthesized with test data to yield final predictions in contrast to following the usual practice of having interviewers make clinical judgments about the job applicant from his test scores and interview performance.[8]

The problem and its solutions therefore may be stated as follows: no matter what, interviews will be held with applicants. To insure that the interviews do as little damage as possible to the accuracy of the entire selection process, it may be best to increase the number of recruits who are tested, thereby reducing the selection ratio and at the same time increasing the likelihood that all those who passed the first test screen, and as a consequence receive interviews, are all fairly good prospects for the job in question. At the same time, the interviewer's judgments should be treated like additional measurements to be combined statistically with test data available on the applicant to provide a final prediction for him. This required change in practice is an organizational question since the interviewer's role is reduced in importance. Resistance is likely particularly if the interviewer has considerable status or experience but in its resolution may lie the major portion of the utility of a selection program.

Training

Commenting on the fads and fashions in training is like commenting about the

[6]K. A. Yonge, "The Value of the Interview: An Orientation and a Pilot Study," *Journal of Applied Psychology* **40**, 25-31 (1956).

[7]H. A. Clampett, Jr., "Psychological Predictions Based on Bayesian Probabilities," Technical Report No. 11, University of Pittsburgh Contract Nonr 624 (14), (March, 1966).

[8]J. Sawyer, "Measurement and Prediction, Clinical and Statistical," *Psychological Bulletin* **66**, 178-200 (1966).

weather and what can be done about it. Nevertheless, organizational matters are vital in the decisions of training programs to be introduced, continued, or abandoned. Let me enumerate some well-known training problems at the interface of personnel and organizational psychology.

1. Trainers have discovered to their chagrin that it is one thing to maintain an effective program which meets its training objectives, but it is another to create a training program which both meets its objectives and obtains the approval of the trainees. Unfortunately, evaluation and continuation of the program are more likely to rest upon the latter rather than the former.

2. Familiar also is the organizational problem associated with the returning trainee. Fleishman provided sufficient evidence that whether or not the effects of the training program made their appearance on the job 6 months after training depended primarily on the attitudes of the boss and the climate of the organization to which the trainee returned.[9]

3. The professional and the manager need to see themselves engaged in "life-long learning" to avoid obsolescence. The organization can help considerably to maintain expectations that its members must continue to keep up with new developments.

4. To a considerable extent much more attention may need to be paid to a basic conflict between management trainer and management trainee. Managers see themselves performing a complex art whereas one may be trying to teach them simple science. A recent unpublished experiment by Alex Bavelas is relevant here and illustrates the tremendous difficulties involved in the training of people under these circumstances. One subject learns to discriminate the slide photos of healthy and sick cellular tissue through appropriate reinforcement of his responses. A second subject receives the same reinforcement schedule regardless of what responses he makes. The first subject forms a few simple hypotheses about what differentiates photos of a healthy and a sick cell; the second subject forms a complex set of hypotheses since his reinforcements have not been associated in any simple way with his different responses. Unfortunately, when the two subjects discuss the matter, the one with the complex art of judgment is more confident, more resistant to change, and less readily influenced than the other subject with the simple hypotheses.

Job Design

As the organization introduces automation, there is a flattening of the distribution of skill demands on newly created jobs and the remaining old ones. More routine jobs as well as more skilled jobs emerge while those at intermediate levels of skill demand are abolished. One can only vaguely foresee the creation of less-fluid worker castes, the unskilled, and the elite, unless some effort is made to intervene with designs for more functional intermediate-level jobs. For instance, electronic data processing (EDP) has created the elite programming job. It has also created the unskilled job of pressing bent IBM cards which are returned by mail.

At the level of the manager, there seem to be two diametrically opposed predictions about how EDP is changing the organization of the future and the jobs within it. On the one hand Leavitt and Whisler see greater centralization decreasing responsibilities accorded middle managers; others see the reverse.[10] Selection and training of future middle managers need to take account of EDP, but how to do so in the face of the uncertain effects of EDP is a dilemma we face at this time. Individual differences play

[9]E. A. Fleishman, "Leadership Climate, Human Relations Training, and Supervisory Behavior," *Personnel Psychology* **6**, 205-222 (1953).

[10]H. J. Leavitt and T. L. Whisler, "Management in the 1980's," *Harvard Business Review* **36**, 41-48 (1958).

an important role here. For instance, younger men at the same level in the organization see that their own jobs are changing as a consequence of EDP much more so than do older men at the same level of management.[11]

Compensation

For too long the questions concerning equitable compensation have been left in the hands of organizational rationalists. We are just beginning to see the full extent of individual differences in attitudes toward compensation. For instance, in a simulation we use for training managers, the managers must award salary increases to 10 engineers each of whom differs in merit and in other attributes. Each has a job somewhat different than those of the others who are to be assigned salary increases. Wide differences appear in the average increases recommended. North Europeans seem to feel that 4–6% is equitable, while South Europeans may push for as high as 36%. Obviously, differences in the rate of inflation in the economies of the different countries in question are of consequence. But just as important are the attitudes toward technicians and engineers that vary greatly from one country to the next. In this same exercise, American, British, and Irish managers generally seem unmoved by the possibility of losing good men to competition and do not feel that counteroffers should be the basis for salary increases. In fact, they sometimes tend to punish men who receive offers from other firms. Contrarily, Flemings, Norwegians, Italians, Indians, and Latin-Americans tend to be more prone to award relatively large increases to men with counteroffers. Even among managers from the same firm, we can see some opting for extremely complex differentials while others insist that regardless of merit or job or sen-

iority, all engineers ought to receive the exact salary increase.[12]

Criteria of Individual Performance

Concern for an employee's performance in a firm must be viewed in terms of his firm's objectives. For example, Smith sells more merchandise faster than Jones, but Smith's customers complain more about their purchases. Smith brings in more new, nonrepeat business, but Jones has more steady, satisfied customers. Who is the better salesman? The answer depends on the firm's goals on what it values most. Smith is the better salesman if the firm is concerned most about its current share of the market. Jones is the better salesman if the firm is concerned about its long-term standing in the market.

We must understand something about how to assess organizational worth if we are to appreciate how individual personnel differ in their contributions to it. Individual differences in the proficiency of executives, for instance, can only be made meaningful if we understand the purposes of their jobs. This in turn entails determining the purposes of the department's divisions and ultimately the purpose of their enterprise.[13] Assessing the adequacy of the performance of a manager can be tricky business indeed. As Shartle pointed out, one may discover 10 years too late that an executive who contributed the most to the firm had been discharged.[14]

ORGANIZATIONAL ISSUES INVOLVING PERSONNEL QUESTIONS

We have seen that the problems of recruiting, application forms, testing, interviewing,

---

[11]J. A. Vaughan and A. M. Porat, "Managerial Reaction to Computers," *Banking* **59** (10), 119-122 (1967).

[12]B. M. Bass, "Combining Management Training and Research," *Training Directors Journal* **21,** (4), 2-7 (1967).

[13]D. W. Fiske, "Values, Theory and the Criteron Problem," *Personnel Psychology* **4,** 93-98 (1951).

[14]C. L. Shartle, *Executive Performance and Leadership* (Englewood Cliffs, N.J.: Prentice-Hall, 1958).

training, job design, and compensation, all ordinarily the primary interest of the personnel psychologist, are likely to contain social issues of interest to organizational psychologists, as well. Now let us reverse roles and look at some problems which usually are the concern of organizational technicians which nevertheless contain significant personnel questions as well: supervision, communications, conflict resolution, team composition, and organization design.

Supervision

For 25 years, there has been major interest by social psychologists in the utility of democratic or permissive rather than directive supervision. But evidence is continuing to accumulate that what type of supervision works best is often a matter of individual and cultural differences. In a number of studies, more directive approaches are favored by subordinates. Indeed, much direction is more often expected in many locales. For instance, in a recent pilot study completed in Spain, those who acted as subordinates were much more favorably disposed toward supervisors who attempted to persuade them rather than who attempted to share the decisions with them, for, they said, a supervisor who does not try to influence his subordinates fails to accord the subordinates the dignity to which they are accustomed by showing that he really does not have sufficient interest to bringing them over to his position. Numerous studies in the United States suggest that those who are highly authoritarian prefer in turn to submit to authority rather than to operate in an environment with opportunities for sharing decisions with their superiors. In turn, they expect to make decisions for their own subordinates.[15]

Communications

In a similar vein, two-way communication is thought more effective as well as more satisfying than one-way communication. Yet, a group of Japanese frustrated an American management trainer who was trying to demonstrate the differences and relatively greater values of two-way communication. Among the Japanese, with whom he was working, the ease of communicating a pattern of rectangles one-way was somewhat greater for the task which was imposed, and as a consequence there was considerable confusion on the part of the students who were ostensibly being taught and shown the value of two-way over one-way communication. We have had similar experiences with engineering students who if they are communicating the pattern of rectangles to others with a great deal of background in mechanical drawing and blueprint reading, may communicate faster and more effectively one-way than two-way. Given individuals with common codes, one-way communication can be more effective and more satisfying than two-way communication.

Conflict Resolution

Some zero-sum games where one party wins only under the condition that the other party loses are situations where conflict resolution is impossible for almost anybody. In some mixed-motive games, resolution will or will not occur, depending on who is playing the game. If one is able to compete with a generous opponent, it is possible to fleece him. If one himself is nurturant, speedy and highly satisfying, resolutions can be achieved.[16] There would seem to be considerable payoff in the study of the interaction of person and structural conditions in various types of ne-

[15]B. M. Bass, *Organizational Psychology* (Boston: Allyn & Bacon, 1965).

[16]J. L. Loomis, "Communication, the Development of Trust, and Cooperative Behavior," *Human Relations* **12**, 305-315 (1959).

gotiating situations. Thus Bass found that task-oriented negotiators were most likely to achieve settlements of high quality in contrast to settlements reached by less task-oriented negotiators.[17]

Team Composition

We are beginning to understand the personal ingredients in the assembly of members of a group required to achieve particular outcomes. For example, evidence accumulated so far suggests if we put together a number of highly task-oriented members, we are likely to generate a great deal of socio-emotional conflict, although at the same time the chances are reasonably good that plenty of work will get done. At the same time if we mix together a group of primarily interaction-oriented personnel, the likelihood is that the group will be most satisfying to the members, there will be much play, but relatively little work will be accomplished.[18]

Organizational Design

To conclude, let us look at what rational organizational designers would suggest as inviolate principles of organizational design and at the same time note the very opposite points of view voiced by behavioralists.

The rationalists would say that an organization should be designed so that someone is responsible for supervising all essential activities. The behavioralists would be primarily concerned with creating structures where leadership was shared.

The rationalists would argue that responsibility for specific acts should not be duplicated or overlapping. The behavioralists would feel that overlapping had much merit, providing opportunities for cross-training,

[17]B. M. Bass, "Effects on the Subsequent Performance of Negotiators of Studying Issues or Planning Strategies Alone or in Groups," *Psychological Monographs* **80** (6, whole No. 614), (1966).

[18]Bass, *op cit.* ("Social Behavior . . .").

backup, and increasing the reliability of the system of interacting workers.

The rationalists would argue for job simplification; the behavioralists would push for the reverse, job enlargement.

The rationalists would insist that responsibilities should be written, clear, and understood by job occupants. The behavioralists would argue that each person brings to a job somewhat different potentials and should be given freedom and flexibility to develop his own particular way of doing the job to make the most of the situation in which he finds himself.

The rationalists would argue that authority to make decisions should be commensurate with responsibility for those decisions. The behavioralists would state that authority cannot be assigned but rather goes with ability and esteem as an individual among associates. Furthermore, they would note that the rationalists' principle of authority primarily makes it easy for some people to shirk responsibility and also increases staff-line conflict.

The rationalists would want authority to be delegated so that decisions take place as close as possible to the point of action. The behavioralists would insist that the rationalists do not mean what they say, for to accomplish this goal they would accept the behavioralists' position that individuals should be responsible for decisions which affect themselves, whereas, in fact, the rationalists design organizations so that such decisions are lodged with the superiors of the individuals who must execute those decisions.

The rationalists have fixed notions about span of control; the behavioralists feel that the span of control creates as many problems as it solves. For example, the smaller the span of control in an organization the taller will be its structure resulting in greater separation of the top of the organization from the bottom. More possibilities will arise for filtering communications that must be transmitted through the organization. There will be greater differences between the goals of those at the top from those at the bottom of the hierarchy. Rather than concern themselves about span of control, the behavioralists would be much more interested in the opportunities for feedback between subordinate and superior; span of control could be much greater where feedback was accurate and easy.

The rationalists insist on a chain of command; the behavioralists say the chain of command is often a fiction interfering with the flow of communication that is needed by the organization, a flow which may be horizontal, diagonal, and in forms quite different than assumed by the rationalists. For example, the relation between the foreman and an assembly-line worker has been likened to that between a travel consultant and his client. The "real boss" in the situation is the machine.[19]

Optimum organizational designs are likely to be found somewhere between rationalist emphasis on predictability and accountability through impersonal structure and behavioralist concern for interpersonal trust and

interpersonal confidence as the bases of organizational stability and growth. Again, one can only agree that organizational design must attend to what has been learned about intrapersonal as well as interpersonal dynamics. Where the optimum lies between the rationalist's and the behavioralist's positions depends on the capabilities, training, and involvement of the personnel in the system. The fully programmed rationalist's organization is closer to the optimum when personnel capability, training, and involvement are low (and the rationalist's organization is likely to keep personnel involvement low). When personnel potential is high, the behavioralist's model becomes more feasible.

The personnel specialist no longer can hide behind his validity coefficients, test blanks, and training manuals. In turn, the organization scientist cannot remain assured of the generality of results from his surveys, field studies, and rational analyses. Models for organizational and personnel research need to take into account sources of variance due to jobs and organizational environment, sources due to individual characteristics, and, most important of all, sources due to the peculiar interactions of individuals and environments.

---

[19]Bass, *op cit.* (1965).

PART TWO

ACQUIRING HUMAN RESOURCES

Today the human resource is the most scarce organizational commodity of all. The handwriting on the organizational wall is clear: As organizations become more complex in the future, this resource will become even more scarce. The increasing complexity of job requirements demands a change in human input, as well as a change in the process of acquiring these resources. In order to meet this challenge, management will have to practice the primary function of management—planning. Since planning is every bit as critical as actual procurement, this section is divided into two parts—manpower planning and manpower procurement.

MANPOWER PLANNING

Proper planning is a major key to organizational effectiveness and success, and the most crucial link in the organization's planning chain is its manpower planning. In other words, if planning is important, the most important part of planning is planning for the procurement of those who will be expected to effect the organization's function in the future. "Manpower—Today's Frontier" discusses the importance of this activity, as well as some of the critical considerations involved. The second article, "The Nature of Long Range Manpower Planning," provides insight into the nature of long range planning in this area.

The third article, "The Growing Role of Manpower Forecasting in Organizations," notes the importance of manpower forecasting as a component of the manpower planning process. The concept of manpower forecasting is briefly discussed, along with the difficulties inherent in achieving optimal forecasts. The future of manpower forecasting is analyzed, and a model of a department manpower forecasting system is presented.

"Planning for a Personnel Reduction" deals with a very specific type of manpower planning problem, while the final article is concerned not directly with manpower planning, but with what was referred to above as "planning for planning." "Job Analysis: National Survey Findings," deals with "planning for planning" as well.

MANPOWER PROCUREMENT

Employee selection is not simply a mechanical process; it is also a human process. "A Behavioral Science Approach to Personnel Selection" discusses the implications of the human process, while "Decision Models for Personnel Selection and Assignment" explores approaches to, and research in, "quantifying" the human variable, which is so much a part of the selection component. An attempt to synthesize the approaches represented by these two articles should provide the reader with a meaningful challenge.

"A Case Study in Effective Recruiting" is included to emphasize the importance of recruiting efforts to the selection process. The last two articles in this section deal with specific devices which may be a part of a procurement program; one explores the use of tests, while the final article addresses the role of the selection interview.

MANPOWER PLANNING

MANPOWER—TODAY'S FRONTIER

Frank H. Cassell

While mammoth advances in science and technology have revolutionized our way of life, our knowledge of how to employ people lags far behind. We can create miracles from molecules. But we are only beginning to get some grasp of what people can do if given the right opportunity and incentive to develop their talents.

A nation's greatness is usually discussed in terms of the state of the arts, literature, antiquities, architecture, scientific achievements, raw materials, or even land-space and scenic splendors. While these continue as measures of greatness, there is a new measure—manpower—which leads, even eclipses, all others. This is not only the numbers of people, but the brains, the talents, and the skills of the work force.

Manpower does not mean much unless it is used. We are self-conscious about the fact that unemployment in western Europe and Japan is lower than at home. The continuing high rate of employment in western Europe has turned that area into a vast international job market, in which workers move from one country to another. Turks and Yugoslavs move to Germany to man steel mills; Span-

iards and Italians fill jobs in Scandinavian countries. Yet, a continuous stream of managers and manpower experts from these countries inspect our factories and offices and seek to learn more about the efficient use of manpower. As full employment is approached, nations can see that it is the quality of manpower—not merely the quantity—the intelligence with which it is deployed, and its willingness to produce that makes the major difference between one country and another.

Most nations of the world face an escalating shortage of high-talent manpower, accompanied by an increase in the excess numbers of people who are untrained and unskilled, or whose skills are not needed. In the future, they will have to cope with urbanization by vast numbers of rural people who are almost totally unprepared for urban life and work. As economies become increasingly sophisticated, it will be necessary to devote more effort to helping the total work force to keep pace (or catch up) with an occupational mix which increasingly reflects the need for minds rather than muscle.

These generalizations apply not only to the highly industrialized countries, but to the newly developing nations as well. It is only prudent for investors of capital, whether in the newly developing nations or in highly sophisticated economies, to invest in the development of qualified manpower. It is the best way to assure economic use of capital.

MOBILITY OF MANPOWER

The International Job Market. We can look forward to a world job market for many occupations. Already we see in western

Europe a continent-wide job market, involving people of practically all skill levels, from laborers to engineers. At the highest skill and professional levels, the job market is intercontinental. High-talent manpower moves more easily than ever before from one part of the world to another.

The highly publicized "brain drain" is a prologue to the wider international job market. There has been a flow of high-talent men to the United States from Europe. Also, they have come from the less developed countries, as in the case of students who do not return home. Of the more than 3 million aliens admitted from 1956 through 1966, 271,873, or 8.5 per cent, were in the professional, technical, and managerial category.

Countries in need of skilled manpower are also importing talent from the United States. The flow includes retired business executives and engineers, itinerant college professors (working out of the international development departments and business schools of our universities), and American technicians sent under contract by their companies.

We are not alone in this. Britain, Germany, Italy, Sweden, Japan, France, Russia, and other industrialized countries are providing technical and economic manpower aid to Asia, Africa, and South America.

The international job market already in existence will increasingly affect both the supply and price of American talent as well as that of other countries. American competition for European technicians is driving up salary levels in Europe, but American talent is also being attracted by foreign inducements.

As the international job market develops and includes lower-skill occupations and as technological change takes hold in the newly developing nations, the emphasis in all countries is certain to shift toward more efficient use of manpower resources.

The supply of talent can be increased by getting it from some other nation. This technique, followed by the United States in the past, contributed greatly to our outstanding economic growth, but time has run out on this course. We and other industrialized nations can increase the supply only by raising the skills and talents of the home work force and by making better use of it.

THE FIRST BUSINESS SCHOOLS

Trends in Training Manpower. American business has a half-century jump on the rest of the world. The United States was the first country in the world to prepare young people, formally and on a large scale, for careers in business. The business schools of the United States are unique. Only recently have such schools been established in Europe.

Our business schools are making new contributions to managerial concepts, and their methods of training people are profoundly shaping business thinking in other parts of the world. The American business schools have been forward-looking and self-critical. This is the reason that a new set of challenges in the manpower field is being placed before them—challenges which evolve out of four pervasive trends in our society.

THE PACE OF CHANGE

The first is the long-term, increasing shortage of high-talent manpower. The world in which we live is more complicated than that of our parents. We need to know more things than they did. Our children will need to know more than we do. The technology needed to cope with the complex problems of modern society or of running a business is already beyond the reach of many of the current generation of business and government leaders.

The pace of change is outstripping our capacity to respond, despite past accomplishments. The curriculum of the schools faces obsolescence.

In fields such as aerospace, missiles, electronic and electrical equipment, and nuclear energy, an engineer's knowledge can become obsolete in ten years.[1] In a recent report on "Obsolescence and Updating of Engineers' and Scientists' Skills," by the Columbia University Seminar on Technology and Social Change,[2] twenty-seven of thirty-four firms said they had significant obsolescence problems, and that most were in the 35-year-old and above category. The long-term shortage is, therefore, compounded of rising knowledge levels, the knowledge lag of individuals, and the rapidly increasing demand for people with recent knowledge.

NEW OCCUPATIONS

The second trend is toward the widening spectrum of occupations in the high-talent category. This has diffused the competition for manpower among a larger number of high-talent occupations.

Today there are twice as many groups in the occupational classifications structure for high-talent occupations—professional, technical, and managerial—as there were ten years ago. Much of this is due to a numerical increase in new types of jobs; some is caused by the movement of relatively obscure occupations to the forefront. The field of mathematics is one example, where the work has become so important to the economy that mathematicians in business are no longer considered mere adjuncts to the other scientists.

The rise of new occupations is creating a form of competition with older, more traditional jobs. There is stiff competition from the professions and from emerging, new service fields. Careers in business are pitted against careers which are essentially non-business and which provide somewhat different satisfactions.

[1]The *Wall Street Journal* of March 28, 1967, says, "A San Francisco consultant figures an electrical engineer with a new Ph.D. degree has about 10 years before he needs to 'have his batteries recharged.' "

[2]Prepared for the Office of Manpower Policy, Evaluation, and Research, U.S. Department of Labor.

The graduating senior has at least twice the number of job options (not offers) open to him as were open to his father when he graduated from college. This happens because he is better educated, which helps open up more job options and because there has been a proliferation of new occupations and careers in business which has increased "intranational" and interindustry competition for all types of engineers, agronomists, economists, sociologists, geologists, physicists, and many others in the high-talent category.

CONCEPT OF EDUCATION

The third trend arises out of the nation's determination to employ its people and to bring an end to poverty. Almost everyone is expected to graduate from high school. This creates a demand for manpower in the education field and for specialists who can cope with the educationally disadvantaged.

In the last few years, as a part of the war on poverty, the nation has begun to educate and train people formerly considered uneducable. We are demonstrating under the Manpower Development and Training Act training programs, that this is perfectly feasible, although old beliefs about the noneducability of a large section of the population persist among some educators in positions of leadership—men and women who were trained twenty or twenty-five years ago and who are attuned to the drum beat of an earlier and more relaxed time.

The decision to end poverty affects more than formal education. It reaches into business. Corporations now operate educational technology. Companies are deeply involved in the process of training people whom we previously discarded as unfit for competitive work.

AN IMPROVED SOCIETY

The fourth trend is the desire to raise the quality of life in the United States. We want higher education of one form or another to be within the reach of all of our children, regardless of their economic background. We also want our living space to be more comfortable, cleaner, and purer. We want to stop the deterioration and decay of our cities. We want our people to live more peacefully together and to have more respect for their neighbors' rights. We want to conserve that which adds beauty to our lives. We want to provide theater, opera, and other cultural advantages. These are things a poor society could not begin to think about. They have become possible in our affluent society.

To realize these dreams, and to have something worthwhile to hand down to succeeding generations, requires development of hundreds of new occupations and careers. These in turn demand more training and more education to respond to new complexities arising out of new knowledge.

A CHALLENGE TO BUSINESS

Career Choice. The broadening scope of occupations and careers will give people a chance to use their wide range of abilities and to fulfill their life expectations. It also extends the dimensions of competition beyond mere wages. Competition now responds to the desires and needs of the human spirit.

It is often alleged that the climate of business is stultifying. It need not be. Competition for the scientist has caused business to alter his conditions of work. These conditions now approximate the university campus and laboratory.

Competition from these new and different industries calls attention to the need to study the conditions which cause an individual to eschew a career in business for one in social service which may pay very much less.

Service fields traditionally have had an appeal because they provide, early in a youth's career, the excitement and responsibility which usually comes much later in

business. It is not infrequent for a Peace Corps volunteer to be given important responsibilities which, due to his youth and lack of experience, a company would consider unthinkable.

Many of our educated young people are concerned with improving society. This appeals to the idealism of youth. The opportunity to better conditions at home and abroad affect the career preferences of some of the best brains coming out of our universities.

As business comes to see that the shortage of high-talent manpower will persist over a long period, the business environment will have to change to meet this competition.

BUSINESS IN THE COMMUNITY

Full use of manpower. We need to employ all of our people as we develop our national resources. Corporations will be involved in aspects of community life never dreamed of by earlier business leaders.

Unemployment and its social consequences, including alienation from the mainstream of American life, touch the lives of all citizens in the community. This includes the corporation. The life of the corporation is inextricably interwoven with that of the community; it prospers or suffers with it.

Cooperation of private enterprise is crucial in eliminating poverty. By training and providing jobs for the poor and disadvantaged, the corporation not only can better the life of the community but also benefit itself directly.

In major cities, where poverty and unemployment abound, deterioration and decay in slum areas have grave social consequences. There is an increasing migration of both people and industry from the cities. The results are predictable: loss of customers from downtown areas, loss of jobs to the suburbs, loss of access of the poor to these jobs, reduction in tax income to support good schools, etc. The trickle from the city may become a torrent. Joining in the exodus will be capital, highly trained manpower, customers, and job opportunity.

Left behind are the poor and the businesses with high fixed investments. Both are saddled with higher taxes which they can least afford.

The distance between races may grow both geographically and socially. The chance for building a viable community will diminish, and with it will go the hope of eliminating poverty. These are consequences that business can ill afford to ignore.

Continued unemployment and poverty eat away like a cancer at the heart of the city, but the city suffers more than the loss of the tax base and the general blight. Loss of leadership and loss of hope are even more serious. Without leadership there is no way out. The poor are trapped, and so is everybody else.

Much of the answer lies in finding ways to bring the disadvantaged poor into the work force. In our culture, whether the individual lives in Harlem or on Fifth Avenue, a job is a badge of citizenship. It is also a means of building for future leadership.

Hundreds of companies across the land from California to New York are aware of these realities. Many have become deeply involved in the renewal of cities. They ask to develop employability among people whom we formerly relegated to the scrap heap or relief rolls. Such people can be retrieved. They form a great reservoir of productive workers. This includes even the mentally handicapped. I am reminded of the restaurant chain in Washington, D.C., and a national department store chain, who employ them successfully.

Employers say they have become involved in the employment of the disadvantaged, the undereducated, and unskilled for the following reasons:

In periods of labor shortage, people with minimum job-readiness are a good source of labor;

use of these workers is an aid in the fight against inflation;

each person employed in private enterprise reduces dependence on welfare;

each person put to work becomes a customer and a taxpayer.

Competitive employment, not "make" work, is what most of the unemployed want. Even the gang kids feel this way. In fact, they are quicker than most to see through the phoniness and the dead-endedness of some of the make-work propositions. Every effort must be made to move them quickly into competitive enterprise.

The seriously disadvantaged can be successfully employed in competitive jobs. However, there is no glossing over the fact that many difficulties and risks are involved. Adjustment to industrial life of people not far removed from the life of a sharecropper is a complex and challenging problem. Fitting rebellious youth to the routines of factory or office is a trial and a challenge.

Productivity may not, at first, be up to a company's standard. It is obvious that bringing the seriously disadvantaged into the work force cannot be accomplished without careful planning. A deep understanding of the human factors involved is needed.

POLICIES FOR TRAINING

Management Adjustments. Reorientation in policy extends from top to bottom. Most of us have been trained, either by experience or by the business schools, to be adept at sorting out the most capable people. We know that the quality of the work force makes the difference, so we recruit and select the best qualified and reject the others.

This is why companies hire personnel managers. The skill with which the personnel officer does this job determines his reward and status in the company. The performance of people under a foreman or supervisor determines his success.

When a company pledges itself to aid in

the retrieval of the disadvantaged or the elimination of discrimination, it must adjust these policies. There are certain practical, hard problems involved in the employment of people with lesser skills.

Hiring these people may be contrary to company policy. What should the company do if the disadvantaged person is over forty-five years of age? In some cities over 80 per cent of the people referred from the unemployment claims offices to the employment services are over forty-five years of age.

Hiring of minority group persons may involve adjustments by the foreman, fellow workers, and the newcomer himself. Most programs which aim to employ the disadvantaged experience high turnover rates in the first few days. Much of this occurs because little attention is given to the adjustment of the work environment. Failure to attend to this problem may involve unfortunate experiences, both for the new employee and for the company.

Employment of the educationally disadvantaged may place a strain upon both the training function of the company and on the supervisor. Corporate personnel have experience in training the educated and well-qualified. The disadvantaged and under-educated have been screened out of the employment channel. People who have failed on other jobs usually will have been eliminated. In many companies, people with police records have been the first to be screened out. The techniques and the skills of the training men often are not attuned to this new clientele.

The company goal of social responsibility and the goals the foreman is accountable for—production, quality, and costs—come in conflict at the work bench. The basic problem does not rest with the foreman. Rather it lies with corporate policy. This must be resolved before any of the programs to employ the disadvantaged can become fully effective.

Many American companies already have faced these problems successfully. In addition to their responsibility for making a profit, they have decided that they have a responsibility to help end the dependence of the poor upon relief and charity. The only way this can be done is to employ these people if they are able to do competitive work.

Patterns of Training and Hiring. The results of programs throughout the United States demonstrate that people can learn more readily than we commonly assume. Those doing the training need skill, understanding, and patience.

People over forty-five do not resist education as much as we commonly suppose. Such people too often have become specialized because of management and production patterns of their companies. They have had little opportunity to diversify their experiences. Affluence has had its disadvantages. Too many people, executives and laborers alike, are lulled and do not prepare themselves for future change.

Management policies for training have not recognized older workers, the disadvantaged, the minorities, the handicapped, youth, and all those whom we customarily reject. We still believe we are operating in an era of manpower abundance. Yet for the last ten years we have had shortages in a wide range of occupations. This is reflected, for example, in the rapid rate of pay increases for engineers. The pay of college professors is rising. In all of the high-talent occupations the growth curve of wages reflects a persistent shortage. This shortage is also reflected in rapidly rising wage levels, sometimes accompanied by labor-management disputes.

There must be a reassessment of the use of those already employed. The steel industry is an example—it has embarked upon a training program to upgrade those in lower job classes. This will add to the industry's talent supply and at the same time open opportunity for thousands at the entry level.

Continuous education has the twin advantages of keeping the work force flexible and the company ready to meet change.

Personnel skills are needed to train and supervise people who are strangers to life in industry, even afraid of it. Their values may not coincide with the disciplines of the 8-hour day, but they can respond when properly instructed and guided.

We shall have to look again at the widening discrepancy between the age of retirement and the length of life. We must ask ourselves if we can afford to turn millions of our citizens out to pasture for as long as thirty years.

Because we believe we have an oversupply of labor, we have depended upon recruitment instead of development to renew the capabilities of our work force.

CONCLUSIONS

Cost and Results. The cost of a work force which revolves from one employer to another is more than the cost of continuous education and retraining. Careful placement and supervision of the disadvantaged can also serve to reduce cost.

At the outset, rehabilitation and training of the hard-core unemployed is a costly undertaking. Yet a nine-month training program and a job will repay the cost twice over in taxes alone in less than two years.

The ultimate cost is the one arising out of human despair at not finding job opportunity. No nation can afford this. Poverty and affluence cannot forever exist side by side; equal opportunity cannot too long be withheld from some Americans. Neither business nor government can ignore these problems.

It takes talent, commitment, and hard work to help people to become employable, independent of the unemployment and relief rolls, and productive members of society.

Government and private enterprise cooperation in the successful employment of the part of our work force which needs special help is being demonstrated in Los Angeles, Houston, Chicago, Newark, and Rochester. Needed now is massive support of business throughout the country to extend these efforts to all parts of the nation.

The business school faces the challenge of the manpower frontier. It has provided intellectual leadership for the most productive system of business in the history of man. It now has the opportunity to provide leadership in helping business build a new manpower system. We need one which takes account of the talents, capabilities, and aspirations of the nation's people, one which relates them in an effective way to the nation's manpower needs. We need to open to all the opportunity to be fully employed in competitive employment.

THE NATURE OF LONG RANGE MANPOWER PLANNING

Eric W. Vetter

Ten years ago, Peter Drucker wrote about the importance of the future manpower resources of the firm. He said, "The prosperity if not the survival of any business depends on the performance of its managers of tomorrow."[1]

For many years the importance and implications of this statement went unnoticed by most firms. Only a handful of companies—primarily those in the oil, aircraft, chemical and utility fields—were willing to commit time and resources to the task of insuring that the managers of tomorrow were both available and qualified to perform. Today many more firms are concerned about this aspect of management. They now realize that the existence of a first class management team doesn't just happen.

Perhaps of greater importance is an awareness by these firms that a sophisticated program of performance appraisal, or management development, or organization planning is inadequate to insure that a proper management team will exist in the future. Without specific long range manpower objectives, each of these programs is inadequate. The development of the manpower planning approach to long range problems now appears to provide the means by which firms

From Eric Vetter, "The Nature of Long Range Manpower Planning," Management of Personnel Quarterly, Summer 1964, pp. 20–27. Reprinted from MANAGEMENT OF PERSONNEL QUARTERLY, a University of Michigan publication read by professional managers throughout the world.

[1]Peter Drucker, *The Practice of Management* (New York: Harpers & Bros., 1954), p. 182.

can effectively integrate specific manpower action programs, such as management development, with the overall long range objectives of the firm and its specific long range manpower objectives.

What is Manpower Planning?

To some companies, manpower planning means employee development. To these firms it is an activity to help executives make better decisions, to communicate more effectively, and to broaden their knowledge of the firm. The purpose is purely qualitative—to make men better managers. Only passing attention is given to insuring that the necessary numbers of managers will be available when needed. The emphasis is on having current managers (whatever their number) skilled in their function and reasonably qualified for promotion. Having *enough* managers is either largely ignored or thought of in terms of having a designated replacement available and trained when a vacancy occurs. Should the organization change in size over time, as most organizations do, the quantity problems posed by this change are met in a stop-gap manner.

In addition, employee development programs often are primarily concerned with short-range qualitative problems. Making managers better managers *today* is the goal. Adequate attention is seldom given to providing the manager today with the knowledge and understanding he will need in the more distant future. More than one firm has wondered why it has so few men qualified for key executive positions after having spent considerable sums of money on management development. The reason is often that the management development programs were designed for short-term payoffs.

In other firms, the entire emphasis on manpower planning is reversed. Here the problem is defined as determining how many managers will be needed at some time in the future.

The goal is to hire certain numbers today to take care of future requirements. The qualitative aspect of development is somehow met by presuming "natural" development will occur within the firm. The premise is that only qualified people will be promoted: presumably nobody will lack the skills and qualities necessary for successful performance of his duties in the future. In fact, future managerial and professional skills requirements are ignored in the planning effort. The guiding principle is only to insure that enough bodies will be available when needed. This approach is engendered by a belief that the firm has never suffered in the past because people weren't capable—manpower hardships result only from a manpower shortage. Thus the emphasis on numeric manpower projection. Unfortunately, this type of thinking persists because nobody in the organization has ever attempted to make valid measurement of the general quality of existing manpower. A common analysis made of manpower quality is one inferred from such data as turnover statistics. For example, a low managerial turnover rate is considered as an indicator that the firm is a good place to work, that people are capable of performing well, and that they do perform well because it is a good place to work with good advancement opportunities.

Another possible and perhaps more realistic interpretation of the same turnover statistic is that the managers aren't wanted by other firms and they can't leave even if they wanted to leave. Whatever the reason for emphasis on numeric projections, the result is a lack of attention to the future managerial and professional skills needed, the level at which the skills will be needed, and the educational and experience quotients required by these persons.

The problems posed by imprecise quantitative and qualitative data are partially overcome by a third group who define manpower planning as organization planning. The approach here is to determine first the ideal future organization *structure*. The boxes in the organization chart are filled with names of current management men who are assigned color codes to indicate their current promotion potential and the quality of their current performance. From this current analysis one of two future organization plans inevitably is developed. If a long range organization plan (e.g., five years) is undertaken, the lack of meaningful quantitative information means the planner can only design the future top management organization structure. He lacks data which will indicate the size, shape and characteristics of the large middle and lower management structure of the future. Similarly, the lack of numerical data forces him to make a short term projection if he attempts to make a detailed organization plan including all levels of management. Without good information on how large the marketing organization will be in five years, for example, the manpower aspects of his plans must not depart too radically from what exists today. Because the planner strives to reduce the uncertainty associated with the plan to give it significance for current decision making, he is thus forced to a short term estimate.

Of great value, however, in the organization planning approach is the attention given the changing nature and structure of the organization. This planner is concerned with the external and internal forces which tend to force the organization to behave in certain ways. Forces such as new markets, new production methods, and new competitive influences combine with many other factors to form a logic that shapes the future organization structure. When this new structural design is integrated with manpower resources, the organization planner is able to focus on some important future management manpower problems.

Each of the approaches discussed—employee development, manpower forecasting, and organizational planning—is inadequate by itself. In combination, however, they form an important part of a good manpower planning effort.

Our definition of manpower planning incorporates elements of all of these approaches. For our purposes it is defined as: *The process by which a firm insures that it has the right number of people and the right kind of people, at the right places, at the right time doing things for which they are economically most useful.* It is a two-phased process involving anticipating the future through *manpower forecasting,* and then developing and implementing *manpower action programs* to meet the implications of the forecast.

This definition embraces all of the traditional activities of the personnel department. And it has as a basic reference point things of economic significance to the firm. This means that manpower planning must be solidly grounded in the profit planning program of the firm. It means manpower planning must be more than an interesting numbers exercise or a currently popular activity undertaken because other firms are engaged in it. It must pay its way or not be undertaken.

What is Unique About Manpower Planning Today?

The significance of both manpower and planning are sometimes debated. The debate is not whether the subjects are important or unimportant, but rather how much attention should be given the subjects. It is difficult to conceive of an organization that does not engage in at least a phase of manpower planning—even if this activity is limited to a development of a work assignment schedule for the next day's operations in order to insure the objectives for that day are accomplished. This activity is perhaps better termed work scheduling than manpower planning. But it does involve the notion of setting up a course of action to insure that an objective is successfully reached.

However, manpower planning of this sort

leaves a great deal to chance. It presumes we have the right people available for the tasks that must be performed tomorrow and that these people are best used on these tasks. It presumes we are neither short of people nor that we are trying to find work to keep people occupied. It presumes, perhaps most of all, that we have the flexibility in the type of persons working for us and a flexibility in our work loads that permits us to schedule activities only a day in advance.

When these conditions actually do occur, it usually is more than a chance situation. More likely, the firm has engaged in a planning activity to insure the necessary flexibility would be present. In brief, a much longer time dimension was at work than a mere twenty-four hours. The time dimension extended back prior to the selection and employment of the persons who are being assigned tasks to perform tomorrow. Ideally, it extended back several years to a time when someone within the organization deliberately set about ensuring that a supervisor could draw up a one-day, one-week, one-month, or one-year work schedule and reasonably expect to have the desired manpower to complete his tasks. It means too, for example, that a director or researcher can assume that when a new research facility is placed into operation he will have both the experienced and newly trained personnel necessary to staff his facility.

Thus today's manpower planning efforts are set in a long-term time dimension. The concern is with five, ten and fifteen year objectives. As a resource and as an investment manpower increasingly requires this kind of attention. Just as capital investment is treated as a long lived asset, increasing recognition is being given the fact that manpower is an asset which pays returns to the firm over a long time period.

The New Time Dimension

This discussion does not mean that American

firms are only now becoming concerned with long-term effective utilization of their manpower resources. Elements of this concern were evident in the early twentieth century when many companies initiated welfare programs for their employees. Even greater concern over long-range aspects of manpower utilization is seen today in the millions of dollars annually spent on long-term employee benefit programs.

It is quite apparent today, however, that few executives are able to show clearly how all of the personnel programs that exist in their firm relate to one another. The management development expert often does not know what talent he should attempt to develop and what the talent should be able to do once developed. Yet he administers programs that are expensive from both an out-of-pocket view and from a time utilization view. The industrial psychologist is in the same position. He may be called upon to design screening tests that will enable the firm to select talent intelligently. We hire a man with the expectation that he will be productive for a long time. The psychologist needs to know what the man might be doing in ten years, at least the level of responsibility he will probably have, in order to answer his basic question "testing for what?". What results is a set of specialized programs designed to service specific problems. But each of the programs tends to operate independently of other personnel programs.

One wage and salary administrator's confession over objectives illustrates the frustration that tends to result from this situation. "Every time we face a manpower problem we slap a new program together to patch up our existing program. Our organization structure is obviously heading in a new direction, but my wage and salary program is tied to our old organization structure—higher management doesn't want to change. In our selection, placement, and promotion programs we do what most of our department managers think is best at the moment. This means we're always changing something in those areas. Our problem is simply that nobody will sit down and map out an overall plan we all can agree on and then follow."

This situation is probably worse than most, but it is not unique. It is a situation that tends to result unless everyone concerned with manpower management knows the manpower goals of the firm and how his activity bears upon these goals.

The evolutionary growth of personnel management probably explains why this situation arises. As firms gained insights into personnel problems, they did not use a common time dimension as the basis for their attack on these problems. New personnel programs were developed to meet specific manpower problems and the need to integrate all of the activities into a unified manpower management activity failed to emerge. They managed to operate because circumstances did not force a change. A review of some of the major influences on personnel management illustrates this point.

The Development of the Personnel Management Function

Beginning with Frederick W. Taylor's experiments at the Midvale Iron Works in the 1880's, research work has proven to be an important influence on manpower policies and practices of the firm. Taylor's concern with man-equipment-task relationships suggested selection policies, training methods and job design of highly repetitive tasks. His work gave direction to the efficiency expert and industrial psychologists who were concerned with fatigue, lighting and safety. The personnel programs that resulted had immediate or short-run economic goals measured by increased production.

Much of our current personnel research work can be traced back to the Elton Mayo research studies at Western Electric. Mayo and his colleagues called attention to employee attitudes and group relationships as significant factors in job performance. Today we are concerned with employee morale and job satisfaction. We study the personality system, the motivational aspects of behavior, the communications process and power structures in order to understand and utilize our employees most effectively. The short-run payoff approach that evolved from the Taylor school is now complemented by a longer-run approach fostered by the behavioral scientists. Training programs are good examples of this. We know that job satisfaction can influence labor turnover. We know effective leadership and supervision can influence job satisfaction. And we know that good communications can help create effective leadership. Thus when we design a current training program for supervisory personnel, we devote attention to improving a supervisor's communication skills because we believe one of the payoffs may be in future lower turnover costs.

In addition to the research influence on manpower management fostered by Taylor and Mayo, other key factors influenced company manpower programs. Industrial cost accounting, the emergence and growth of the decentralization concept, the demands of two World Wars, and the growth of unions caused new personnel policies and techniques to be developed. On-the-job training programs, selection tests, college recruiting, manpower cost studies, fringe benefit plans, and labor relations programs emerged. Each new policy and technique added to the large number of items of concern to the firm in its manpower effort. *But the time dimension for each of these programs was different.* The college recruiting task, for example, tended to require a nine month program, the labor contract a two or three year period, and the pension plan a ten to thirty year program.

Because the programs arose at different times and because each had a unique time element, common objectives and direction were lacking in manpower efforts of the firm. Only when a manpower shortage posed serious economic problems did unity of effort become important. This situation usually occurred during war or mobilization. At other times manpower shortages were met by raising wages to attract workers, by recruiting workers in other locations, or by instituting training programs to produce the needed talent. Management could direct its recruitment and selection activity at most problems and solve them. And if difficulties arose with the union, the industrial relations expert was told to settle the differences.

Technological Factors

The situation is changed today because of two major developments. The first is the impact of modern technology on the size and composition of the work force. The rapid replacement of men by machines since the late 1950's has created long-term problems for the firm and society. Manpower planning is helping the firm meet the human problems of automation and at the same time is helping society solve unemployment problems.

The second new development also involves technology. It centers on the great emphasis on research and development activity by government, industry and universities. The drive for technical knowledge is constantly increasing and each new discovery opens up new avenues for further research. As this occurs, the business firm is forced to even greater research effort in order to survive. The Schumpeterian concept of "creative destruction" is acting as a driving force in research laboratories across the nation. As competitors develop new ideas and products, firms face potential destruction unless they can also develop new ways of creating demand or reducing costs.

This research emphasis means an increased demand for professionally trained scientists, engineers and managers. The services of these men cannot always be purchased by raising wages and the firm cannot hire an untrained person and expect to make him a qualified professional by training him for two weeks or six months. A potential shortage of highly trained persons thus poses a new set of problems for the firm that cannot be met by wage and training policies that were adequate in an earlier day. But the problems posed by technology are even more complicated than this. Advances in knowledge occur at such a rapid pace today, that it is now difficult for a qualified professional to maintain his technical proficiency. Obsolescence of technical manpower is a serious threat to the growth capabilities of many firms and to the nation as a whole. Returning experienced engineers to the college classroom is a solution to the problem for some firms. Other firms are doing nothing about the problem.

The very serious aspect of the entire problem, however, is the outdated selection criteria used by many firms in recruiting new talent from the colleges and universities. Unless campus recruiters make decisions on the basis of long-range qualitative requirements, a large percentage of the fresh manpower talent of a firm may be obsolete in a few years. We know, for example, that mathematical tools are extremely valuable in business decision making. The manager of the future must, as a minimum, be able to recognize a problem that can be approached and solved through the use of mathematics and statistics. Yet we know that many graduates of business schools have little if any understanding of the use of mathematical and economic models for decision making. Many of these men have never used a computer or know its capabilities when an expert makes use of it. Especially serious, then, is the fact that the professional curricula of many business, engineering and other disciplines, are obsolete today and totally inadequate for the needs of the future. Yet these schools fail to make the necessary adjustments because the business community has often failed to recognize and communicate the educational needs to manpower resources—the nation's colleges and universities. By continuing to

recruit men with an education inadequate for the future demands of industrial activity, firms do not exert the pressure necessary to help force changes in our higher educational system.

WHY ENGAGE IN LONG RANGE MANPOWER PLANNING?

The problems created by modern technology must be attacked several years in advance for successful solution. To solve the manpower obsolescence problem, selection and placement programs must anticipate future problems. This means time, money and effort must be expended in the near future to avoid the expenditure of larger sums of these factors at some later date. An examination of some of the identifiable problems that will face the firm and the nation during the next decade reveals the need for this planning effort.

The Future Supply of Manpower

Estimates of our future labor markets point out some very important facts.[2] Here are some of the things we know about the future.

The low birth rate during the 1930's in the United States means that a relatively small percentage of our population will be between the ages of 30 and 45 during the next ten years. This is the age group which is especially significant in middle management and professional jobs. It is from this pool that most of our top managers in the 1970's will be selected.

In 1955, the 30-45 year age group constituted 14% of the population. In 1970, the Department of Labor estimates that the group will constitute only 11% of the population and that it will fall to 10% by 1975. As this happens, business needs for capable

[2] The three leading groups studying future manpower problems are The Department of Labor, The National Science Foundation, and The Office of Education of the Department of Health, Education and Welfare.

managers will be expanding. We can expect the competitive pressures of technology and foreign competition to be greater. We know that the desire for diversification by firms creates more difficult planning, organizing, coordinating and controlling tasks for management. The legal, political and social environments of business firms will be still more complex in the future than it is today. The consumer demand sector of the economy will be bigger than ever and the servicing of it will also be more complex. All of these factors will press heavily on the competency of the firm's manpower. Although some experts foresee a decline in the importance of the middle management group because of computer technology, we may find that this increased complexity of business management will increase the burdens of the staff specialists and middle-level professional employees. And our statistics indicate that the men of an age normally used in these positions will be in relatively shorter supply than ever.

Some firms have discovered the age distribution factor is already a real problem. During the depression years of the 1930's these firms refrained from hiring new management personnel in order to provide jobs for those already employed. World War II then meant another five years of reduced hiring of young managerial talent because of the manpower scarcity. As normal retirements in the 1960's drain off the men hired during the 1920's, these firms are becoming aware of a shortage of experienced executives in the fifty year age class.

A problem facing many more firms is the supply of engineers and scientists that will be available during the late 1960's and early 1970's. The National Science Foundation estimates that 20%, or about 210,000, of the current number of engineers and scientists will leave the labor force due to deaths or retirements in the 1960's. In addition, they estimate that as many as 100,000 will transfer to non-engineering work. Offsetting this exodus will be an increased supply of college

trained persons. College enrollments are expected to increase by 70% during the 1960's over the 1950's. But the new talent may not be enough to fill the expected three to four million professional and technical jobs according to Department of Labor estimates. The Department of Labor, the Office of Education, and the National Manpower Council also foresee a potential serious shortage of professional manpower.

The National Manpower Council some time ago saw the situation developing and said, "The manpower pool is relatively shallow in our post-war economy—the economy, including our military force, is in continual danger of running aground on real shortages of highly trained talent."[3]

The Demand for Future Manpower

The supply figures cited above indicate only part of the potential problem that the nation and its business firms face. An examination of the expected demand for manpower provides some further insights.

The Department of Labor expects a 64% increase in the demand for professional, technical and kindred workers will occur in the United States from 1960 to 1975. A 40% increase is expected in the demand for managers, officials and proprietory workers during the same period. These figures are but a part of the increasing demand for manpower that will take place in the next several years.

The impact of this demand among professional workers will be felt greatest by scientists and engineers as opposed to medical, legal and military personnel. The demand for engineers, for example, is expected to be around the two million mark in 1975 as compared to 850,000 in 1960. Business firms thus increase their demand for engineers at

[3]Thomas Page, "Studies of National Manpower Problems," *Personnel Administration*, **XXI** (3), 16 (May-June, 1958).

a rate considerably greater than the entire professional group.

The same situation is true for managerial employees. Government statistics classify proprietors of service and retailing establishments as managerial employees. The number of proprietors is expected to grow at a slower rate than for the managerial group as a whole. "At the same time the number of managers and other salaried officials in business organizations and government is expected to increase at a relatively rapid rate."[4]

The future manpower demands of government and educational institutions is especially significant. Government employment rose by 178 per cent from 1929 to 1960 while the labor force as a whole rose by 43 per cent. Federal government officials have shown an increasing awareness for the need to attract top quality men from the nation's campuses in order to increase the efficiency of government operations. Higher salaries and improved recruiting techniques are two devices the government is using to attract top graduates. In addition, the many government scientific programs are a source of increased demand for engineers and scientists.

The nation's schools and colleges constitute still another pressure on the available professional and managerial talent. A National Science Foundation study indicates a 57 per cent increase in the demand for scientists and engineers by colleges and universities between 1959 and 1970. This study also projects a 75 per cent increase in the demand by government agencies for scientists and engineers.

Testimony to this impact of government and educational institutions on the supply of professionals to business firms is given by an executive of a major chemical company which employs large numbers of scientists.

This executive says:

We're having a much more difficult time filling our requisitions for scientists. Not only have other firms stepped up their activity, but we find that the federal government is a much more effective bidder for talent than ever before. In addition, the top schools in the country are offering their Ph.D.'s professorships, combined with almost unlimited research money for projects of interest to Washington and financed by government money.

An important feature of the demand characteristics of the future labor force is the changing occupational requirements. Technology has made its greatest impact on the unskilled hourly and clerical worker, but many skilled workers have also been affected. Experts disagree as to whether this has meant an overall upgrading of the work force. They agree, however, that new and different skills are required by technology.

The machine operator who had to use considerable judgment and skill in tending one or two pieces of equipment is being replaced by a magnetic tape unit, a control console, and a worker who monitors dials to insure that his six machines are performing properly. In one firm this type of operation meant the layoff of several highly skilled workers. When finally recalled to work most of the men were placed in lower job classifications because they could not make the necessary mental adjustments to the new job demands. Younger men without any of the old job skills were moved into the higher rated jobs.

Among managers, obsolescence is not as easily detected. Firms may operate for a considerable period without realizing they are falling behind competitors in improved scientific, technical and managerial techniques. A typical example centers around capital investment decisions. The firm that has specialists using present worth, discounted cash flow and common dollar valuation techniques in these calculations often thinks it is ahead of or abreast of its competitors. When it finds that competition is using the

[4]U.S. Bureau of Labor Statistics, Division of Manpower and Employment Statistics, *Manpower Needs and Resources of the United States: 1960-1975*, (Washington, D.C.: U.S. Government Printing Office, 1960), p. 16.

computer to examine a wider variety of alternatives in greater depth and with fewer man hours they are unpleasantly surprised.

The unemployment situation of the early 1960's indicates that it is not a general shortage of persons that pose manpower problems for management. It is the shortage of particular skills that creates problems. An estimate of future skill requirements is essential for a firm to avoid this type of problem in the future.

Optimum Utilization of Company Manpower

The challenges posed by supply and demand considerations are responsible for the emphasis on greater work force flexibility in all wage classifications through revised selection and development programs.

At the executive level flexibility is sought by job enlargement and job rotation. Among hourly rated employees it may mean selection based on the ability to learn new skills rather than emphasis on skills already possessed. Whatever the method employed, this flexibility drive is designed to permit the firm to fill key vacancies with current employees, to reduce manpower obsolescence, and to avoid the misuse of current manpower.

With high talent manpower, this means carefully thought out programs tied to the future. As Hill and Harbison have said, "Of all economic resources, high-talent manpower takes the longest time to develop, and thus it demands the most careful consideration in planning for the future."[5] This means, for example, that management development programs must have a long-term time horizon with specific objectives in mind. It means that constant evaluation of past programs is necessary to insure that proper development is taking place. And it means that the firm must constantly stand ready to revise even the most carefully planned programs

when new information about the future indicates changes are necessary.

The situation in one firm clearly demonstrates this need. An executive in a position to observe management manpower trends reported his firm is still guided by the notion that it "can never have enough engineers." "This worked for us during the last 10 years but it won't work during the next 10 years," he said. "What we need are some first class marketing and finance men. We're moving out of our production phase but nobody wants to admit that a good production engineer may not be a good promotion man."

Investment in Human Resources

The final and perhaps most important reason for manpower planning is the investment that a firm has in its manpower resources. The remark by Peter Drucker cited at the beginning of this article indicates the importance of the manpower resource to the firm. The continual improvement in the quality of the manpower talent in the firm is a necessary investment for survival.[6]

In a major division of one of the largest firms in the United States the average cost of recruiting one new engineer from college is $13,000. The firm estimates that new college graduates constitute a net expense item for the firm for at least two years. Close to $20,000 is thus invested in each new man before he can be considered an asset contributing to profits. Like many other companies the firm continues to invest in these men throughout their career with the firm through training and development programs.

[5]Samuel E. Hill and Frederick Harbison, *Manpower and Innovation in America* (Princeton, N.J.: Princeton University, 1959), p. 64.

[6]The idea of investment in human resources was given its current impetus by Theodore W. Schultz of the University of Chicago. Dr. Schultz' interest has been in the investment the nation as a whole makes in its manpower resources through education and other programs, including company sponsored or supported training and education. See, T. W. Schultz, "Capital Formation by Education," *Journal of Political Economy* **LXVIII,** 571-583 (December, 1960); and "Investment in Human Capital," *American Economic Review,* **I.I,** 1-17 (March, 1961).

Unlike most other assets of the firm, manpower has the potential to *appreciate* in value through utilization. In fact, the more intensively it is utilized with respect to its capabilities and capacities, the more valuable it tends to become. For example, a manager who is forced to use his abilities to their fullest tends to develop into an even better manager for the firm. The manager whose work is so uninspiring and unchallenging that he operates below capacity may actually depreciate in value through lack of use.

The dollar value of a trained, flexible, motivated and productive work force is difficult to determine. It appears reasonable to assume, however, that the quality of the managerial, professional, clerical and hourly work groups can cause significant differences in short- and long-run performance among firms. Money may enable a firm to duplicate reasonably a competitor's physical facilities. But money alone cannot enable a firm to duplicate the quality of a competitor's manpower. The additional factors needed to do this include a management policy regarding the importance of manpower, basic supervisory attitudes, time, and a program designed to accomplish the objectives of manpower training, motivation, flexibility and productivity. And these elements are key elements in any manpower planning program.[7]

MANPOWER PLANNING AND SOCIETY

An important aspect of manpower planning is the impact the process has on society. The inefficiencies and losses firms suffer from inadequate manpower staffing are a loss to the nation. When these individual losses are added up, the total losses may be very significant to the economy of the nation.

[7]An interesting and valuable source of information on this topic is *The Production and Distribution of Knowledge in the United States* by Fritz Machlup, (Princeton, New Jersey, Princeton University Press, 1962). See particularly Chapter Four on "Education" and Chapter Five on "Research and Development."

Even if the nation as a whole should develop enough highly trained individuals during the next decade to meet total demand, serious regional imbalances will exist. If firms can avoid overstaffing themselves with competent professionals, firms having difficulty obtaining key talent will have their problems eased.

Two trends indicate that the allocation of available resources will become less efficient before it becomes better. Defense contracting procedures often require a firm to stockpile key talent in order to obtain major contracts. This "capability" aspect of defense and space work has a reason. It assures the government that the successful bidder will be able to perform in accordance with the contract. It is an insurance factor vital to the government. At the same time it requires major space and defense contractors to carry large numbers of technically trained personnel on their payroll in order to bid on future contracts even if the personnel are not currently needed. A partial cost benefit results to the bidder when he is successful. He is able to reduce some turnover costs by having fewer layoffs between defense contracts. If unsuccessful in bidding, however, he is not so fortunate because the delayed layoffs finally take place. The geographic dispersion of defense work along the East, West and Gulf Coasts also complicates the nation's allocation problem of high talent manpower. When the large West Coast firm fails to win a large defense contract several thousand professionals are out of work unless and until another West Coast firm wins a contract requiring the hiring of thousands of professionals. To avoid unemployment, the professionals may have to journey East or South to another defense complex where hiring is taking place. Professional placement agencies are helping with this problem but the degree of frictional unemployment among professionals has risen greatly in recent years and now constitutes a significant annual talent loss to the economy.

Another form of manpower insurance is engaged in by a number of our larger companies. A mathematician for one company described the policy as "putting them (the scientists and engineers) in 'deep freeze' on some long term research until we actually need them. Then we pull them out and put them to work on economically significant problems." "Deep freezing" key manpower assets is not a new practice. But if it becomes more prevalent in industry, the allocation problems the nation faces will become more severe.

If firms are able to forecast their future needs with greater accuracy, the economy will be able to do a better allocation job. Scientists will be hired because the prospects of their doing economically significant work are high. Manpower insurance programs will not disappear, but the premium paid will be lower because the uncertainty factor has been reduced.

Another valuable use of manpower forecasting and planning is the information that can be furnished local agencies engaged in training manpower. The $435 million dollar federal manpower retraining program suffered because state employment agencies had little information on the types of skills for which training was needed. Firms that furnish these data are able to obtain trained personnel for jobs requiring skills in short supply.

Dissemination of this type of manpower information to our secondary school system is perhaps of great long-run significance to the economy. The number of teenagers from 15 to 18 years old will increase by 23% from 1961 to 1966—the sharpest rise for this age group on record. In addition, high school enrollments will rise by nearly 50% during the 1960's, and college enrollments by 70%.

School administrators, teachers and counselors need information on future occupational opportunities in order to plan curricula, facilities, and staffing. The City of Detroit, with one of the nation's first-class school systems, heard some unpleasant facts by a special committee investigating the educational needs of the city. The committee reported, "To put it very bluntly, the present course offerings are less than adequate to prepare youth for employment in today's labor market."[8]

Unless there is frequent and accurate communication between the employers in a community and educators, the frank appraisal made by the Detroit Committee may become a common experience in the United States. Misdirected effort in education is a loss to the student, to society, and to those financing the educational system. Recognition of this situation is explicitly made by the Department of Labor which has instituted an "early warning system" on "impending technological changes and their probable effect on employment opportunities and training requirements in different industries and occupations."[9] Industry cooperation is vitally needed so that the Labor Department and the United States Employment Service can assist educators in preparing young men and women to enter the work force.

CONCLUSION

The manpower problems created within firms because of the onrush of modern technology are requiring a new approach to the effective utilization of the manpower resources of the firm. A longer-term time horizon is dictated by this technology if these problems are to be anticipated and adequately solved. Prior to this modern industrial (or scientific) revolution, business firms were able to meet special manpower problems with special manpower projects of vary-

[8]The Board of Education of the City of Detroit, *Preparing Pupils for the World of Work*, (Detroit: Detroit Public Schools, 1962).

[9]U.S. Department of Labor, Manpower Research Bulletin No. 1 (Rev.), *Mobility and Worker Adaptation to Economic Change in the United States* (Washington, D.C., U.S. Government Printing Office, July, 1963).

ing time dimensions. A wealth of statistical evidence indicates, however, that today's problems may become extremely acute for individual firms and our nation as a whole. A manpower planning program which economically evaluates quantitative and qualitative manpower factors can help solve these problems for the firm. And in solving their own problems, firms can help society solve its manpower problems.

THE GROWING ROLE OF MANPOWER FORECASTING IN ORGANIZATIONS

Richard B. Peterson

Within the past few years increasing attention has been given the area of manpower forecasting. This is particularly the case at the national level where the government has attempted to provide more effective utilization of manpower resources. In a period of unprecedented prosperity we still find a minority of the labor force either unemployed or underemployed. The government has attempted to improve this situation through such legislation as the Manpower Training and Development Act and the Economic Opportunity Act. In conjunction with these various programs, the Department of Labor has attempted to estimate the long-term needs for various occupations. In the past, these forecasts have suffered from the lack of meaningful information at the firm level.

This article has several purposes. First, it seeks to point out the importance of manpower forecasting, both to the economy and to the individual firm. Secondly, the literature on manpower forecasting is surveyed. And finally, we shall present a manpower forecasting model used by a major American corporation in a dynamic environment.

Reference has been made above to the paucity of forecasting information at the firm level. This situation has been somewhat improved by the results of a study of job vacancies carried out by the National Industrial Conference Board under a Ford Foundation grant.[1]

The NICB study showed that it was possible to arrive at a workable system of determining job vacancies at the firm level. During 1965, 400 firms were studied in the Rochester, New York, labor market. Investigators visited the plants three times (February, May, and August) to determine what job vacancies existed at that point of time. A job vacancy was defined as "an unfilled job that an employer is actively seeking to fill by hiring a person outside of the organization."[2] The researchers were able to ascertain not only the number of available positions, but the specific occupation (using the Dictionary of Occupational Titles) and skill and educational requirements. Should the federal government decide to carry out this job vacancy study on a national scale, the information will be helpful in determining the short-term needs for manpower in our country. However, the results will have somewhat less meaning for the long-term projections concerning the composition of our labor force.

TERM DEFINED

The term *manpower forecasting*, as used here, refers to research for the purpose of estimating the size and characteristics of the work force at some future point of time. This definition precludes consideration of manpower development within the firm. This does not mean that manpower training has no importance for the future work force. Rather, the author wishes to emphasize the need for management to first ascertain the number of workers and skills that will be required. Only at that point can effective training and retraining be carried out.

From Richard B. Peterson, "The Growing Role of Manpower Forecasting in Organizations," pp. 7–14, MSU Business Topics, Summer 1969. Reprinted by permission of the publisher, Division of Research, Graduate School of Business Administration, Michigan State University.

[1] Robert Ferber et al., *The Measurement and Interpretation of Job Vacancies* (New York: National Bureau of Economic Research, 1966). See chapter by John G. Myers, pp. 405-45.

[2] "The NICB Job Vacancy Study," *The Conference Board Record*, p. 20 (September 1966).

What has been the experience in manpower forecasting in industry? The field research that has been undertaken in the past emphasizes the fact that, with few exceptions, systematic plans for future manpower do not exist in American industry. Hill and Harbison made this conclusion in the late 1950s after interviewing a number of firms.[3] They pointed out that even in those firms that were using long-range forecasting of manpower, the system was rarely being revised to recognize the changes taking place in the organization. One example was given where a firm had made a five-year forecast in 1955. Within two years the manpower estimate had been exceeded, but no modification had been made to recognize this fact. The authors concluded by stating that:

> Possibly the most important implication for company policy-makers suggested by this study is the need for companies to appraise their future development not merely with reference to markets, processes, and financial resources, but also in terms of the human resources that will be required.[4]

It is evident that this recommendation was not taken seriously by most firms. Two more recent studies illustrate this conclusion. The first research was carried out by the Bureau of Industrial Relations at the University of Michigan. It was found that most firms were doing nothing in terms of manpower forecasting. What work was being done was limited primarily to the aircraft, chemical, petroleum, and utilities industries.[5]

The most recent research was performed by the School of Business at the University of Indiana for the American Society for Personnel Administration.[6] Only a small number of the original sample of firms were doing significant work in the field of manpower forecasting. Of the original group of forty firms that might be doing something in this area, eight firms were chosen. Only five of the final sample firms were doing significant work.[7]

SOME OBSERVATIONS

A number of observations were reached with regard to the extent of manpower forecasting activities in these firms studied. First, manpower forecasting was more formal and extensive in rapidly growing firms and industries. Second, a variety of approaches to forecasting was used, varying from simple surmising to highly involved statistical techniques. The third important conclusion was that the firms were essentially concentrating on the replacement of present managers rather than attempting to estimate the degree of creation of new positions in the future. Finally, the researchers concluded that even in many cases where personnel executives realized the need for forecasting, the view was not shared by top management.[8]

It is surprising that so little meaningful work has been performed in the area of manpower forecasting at the firm level. Particularly is this the case when one realizes that most companies regularly prepare long-range forecasts or plans in the areas of marketing, research, manufacturing, and product development. The cost of ineffective utilization of manpower clearly justifies increased

[3]Samuel E. Hill and Frederick Harbison, *Manpower and Innovation in American Industry* (Report Series No. 96, 1959), 85 pp. For a short summary of this report see Frederick Harbison, "Manpower and Innovation," *Personnel*, pp. 8-15 (November-December 1959). In the few cases cited where planning existed, the figures were based upon erroneous assumptions that technology would remain the same.

[4]Frederick Harbison, "Manpower and Innovation," *Personnel*, p. 15 (November-December 1959).

[5]"How to Forecast Your Manpower Needs," *Nation's Business*, p. 102 (February 1964). The article suggested the need for past productivity data, employment and occupational trends, and managerial and professional work force data.

[6]Albert N. Navas, et al., "Managerial Manpower Forecasting and Planning," *American Society for Personnel Administration* (Research Project Report 1965), 13 pp.

[7]*Ibid.*, p. 2.

[8]*Ibid.* This list represents only a few major observations and tentative conclusions based upon the research. For more detail, see p. 2.

attention for manpower planning. Today, many firms are saddled with a certain percentage of employees who are technologically obsolescent, partially as a result of this negligence. This situation is particularly true for scientists and engineers. Effective manpower plans could recognize this danger and provide systems for retaining these employees.

It has been estimated that many of the existing jobs in industry will be obsolete or materially changed within the next ten to twenty years. If this is true, it behooves management to focus attention on the skills likely to be required. Only in this way can these skills be integrated into the educational process so that the required manpower will be available. For example, General Electric recognized that many of their older engineers were technologically obsolete. The result was periodic training programs to give such employees some conception of recent developments in engineering.

Increased attention to manpower forecasting systems also would provide benefits in terms of lowering the rate of employee turnover. To the degree that the most capable employees are retained, there is a considerable cost savings to the firm. It has been estimated that the cost of hiring a professional worker varies from $250 to over $1,000 (moving expenses not included). If a firm hired fifty engineers each year, the total cost would vary from $12,500 to over $50,000. Finally, though estimated costs are unavailable, the hiring of certain key professional employees may contribute substantially to the success of specific programs.

INHERENT DIFFICULTIES

In fairness to many companies, it should be recognized that there are many inherent difficulties in attempting to estimate future manpower needs. Particularly this is the case where one is trying to determine the type and number of jobs which might exist five or ten years hence. No doubt, many firms

try to translate production forecasts into the estimate of the number of production workers required during the next fiscal year. However, with the anticipated rapid increase in salaried employment in the coming years, there is a pressing need to emphasize this sector as well.[9] It is in the managerial and professional categories that the problem may be most acute because of increasing demand for these personnel.[10] The primary emphasis of this article concerns the managerial, technical, and professional needs in organizations.

Enough has been said about the need for research in manpower forecasting. Although this need exists at all levels of the organization, the problem is especially acute at the managerial and professional levels. The next question concerns how to properly develop a systematic approach to manpower forecasting for these personnel.

There is no simple formula which can be universally applied. Each firm must develop its own system in light of its own particular experiences.

Considerable research is required if the manpower forecast will roughly approximate the actual manpower needs of the firm one to ten years hence. It should be expected that short-range projections of up to one year should be more accurate than long-term estimates. W. S. Wikstrom suggests that the forecast will be satisfactory if it estimates within 15-20 percent of the actual requirements for personnel.[11]

It must be stressed that manpower planning will be effective only to the degree that

[9]"BLS Forecasts Big Increase in White Collar Jobs," *White Collar Report,* Bureau of National Affairs, September 22, 1966, pp. B1-B3.

[10]*Ibid.,* p. B-1. Between 1964 and 1975 it is expected that there will be a 54 percent increase in the category of professional, technical and kindred workers. For the managerial group, a 23 percent increase is expected. When considering all white collar workers, the figure is 38 percent. This compares with an estimate of 17 percent increase in the blue collar sector.

[11]W. S. Wikstrom, "Planning for Manpower Planning," *Business Management Record* (National Industrial Conference Board, August 1963), p. 33.

such work is an integral part of the entire corporate planning process. If top management is unwilling or unable to see this point, then the forecast degenerates into a mass of meaningless data.

On the other hand, if top management recognizes the gains to be made by effective manpower forecasting, important results can be attained.

The following information should normally be considered essential to the preparation of a worthwhile manpower forecast: (1) analysis of past and present product and process development, (2) evaluation of major corporate plans regarding future products, processes, and services, (3) awareness of technological developments in other industries that may affect your own organization, and (4) evaluation of past and present work force.

One of the first questions that manpower planners must ask themselves is the degree to which the company has developed technologically. In such industries as aerospace one finds major changes in technology. Many of the specific job titles held by present-day engineers were virtually unknown a generation ago. Another illustration is the computer industry where the job skills in such firms as IBM and Remington Rand are considerably different than when they manufactured office machines.

Estimating manpower requirements is considerably easier for those firms in which limited technological advances have taken place. But for the more dynamic firms, rapid changes at present likely will continue into the future.

THE FUTURE?

The future of manpower forecasting hinges on the amount of information provided by other functional areas concerning short-term and long-term planning. This requires that key personnel responsible for this activity be continually informed relative to research,

product development, marketing, and manufacturing plans. Furthermore, where the firm is acquiring or merging with other companies, this information is imperative.

On the plant level, knowledge of improved processes or increased sales estimates can be translated into a need for a specific number of new employees in specific categories. Particularly is this true for direct production workers. The problem is more complicated when one seeks to translate projections for company growth into the need for specific numbers of professional and managerial personnel with specific job skills.

Worthwhile long-range planning requires considerable understanding of developments taking place in other industries as well. The recent developments in data-processing equipment have had significance on the level and skill mix of employees in particular firms. Though research has been inconclusive so far, the computer may affect the design of the organization and create new positions.

Another illustration emphasizes the need to recognize the effects of competition on the work force. Until recent years, the steel industry was the principal producer of cans for storing oil and various consumer products. During the early 1960s, the aluminum companies developed cans that were directly competitive with steel for packaging oil, beer, and other products. This innovation not only affected the profit position of the competing industries, but also the level and types of work force.

One of the major sources of information consists of analyzing the firm's work force over a number of years to detect major trends in level and skills required. This procedure has particular relevance when the company seeks to ascertain the manpower needed to replace employees leaving the organization over a period of time. Review of the company's turnover experience, in light of economic conditions, provides some important insights for future recruiting purposes. See Table 1 for an outline of the major consid-

TABLE 1   MODEL OF DEPARTMENTAL MANPOWER FORECASTING SYSTEM

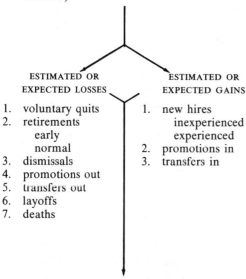

INVENTORY OF PRESENT WORK FORCE

1. age
2. job title
3. level of experience
4. evaluation of employee potential

EXPECTED GROWTH OF DEPARTMENT WORK

(taken from one and five year plans as approved by top management)

1. number of new projects
2. size and responsibility of new projects
3. expansion of present projects
4. technical developments in other departments
5. technical developments outside the company
6. developments in professional education (universities)

ESTIMATED OR EXPECTED LOSSES

1. voluntary quits
2. retirements
   early
   normal
3. dismissals
4. promotions out
5. transfers out
6. layoffs
7. deaths

ESTIMATED OR EXPECTED GAINS

1. new hires
   inexperienced
   experienced
2. promotions in
3. transfers in

PROJECTED DEPARTMENTAL WORK FORCE
(estimates compared to past experience)

1. one year projection
2. five year projection

REVISION OF FIVE YEAR PROTECTION
ON BASIS OF YEARLY PROJECTION
RESULTS

erations for a departmental manpower forecasting system.

The compilation of such information has become considerably eased with the use of data-processing equipment. Today most medium and large firms can quickly determine specific characteristics of their work force. Turnover figures by specific categories such as voluntary quits, dismissals, retirements, layoffs, transfers, and deaths are readily accessible. For an example, see the IBM manual *Personnel Data System*. Estimates of likely future turnover can be developed through trend projections. Furthermore, replacement charts help in determining effects of promotions and retirements.

By careful analysis of strengths and weaknesses of present personnel, the manager can foresee the needs for additional employees to complement the present work force. Based upon the author's preliminary field research, firms in the aerospace industry have attempted to translate new contracts into specific manpower needs.

There is an additional bonus in keeping comprehensive records of employee turnover in light of changing production demands. By studying the past use of manpower it is possible to determine the costs of certain alternatives. Recent articles by Eckley and Garbarino have dealt specifically with this subject. Though the application has concerned the plant force in particular, it raises questions for those firms where there is fluctuation in the salaried force as well.

R. S. Eckley raises the question of whether layoffs are not more costly to the firm than other alternatives when there is a lowered demand for the company products. Such factors as higher unemployment taxes, selection and training expenditures, and difficulty in rehiring laid off workers are important considerations. He suggests that employers can even out the fluctuations in business by such means as: elimination of overtime used to achieve peak output; retrieval of work previously subcontracted; and absorption of annual attrition in the work force.[12]

COMPARATIVE COSTS

Garbarino also treats the question of comparative costs, but in terms of handling peak loads rather than surplus labor supply. Because of the increased percentage of fringe benefits to total compensation, the question has been raised as to comparative costs of overtime vs. hiring of additional employees. Though conditions will vary among firms, many employers believe that the costs of hiring additional workers (interviewing, training, social security contributions, unemployment taxes, etc.) may exceed costs of the alternative device of using overtime work.[13]

This question has particular significance to the hiring of professional employees in the aerospace industry. According to a recent publication, the average cost of hiring such workers in 1965 was $1,251. The figure was $2,857 if moving costs were included.[14] It is obvious that proper utilization of scarce resources (scientists and engineers) has an economic advantage to the firm.

It has already been suggested that manpower planning is a corporate-wide responsibility. More than anything, it requires the support of the chief executive and his top management staff. For it is only through their acceptance that functional managers will provide the necessary information.

Who should have the day-to-day responsibility for preparing and revising the manpower forecasts? The answer may vary with the firm. However, the most common practice centers on the personnel department or organization planning where this activity is a

separate function.[15] Whatever the decision, there must be a close relationship between these personnel and other key officials of the firm.

Manpower forecasts should not be limited to internal use only. The data have relevance to determining occupational needs for the economy in general. To the degree that we have improved occupational forecasting at the firm level, there will be more effective allocation of the nation's entire work force.

MODEL IS USED

Let us now turn our attention to outlining the major components of an ongoing manpower forecasting system. This model is used by one of the major American corporations, operating in a highly dynamic environment, with rapid change both in product mix and sales. It has been developed within the last few years at this major corporation. As will be shown, manpower planning and forecasting is very much integrated with total corporate long-range planning. In fact, there is a great deal of coordination between manpower planning and corporate planning at the headquarter's level.

Perhaps the best way of illustrating the total long-range planning system is by way of a diagram. Figure 2:1 provides a general outline of the various inputs which eventually are incorporated into the approved plan.

Starting in July of each year, the major divisions or the organization prepare *A Long-Range Planning and Review Report* which encompasses the planning for that particular division during the coming five years. There are three major inputs in determining long-range planning for the corporation. First, they discuss alternative business opportunities for the division. Secondly, they

[12]R. S. Eckley, "Company Action to Stabilize Employment," *Harvard Business Review,* pp. 51-61 (July 1966).

[13]Joseph Garbarino, "Fringe Benefits and Overtime Barriers to Expanded Employment," *Industrial and Labor Relations Review,* pp. 426-42 (April 1964).

[14]Deutsch and Shea, Inc., *Technical Manpower Recruitment Practices* (1965-1966), 44 pp.

[15]See Edwin Geisler, "Manpower Planning: An Emerging Staff Function," *Management Bulletin #101* (American Management Association 1967), for study of unit responsible for manpower planning function in surveyed corporations.

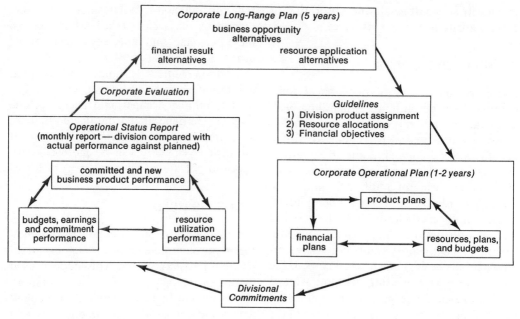

Figure 2.1

determine alternate plans for resource allocation, including manpower and equipment. Finally, they determine the financial position of the company, which plays a major role in evaluating future alternatives.[16] This report is then reviewed by corporate headquarters to determine its feasibility when compared to the demands placed on the corporation from other divisions. The final approved report is usually completed by late October.

The next step is for each division to prepare *An Operational Planning and Review Report* based upon the approved *Long-Range Planning Report.* This operational plan is usually submitted and approved during the months of November and December. Although the plan constitutes divisional objectives during the next two year period, the primary focus centers upon the first twelve month period.

[16]The group plan is based on (a) results of market survey and (b) division forecasts based on market survey statistics. At the same time the personnel department develops a training and employee budget for the following twelve months. This budget is based not only on market survey reports but the budgets for research and development as well.

This approved *Operational Planning and Review Report* is updated in May of the following year to insure that it is current.

Finally, the *Monthly Operational Status Report* is submitted by each division. The corporate staff can now compare actual to planned performance.

Our primary interest here is to study the way the organization determines the need for its manpower. Manpower requirements are determined according to certain formulas developed for measuring specific needs.

Each division is responsible for preparing its manpower requirements. Divisional manpower planning personnel first outline their needs by program. The manpower forecast is broken down into three major programs: first, direct (non-overhead) personnel required to meet present product requirements; secondly, personnel required to carry out research and development work (new business); and finally, requirements for indirect (or overhead personnel) to provide staff services.

The next step is to divide the manpower budget into three major categories. They are engineering, operation (production), and administrative and support services. The budgets are further broken down into direct and indirect budgets for the first two functional groupings.

The fourth step is for the division to determine what work will be done within the corporation or division as opposed to work done by other divisions or outside contractors.

FINAL STEP

The final step is for the division to break down its manpower needs into specific payrolls such as engineering, manufacturing, quality control, material, facilities, and all other personnel. The company has developed certain yardsticks as to typical wages and salary for different levels of personnel. This payroll is then further broken down for each payroll into hourly, general office professional-technical, and managerial.

After the divisional reports have been approved by corporate headquarters, the corporate manpower planning group then develops forecasts for specific occupations. At present, they maintain skills forecasts for thirty-two hourly positions. Not all of these positions are necessarily critical; however, the majority fall into that category. In the professional-technical sector, they maintain specific forecasts of approximately fifteen to twenty job classifications.

The corporation has developed a rather comprehensive way of determining the need for particular groups of personnel under different circumstances. For instance, they have developed a meaningful relationship between weight of product and need for particular personnel, such as operatives, designers, and other engineering support personnel. Furthermore, they have found considerable success with developing learning curves; and depending on the skill mix of employees and the local labor market, determining the applicable learning curve to apply at that point of time.

In discussing the impact of the manpower forecasting system, the members of the corporate group felt that this system provided a helpful means for the division in legitimizing their need for additional personnel. As yet, it is too early to measure the accuracy of the estimates, but the manpower planning group feels that the system provides measurement devices to insure more effective utilization of manpower within the corporation.

PLANNING FOR A PERSONNEL REDUCTION

Thomas H. Sebring

While personnel managers generally cheerfully assume that hiring people is the normal function of a personnel operation, occasionally business conditions force them into the more unpleasant role of handling personnel layoffs. Many articles and publications are regularly written for and by personnel people covering every imaginable facet of personnel selection and placement. However, little thought is generally given to the layoff problem until the unpleasant certainty is suddenly before the personnel manager and an emergency program has to be undertaken. At this point of time, the need of immediate action frequently precludes the careful planning necessary to handle a personnel reduction with a minimum of problems.

This is highly unfortunate, because failure to handle a personnel reduction smoothly can destroy almost overnight the good will and credibility the personnel operation has built up in its other work areas over a period of years. It may even have a disastrous effect upon the entire company's image in the local community. However, very few companies have developed a comprehensive personnel reduction plan which could be applied with little delay, when the need for a reduction actually develops. This is not to imply that most companies have no policies or procedures governing personnel reductions. The average company usually has a number of detailed procedures relating to termination pay, length of notice, etc. However, these policies and procedures are insufficient unless

From Thomas H. Sebring, "Planning for a Personnel Reduction," Personnel Journal 44 (4), 179–183 (1965). Reprinted by permission.

incorporated into a comprehensive, well considered reduction plan.

Any specific manpower reduction plan depends to a large degree upon the nature of the company, the type of business, and the composition of the work force. It is manifestly impossible, therefore, to develop a plan which would be applicable to all companies under all conditions. It is not the purpose of this paper to attempt to formulate a detailed reduction plan which your company can install.

However, there are a number of significant considerations which must be covered in establishing any personnel reduction plan. These include: (1) Communication; (2) Equitable identification of those to be affected by the reduction; (3) Treatment of long service employees; (4) Placement effort; (5) Record keeping; (6) Exit interviews. Some brief comments follow concerning these considerations.

COMMUNICATION

One of the most important aspects of any personnel reduction is complete and timely employee communication. The tendency frequently exists for a company to delay giving any information at all to its employees concerning an impending manpower reduction until it can give them "all the facts." This overlooks the fact that employees always have their own informal channels of communication and will undoubtedly know about the forthcoming layoff shortly after management makes the decision.

Failure to release all available information to the employees immediately will usually result in the rapid development of rumors which will considerably magnify and distort the actual facts. An actual reduction of 200 people may be rumored to be a thousand-man layoff, or even a plant shutdown. The best way to forestall the development of wild rumors is to announce the reduction immediately, describing the business conditions which make it necessary, the probable number of people to be affected, and the expected timing of the action.

In addition to the general communication directed to all employees mentioned above, it is usually advisable for each manager to let all the people in his sphere of operation know where they stand, both individually and as a group. Each individual whom the manager feels will or will not be affected by the layoff should be personally informed of his prospects, and all the employees should receive all the information the manager has on the nature, size and timing of the layoff. If complete and prompt information covering the layoff is not made available to employees, some people whose jobs are actually secure may take precipitate action to find a new position based on distorted rumors as to what is going to occur.

EQUITABLE IDENTIFICATION OF THOSE TO BE AFFECTED BY THE REDUCTION

In some cases, particularly in regard to hourly employees where pure seniority tends to weigh heavily, the criteria for selection of those to be released in a manpower reduction are already firmly established. However, in cases where the rules are less definite, there exists a significant opportunity for personnel people to make a valid and frequently unrecognized contribution to the equitable selection of those to be affected. For example, insuring that managers give merit, future potential, and length of company service proper balance in determining those to be "surplussed" is a responsibility of the personnel function. As a matter of fact, to the extent that the criteria for layoff seem inequitable to those affected, the personnel operation will be charged with a major share of the blame, whether they established the ground rules or not.

While past performance should be a key factor in layoff selection, it is questionable

whether most formal merit rating systems seem to those affected to be consistent and objective enough to be used as the sole reduction criteria. Consideration of which of two employees with similar backgrounds from different units is to be laid off might be made difficult by differences in the rating tendencies of the managers concerned. A system which provides for performance ranking by the managers of all the employees in the same job classification in the organization, and which also takes into account length of service considerations, sometimes proves to be useful. It is especially important, regardless of what type of system is utilized, that the factors taken into account in selecting those employees to be released be consistently applied across the entire organization and carefully explained to the affected employees.

TREATMENT OF LONG SERVICE EMPLOYEES

One of the problems most difficult to resolve in a manpower reduction occurs when the question arises of "surplussing" long service people. The definition of "long service" depends to a large extent upon the organization itself and the average service of its employees. However, one frequently accepted definition for long service is ten or more years continuous service with the company.

If possible, of course, any company would prefer not to place long service employees on layoff notice. Personal problems arise with long service employees which are especially difficult to solve: (1) Frequently longer service employees have achieved an age which makes it difficult for them to find a suitable job with another company. (2) Since their children may be well along in school, they may find it more difficult to uproot them than will a family with younger children. (3) The skills which they have obtained over a long period of time with the company are not always easily transferable to another organization.

In addition to the personal problems involved in releasing long service people, which, of course, are paramount, there is also the question of the effect which their release may have upon the morale of other people in the work group. There is a tendency in such a situation for the other employees to identify with the unfortunates and wonder what sort of treatment they themselves would receive in a similar situation. Releasing long service personnel may also have a very unfortunate effect upon the company's public image in its community. At a time when it is popular to classify corporations as cold, ruthless, profit machines, the release by a company to the open labor market of older employees with extensive service with the company can only seem to confirm the image.

A case which occurred several years ago illustrates the problem very well. As a brand new recruiter, the author was representing his company at the plant of a nationally known corporation which was then experiencing substantial layoffs. The firm was extremely interested in placing its people and had invited in outside concerns to interview the affected people in its facilities. In looking over the résumés which they had prepared for review, it was surprising to note that about a half dozen of these people had service with this company of from twenty to thirty years. When asked about this, the personnel representative handling the placement of these people stated that, while they were unhappy about laying these people off and had delayed it as long as they could, business conditions would not permit their continued employment. An interview with several of the men found them to be in a state of numbed disbelief that this could happen to them.

To this day I have never felt the same about that company. Even though there was no way of knowing the full scope of their business problems at that time, it seems that there must have been an alternative course other than the layoff of these long service people. And if an outsider were so shocked by the release of these men, it is a reasonable assumption that it may have had an even more unfavorable impact upon the local community in which they had lived for so many years. And, to the extent that the community's disappointment with the company affected its buying habits in regard to the company's products, a decision which, on its face, seems an unsatisfactory handling of a human problem may have also turned out to be a bad business decision. While it may be argued that a corporation's primary *raison d'etre* is to make a profit for its stockholders, it is also true that industrial concerns are expected to exhibit a social concern today which was not expected of them fifty years ago. Failure to exhibit this concern in its dealings with its employees, consumers, or the public may turn out to have an adverse effect on the corporation's profitability.

While it may sometimes be impossible to maintain long service employees in their jobs when business reverses occur, there are usually alternatives to laying them off. For example:

(1) Even though the company may not follow a straight seniority system, it may be possible to displace shorter service people in the same job category.

(2) In a multi-plant company, they may often be successfully transferred to another location.

(3) If there is no alternative to their release from the company, it might be possible to give them extended notice of termination with the understanding that they will not be released until they have located a new job.

(4) If they lack skills which are still in demand elsewhere in the company, it may be possible to retrain them to qualify for these positions.

Regardless of how the problem is handled, it is critical to the success of the personnel reduction plan that a system for handling long service personnel be developed which is generally accepted as equitable by the affected employees, other employees, and the general community.

PLACEMENT EFFORT

One of the first questions which arises in a personnel reduction is the delineation of responsibility for finding new jobs for the surplus people. Should the individual be turned loose to find a job on his own? Should the personnel operation engage in a concerted placement campaign? What placement responsibility should the employee's manager bear? In handling a manpower reduction of over a thousand people in 1963, our organization found the best results were achieved when all three parties were given specific placement responsibility.

Our personnel operation contacted all other locations of our company in order to develop any openings which might be available. In addition, we sent over a hundred outside firms both within and outside our local area a description of the types of people available and extended them an invitation to interview these people on our facilities. (This was done in spite of the concern which some of our managers had that inviting other concerns to our plant might result in "under-the-table" contacts with some of our non-"surplus" people whom we could ill afford to lose. This concern turned out to be unnecessary. The company representatives who visited our plant handled themselves very circumspectly.) In addition to the visit invitations to other corporations, contacts were established with any governmental agency or other organization which could prove of service. For example, both the local office of the State Employment Bureau and the local manufacturers association proved to be a productive source of job openings.

The managers of the employees affected were also asked to make placement contacts of their own for their people. Being particu-

larly familiar with both the work experience and personal characteristics of their people, they frequently are capable of making quicker and more appropriate placements than the personnel operation. In addition to their knowledge of the people working for them, they often have a good feel as to which companies in the area (or other geographic locations of their own company) have comparable jobs and they often have an easier entry to the managers possessing these openings than the personnel people.

While a great deal of assistance can be given to an individual in the job-hunting process by his personnel operation and by his immediate manager, the final responsibility to relocating a new position lies with the individual himself. In this regard it is surprising how little knowledge of the job-hunting process many people possess. Most people do not look for a new position very frequently and are, hence, relatively unsophisticated in the process of résumé writing and in interviewing, etc. (This does not necessarily apply to engineers, particularly those in the aerospace industry, many of whom tend to change jobs more frequently.)

It is important that the personnel function provide professional counsel and help in job-hunting techniques to those desiring it. Advice to an individual on the proper construction of a terse but comprehensible résumé, and helpful tips on how to approach the job interview can be of invaluable assistance. Another area in which the individual frequently needs help, but may not even have realized it himself, is in developing the proper attitude to make a success of his job-hunting efforts. The first reaction of many people placed on layoff notice is humiliation that it could happen to them. Though the cuts might have been extremely deep, and many highly qualified people affected, the feeling frequently exists that being "surplussed" is somehow a reflection upon their performance. This initial attitude may actually impede the employee's job-hunting efforts to the extent that it lowers his self-confidence and, hence, his presentation of himself to prospective employers. It is necessary, therefore, to reassure the employee that the layoff in no way reflected upon him as a desirable employee. A technique which was used with some success in our organization during layoff situations is the "Self-Help Job Clinic." This consisted of a seminar composed of eight to ten surplus employees, a placement representative from the personnel function, and a psychologist from our psychological services operation. The seminar had two main purposes. One was the presentation to the group by the personnel representative of specific information on résumé writing and interviewing. The second was, through group discussion of their problem, to help each of the employees to achieve a frame of mind commensurate with the job-hunting process. By realizing that he was not alone in his predicament, and by discussing his problem with a group of people in the same situation with comparable backgrounds, the employee is frequently helped to develop a more positive attitude toward himself and thus improve his placement prospects.

RECORD KEEPING

An important aspect of any personnel reduction is the maintenance of accurate records. Since the number of people in the organization was originally a critical enough element to make a reduction necessary, maintenance of accurate records as to how many people were actually "surplussed," on what sort of time schedule, and where they went, is also highly important. These statistics will be frequently required by people outside of the personnel function and are exceedingly difficult to compile unless a record system has been maintained from the very inception of the reduction. Detailed records should be kept, if possible, of the names of all people affected, the job sources to which they were referred, the number of interviews

and offers received by each, and the final disposition of each case.

In addition, keeping detailed records provides the means for obtaining measurements as to the effectiveness of the overall placement effort, and of each of the job sources exploited on behalf of the affected individual.

EXIT INTERVIEWS

One of the final, but by no means the least important, elements of the personnel reduction plan is the exit interviewing of those leaving. A properly conducted exit interview by a trained interviewer can serve several purposes: (1) It can provide spontaneous information from the employee concerning his attitudes toward the company, his co-workers, his supervision and his job. (2) It can provide the employee's evaluation of how fairly, effectively, and humanely the layoff was conducted, and may develop from the employee some valid suggestions for handling future reductions differently.

In order to obtain any indication of an employee's real feelings about the items above, it is necessary to overcome the employee's fear that any critical feelings which he expresses will be carefully documented by the interviewer and inserted in his personnel folder with a resulting adverse influence on his chances of being recalled to the company when business conditions improve. This fear can frequently be overcome if the interviewer carefully refrains from making even the simplest written notes until after the interview is concluded.

GENERAL COMMENTS

The preceding discussion has reviewed a few significant points to consider in planning a manpower reduction. It has not provided, nor was it intended to provide, a detailed blueprint for handling layoffs. The prime criteria for handling a reduction properly, of course, is that the company management recognize that this is a highly critical activity which deserves the full support of the entire management organization.

It is important that an equitably planned and humanely administered layoff, providing all the help to the affected employees possible, be regarded not as a philanthropic action on the company's part but as an element of sound business judgment. Failure to exercise good judgment in planning a layoff can have a disastrous effect upon the company's reputation as a fair employer and even affect the sales of its product in the community affected.

JOB ANALYSIS: NATIONAL SURVEY FINDINGS

Jean J. Jones, Jr.
Thomas A. DeCoths

In the summer of 1968, the Bureau of Business Research, California State College, Long Beach and the Job Analysis Research Staff of the California State College, Los Angeles Foundation conducted a nationwide survey to determine current uses, methods, and practices of job analysis.[1] Job analysis is the process of gathering information about jobs: specifically, what the worker does; how he gets it done; why he does it; skill, education, and training required; relationships to other jobs; physical demands; and environmental conditions. It is the basic tool manpower managers use to generate job descriptions, job specifications, job evaluations, and information for collective bargaining, personnel appraisal, training, and manpower planning and organization.

Questionnaires were mailed to a nationwide sample of 1805 firms listed in the 1968 *College Placement Annual* (published by the College Placement Council). Responses were received from 899 firms. Organizations in the sample range in size from less than 500 em-

From Jean J. Jones and Thomas A. DeCoths, "Job Analysis: National Survey Findings," Personnel Journal 49 (10), 805–809 (1969). Reprinted by permission.

[1]This survey was undertaken in connection with job analysis research being conducted jointly by the two institutions mentioned for the California State Department of Employment, with funds provided by the U.S. Department of Labor. The authors wish to express their gratitude to Dr. Dale Yoder and Dr. C. Harold Stone, co-directors of the research project, and other members of the research committee, Drs. Carl E. Gregory, James J. Kirkpatrick and William F. Long for their contributions, without which this article would not have been possible. The research committee is credited with the design and construction of the questionnaire.

ployees to over 100,000 and include all the major industrial classifications with the exception of agriculture. The questionnaire distinguished between job analysis programs for salary-rated and hourly-rated employees. About 37 percent of the 681 respondents *using* job analysis indicated they have programs for salaried only, 6 percent for hourly only, and 57 percent include both.

This article highlights several significant findings of the survey and suggests possible reasons for some of the responses.

SOME FIRMS DO NOT USE JOB ANALYSIS

Approximately one-fourth of the respondents do not have job analysis programs. One-third of these respondents expect to establish a program in the future. Reasons most often cited for not using job analysis are: (1) "it would serve no useful purpose," (2) "an acceptable system has not been found," (3) "it is too expensive," and (4) "it takes too much time."

The survey shows that firms with fewer than 500 employees are less likely to have job analysis programs than larger firms. At the extremes, firms in durable goods manufacturing are *most* likely to have job analysis programs, while those in service industries are *least* likely to have them.

USES OF JOB ANALYSIS INFORMATION

The major uses of job information are for job evaluation, recruitment and placement, labor relations, manpower utilization (e.g., organizing, planning, and avoiding task duplication), and training. Table I summarizes the extent of these uses among respondents.

The four groups making the most use of job descriptions are personnel staff, management, first-line supervision, and training personnel. Two-thirds of the respondents indicated they use job descriptions at least weekly, with one-half claiming daily use.

TABLE I. **MAJOR USES OF JOB ANALYSIS INFORMATION**

	PROGRAMS FOR SALARY-RATED	PROGRAMS FOR HOURLY-RATED
Job Evaluation	98%	95%
Recruiting and Placing	95	92
Conducting Labor and Personnel Relations	83	79
Utilizing Personnel	72	67
Training	61	63

Job information is used in hiring the handicapped in 17 percent of the programs for salary-rated employees and 25 percent of the programs for hourly-rated employees. One-fourth of the respondents reported that they use job information for enriching jobs and for vocational counseling. About three-fourths apply job information when writing job specifications for recruiting and placing. Less than half indicated the use of job analysis for development of performance standards, which, of course, are vital in the areas of personnel appraisal and training.

For the most part, job information is used for the same purposes in programs for salary-rated personnel and programs for hourly-rated. However, some differences deserve comment. For salary-rated employees, job information is more frequently used to appraise personnel and to establish authority, responsibility, and accountability than in programs for hourly-rated workers. In the latter, it is used more often in labor negotiations and to administer labor agreements than in programs for salaried employees.

FACTORS COVERED BY RESPONDENTS' JOB ANALYSIS PROGRAMS

With respect to factors included in job analysis programs, substantial differences exist between programs for salary-rated and hourly-rated employees. Programs for hourly-rated employees more often emphasize factors of environmental conditions (e.g., work space, comfort variables, and hazards); what the worker uses (e.g., tools, equipment, materials, supplies, and special clothing); responsibility for materials, equipment, and safety; physical attributes; and the incumbent's "functional relationship" to physical objects. In contrast, programs covering salary-rated personnel more frequently include factors of "functional relationships" to data and to people;[2] social skills, responsibility for money and confidential information; company policies; and organizational relationships to other jobs.

Factors which occur with about the same frequency in both types of programs are what the worker does, supervision received, experience, training, education, and mental skills. Only about half the respondents reported that they have developed standard definitions for job analysis factors.

Despite the abundance of "human relations" theory in management thinking during recent years, information for its practice is gathered by relatively few of the respondents' job analysis programs. In Table II, the low percentage of response for the human relations factors "Interests, Motivation," "Personality," and "Social Skills" relative to other worker attributes illustrates this point.

The possible reasons for this limited emphasis on human relations are a lack of standard definitions, the difficulty of measuring human relations activity, and the amount of research required to develop valid and reliable information-gathering instruments.

[2]Workers' "functional relationships" to physical objects, data and people serve as one of two bases of classification in the *Dictionary of Occupational Titles*. For an explanation of these functional relationships, see U.S. Department of Labor, *Dictionary of Occupational Titles* Washington, D.C.: U.S. Government Printing Office, 1965) 3rd ed., Vol. II, pp. 649-650.

TABLE II. OCCURRENCE OF WORKER ATTRIBUTE FACTORS IN RESPONDENTS' JOB ANALYSIS PROGRAMS

	PROGRAMS FOR SALARY-RATED	PROGRAMS FOR HOURLY-RATED
Aptitudes (Type, Level)	39%	41%
Experience (Job Knowledge)	89	86
Interests, Motivation (Activity Preferences)	24	19
Manual, Manipulative Skills (Dexterity, Accuracy)	40	71
Mental Skills (Adaptability, Judgment, Initiative, Creativity, Technical)	77	71
Personality (Adjustment to Job Situations)	27	21
Physical (Strength, Coordination, Senses)	32	69
Social Skills (Human Interactions)	39	23
Training, Education (Level, Type, Time)	83	84

RESPONSIBILITY FOR PERFORMANCE OF JOB ANALYSIS AND TIME REQUIRED

The respondents were asked to indicate the department which performs job analysis in their organizations. Table III summarizes their responses.

TABLE III. THOSE RESPONSIBLE FOR PERFORMANCE OF JOB ANALYSIS

	PROGRAMS FOR SALARY-RATED	PROGRAMS FOR HOURLY-RATED
Consultant Analyst	3%	2%
Full-Time Analyst	18	15
General Personnel	37	35
Industrial Engineering	2	11
Labor Relations	3	14
Organization-Planning Personnel	10	6
Part-Time Analyst	5	6
State Employment Service Analyst	1	1
Wage and Salary	55	45
Other	4	3

The frequent assignment of responsibility to "Wage and Salary" and "General Personnel" groups for the performance of job analysis is not surprising. The two most frequent uses of job information are in job evaluation and recruitment and placement—traditionally the functions of the above-mentioned groups. However, the extremely low response indicated for the use of "State Employment Service Analyst" *is* surprising in light of the skills possessed by state analysts, services offered, and the low costs involved. A possible explanation for this small response may be that firms are unaware of services offered by State Departments of Employment.

One of the parameters measured in the survey is the time required to complete one job analysis and write a job description. For both salary-rated and hourly-rated programs, approximately three-fourths of the respondents reported a time of 8 hours or less. Only 5 percent of the respondents indicated they spend 17 hours or more.

EDP IN JOB ANALYSIS

About 10 percent of the respondents using job analysis employ electronic data processing for storage and retrieval of job information. However, less than 2 percent use computers for more difficult applications such as job structuring, estimating time spent on tasks, task ranking, or ascertaining frequency of tasks. In general, industry has yet to develop the sophisticated information systems necessary to harvest the benefits of computer applications in manpower management. There are at least three primary reasons why.

The first is technical. Most information obtained through job analysis concerns the incumbent's duties. The survey discloses that prevalent practice is to describe these duties in a narrative form. Unfortunately, that form is not as amenable to computerization as numeric information. Alphabetic data usually require twice the computer memory space as numeric data, and words are much more difficult for most computers to interpret and manipulate than the relatively simple language of numbers. Thus, where attempts have been made by industry to computerize job analysis procedures, difficult conceptual design problems have been encountered.

The second reason for limited EDP application is one of feasibility. Job duties and elements vary significantly from job to job, even within an occupational group. The wide variance between jobs makes identification, standardization, and codification of job variables difficult and arduous. The difficulty of attempting to deal with job variables is magnified by the diversity and changing nature of jobs in the economy. (The United States Employment Service lists over 30,000 job titles[3] and describes in excess of 13,000 jobs in the *Dictionary of Occupational Titles.*) It is obvious that the adaptation of EDP to job analysis for the individual firm presents not only conceptual design problems but also real questions of feasibility and economy.

The third reason is one of priority in allocation of resources. Over half of the respondents indicated that they would be interested in experimenting with new techniques for improving job analysis. The question remains, however, whether firms are willing to commit the resources required to develop comprehensive, theoretical job analysis models. The research and man-hours required to develop such models suffer the same handicap inherent in most non-product related research—the problem of identifying their worth to the organization in financial terms.

MAJOR DISSATISFACTIONS

Respondents were asked to rate various factors in their job analysis programs as "very satisfactory," "satisfactory," or "unsatisfac-

[3]U.S. Department of Labor, *Dictionary of Occupational Titles* (Washington, D.C.: U.S. Government Printing Office, 1965) 3rd ed., Vol. I, p. xv.

tory." The two areas most frequently rated as unsatisfactory are currency of job information and multi-purpose or broad use of job analysis programs.

The dissatisfaction with currency of job information is traceable to the traditional methods of performing job analysis. The survey reveals that the most common methods used to gather job information are interviews (of supervisors and/or job incumbents), old job descriptions, observation, and supervisor written narratives. Table IV lists these and other methods and extent of their use.

TABLE IV. METHODS RESPONDENTS USE TO PERFORM JOB ANALYSIS

	PROGRAMS FOR SALARY-RATED	PROGRAMS FOR HOURLY-RATED
Check Lists of Tasks and Duties	19%	23%
Check Lists of Worker Behavior	2	2
Critical Incidents	3	2
Daily Diary by Employee	3	4
Employee Written Narrative	41	22
Interviews	85	84
Of Groups	11	9
Of Supervisors	79	78
Of Workers	69	61
Job Training Standards Review	2	3
Key Question Interview	26	20
Observations	57	72
Observation-Interview	34	39
Old Job Descriptions	59	58
Questionnaires	43	30
Recall from Analyst's Experience	18	17
Supervisor-Written Narrative	54	42
Technical or Supervisory Conference	20	17
Time and Motion Studies	4	13
Work Participation by Analyst	8	7
Other	1	1

The traditional methods of gathering job information are time consuming and difficult to perform with anything more than a modicum of consistency and currency. As a result, necessary up-dating of job information often proves costly and impractical. An additional shortcoming of traditional methods is that their subjective and narrative nature severely limits their adaptability to automation and the computer attributes of speed, mass data manipulation, and standardization.

The dissatisfaction with versatility of job analysis programs is related to the difficulty of adapting a common method of gathering job information for diverse purposes. It may be that some of the respondents' job analysis programs lack the necessary sophistication demanded by the more rigorous applications. Such applications are inherent in the construction of vocational tests, development of training courses, job dilution, and job restructuring. Industry's current emphasis on training the handicapped and the hardcore unemployed gives added impetus for sophisticated job analysis techniques.

CONCLUSION

Three important conclusions may be drawn from information provided by this survey. First, there is widespread dissatisfaction with present job analysis programs, particularly with respect to currency of job information and versatility for diverse purposes. The reasons for this dissatisfaction may be attributed to lack of standardized, quantifiable techniques for gathering, recording, and presenting job information, and limited use of EDP. Second, most job analysis programs are characterized by relatively little emphasis on human relations type job variables. Third, due to the rapidly growing work force, the current emphasis on upgrading the unemployed and underemployed and the impact of technological change on the nature of work, the traditional techniques of job analysis may no longer be adequate to meet the needs of the economy.

These conclusions suggest the need for a two-pronged research effort in job analysis. One aspect of the research should attempt to develop a comprehensive model for improving job analysis procedures. The objective of this research should center around quantifying job information, increasing its validity, eliminating its subjectiveness, and reducing the costs of its collection. In addition to standardizing job analysis methods, the successful implementation of such a model will greatly facilitate updating of job information. The other aspect of the research should examine ways to help job analysis practitioners define and measure psychological and sociological job related variables. Increased availability and validity of human relations type job data will enable manpower managers and planners to more effectively deal with the human aspects of technological change.

MANPOWER PROCUREMENT

A BEHAVIORAL SCIENCE APPROACH TO PERSONNEL SELECTION

Everett G. Dillman

INTRODUCTION

The process of selection of personnel is an essential procedure for any organization. The effectiveness of the selection procedures will often determine the long-run ability of the organization to achieve its objectives. Many organizational problems—such as labor strife, turnover, excessive absenteeism, low or poor quality production—may be minimized by the use of proper selection procedures. Selection itself will not insure organizational success but is a critical first step toward obtaining it.

Traditional Selection Techniques

The principle of "fitting the man to the job" has formed the basis for the selection procedures used by many personnel organizations. By this is meant that an individual's abilities, capacities, and aptitudes must be such that he will be able to perform the *tasks* called for by the job.[1]

The sociological implications of work are recognized by some experts in personnel. The personnel selection procedures used by many organizations are designed to consider how well an employee will "fit in" with his fellow workers.[2] In addition, it has been generally recognized that psychological variables of an individual, including his personality, aptitudes, and intelligence, play important roles for adequate performance of most jobs. Many present-day selection techniques purport to consider these factors and try to appraise the important personality and intelligence variables through the use of various psychological tests and interview techniques.[3]

The validation of the various traditional selection procedures (including psychological tests) usually relies on some measure of performance as the dependent variable, i.e., that which is to be predicted. In other words, scores on a psychological test—say a personality test—are correlated with some measure of job performance. If a reasonably high correlation is obtained—e.g., if the high scores on the test are associated with high scores on the performance rating—the test is considered to be valid and therefore useful.

In practice, however, the measurement of many psychological variables has been found to be elusive. In many cases the correlation of a selection technique to performance has tended to vary—the relationships are often situational.

The shortcomings of tests and other traditional selection techniques in consistently

From Everett G. Dillman, "A Behavioral Science Approach to Personnel Selection," Academy of Management Journal 10 (2), 185–198 (1967). Reprinted by permission.

[1]For instance, see Michael J. Jucius, *Personnel Management* (Homewood, Ill.: Richard D. Irwin, Inc., 1959), 4th ed. Chapter 6, "Job Requirements," considers no aspect of the job other than the tasks to be performed and the abilities required by the individual to perform these tasks.

[2]Richard P. Calhoon, *Managing Personnel* (New York: Harper and Row, 1963).

[3]C. Harold Stone and William E. Kendall, *Effective Personnel Selection Procedures* (Englewood Cliffs, N.J.: Prentice-Hall, 1956).

predicting job performance may be explained when it is recognized (a) that the performance variables themselves are frequently unreliable, (b) that the performance measures are frequently not valid measures of "true" performance, and (c) that job performance is frequently dependent upon factors over which the individual has little or no control.

In summary, then, most of the presently used selection techniques are designed to best fit the man to the job. Sociological and psychological variables are frequently considered, but short run, on-the-job performance is the criterion by which the selection procedure is evaluated. The obvious deviates from "normal" behavior, among the candidates, are usually screened out by the selection process, but still many individuals are hired who prove to be troublesome to the organization in many different ways or who become so frustrated with the job situation that they are forced to leave.

Although the present approach to selection is indeed a vast improvement over the early approaches, it is the thesis of this discussion that the perspective of the present approach is too narrow and, as such, the techniques used are less effective than they could be. A broad perspective can be gained through the use of a behavioral conceptual model. The proposed model will consider both the formal and the informal organization. Behavior is analyzed at three levels of abstraction: (a) the individual level, (b) the work group level, and (c) the level of intergroup relationships.

AN ORGANIZATIONAL MODEL OF EXPECTATIONS–CONSTRAINTS

The objectives of a formal organization form certain restrictions on the behavioral alternatives available to the personnel within that organization (1). (The numbers within the parentheses refer to specific arrows on the model.) These restrictions are known as *formal constraints* and consist of (a) the formal

organizational structure, (b) the job assignments, (c) the formal rules and regulations, and (d) the physical environment. In addition to the restrictions on behavior, these formal elements require certain minimum behavior. These are known as expectations. The expectations, then, may be thought of as forming the lower limit to performance and the constraints the upper.

The set of expectations-constraints may be viewed as restrictions on the behavioral alternatives available to personnel within the organization. Supervisory behavior must operate within these, so it may be said that supervision is greatly affected by the formal set of expectations-constraints. Supervisory behavior, in turn, affects the formal set of expectations-constraints through modifications in the organizational structure and changes in the rules and regulations and the job assignments (2).

Leadership behavior has a direct influence on the behavior of the individual operative (3). Organization expectations-constraints also will affect the operative performance, independent of supervisory behavior. On the other hand, both leadership behavior and the set of expectations-constraints (including the informal set) are affected by the operative—his attitudes and actions.

The individual is most frequently a member of a work group (primary group) which has its own characteristics, dependent upon but often different from those of its membership. The influence of the individual upon the group is considerable, as is the reciprocal influence of the group on the individual (5). Supervisory behavior and the set of expectations-constraints both influence the characteristics of the group and are influenced by it (6, 7).

There is usually more than one work group within an organization. It has been shown that intergroup behavior has characteristics unique from those of the individuals or the groups which comprise it. Intergroup behavior is affected by, and affects, the constraints

(8), leadership behavior (9), the work group (10), and the individual (11).

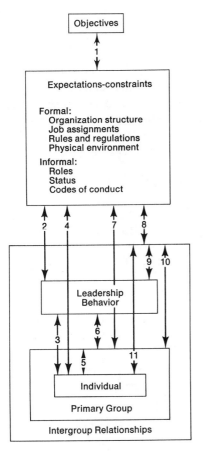

Figure 2.2

The model, then, can be shown as a series of interrelated organizational elements. The model should be considered as a system with the arrows indicating inputs and outputs between and among the various organizational elements. It should be noted that the organizational elements relate in interaction. Each of the arrows in the model may be thought of as a point of interaction. The arrow indicates the direction of the effect; double arrows indicate reciprocal effects.

The behavioral approach to selection can be viewed as an attempt to fit an individual into this dynamic model. It is the thesis of this analysis that the effectiveness of the selection process will be much greater if it is viewed in terms of the entire organizational system. It should be realized that the organization is composed of a series of interrelated subsystems and that the individual must fit into all elements of the system—the formal and the informal.

A BEHAVIORAL PERSPECTIVE

Selection should be based upon an understanding of the set of expectations-constraints present in the specific position.[4] This requires, of course, knowledge of all relevant expectations and constraints, formal and informal, at each of the several levels of analysis. It must be emphasized that since all elements in the model are interrelated no one expectation or constraint may be considered in isolation. In addition, the constraints exist in reality only as they are perceived by the individual.

The test of selection, therefore, is:

1. To determine the objective set of expectations-constraints which is imposed by the formal and the informal elements interacting within the organizational framework,

2. To appraise the way these expectations-constraints will be perceived by the individual being considered,

3. To evaluate the effects the expectations-constraints will have on the individual, and

4. To appraise the effects the individual

[4]The typical job analysis does not discover these expectations (except the formal task expectations) and does not deal at all with the constraints directly, but instead concentrates on the duties of the job. Consequently the job descriptions and the job specifications are generally deficient in outlining the boundaries of the job.

will have upon the system of expectations-constraints.

The difference between the approach using the behavioral perspective and that using the traditional point of view should be clear. *All* elements of the job are considered in behavioral selection, while traditional methods look only at the job tasks and conditions. Under the behavioral approach it is important to realize that each individual not only must be capable of meeting the expectations of the job (including the task expectations) but must also be psychologically able to withstand the job constraints, including the informal constraints.

The Objective Set of Expectations-Constraints

Each position in an organization has an "objective" set of expectations and constraints associated with it. An objective set of expectations-constraints may be operationally defined as the set which has a reality in the perceptions of "most" individuals subject to the set. When a manager evaluates the physical environment of the job, certain elements of the environment appear to be constraining. Not only does he think so, but so may most of the people who work under these conditions. The fact that the particular constraint is not really "true" (e.g., a certain danger may be thought to exist by everybody and therefore will influence behavior even though the particular danger may have no basis in fact) is not the point at issue. Neither is a value judgment as to the propriety of the constraint a valid criterion for determining whether a constraint exists. For instance, management may not like a particular group norm, but it still may have a very strong constraining influence on the behavior of the group members. If it does, the selection process should take it into account. Something is an "objective" expectation or constraint, then, because a number of persons perceive it as such.

The constraints on behavior within the organization may be viewed as a narrowing of the repertoire of choice alternatives available to the personnel within the organization. The most stringent constraints would exist when one, and only one, behavioral pattern would be open to the employee. On the other hand, the most liberal set of constraints would exist when there were no restrictions on behavior (except the community moral code of behavior). It should be recognized that in any society the status of no constraints can exist only with complete anarchy. As a matter of reality some constraints on behavior will always exist.

As seen in the model the constraints and the expectations which influence organizational behavior can be classified into those which are derived from the formal aspects of the organization and those which have their derivation in the informal aspects.

1. Formal Expectations-Constraints
   1.1 Organization structure
   1.2 Job assignments
   1.3 Formal rules and regulations
   1.4 Physical environment
2. Informal Expectations-Constraints
   2.1 Roles
   2.2 Status
   2.3 Codes of conduct (norms)

The formal organization may be defined as the scalar hierarchy of responsibility and authority which has been blueprinted for the organization. The formal organizational structure is the basic framework within which all interpersonnel relationships (behavior) must take place. Established authority relationships can be seen to greatly affect the action alternatives available to the job incumbent. One can do (formally) only what he has the authority to do.

The tasks which are assigned to each job form definite expectations and constraints on behavior. These tasks are expected to be performed. Activities not specifically assigned to the job are normally considered to be outside of the formal job assignment. Frequently the job tasks are set forth in a job description and a job specification which further limit the allowable behavioral patterns.

Formal rules and regulations (including budgets and other control devices) form definite constraints on performance. The very purpose of the rules and regulations is to regulate and to control behavior by restricting undesirable choice alternatives and requiring other more desirable behavior.

The formal organization dictates where each job will be performed and the tools and equipment to be used. These conditions may be thought of as constituting the physical environment of the job. The location of the job constrains a person by limiting his choice of associates and by putting him into contact with specific physical and social conditions.

In addition to the formal set of expectations and constraints under consideration, the informal constraints and expectations play a large part in determining organizational behavior. The first expectation-constraint to be considered is that of the concept of role. A role may be defined as "a specification of some, but not all, of the premises that enter into an individual's decision"[5] and thus affect his behavior.

The formal organization dictates only part of the role behavior of each individual in the organization. Every person in the organization expects those with whom he has contact (superiors, subordinates, and peers) to behave in certain ways with respect to him. This is known as a role expectation and is a key concept in the study of organizational behavior. Role expectations are part of the informal organization and, as such, are af-

fected by both the individual and the group. It is important to note that role expectations may or may not be congruent with the formal job demands. If they are not congruent it can be expected that a conflict between the informal and the formal organization will exist.

Status may be defined as "... a relative position of worth or standing accorded a person by some other person or group of evaluators."[6] The status ascribed to an individual in a group is a restraining influence on that individual. Status affects individuals in two basic ways—status seeking and status maintenance. Few generalizations may be made about the specific behavioral requirements any one group will hold as the determinants of a specific status. It can be said that some criteria will exist, however, and that these will affect the behaviors of those who are seeking to maintain a status position as well as the behaviors of those who are attempting to attain it, although the behavioral patterns of these two groups will probably be different.

The informal organization tends to develop certain codes of behavior which act to regulate the performance of personnel within the organization. In every organization certain things are "just not done" although there may not be any formal rules against the behavior. These informal rules of conduct (i.e., norms) act as behavioral controls which constrain behavior deemed by the group to be undesirable. The strength of these informal constraints should not be underestimated.

Adequate selection, therefore, requires knowledge of the existing set of formal and informal expectations-constraints. The procedures for determining the set clearly must encompass much more than the traditional job analysis although the same method may be used.

---

[5]Herbert A. Simon, *Administrative Behavior* (New York: The MacMillan Co., 1958), 2nd ed., p. xxx.

[6]Waldo W. Burchard, "The Status of Status," *Sociology and Social Research,* **XLIV** (6), 420 (July-August, 1960).

Perceptions of the Structure of Expectations-Constraints

Although each job will have a set of "objective" expectations-constraints associated with it, the personal significance of this set—in fact, the delineation of the set itself—can be expected to differ from individual to individual. This was borne out by a study of 203 teachers conducted by Raymond Kuhlen. It was found in this study that there was considerable variation in the ways the various teachers perceived their job.[7] The interpretation of the particular "objective" set of expectations-constraints is "filtered" through the individual's cognitive world, that is, through his image of the world. This image is a product of (a) his physical and social environments, (b) his physiological structure, (c) his wants and goals, and (d) his past experiences.[8]

Even though each individual has a somewhat different cognitive world there are many common features in the cognitive worlds of all people, especially when the individuals are subject to a common social environment. It should be noted that the physical and social environments, the wants and goals, and many experiences are shaped by the society in which one lives. Even though each individual in that society will be subject to somewhat different forces, the general forces will be substantially the same.

It is important, in the selection process, to evaluate the individual's perceptions of the legitimate base for organizational authority. In a study of several organizations Peabody found that the legitimacy of the authority relationship was viewed by individuals in several different ways. In some instances the base for authority was seen to rest in the office. In other cases authority rested in pro-fessional competence, experience, and human relations skills which either supported or competed with formal authority.[9] The implications of these differences in perception of authority for the selection process are great. It may be hypothesized that if an organization is authoritarian in its structure, e.g., the military, its authority relationships will probably have to be perceived by the individuals in the organization as being vested in the office. In other more permissive organizations, such as research and development laboratories, the legitimate base should be viewed as resting in the professional competence of the supervisor. It is essential that the individuals selected perceive authority in a manner consistent with this essential element of the expectations-constraints structure.

The concept of situs can be a very useful tool to determine or to infer the way an individual will perceive the structure of expectations-constraints. A situs may be defined as "an occupation grouping of categories of work which are differentiated in some way but are not invidiously compared."[10] Each situs category contains occupations ranging from the highest to the lowest status.

Morris and Murphy have identified the following ten civilian occupational situses: (1) Legal Authority, (2) Finance and Records, (3) Manufacturing, (4) Transportation, (5) Extractive, (6) Building and Maintenance, (7) Commerce, (8) Arts and Entertainment, (9) Education and Research, and (10) Health and Welfare.[11] Within each one of these occupational situses a set of values, norms, and expectations tends to develop. In many respects, each situs may be thought of as a sub-culture.

[7]Raymond G. Kuhlan, "Needs, Perceived Need Satisfaction, Opportunities, and Satisfaction," *Journal of Applied Psychology,* **XLVIII,** pp. 56-65.

[8]David Krech, Richard S. Crutchfield, and Egerton L. Ballachey, *Individual In Society* (New York: McGraw-Hill, 1962), pp. 17-18.

[9]Robert L. Peabody, "Perceptions of Organizational Authority," *Administrative Science Quarterly,* pp. 465-466 (March, 1962).

[10]Richard T. Morris and Raymond J. Murphy, "The Situs Dimension in Occupational Structure," *American Sociological Review,* **XXIV** (2), 233 (April, 1959).

[11]*Ibid.,* pp. 236-237.

Since a common set of values, norms, and expectations can be expected to develop within each of the situses, it can be expected that mobility within the situs would appear easier to the individual than would inter-situs mobility. Reiss has observed that "... the difference between inter- and intra-situs mobility is considerable. Inter-situs movement is characterized by increased risk and intra-situs movement by increased security."[12] It can be expected, then, that the perceptions of the particular set of objective expectations-constraints will be influenced, to a great extent, by the particular situs background of the individual under consideration for selection. Individuals who have previously held positions in the same situs category could be expected to have clearer perceptions of the "objective" structure than those individuals who had been exposed to situses with vastly different value systems.

The importance of studying the situs background of applicants was pointed out in a study of the occupational backgrounds of applicants for two police departments.[13] In this study it was found that more of the occupations previously held by the job applicants fell into the Building and Maintenance and the Commerce situses. Surprisingly few of the applicants had held jobs in the Financial and Records situs. The data indicated that the job of a policeman was being perceived in different ways by the different applicants and that the perceptions depended upon occupational value systems held. It was concluded that certain occupational groupings are more likely to be attracted to the job of patrolman. The ease of inter-situs mobility will be greatest from situses where the values, norms, and expectations differ only slightly from those to be expected in the Legal Authority situs.

As a general rule, the selection procedure should be designed to examine very carefully the situs background of each applicant in an effort to determine the extent of prior inter- and intra-situs mobility. An individual who has remained in one situs for a considerable length of time can be presumed to have developed the common value system of that situs. If the occupation for which he is applying has a vastly different value system than that to which he has been accustomed, some problems may be anticipated in the integration of the individual into the structure of expectations-constraints.

An individual's satisfaction with the job will depend, to a great extent, upon the particular set of expectations brought with him to the work situation. Although group membership is frequently mentioned in the literature as being an important motivation force (i.e., satisfying a basic need), the employee's attitude toward the group may depend upon the experience of group success or failure to attain what he perceives as a prize.[14] Group membership is important to the individual, but its importance lies in satisfying his need structure. The selection process should consider this. The classification of "goals" set forth by Zander, Natsoulac, and Thomas provides an appropriate analytical tool for determining the congruency of the individual and the group goals. They note the following classifications: (a) *the member's goal for the group,* (b) *the group goal,* (c) *the group's goal for a member, and* (d) *the personal goal.*[15] The goals may be said to be highly congruent if the group goal for a member is close to the member's personal goal. It is desirable to try to achieve such congruity through selection.

[12]Albert J. Reiss, Jr., *Occupations and Social Status* (New York: The Free Press of Glencoe, Inc., 1961), p. 257.
[13]Everett G. Dillman, "Analyzing Police Recruitment and Retention Problems," *Police* (May-June, 1964).

[14]Morton Deutsch, "Some Factors Affecting Membership Motivation and Achievement Motivation in a Group," *Human Relations,* **XII** (1), 81-95 (1959).
[15]Alvin Zander, Thomas Natsoulac, and Edwin J. Thomas, "Personal Goals and the Group's Goals for the Member," *Human Relations,* **XIII** (4), 334 (November, 1960).

In summary, then, the selection procedures must recognize that the perceptions of the structure of expectations-constraints are colored by the particular cognitive world of the individual. Included in this cognitive world are subsets of expectations, beliefs, values, norms, needs, and goals. Each of these must be appraised to determine how they will affect the perceptions of the set of "objective" expectations-constraints associated with the particular job.

The Effect of the Structure of Expectations-Constraints on the Individual

It has been shown in the previous discussion that the objective expectations-constraints present in any job are filtered through the cognitive structure of the individual. If these expectations-constraints are determined (by the individual) to be incongruent with his self-concept—e.g., the cognitive structure which determines how the individual will view himself, including his evaluation of his abilities and capacities—some frustration can be expected.

It must be recognized (indeed, it is a basic concept of a behavioral orientation to selection) that any given set of expectations-constraints will have differential effects on various individuals. Because of this the selection process must be so designed as to appraise these individual differences and to predict the effects of the structure on the particular individual. The following are important considerations in making such an appraisal:

1. *Each individual will perceive the set of expectations-constraints in a somewhat unique manner* (as we have already noted in the previous discussion). It is important to emphasize, at this point, that the perceptions of the individual are shaped to a great extent by social conditioning. The particular way an individual will perceive certain relevant organizational variables may be inferred from a study of his work and life history

(including an examination of the situs categories already mentioned.)

The model may be used in making an analysis of the probable perceptions. Since each element in the model has been hypothesized as constituting one aspect of a set of expectations-constraints it is possible to derive measures which will evaluate how an individual will react to the structure.

2. *The self-concepts of each individual differ.* It is important to realize that each individual will measure his life and progress in an organization against his self-concept and his need structure. If organizational reality forces behavior which is vastly different from the image of the self held by the individual, it can be expected that conflict will occur. It should be recognized that the constraints forced by the organization are the greatest limiting factors to the full achievement of the higher order needs of most individuals. Argyris has maintained that an organization forces immature behavior on generally mature individuals (who presumably have a mature self-image) and in the process creates conflict and frustration.[16]

The self-concept held by an individual will determine, to a great extent, what he will expect from the organization.[17] Vroom has shown that the ego-involved individual performs better than those who are not so involved.[18] It might be noted that ego-involvement will come about when the organizational environment is consonant with the individual's self-concept and his expectations.

3. *The basic personality structures of individuals will differ.* The primary aspect of the

[16]Chris Argyris, *Personality and Organization* (New York: Harper and Row, 1957).

[17]Uriel G. Foa, "Relation of Workers' Expectations to Satisfaction with Supervisor," *Personnel Psychology,* **X,** 161-169 (1957).

[18]Victor H. Vroom, "Ego-Involvement, Job Satisfaction and Job Performance," *Personnel Psychology,* **XV** (1), 159-177 (Spring, 1962).

personality structure which is important for selection is the ability of the individual to withstand frustration. This ability affects the willingness of the individual to accept different levels of authority and pressure.

One important personality variable which can be used to appraise the susceptibility to authority and pressure is the authoritarian-equalitarian continuum.

Authoritarians behave in ways that reveal compulsive conformity based upon a view of the world as menacing and unfriendly. Though they are not necessarily people of low intelligence, they think in relatively few channels, from which they cannot be moved. In addition, they seek security through the exercise of authority or, better still through surrender to some powerful authority figure.[19]

In a laboratory experiment conducted to test the differential effects of group pressures on authoritarian and nonauthoritarian persons, Canning and Baker found that "Comparisons between subjects with authoritarian and those with non-authoritarian personalities validated the hypothesis that the authoritarian would be influenced to a greater degree by group pressure than the non-authoritarian."[20] It was found that although both groups responded to group pressure the authoritarian group was influenced to a greater extent than the non-authoritarian. The most commonly used measure of authoritarianism is the California F-Scale.

In a study of the effects of participation in decision making on persons with different personality structures, Vroom noted that equalitarians (non-authoritarians) and those with strong independence needs developed more positive attitudes toward their jobs and increased in performance through partici-

pation.[21] If the job has a wide latitude for decision making (i.e., if the constraints are broad) an equalitarian personality would be more likely to adjust and to avoid frustration.

There is some evidence to indicate that the equalitarian will be more able to distinguish differences between himself and others in the group than will the authoritarian. The evidence is not clear, however, as to how this clearer perception of differences will affect the interactional patterns. As a general rule, equalitarians will tend to be more tolerant of the perceived differences than will authoritarians. The authoritarian personality may not be able to distinguish small differences between himself and others in the group but will tend to be less tolerant of those differences that he does perceive. Steiner notes that an authoritarian personality may be unwilling to believe that "good people" possess a mixture of good and bad traits.[22]

Kahn and Wolfe have noted that the following personality dimensions can act to modify the pressures of the expectations-constraints structure.

1. *Flexibility:* the flexible individual is sensitive to early signals of pressure and will experience tension as a result. The rigid individual is less sensitive and therefore reports less tension.

2. *Introversion:* the introverted person feels more tension, trusts and respects his associates less, and attributes less power to them. The extrovert feels about the same amount of tension regardless of pressure; his trust and respect for his associates is much less

---

[19]Robert T. Golembiewski, "Three Styles of Leadership and Their Uses," *Personnel,* **XXXVIII** (4), 36 (July-August 1961).

[20]Ray R. Canning and James M. Baker, "Effect of the Group on Authoritarian and Non-Authoritarian Persons," *The American Journal of Sociology,* p. 580 (May, 1959).

[21]Victor H. Vroom, *Some Personality Determinants of the Effects of Participation* (Englewood Cliffs, N.J.: Prentice-Hall, 1960). Also see Arnold S. Tannenbaum, "Control in Organizations: Individual Adjustment and Organizational Performance," *Administrative Science Quarterly,* **VII** (2), 236-257 (1962).

[22]Ivan D. Steiner and Homer H. Johnson, "Authoritarianism and 'Tolerance of Trait' Inconsistency," *Journal of Abnormal and Social Psychology,* **LXVII** (4), 388-391 (1963).

impaired under pressure.[23]

The specific mental and physical abilities, then, must be appraised in light of the requirements of the structure of expectations-constraints. The effect of the structure on the individual is of great importance. If these effects are not correctly predicted the individual will probably experience frustration and consequently present problems.

Effects of the Individual on the Structure of Expectations-Constraints

The expectations-constraints model, underlying the behavioral perspective to selection, has been presented as a system—a series of interrelated formal and informal organizational elements. Although the particular influences between and among the elements have not been quantitatively defined, their existence has been postulated. In terms of the model, then, a change in one element of the system will introduce changes in the other elements of the system.

The process of selection will affect the various elements of the organization by introducing a new element (the individual) into that system. The probable changes to the system must be evaluated as an essential part of the selection procedure. If an organizational system is functioning reasonably well and if no major changes in the structure of expectations-constraints are desired, it will be necessary to select an individual who not only can operate within this structure (without experiencing frustration) but who will introduce little change in the structure.

In making an inference as to the probable changes in the system it should be kept in mind that the structure of expectations-constraints is formed in the interactions among the elements (levels of abstraction). It will be necessary, then, to appraise the value

[23]Robert Kahn and Donald Wolfe, "Role Conflict in an Organization," *Conflict Management in Organization* (Ann Arbor, Mich.: Foundation for Research on Human Behavior, 1961), pp. 21-31.

orientations held by each of the elements. The most critical points of interaction for the selection process are the individuals, the groups, and the formal leaders. The value system of the individual under consideration must be congruent with the systems held by the group and by the leader. In short, he must accept, be acceptable to, and be accepted by, the system.

Of course, it may be desirable in some instances to intentionally try to change the existing set of expectations-constraints by introducing some dissonance into the system. It should be pointed out, however, that the effects of such an introduction into the system may be difficult to predict. Unless predictable effects can be traced through all elements of the system it would be preferable to introduce only mild levels of dissonance at any one time. If large changes are to be made they may be made in steps, each of which is relatively small. This will allow the system to return to equilibrium after each change.

SUMMARY AND CONCLUSIONS

The traditional methods for the selection of personnel have generally been preoccupied with appraising the ability of the candidate to perform the tasks of the job. Although it is indeed essential that the individual be able to perform the job duties, the behavioral approach to selection recognizes a need for taking a broad perspective of the job.

The behavioral approach to selection presented in this report conceptualizes a position as being subject to a set of "objective" formal and informal expectations and constraints. This structure determines the minimum behavior and restricts the patterns of behavior that remain open to the individual.

The behavioral selection process has been described as the attempt to determine (a) the set of "objective" expectations-constraints associated with the job, (b) the way the candidate will perceive this set, (c) the effects of the structure of expectations-constraints on the individual, and (d) the effects of the individual on the structure of expectations-constraints.

Although this report does not give the personnel administrator a complete set of analytical tools for selection, a broad model has been presented which should serve as a framework within which the tools may be developed. It is felt that the broad approach taken in this report will meet the expectations of the organization while satisfying the individual employee's own structure of needs and goals.

DECISION MODELS FOR PERSONNEL SELECTION AND ASSIGNMENT

Lawrence J. Clarke

In recent years there has been an earnest effort by personnel managers to improve the quality of decisions and to reduce the cost of the decision-making process. Personnel managers would like to have decision-making aids that are inexpensive and easy to manipulate.

In the last decade, formal decision models have proven to be a valuable tool as a basis for effective decision making. This formal decision-making approach to problems involves, broadly, a five step procedure:

1. Define the problem and state the objective(s);
2. quantify the variables;
3. develop a model of the system under study;
4. test the model;
5. implement the quantitative tool.

Formal decision models offer management many advantages. They force management to define organization goals and results in clearly defined problems. They can result in an optimal use of resources, reduced costs, better communication between organizational departments, and more effective control (actual outputs can be measured against forecast outputs).

On the other hand, there are limitations to this formal approach to business problems. The cost of designing and implementing a

quantitative system can be very expensive. A quantitative approach is not necessarily the complete answer to business problems; it is only a tool in the decision-making process. Moreover, the quantitative approach can be designed for the "snow job" effect; that is, it may be accepted only on the basis of its being the new scientific approach to business problems.

A mathematical model may be defined as an abstraction or an explicit representation of reality. For example, a selection model is a mathematical representation of the personnel selection process. The purpose of the model is to determine an optimal strategy or solution to the quantified process. All solutions will depend on some set of costs, whether measured in dollars or in utilities. The accuracy of the solution is dependent on the accuracy of measurement of these costs or utilities. The validity of the model is predicated on the number of variables that must be considered. That is, these variables must be quantified, and their interrelationships must be mathematically defined.

The advantages and limitations of mathematical models have been summarized succinctly by Cronbach and Gleser as follows:[1]

> The advantages lie in the precision with which conclusions can be stated, the finality with which they can be established, and the wide range of circumstances to which a derivation can apply . . . The disadvantage of the mathematical attack is that it involves assumptions about postulated variables that have never been observed.

PERSONNEL SELECTION

Mathematical personnel selection has been based on the identification and validation of relationships between predictor and criterion measures of a given population.

In the past, this approach has failed to consider the costs involved in the selection

[1] L. J. Cronbach and G. C. Gleser, *Psychological Tests and Personnel Decisions* (Urbana: University of Illinois Press, 1965), p. 5.

process. In any personnel selection program it is important that the resultant organizational benefits exceed the cost of the program. Brogden points out that the costs of a testing program per applicant hired must be considered to ascertain the profitability of the program.[2] The rationale proposed involves converting production units, errors, time of other personnel consumed, etc., into dollar units thus establishing a dollar criterion scale. The important concept is that there is a point where further testing may incur more costs than the company receives in benefits.

Arbous and Sichel have developed a pre-screening model to reduce the costs of testing.[3] The aim was to develop a test that was easy to administer and utilizes a predictor that will correlate highly with the final battery score. The model was developed and tested on Army recruits, and the results compared favorably with the theoretically predicted results.

Cronbach and Gleser have developed a selection (and placement) model where the expected utility of decisions is obtained by summing the expected payoff (benefits) over all persons tested (or per man accepted) and subtracting the cost of testing.[4] The object is to determine the strategy that maximizes utility.

The main assumption of this model is that a person's contribution to a company, and the costs of testing, can be evaluated and quantified on a common unit of measure. Roche, as reported in Cronbach and Gleser, demonstrated that the teachings of Brogden's "dollar criterion" is applicable to the Cronbach and Gleser model. However, there were many arbitrary cost allocations which tend to cloud the results. Also, the cost of testing was difficult to ascertain as was the measure of job performance.

Van Naerssen's model for the selection of drivers, as reported in Cronbach and Gleser, points out the problems of translating different criteria into utilities and allocating dollar values to different variables. This approach is not practical, since it is extremely difficult to convert different criteria to a common measure of utility. Cronbach and Gleser summarize[5]:

This draws attention to the marked difficulty of a dollars-and-cents analysis where selection affects several diverse criteria. Our model calls for reducing all criteria to a common scale, rather than considering the criteria separately. But Van Naerssen's criteria are very nearly incommensurable, and it would be extremely difficult to work out the optimum selection ratio, for example, considering all information.

Blumberg developed a screening model to determine whether enough evidence of a disease condition exists to warrant further diagnostic examination by a physician.[6] However, the model may be used to identify healthy rather than sick individuals. Blumberg points out that this model is advantageous in selecting people for the armed forces as well as the screening of life insurance applicants.

The primary weakness of this model is that the assignment of values to true and false positives (true positive—selection of a candidate who would have been acceptable; false positive-rejection of a candidate who would have been accepted) and negatives (true negative—screen out an individual who is not acceptable; false negative—accept an individual who is not acceptable) is based largely upon judgment. Blumberg indicates that this assignment should be a quantified procedure. Also, it is extremely difficult to accurately

[2]H. E. Brogden, "When Testing Pays Off," *Personnel Psychology* XXXVII, 65-76 (1946); H. E. Brogden and E. K. Taylor, "The Dollar Criterion—Applying the Cost Accounting Concept to Criterion Construction," *Personnel Psychology* III, 133-154 (1950).

[3]A. G. Arbous and H. S. Sichel, "On the Economics of a Pre-Screening Technique for Aptitude Test Batteries," *Psychometrika* XVII, 331-346 (1952).

[4]Cronbach and Gleser, *op. cit.*

[5]*Ibid.,* p. 157.

[6]M. S. Blumberg, "Evaluating Health Screening Procedures," *Operations Research* V, 351-360 (1957).

measure these costs.

Kao and Rowan examined the problem of filling a personnel quota where the quota is stated in terms of people productivity on the job, rather than in terms of people hired.[7] The model was developed to determine the optimum strategy (the number of people recruited and the minimum acceptable score on the selection test) that will minimize costs, subject to a given probability that a specified number of satisfactory (or successful) employees be hired.

One of the constraints of this model is that it is extremely expensive to hire a person who turns out to be unsatisfactory. The determination of costs are the same as Brogden's approach, only costs are not constant per applicant. This model emphasizes the importance of enlarging a personnel model to incorporate more variables than are presently considered in personnel selection. One of the model assumptions is that the correlation between the criterion and the test is known. This is not true in actual practice. The broad assumptions made in order to incorporate all the variables preclude the application of this model to complex systems.

Mahoney and England discuss the drawbacks of traditional methods of statistical decision rules for employee selection[8]:

These traditional approaches . . . are inadequate since they fail to consider the cost consequences of their application. The maximum differential approach, for example, implicitly assumes that errors of accepting a failure candidate and of rejecting a successful candidate are of equal consequence . . . Realistically, there should be a balancing of recruitment costs and misclassification costs in the determination of the selection decision rule without a focus solely on one cost or the other. Further, the relative costs . . . or misclassification error should be explicitly taken into account and permitted to vary with the situation.

The model incorporates the costs of hiring an acceptable and/or a failure candidate. However, it must be noted that the proportion of candidates being successful or failures is based on estimates. The primary assumption of the model concerns the criterion. The criterion of employee effectiveness is dichotomous (i.e., an employee is acceptable or a failure) rather than a continuous variable, a fact which severely limits its applicability. Kao and Rowan state that when it is possible

JOBS

		1	2	3	4
	1	1	9	4	1
	2	5	8	6	6
INDIVIDUALS	3	4	6	4	2
	4	4	1	6	4

Figure 2.3 Figures within matrix represent predicted performance times for each individual to do each job.

[7]R. C. Kao and T. C. Rowan, "A Model for Personnel Recruiting and Selection," *Management Science* **V**, 192-203 (1959).

[8]T. A. Mahoney and G. W. England, "Efficiency and Accuracy of Employee Selection Rules," *Personnel Psychology* **XVIII**, 361-377 (1965), see pp. 366 and 367.

to measure the productivity of a new employee and to relate this productivity to the costs of selection, a dichotomous treatment would not be an efficient one.[9] However, the dichotomous treatment in the Mahoney and England model would be applicable in measuring sales applicants.

One of the main problems in personnel assignments is lack of knowledge of job applicants' performance with respect to job vacancies. Predictive measures are used to determine if an applicant will prove to be successful on the job. The assignment process is to allocate personnel optimally to job vacancies in order to provide maximum value to the organization.

Flood defines the assignment problem:[10]

In its most familiar application to personnel management, the assignment problem is to assign N men optimally to N different jobs. In this

application, it is supposed that a numerical performance rating is given for each of the N^2 man-job combinations and an optimal assignment is one that minimizes the sum of the N applicable ratings. For example, the ratings might be estimated times, or costs, for the various man-job combinations.

An example of the linear programming assignment problem is shown in Figures 2.3 and 2.4. Figure 2.3 shows a 4 x 4 matrix of predicted performance times for each individual to do each job. The problem is to assign each individual to a job so that the sum of the rows and columns are minimized. That is, allocate the individuals to jobs that they can do the best consistent with attaining a total minimum time. If costs were used, instead of performance times, then the object would be to minimize costs. Figure 2.4 shows the optimal allocation of the individuals utilizing the linear programming approach to the assignment problem.

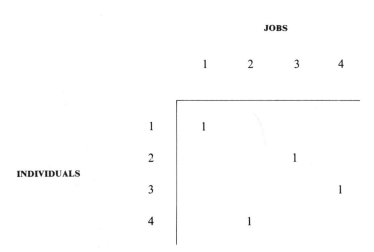

Figure 2.4 Optimal allocation of individuals to jobs, i.e., allocation of individuals to jobs that they can do the best consistent with attaining a total minimum time, utilizing the linear programming approach.

[9]Kao and Rowan, *op. cit.*, p. 202.

[10]M. M. Flood, "The Traveling-Salesman Problem," *Operations Research* **IV** (4), 61-75 (1957), see p. 61.

Kuhn describes the Hungarian method,[11] which is an algorithm for solving the assignment problem based on the work of D. Konig and J. Egervary. Konig treats the assignment problem using only two ratings (1 and 0), meaning that the job candidate is either qualified or not qualified. In a later article,[12] Kuhn presents a geometrical model to define and compare alternative mathematical solutions to a modified Hungarian model. Belinski and Gomory developed a "dual" to the Hungarian method.[13] Since the Hungarian method is the dual, the model becomes a primal and has a feasible solution at each iteration of the linear programming technique.

Table 1 shows the various methods of solution to the personnel classification problem.[14]

Votaw defines the quota problem as:[15]

Given a number of job categories with quota and a group of persons, where each person is regarded simply as qualified or not in each job category, the problem is to find, if one exists, some allocation that will place each person in the job for which he is qualified.

Lord developed a model for the assignment of N men to N jobs when the proportion of men to be assigned to each job is specified in advance.[16]

Votaw also considered priority sequenced allocation:[17]

Given a group of persons and N occupational areas with quotas, and given a predictive score for each person with regard to each area; find a satisfactory set of minimum qualifying scores.

Votaw considers the quota problem where it is assumed that there is complete knowledge of all applicants with regard to each job category (qualified or not qualified).[18] The model considers the job categories and allocates the personnel available. The structure of job categories can be reduced and priorities placed on the personnel (i.e., personnel cannot be allocated to job 2 until job 5 requirements have been met). The purpose of this model is to reduce a large allocation problem to a series of smaller problems. This is ideal when computer facilities are not available. The dichotomous approach used here fails to utilize efficiently a test or performance score in the optimal allocation of personnel.

MINIMIZE IDLE TIME

Miller and Starr illustrate a method of determining the optimal size of maintenance crews.[19] The object is to minimize the maintenance crew idle time. Shuchman solves the same problem by simulating the maintenance process using the Monte Carlo Method.[20] Birnbaum and Maxwell, as reported in Cronbach and Gleser, describe different methods of classification using Bayesian statistics. The approach is very general and does not utilize constraint equations. The predictive ability of these models is based on the accuracy of historical data to determine statistical relationships. These models emphasize the importance of retrieving accurate

[11]H. W. Kuhn, "The Hungarian Method for the Assignment," *Naval Research Logistics Quarterly* **II** (1 & 2), 83-98 (1955).

[12]H. W. Kuhn, "Variants of the Hungarian Method for Assignment Problems," *Naval Research Logistics Quarterly* **III** (4), 253-258 (1956).

[13]M. L. Belinski and R. E. Gomory, "A Primal Method for the Assignment and Transportation Problem," *Management Science* **X** (3), 578-593 (1964).

[14]D. F. Votaw, Jr., *Review and Summary of Research on Personnel Classification Problems,* Research Report AFPTRC-TN-56-106, ASTIA DOC. No. 098881 (Lackland Air Force Base, Texas: Air Force Personnel and Training Research Center, 1956).

[15]*Ibid.,* p. 2.

[16]F. M. Lord, "Notes on a Problem of Multiple Classification," *Psychometrika* **XVII**, 297-304 (1952).

[17] Votaw, *op. cit.*

[18]D. F. Votaw, Jr., "Solution of the Quota Problem by a Successive-reduction Method," *Operations Research* **VI** (1), 56-64 (1958).

[19]D. W. Miller and M. K. Starr, *Executive Decisions and Operations Research* (Englewood Cliffs, N. J.: Prentice-Hall, 1960).

[20]A Shuchman, *Scientific Decision Making in Business* (New York: Holt, Rinehart and Winston, 1963).

historical data in order to define, quantify, and interrelate the model variables.

Dwyer developed a linear programming model for the group assembly problem.[21] A group, in this case, consists of N men each of whom has been trained to perform only one job in a group. This model optimally allocates personnel to attain optimal group assemblies. Votaw and Orden considered the possibility of using computers to perform the linear programming (simplex method) solution to personnel assignment problems in the Armed Forces.[22] However, the limiting factor in this case is the size of the computer memory.

McCloskey and Hanssman designed a linear programming model to schedule optimally a stewardess school operated by an airline.[23] Some of the factors considered were: stewardess requirements, capacity of the school, selection, process and training time of the stewardesses, high turnover rate, illness, vacation and airplane flight schedules. The model was implemented with good results. However, it did take over a year to design, manipulate, and implement the model. This application has made the extremely difficult transition from theoretical design to implementation in a business environment.

Karush and Vazsonyi developed a model to determine an employment schedule of a given type of labor which minimizes costs over a specified time interval.[24] The costs considered were: (1) the wage labor cost, including part-time help and overtime; (2) the cost of varying the employment level; (3) the cost of hiring and terminating a worker. The model utilizes a dynamic programming procedure which is a multi-stage decision process. The basis of the model is fourth degree cost equation, which is quite difficult to handle in an industrial situation.

Ward presents a Decision Index theory for determining the optimal assignment of personnel to jobs (one at a time).[25] Ward states that automated personnel decisions will be quite difficult to see; and thus, there will be a need for counseling in the assignment problem. This approach suggests introducing more information concerning personnel to be assigned in the form of an index, which would result in more effective personnel utilization. However, it is not clear what information is needed to develop the necessary indices. The approach appears to be too theoretical to apply to an industrial situation.

KING ASSIGNMENT MODEL

King developed a unique personnel assignment model.[26] Personnel assignment can be considered a two-stage process: (1) prediction on the basis of test results; (2) optimal allocation of personnel to job vacancies. King has attempted to integrate the two phases into one model. The model utilizes "value" judgments in developing the model (i.e., the value associated with unsuccessful performance of each job may be taken to be zero). The object is the maximization of the expected value to the organization based on qualitative judgment of job performance. A job of allocating a large number of people to various jobs would mean a near impossible job of ascertaining hierarchical value judgments.

The majority of the allocation problems are based on linear programming techniques.

[21]P. S. Dwyer, "The Mean and Standard Deviation of the Distribution of Group Assembly Sums," *Psychometrika* **XXIX** (4), 397-408 (1954).

[22]D. F. Votaw and A. Orden, "The Personnel Assignment Problem," *Symposium on Linear Inequalities and Programming* (U.S. Air Force, Project SCOOP, 1952).

[23]J. F. McCloskey and F. Hanssman, "An Analysis of Stewardess Requirements and Scheduling for a Major Domestic Airline," *Naval Research Logistics Quarterly* **IV** (3), 183-199 (1957).

[24]W. Karush and A. Vazsonyi, "Mathematical Programming and Employment Scheduling," *Naval Research Logistics Quarterly* **IV** (4), 297-320 (1957).

[25]J. H. Ward, Jr., "The Counselling Assignment Problem," *Psychometrika* **XXIII** (1), 55-65 (1958).

[26]W. R. King, "A Stochastic Personnel-assignment Model," *Operations Research* **XIII**, 67-81 (1965).

TABLE I   METHODS OF SOLUTION OF THE PERSONNEL CLASSIFICATION PROBLEM

METHOD	BIBLIOGRAPHY ITEM*
1. Approximate methods (e.g., random allocation, array maximal procedure, inspection)	Shutzenberger, 1951 Votaw & Dailey, 1952
2. Bounding—Set method	Dwyer, 1952 Smith, 1951 Votaw & Dailey, 1952
3. Critical rejection score method	Dwyer, 1952 Brogden, 1946 Dwyer, 1954
4. Easterfield's adjustment	Easterfield, 1946
5. Inspection of all possible allocations	Dwyer, 1952 Votaw & Dailey, 1952
6. Interchange methods	Dwyer, 1952 Votaw & Dailey, 1952
7. Optimal regions method	Dwyer, 1952 Dwyer, 1954
8. Programming methods (other than simplex)	Orden & Goldstein, 1952
9. Simplex method	Orden & Goldstein, 1952 Dwyer, 1952 Smith, 1951
10. Successive addition method	Dwyer, 1952 Smith, 1951 Shutzenberger, 1952

*See secondary references.

Brogden, H. E. "An Approach to the Problem of Differential Prediction," *Psychometrika* **XI,** 139-154 (1946).

Dwyer, P. S. *Statistical Methods for Assignment Among a Variety of Jobs: II, Optimal Assignment of Men* (Washington: The Adjutant General's Office, Department of the Army, November 1952, (unpublished)).

Dwyer, P. S. "Solution of the Personnel Classification Problem with the Method of Optimal Regions," *Psychometrika* **XIX,** 11-25 (1954).

Easterfield, T. E. "A Combinatorial Algorithm," *Journal of the London Mathematical Society* **XXI,** 219-226 (1946).

Orden, A., and Goldstein, L., eds. *Symposium on Linear Inequalities and Programming* (Washington: Planning Research Division, Director of Management Analysis Service, Comptroller, Headquarters United States Air Force, April 1952).

Schutzenberger, M. P. *"On the Determination of the Maximal Value of the Spur within a Set of Equivalent Numerical Matrices with Reference to a Problem in Personnel Orientation,"* (1951, Unpublished).

Smith, R. B. *Hand Computational Methods for the Classification Problem* (New Haven, Conn.: Yale University, September 1951 (mimeographed)).

Votaw, D. F., Jr., and Dailey, J. T. *Assignment of Personnel to Jobs* (Lackland Air Force Base, Texas: Human Resources Research Center, August 1952 (Research Bulletin 52-24)).

It is important, in evaluating these models, to consider the advantages and limitations of this quantitative technique. Linear programming results in an optimum allocation of personnel. It also forces management to thoroughly analyze the problem.

However, there are certain modeling aspects of linear programming that must be considered. There is the possibility that no solution exists. Consideration must be given to the very difficult task of combining two or more objectives. Is it possible to define a common unit of measure for the system variables? Are the relationships between the test and the criterion linear? These questions must be answered in the context of each model application. If a problem is accurately stated, mathematically, there may not be any limitation to the model; but from a practical point of view, there may be numerous limitations.

Votaw points out that in practical problems, there is uncertainty relative to the amount of predicted production on the job.[27] He states that this is not surprising when one considers the difficult scaling problems and the general absence of perfect correlation between predictors and criteria. In his review of the personnel classification problem, Votaw came up with three conclusions:

1. Tryouts of computational methods on practical problems are desirable.
2. Computational methods could be improved.
3. The practical problem of predicting the amount of production that would result from placing a given person in a given job needs further research.

CONCLUSION

The Mahoney and England model is the most applicable to personnel selection when evaluated in terms of model implementation in

the business environment. However, the model is only applicable to situations where the selection variable is a dichotomous measure. The model is not capable of evaluating personnel when the measuring variable is continuous (i.e., where there are various levels of success or failure). The fact that the measure of success and failure is based on estimates illustrates the importance, and necessity, of an accurate data base to evaluate the model results effectively.

In the area of personnel assignment the McCloskey and Hanssman model has been implemented with success. The length of time needed to implement the model points up some of the problems that face a personnel organization prior to the design or implementation of the model. Of primary importance is to evaluate the time needed to implement the model and solve the problem.

The majority of the models discussed failed to consider the aspect of actually making the model a decision aid of the personnel organization. This requires an analysis of the model and an awareness of the problems of implementation.

Model acceptance requires that the user organization agree to the decisions and assumptions made in the development of the model. Some of the questions that must be answered are: (1) Is there an accurate data base for criterion measurement? (2) What is the common denominator used in evaluating and comparing various jobs, and how do you allocate dollar values to system variables? Consideration must be given to the accuracy and validity of the model assumptions to the actual environment. The user organization must accord to these assumptions; thus, each model must be tailored to the unique organization under study.

The measure of effectiveness of any model is its predictive ability. The true test of any model is to use past data in the model and compare the model results with the actual results. However, in an assignment problem the model results will probably vary a great

[27]Votaw, *op. cit.* (1956).

deal from the actual assignment. The problem then is to determine if the model results would have been more beneficial to the organization than the actual assignment made.

Many of the models discussed emphasize that the model is based on a particular selection procedure. If this procedure were changed, the decision rule would have little relevance in the model. An effective model should be able to adapt to changes in the system. That is, the model must accurately reflect the impact of change when one (or some) of the variables change.

CAN MODEL BE IMPLEMENTED?

Most of the models failed to consider the important aspect of model implementation. The first question that must be answered is: Can the model be implemented? Will the implementation of the model provide value to the organization using the model? That is, will the benefits of implementing the optimal decisions exceed the costs of designing and using the model? Also, what effects will using the model have on the user organization?

Mathematical modeling is ideal for very simple systems. However, in a complex personnel model, it becomes very difficult to evaluate all the variables simultaneously. Thus, it may become too complicated for management to grasp and manipulate. One can readily see management resistance to endorsing a policy of detailed, and complicated, mathematical analysis.

The majority of the research has explored the use of Operations Research only in personnel selection and assignment. A great deal of research needs to be done before these models can be utilized on a day-to-day basis. However, some of the teachings of the quantitative approach are now being utilized effectively in personnel systems, and more widespread use of formal decision models appear to be likely in the future, as management improvement techniques are applied in personnel management.

A CASE STUDY IN EFFECTIVE RECRUITMENT

Stephen Gould

A number of Federal departments and agencies are disproving the commonly accepted belief that the Government is in no position to compete with industry and the professions in attracting well qualified college students to its ranks. The Internal Revenue Service, Housing and Home Finance Agency, Agricultural Research Service, Army Ordnance Missile Command, and many others are demonstrating their recruiting capabilities every day.

The Treasury Department's Internal Revenue Service is a prime example of an agency that is getting its fair share of the annual crop of collegians by the dint of hard work, a well-organized, decentralized recruiting program, a top quality series of brochures, and a factual soft-sell approach. During the seven-year period since it started an expanded recruiting program IRS has increased its intake from 460 recruits for the single occupational category of internal revenue agent to slightly under 4,000 appointees for fiscal year 1962 distributed among 10 principal kinds of program positions.

College recruiting in IRS is decentralized to the lowest practicable level. The Service has 9 regional offices and 62 district offices, each of which has a personnel office with delegated appointing authority. The policy and procedural development responsibility, as well as nationwide coordination of the entire program, is vested in the position of

IRS College Recruitment Coordinator in the National Office in Washington. Each of the regional offices has a recruitment coordinator who assists, advises and generally directs recruiting in about seven district offices. It is at the district level that the actual recruiting job is done. Direct contacts with college placement officers, faculty members and students are made by the district recruiter and the program officials of the office. All of these contacts are arranged for and coordinated by a District Office Recruitment Coordinator. But it is in the operating men that the true strength of the program lies. IRS considers college recruiting to be a line responsibility in which program people must participate. The success of the revenue program is in their hands, the best knowledge of the progress and future of the agency is theirs, the final selection of new people is theirs also. Therefore, it is essential that the responsibility for explaining the program, creating an interest in the Service, and interviewing prospects be theirs.

RECRUITING BROCHURES

A major factor in the success of IRS college recruitment has been its series of excellent recruiting brochures. After considerable experimentation since 1958, a series of brochures has now been developed that is not only producing favorable results where they count the most—among college students—but has also received official recognition in the trade. A review committee of the College Placement Council has given a "superior" rating to the IRS brochure series.[1] Internal Revenue was the only Federal agency among a group of 15 organizations that received this top rating.

Let's take a bird's-eye view of a typical year's program under Internal Revenue's present system. During the spring of the year

[1]Joan Fiss Bishop, "What Makes Employer Recruiting Literature *Good . . . Better . . . Best,*" *Journal of College Placement,* p. 20 ff. (April 1962).

87

the National Office revamps its pamphlet series, updating and revising text as necessary, varying artwork, preparing new covers. The new or revised set is printed during the summer. The basic brochure, called "Careers," is an 8″ by 10″, 18-page, three-color job with glossy cover and of high quality throughout. It presents an over-all picture of the Service and discusses briefly the five principal occupations for which recruitment is to be conducted. 120,000 copies are printed. A set of 6″ by 9″ brochures covers each of the five specialized positions, expanding the material in "Careers" and providing simple, factual employment information. Each of these is printed in quantities of 45,000. An additional larger brochure is published to feature the administrative intern program.

Exhibits are redesigned, advertising material is developed, and new and revised film strips are prepared with accompanying narration and music. The National Office also effects program improvements including negotiations with the Civil Service Commission that will enable the Service to accomplish its recruiting objectives more effectively each year.

CAMPUS CONTACTS

Meanwhile at the local level, recruitment coordinators are making their contacts with college placement officers to discuss the results of the previous year's program and pave the way for the coming year. During this period of greater leisure for college placement people, considerable headway can be made in cementing relations and correcting any weaknesses that may have occurred previously.

Shortly after the school year opens, distribution of brochures is made. "Careers" is sent from a National Office service center directly to seniors, where individual names and addresses are available, or by district offices to college placement officers for distribution. Each brochure contains return postal cards which are to be mailed to the nearest IRS office. This brochure has produced about a 7% return. A specialized brochure is subsequently sent to each of these same seniors according to his major subject interest, or to placement officers for distribution to students. These have brought a return of more than 8% in addition to the initial results from the general brochure.

Personal visits are then made, starting in the fall, to campuses within the geographical area covered by each district office, with more than 500 colleges and universities being visited nationwide. The recruiting team consists of program people and the district recruitment coordinator, with the latter serving as team leader. Interviews are conducted with students primarily to create interest in the IRS program and in career opportunities. Every attempt is made to overcome the apathy that many students have toward the Government. Information is provided, questions are answered, and students are told how to file for the examination that is appropriate for their field of study. As appropriate, applications for Board examinations or for the Federal Service Entrance Examination are picked up and filed for the students. Commitments are rarely made at this early stage, even subject to passing an examination. As Gordon VanLeer, National Office Coordinator, says, "The critical importance that is given to being able to make an on-the-spot commitment is highly overrated. College students don't expect to be given a commitment in October, and certainly not after a half-hour interview. They're not ready to make up their minds that early and are wary of the recruiter who can talk to them for just a few minutes and make a firm offer."

Follow-ups are made with students who have expressed an interest either by their use of a return card or when interviewed. Others who seem promising are also contacted further. The principle of repetitive coverage is followed wherever possible through correspondence, recruiting literature, and personal visits. Career opportunities are stressed together with information about training programs and the developmental advantages that exist in the Service. Full participation is made in college career days and exhibits and film strips are shown.

PANEL INTERVIEWS

Internal Revenue looks for quality people, just as all other employers do. However, it cannot base selection entirely on high scholastic averages. Most of the assignments which new employees will be called upon to perform during their careers with the Service will involve personal relationships with the public. Therefore, the ability to get along with people, to make a favorable first impression, to have the knack of selling themselves is considered much more important than having straight "A's." In order to determine this public contact ability, IRS makes extensive use of panel interviews and has developed both a trainee's guide and an instructor's guide for oral panel interviewing.[2]

As students refine their thinking during the spring months, commitments are made. By this time, interested seniors have taken Federal examinations and both parties are ready to close the deal.

BUDGETING FOR RECRUITMENT

Obviously, an absolute necessity at this stage is to have all of the internal agency machin-

ery properly greased so that students may enter on duty immediately after graduation in June. This is the worst time in the year insofar as Federal agency budgets are concerned. Money has not yet been appropriated for the fiscal year starting on July 1, and even if it had been it would not cover the last few weeks of the previous fiscal year. There is usually no advance knowledge of exactly how much personal services money will be available for each of the program areas during this year-end period. All of this means that planning must be accomplished as much as two years before the entrance-on-duty date of this year's college recruits, since a request for funds must have been included in the budget that was prepared in the agency in 1960 in order for it to be available in June 1962. Adequate advance plans for financing college hiring cannot be stressed too much.

In IRS very close contact is maintained between the National Office and the regional and district offices throughout the entire period of budget processing. Field people initially assume that their hiring needs for the following fiscal year will be comparable to those of the present year and plan on that basis. The National Office informs them of jobs that have been included for them after review by the Bureau of the Budget. Additional information is disseminated after the House of Representatives Appropriation Committee has taken its action. Similarly, after Senate review of the budget request a further reading is taken and the field is given authority to proceed. These several analyses in the National Office involve coordinating the thinking of the personnel, financial, and line management people, and having top management give the go-ahead signal to the district offices as soon as possible so that hiring may be effected no later than early July. Continuing effort must be made to see that all parties concerned work closely to-

[2]John J. Logue, "Training Panel Interviewers," *Public Personnel Review*, pp. 135-138 (April 1962).

gether and that each field office is kept informed of its recruiting authority from a staffing and financial viewpoint.

Internal paperwork requirements of obtaining properly approved personnel action requests must also be arranged so that there will be no last minute delays in the prompt processing of recruits. In addition, those personnel people who are responsible for the orientation of new employees and for coordinating the in-service training program into which all recruits are placed, must be alerted sufficiently in advance so that everything is ready to receive the appointees when they arrive. This ends the recruiting cycle in the field, while the National Office has already been preparing for the following year's program.

The need to develop the program carefully and sell it successfully within the Service, caused the recruitment staff to concentrate on only one occupational area during the first year. The immediate success of this attempt sold the program to operating officials. The noticeably improved quality of recruits in the first categories that were filled caused other field managers to want to participate. As a result, the initial accession figure of 460 increased to about 1,000 by 1958, almost doubled by 1961, and has approached 4,000 for 1962.

The problem of coordinating the efforts of 62 recruiting offices so that the growing needs of the entire Service and varying local requirements could be met was not an easy one. Maximum utilization of an excess supply of specialists in one district by referring them to other offices, meeting the geographical desires of students who attend colleges on the East Coast but want to work out West, and attempting to equalize or raise the caliber of input in areas where fewer high ranking students are available necessitate maximum cooperation among district and regional coordinators. But all of this can be done under a well organized program.

ANALYSIS OF QUALITY

With numerical needs being met the next question that arises concerns the quality of recruits. IRS statistics are not yet complete on this point although impressions are. Internal Revenue appoints about 40% of its recruits at the GS-5 level and 60% at GS-7. However, this does not mean that 60% of all recruits have obtained "B" averages or are in the top 25% of their classes. The reason for this is that not all of each year's appointees come from that year's graduating class—a great many have been out of college for a year or more and qualify for the higher grade because of additional education or work experience. A survey is being made of last year's group to obtain detailed information about scholastic honors, extracurricular activities, reactions to recruiters, brochures and correspondence, and motivating factors which caused college people to select IRS as an employer. Operating officials are impressed with the high caliber of the recruits who are entering the agency. The correlation between what IRS considers to be high quality people and their scholastic achievements will be of great interest.

INCREASING THE SUPPLY

Recruitment people see their job as a never-ending one in IRS. One of the major subject matter areas from which they draw is accounting which is a requirement for the highly populated occupation of internal revenue agent. Studies made by the Department of Health, Education, and Welfare show that the increased number of students who take accounting courses is far below the expanding national requirements for this specialty. Internal Revenue has prepared a brochure called "Careers in Tax Work" which has been distributed to high school instructors throughout the country who give a course on "Teaching Taxes." The potential exposure of this brochure is 2½ million. It is hoped that creating interest in a tax career at the high school level will permit the Service to keep its 12,000 revenue agent positions filled and provide a sufficient supply of newcomers to enable the staff to increase to its ultimate strength of 20,000. Advance planning such as this is essential if an agency is to meet its long range goals which only too soon become immediate problems.

There has been considerable concern of late about the image of the public service and the need of improving Federal college recruitment programs. The Internal Revenue Service is well aware of student apathy and directs much of its recruiting attention to developing interest in the Government and in IRS programs and careers. Its efforts have proved that it is possible to overcome adverse impressions and to attract bright college students to the Government. As they say down at the tax office—Uncle Sam *can* recruit successfully.

USES AND MISUSES OF TESTS IN SELECTING KEY PERSONNEL

Herbert H. Meyer
Joseph M. Bertotti

During the past few years, we have seen a growing interest in the use of more systematic methods for the selection and placement of key personnel in business and industry. Many managers are beginning to feel that, since the systematic approach has contributed so much to the success of other business functions, perhaps it can also be applied to the solution of critical personnel problems.

Throughout industry, increasing attention is now being given to the use of such systematic methods of selection and placement as (1) carefully patterned interviews; (2) thorough reference checks and investigations; and (3) objective psychological tests designed to measure certain abilities and interests.

Practices among companies in this respect vary considerably, however. Some have established procedures for carefully screening *all candidates* considered for employment or promotion, including a complete analysis by a trained evaluator. Others have made little or no use of such techniques, preferring to rely on their own historical methods of evaluation and selection.

As is usual with every innovation, there has been considerable misunderstanding regarding the use of these new selection methods, not only among those responsible for making the selections, but also on the part of the people who have been asked to undergo the evaluation procedure. This paper

Reprinted by permission of the publisher from Person-nel © November 1956 by the American Management Association, Inc.

will deal with some of the major questions that have arisen in this area.

As part of a systematic personnel evaluation procedure, candidates for managerial and other key positions in industry are sometimes asked to take a battery of psychological tests. The use of such tests has probably been accompanied by more questions and misunderstandings than has happened in the case of any other selection tool. While in the eyes of the professional evaluator a candidate's test results may be a very minor part of the appraisal, the candidate himself may very well regard the tests as the most critical and decisive part of the evaluation.

Most of us associate tests with our school days, where they are usually a "pass or fail" matter. Consequently, we are likely to be apprehensive about taking tests, since we are apt to feel that our futures will be decided largely by our performance on the tests, regardless of assurances to the contrary.

PSYCHOLOGICAL TESTS AS A SELECTION TOOL

Because of these questions and possible misunderstandings, certain facts regarding the application of psychological tests should be made clear.

1. *What is a test?* A psychological test may be considered as *a sample of performance taken under standardized conditions.* As a general rule, this sample is very carefully selected to be *representative of a broad area of performance.* This is a very important point, for the criticism often leveled at tests is that they don't measure practical performance. We sometimes hear the complaint, "What difference does it make whether or not a man can solve some simple paper-and-pencil problems? He doesn't have to do anything like that on the job." True enough; but years of experimentation have shown that the ability to solve these paper-and-pencil

problems is definitely related to the ability to perform certain practical tasks.

The word "standardized" in our definition also deserves emphasis. A psychological test presents a series of tasks to be performed under uniform conditions by each candidate. Thus we can directly compare the performance of any one candidate with that of others. This is one of the main advantages of a test, since "standardized conditions" do not hold for the interview, performance appraisals, or other means of evaluation.

2. *What can tests measure?* Research studies indicate that tests are of most value in measuring certain *abilities or aptitudes*. The most widely used tests for screening candidates for higher-level positions are those designed to measure "general intelligence" or general learning ability. Studies have shown that it is very difficult to judge intellectual capacity or "ability to learn" on the basis of an interview—or even on the basis of observed job performance. Yet basic intellectual capacity is essential to success in a complex, higher level job assignment.

Years of experimentation confirm that the intellectual tasks in a "general ability" test are predictive of certain aspects of practical performance. In other words, persons who score high on general ability tests generally have the *capacity* to use good judgment, to think ahead, and to make wise decisions quickly in a variety of situations—all the activities generally thought to require "intelligence."

Tests can also provide a fairly accurate measure of other abilities of importance for specific jobs, such as the ability to understand mechanical concepts, to visualize objects in space or to work with figures or facts. All these qualities are difficult to assess accurately by means of an interview or other selection tools.

3. *Personality and Interest Tests.* Tests are also used quite often to measure interests and personality characteristics. In these areas, considerable caution must be exercised, however, in interpreting test results. While interests and "personality" are usually important factors in determining job success, psychologists have not been so successful in developing valid measures of them as they have been in developing measures of abilities.

A diagrammatic representation of the degree of accuracy with which different human characteristics can be measured is shown in the accompanying exhibit. As may be seen, certain physical characteristics can be measured with a *high,* and abilities, aptitudes, and skills with a *fair,* degree of confidence; interest measures are less accurate, while personality traits are at the bottom of the scale.

One reason why personality tests often fail to provide valid predictions is probably that personality "traits" themselves are not always highly consistent. Our personalities vary somewhat with the situations in which we are placed. We are all "retiring" in some situations and "aggressive" in others. We may show great "perseverance" in one kind of activity and very little in another.

A second shortcoming of both personality and interest tests is that most of those that are in use today are rather "transparent" to the applicant with reasonable intelligence. A job candidate eager to make a good impression can usually see through the test, at least to some extent. He can indicate certain interests or personality characteristics which he thinks will put him in the most favorable light, whether he actually possesses them or not.

Though a trained psychologist can pick up some valuable clues from interest and personality tests, he also knows that he cannot place too much faith in the validity of the raw scores that are obtained. For this reason, most reputable test publishers refuse to sell personality and interest tests to any but well-trained, highly qualified psychologists and personnel specialists. Literal interpretations by untrained persons of personality test scores can be highly damaging to the individual tested.

OTHER LIMITATIONS OF TESTS

Some other limitations of the use of tests in selection and placement should be noted here:

1. *Tests are designed to supplement other screening methods, not to replace them.* Tests cannot measure all the factors which must be considered when a selection or placement decision is made. There are many important qualifications which can be evaluated only on the basis of past performance, or from the candidate's education, special training, or demonstrated interests.

Even in the matter of abilities, tests indicate only what a man should be able to do—they cannot measure what he *will* do. This point cannot be emphasized too strongly. However much ability an individual possesses, it is of little value to him if, for some reason, he is incapable of applying it to the performance of his job. Even a top score on an "intelligence" test, for example, will not compensate for lack of drive.

2. *Test scores have a relatively high margin of error.* A further limitation arising from the use of tests is the natural tendency to accept the numerical scores obtained as precise and exact measures. We are all accustomed to dealing with physical measures where the margin of error is insignificant. If a table measures, say, 36 inches in length, for all practical purposes we can accept its length as 36 inches. With a psychological test, on the other hand, a score of 36 may mean a true score of something between 30 and 40. Hence, small differences in scores between candidates are relatively meaningless.

3. *Tests alone are inaccurate predictors of job success.* Even more important is the fact that test results are still less accurate in *predicting* the behavior they are designed to sample. A test may provide a reasonably accurate measure of mechanical aptitude, for example, but its accuracy as a predictor of success in a mechanical job may be relatively low. It is much like the problem of predicting weather from a barometric reading. The barometer may provide an accurate measure of air pressure, but a prediction of future weather conditions based solely on this measure of air pressure may be relatively unreliable.

Let's carry this analogy a step further. While the barometer is not a highly accurate predictor of weather, with it we can do a better job of weather forecasting than without it. The same principle applies in the use of tests for predicting job success, *provided the characteristics tested are required in the job.*

This warning deserves special emphasis. Obvious though this principle may seem, tests are often used without sufficient attention being paid to specific job requirements. Unless we have an accurate "Man Specification" for the position to be filled, even the most reliable appraisal tools will be of little value in predicting success on the job.

A common error along this line is to assume that the higher the score on any test the better the chances for success on any job. In some jobs, precisely the opposite holds true. Thus, persons who score high on intelligence tests often make a poor adjustment to relatively routine work. Even in screening college graduates, we sometimes find that a high test score is the clue to a liability. A very high intelligence test score, accompanied by a mediocre record of achievement, for example, may indicate that the applicant is lazy, has poor work habits, or possesses personality problems which interfere with his efficiency. This clue we would try to verify, of course, in the interview or through reference checks.

In one research study of tests for selecting

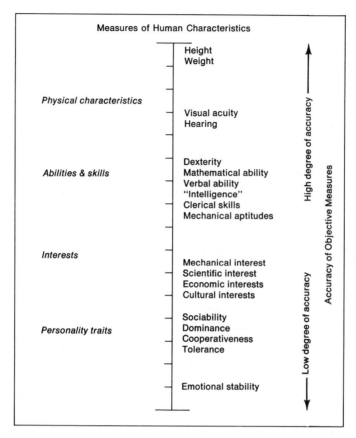

Figure 2.5

supervisors,[1] the applicants who scored either very low *or* very high on a test of "supervisory judgment" were found to be the poorer performers in supervisory jobs. In this case, the research study showed that applicants scoring in the middle range on this particular test were the best bets, even though the test seemed to be measuring desirable supervisory knowledge—or at least the "right" supervisory attitudes.

PRACTICES TO BE FOLLOWED IN USING PROFESSIONAL EVALUATIONS

While it is important to recognize the limitations enumerated above, experience has

[1]"An Evaluation of the G.E. Supervisory Selection Program," unpublished report for General Electric Company Management (1954).

shown that the proper use of tests and related professional evaluation services can enable a manager to make wiser selection and placement decisions than he can make without the aid of these tools. Experience has also shown, however, that the use of these evaluation tools of the professional should be accompanied by:

1. *Accurate "Man Specifications" for the Positions for which Candidates Are Evaluated.* We cannot hit the bull's eye if we have not clearly defined the target. Appraisal information does not have general validity. It has value only for predicting success in specific situations. The same ability or trait may be an asset in one position and a liability in another.

Hence, the specific key requirements for success on the job should be spelled out, and the evaluation results interpreted in the light of these requirements. Measures of little or no value in determining performance on the job should be ignored.

2. *Past Performance Records and Other Background Appraisal Information.* Test results should be presented as a *supplement* to these other appraisal sources, in order to insure that test findings are not given undue weight in arriving at personnel selection or placement decisions.

3. *Strictly Confidential Handling of Test Results and Other Evaluative Information.* Appraisal findings passed on indiscriminately can easily be misinterpreted or misused and might be highly damaging to the reputation of the individual involved. All such information should be treated as strictly confidential.

Particular care should be used in passing on an evaluation for a specific job opening, when the same man subsequently becomes a candidate for another job. Negative findings on a candidate for a highly technical position, for example, may not apply at all to the same man when he is being considered for a managerial position.

4. *Careful Selection of Outside Consultants.* More and more companies are turning to outside experts for help in arriving at difficult selection decisions. Unfortunately, while many of the firms offering evaluation services are staffed by reputable professionals who use well-proven techniques, there are also a few "operators" in this field who often do a more effective selling job than their better-qualified competitors. Particularly open to suspicion are all alleged panaceas, and the practitioner who makes extravagant claims for the validity of his techniques. There are no magic answers to this difficult problem of appraising human potentialities.

Unless the manager has a trained person on his staff to interpret test findings properly, he would be well advised to select a consulting firm whose evaluations are based on something more than *tests alone.* A great deal of importance is likely to be attached to the expert's findings. *If the expert uses tests alone, he cannot provide a complete and accurate picture of an individual's potentialities.* The manager should be especially cautious about consultants who claim to be able to pick people without even seeing them.

5. *Cautious Interpretation of "Personality" Test Findings.* As has been pointed out, personality tests have generally proved to be less valid than tests of abilities or aptitudes. On the other hand, *if we accept "testimonial" evidence, personality tests seem to be very valid.* This is because personality traits are so nebulous that almost any pattern of findings will seem to fit a candidate very well. In other words, we tend to see in a candidate the traits which the test results say are there. If test results inaccurately point up personal liabilities, the reputation of the individual involved might be unjustly damaged.

In any case, even if we could measure personality traits accurately, we do not know what constitutes the ideal "personality" for an accountant, a salesman, a lawyer, a manager, or even a company president. Research studies have shown that men with entirely different personalities have often been successful in the same positions.

6. *Avoidance of Emergency Evaluations.* All too often, an employee has little or no experience with tests until some emergency arises and a personnel change which would affect him must be made. Perhaps his department is being reorganized, or a specific promotional opportunity arises. If, at this time, he is asked to undergo a formal "evaluation," it is difficult to convince him that his future status will not be decided on the basis of the "evaluation" results alone. Such "emergency" evaluations often give rise to complaints, especially by long-service employees.

They may feel that more weight will be given to the test results than to their record of performance.

Some companies have followed the practice of conducting a complete audit of the abilities and other qualifications of all managers and key specialists as part of their regular "Personnel Development" program. The primary purpose of such evaluations is to aid each individual evaluated in planning his own self-development. When subsequent promotional or transfer opportunities arise, the evaluation data can also aid his superior to place him where he can capitalize on his strengths.

7. Careful Explanation of the Program. Each individual to be tested or otherwise appraised by the "expert" should be given a thorough explanation of the program, the part which the tests or professional evaluation will play in arriving at personnel decisions, and the potential value of the program to him personally.

In fact, when formal appraisal procedures are used to any extent within a department, it is well to *provide an explanation of the program to all persons who might be involved.* This will help to prevent the misunderstandings which are now prevalent in many companies regarding the use of such tools.

The important part played by other sources of appraisal information should also be stressed. It is especially damaging to the reputation of the testing program if test results are used as the "scapegoat" when the manager has the undesirable task of explaining to an unsuccessful candidate why he did not qualify for a particular assignment.

8. Feedback of Evaluation Findings. Provision should be made for the results of an evaluation to be communicated to the candidate. Failure to report back often causes unnecessary apprehension about the implications of the findings.

Though every person who takes tests or is subjected to a professional appraisal can *benefit from the findings* if they are presented to him properly, it is well to recognize, however, that this feedback of appraisal results is not easy. If poorly handled, it can do more harm than good. In some companies where professional consulting firms are extensively used for executive appraisals, the same consultants are employed to perform the additional counseling service of discussing each man's appraisal results with him. In other companies, personnel department specialists provide operating managers with the materials and training necessary to perform this feedback task properly.

RAISING OUR BATTING AVERAGE

Though tests may appear to offer an easier and quicker way of making selection and placement decisions, unfortunately this is not the case. Properly employed, tests do not provide a short cut. In fact, with the adoption of more thorough and systematic methods in the evaluation program, the manager may very well find that he *spends more time* on personnel decisions.

Furthermore, the use of tests does not necessarily make selection decisions any more clear-cut and automatic. *Tests cannot be used as a substitute for good judgment.* Actually, the additional information provided by tests will sometimes make the selection decision more difficult. However, though the use of tests may necessitate more discerning judgment, the additional information they provide should also make our judgments more accurate.

Finally, it should be emphasized that the use of more systematic procedures for evaluating human characteristics will not result in perfect predictions of human performance. Even if our measures were perfect—which they are not—human behavior is not consistent enough to enable perfect predictions to be made. Despite the aid of the most advanced procedures, we shall continue to make some mistakes. The important point is: Do we make fewer mistakes when objective and systematic methods are applied?

The GE research study previously referred to showed that supervisors selected on the basis of the "expert's" evaluation, in conjunction with management's own appraisal of potential, were about four times less likely to be rated "poor" in subsequent job performance than were a comparable group of supervisors selected without recourse to the evaluation of an expert.

On the findings of this study, we may conclude, therefore, that the use of more thorough and objective methods should raise our batting average and so help to achieve a better qualified management team.

Bearing in mind that the misuse of tests can set us back materially in the progress made in this field thus far, we can consolidate our gains by taking every precaution in the use of the formal or systematic screening tools discussed in this paper. On this foundation we can continue to develop still better methods for insuring that each individual is placed in the job for which he is well qualified and in which he can make the maximum contribution to his company's success.

WHAT DOES THE SELECTION INTERVIEW ACCOMPLISH?

Calvin W. Downs

"Selection interviews are not really useful. They are neither valid nor reliable."—Participant in a recent seminar on interviewing.

Such criticism has caused a number of people to make concerted efforts to eliminate some of the confusion about the interviewing process.

Many experimental studies have been conducted to test such items as the honesty of people in answering questions, the effects of structuring an interview, and different ways of asking questions.[1] More of this kind of research is needed. The purpose of this study, however, is to analyze what happens in *actual* interviews and to find out what impressions the interviewers and interviewees have about the interviewing process.

Three techniques were used to obtain information. First, a comprehensive questionnaire was distributed to 76 professional college recruiters who came to Northwestern University's Graduate School of Business during the winter of 1967. Second, after the interviewing season was completed, a similar questionnaire was given to students at the graduate schools of business at Northwestern and the University of Chicago. Third, approximately 40 interviews were taped for analysis.

Reprinted by permission from the May–June 1968 issue of PERSONNEL ADMINISTRATION. Copyright 1968, Society for Personnel Administration, 485–87 National Press Building, 14th and F Streets, N.W., Washington, D.C. 20004.

[1]For a comprehensive review of the research on interviewing, see Eugene C. Mayfield, "The Selection Interview—A Re-evaluation of Published Research," *Personnel Psychology* **XVII**, 239-260 (Autumn 1964).

OBJECTIVES

In order to evaluate whether an interview, for example, is invalid and unreliable, the evaluator must first know the purposes of the interviewer. Consequently, the first step in this research was to ask what the participants in an interview were *trying* to accomplish.

Table A gives the responses to the question, "What is the *primary* objective of the interview?"[2]

The overwhelming emphasis on "what kind of person" he is indicates that the interviewer is very much interested in the candidate as a whole rather than being interested only in his job qualifications. Dr. James McBurney, Dean of the Northwestern School of Speech, once stated it this way: "I want to see whether I can live with him." There is, of course, no objective means of measuring the total individual. Perhaps the interviewer really looks only at the way a candidate interacts with the interviewer, and such analysis will always be somewhat subjective. No one can deny, however, that these subjective social relationships are important on the job.

Because of its subjectivity, the interview as a means of selecting candidates must be kept in perspective, and the information derived from it should be complemented by the information derived from application blanks, resumes, tests and letters of recommendation. Nevertheless, the interview performs an important function in the selection of a candidate because interviewers and interviewees both feel that the interview situation allows them to accomplish something that could not be accomplished in any other way.

The interviewers and candidates were asked, "What do you think that the interview accomplishes that could not be accomplished

[2]The student version of the question was: "Which do you think is the greatest objective of the interviewer in an interview?"

TABLE A OBJECTIVE OF THE INTERVIEW

OBJECTIVES (MORE THAN ONE COULD BE CHECKED)	INTERVIEWERS	CANDIDATES
To provide information about the job	7%	14%
To determine a candidate's non-personal qualifications	30%	16%
To find out what kind of person the candidate is	78%	68%

by written materials?" Their answers can be summarized as follows.

A. The interview offers an opportunity to exchange information about the candidate.

1. The interviewer may ask the candidate personal questions that might not be answered otherwise. Previous research indicates that answers to the same questions by the same respondent differ when the answers must be written and when they are given orally. Furthermore, answers can be explored in more detail in the interview than is possible on a written form. Typical comments follow.

The interviewer can ask "why" about information on the resume and other written forms. (Recruiter)

The definitions of terms and positions are important. The words "marketing" or "process development" have as many meanings as there are companies. The interview allows you to explore what these mean to the candidate. (Recruiter)

Many questions can be explored more specifically than can be covered on the written forms. (Candidate)

The interviewer can explore your interests in the company and in other activities. (Candidate)

2. Face-to-face encounters are most desirable, since it will be a face-to-face encounter on the job.

B. The interview offers an opportunity to exchange information about the company and job.

1. The interviewer can eliminate much of the ambiguity contained in brochures.

No brochure can be all things to all people. It cannot be specific and brief at the same time. The brochure is designed to get people to sign up for an interview, and they always "read" better than the actual situation. (Recruiter)

My company is more unstructured than we have

been able to indicate in the brochures so far. (Recruiter)

Written material tends to stress only the good things about a company. If an interviewer cannot mention negative points, he is not honest. (Candidate)

Details of a particular program or a particular job are necessary. (Candidate)

Information in the interview may be more current. (Candidate)

2. The candidate can ask specific questions relating to his particular interest in the company.

I can ask pointed questions about things about which I am in doubt or which are not covered in the written materials. (Candidate)

Answering specific questions makes the company appear stronger and more realistic. (Recruiter)

One can relate specific interests to a certain job, personalities, goals and objectives. (Recruiter)

The interview is less propagandistic. Answering specific job questions gives a certain validity to the answers. (Candidate)

The company literature is of negligible value. In the interview I can ask what type of person the company wants and what type of person they are likely to hire. (Candidate)

C. Judgments are made about the candidate on the basis of the interview.

1. A candidate reveals his personality in the interview.

One gets an indication of personal characteristics which are not evident in written material. (Recruiter)

Everyone's resume tends to look the same. It is not a true picture of him. (Recruiter)

My company is one in which a strong salesman for his own ideas succeeds whereas a weak personality, despite the value of his ideas, will fail. This quality of human relations I find impossible to determine from written forms. (Recruiter)

Whether or not I am the type of person they want

cannot be determined from my record. (Candidate)

The interview serves to show the personality adaptability of the candidate to the potential company environment. (Candidate)

The personal contact allows me to use my "whole man" concept in making my evaluations. The personal factors are as important as technical factors. (Recruiter)

The answers to this question indicate that both recruiters and candidates feel that "personality" can be judged from the interview. Rarely, however, do they pinpoint specifically what about the personality is revealed.

In his report on research in interviewing, Mayfield states, "With respect to traits or characteristics which can be estimated reliably and validly from interviews. It seems that only the intelligence or mental ability of the interviewee can be judged satisfactorily."[3] When asked if they agreed with this statement, however, an overwhelming percentage of the interviewers (88%) and candidates (94%) disagreed with it.

Furthermore, the Arco manual for the employment interviewer, a study guide for Civil Service examinations, maintains that mental ability should be rated by objective tests, whereas other characteristics may be appraised in the interview.[4]

What then can the interviewer determine about the interviewee's personality? "Traits which do not enter specifically into the behavior of the applicant during the interview cannot be judged with any accuracy."[5] While such characteristics as loyalty or honesty cannot be judged unless such information is specified in the interview, an interviewer may well make some estimates about the individual's motivation, enthusiasm, ability to get along with others, and his regard for himself. These estimates will be made from the information a candidate reveals about himself and

from his behavior in the interview. Perhaps more objective measures of personality are needed, but in the meantime it would be helpful to an interviewer if he would analyze his own means of measuring personality in order to improve his estimates.

2. A candidate reveals his ability to communicate orally in the interview but not on written forms.

A candidate's articulateness and how he reacts to questions is important. (Recruiter)

I must hear a man express himself in order to evaluate properly his potential and his enthusiasm. (Recruiter)

The interviewer can get an impression of how the candidate thinks and how quickly he comprehends. Is he analytical? (Recruiter)

The company would not want to hire a man who could not converse with others in an acceptable manner. (Candidate)

The interviewer can study your abilities of articulation, logic and thinking power. (Candidate)

The candidate is appraised on his abilities to think on his feet and to work in a dedicated manner rather than on his grades and experience. (Candidate)

Not only are the interviewers examining how well one articulates, but they also judge how he thinks, how well he listens and comprehends, and how well he can express his ideas. Anyone who has ever judged a speech contest knows that the judges frequently disagree over the "effectiveness" of a speech. The same phenomenon will be true of various interviewers as they judge a candidate's ability to communicate orally. Nevertheless, this is a tangible ability that lends itself to objective measurement better than does an intangible characteristic such as personality.

3. Estimates are made of a candidate's poise and behavioral skills in the interview.

An interview is a "must" for determining motivation and energy level. (Recruiter)

The interview gives some implications as to the behavior of the candidate with our customers. (Recruiter)

You can tell in an interview how well the can-

---

[3]Mayfield, *Ibid,* p. 252.

[4]Arco Editorial Board, *Employment Interview* (New York: Arco, 1966), p. 50.

[5]*Ibid.*

didate can handle himself. (Recruiter)

Like ability to communicate, poise and behavioral skills are somewhat tangible and are, therefore, amenable to measurement by an interviewer. Again, the judgment will be based almost exclusively on how the interviewee interacts within the interview situation. Nervousness is easy to spot generally, and most interviewers claim that they try to put the candidate at ease and let him demonstrate his normal behavior. One might question whether or not the poise (or lack of it) demonstrated in an interview is really typical; nevertheless, both recruiters and interviewees recognize that it is all-important in determining the estimate.

4. A candidate's appearance may be seen and evaluated in the interview.

A certain type of appearance is sometimes quite important to a particular kind of job, and whether or not the candidate meets the requirements may be established easily enough. Recruiters sometimes find themselves generalizing from appearance as an indicator of other qualities such as cleanliness, neatness, orderliness, and even honesty. Such generalizations should be avoided until they are corroborated by other evidence. It is important to note here, too, that the literature is quite specific in instructing candidates how to dress for an interview, and the appearance of a given candidate at an interview may not be typical at all.

A student once posed this question to me, "If a person is otherwise qualified for a job but does not dress properly, why could he not be hired and taught how to dress?"

D. Judgments are made about the company on the basis of the interview.

The interview personalizes the company.

The interview makes the contact with the candidate a personal one which dispels the impersonal image, and it lets the interviewer establish empathy with the interviewee. (Recruiter)

One cannot evaluate management until he meets them. (Recruiter)

The interviewer is an extension of the company, and the candidate gets an insight into the type of person who works for the company. (Recruiter)

I am a personal representative, and my knowledge, spirit, and enthusiasm personalize the situation. (Recruiter)

The interviewee wants some idea of the personality of the company. The interviewer is this impression. (Candidate)

The progressiveness of the company is projected by the type itself. (Candidates)

It is an opportunity to learn about the working climate and the character of the company through someone's opinions. (Candidate)

The candidate's estimate of the personality of the company on the basis of an interview is just as subject to error as the interviewer's estimate of the personality of the candidate. The interviewer becomes the symbol for the company, and yet he represents a sample size of only one. Nevertheless, the candidate often places more importance on his estimate of the "representative of the company" than on his judgments based on the company literature.

CONCLUSION

Of what utility then is the selection interview? There can be little doubt of the utility of the interview as an opportunity to exchange vital information that would not easily be exchanged in any other way. There is doubt, however, of the reliability of the judgments made in the interview, and the interviewer should be constantly aware of the limitations of the interview.

The highly subjective nature of the judgments leaves them open to much criticism, but these judgments are no less useful than other subjective judgments which we make about speechmaking, the writing of books, and similar communications. Furthermore, it would seem that skillful interviewers should be able to gauge at least three of the characteristics sought—ability to communicate orally, poise, and appearance—with a great deal of reliability. While the interviewer should continually attempt to make his judgments as objective as he can, ultimately he is "paid for setting up criteria for what is good and for applying them."[6] The task of future research is to determine how extensively an interviewer can actually accomplish what he says he is trying to accomplish.

Although the interviewers themselves express confidence in their ability to make discriminating judgments among candidates, they also express some reservations about many of the decisions which they must make. They were asked: "After the interview, how confident are you of your decision?" The results in Table B indicate that most of them have some reservations. Their uncertainty seems to lie with judgments about average candidates, for many of them expressed a

[6]This statement was made by a recruiter whose name is withheld by request.

high degree of certainty about candidates who were either "outstanding" or "very poor."

TABLE B. CONFIDENCE IN DECISIONS

CONFIDENCE LEVEL	% OF INTERVIEWERS
60%	4%
70%	5%
75%	29%
80%	22%
90%	27%
100%	3%
Other	10%

Finally, it is encouraging to note that recruiters in general indicate a strong motivation to improve. In the final analysis, the degree of validity and reliability does not depend upon the interview as a communication process. It depends, rather, upon the skills of the individual interviewer.

PART THREE

DEVELOPING HUMAN RESOURCES

There is a very direct relationship between manpower procurement and manpower development. The more effective an organization is in acquiring the optimal human resources, the easier it is to manage the development of those human resources. Under the very best of conditions, however, training and development will not take care of themselves. Neither is it a one-shot process. Developing people is an on-going process not only for those entering the organization for the first time, but for those already in it as well. The process begins with orientation procedures, which is the topic of the first article in this section, "A Systems Approach to Orientation." After orientation, it is a continuous process which lasts as long as the employee remains in the organization.

The second article, "The Application of Behavioral Science Theory to Professional Development," presents scientific findings which are useful to the administrator of a professional development program. The article is particularly relevant in that it views professional development as a system itself and explores the possible consequence to the organization of propositions developed by the author. Since, however, developing people must be viewed from a comprehensive frame of reference, and we are attempting to integrate different approaches to human resources management, we have included the article "Management Development: A Systems View." This article takes a systematic approach to the development process.

"Guidelines for the Design of New Careers" focuses on the restructuring of dead-end and lower level jobs. A comprehensive approach is outlined for developing the personnel entering these jobs, and for restructuring jobs into career ladders in order to provide increased opportunity for occupational and personal growth.

The final selection outlines the problems of training unemployed, unskilled workers and proposes an approach to the solution of these problems.

A SYSTEMS APPROACH TO ORIENTATION

Otis Lipstreu

Would you believe that apart from obtaining certain "tombstone" and classification data, companies can attain more effective employee-adjustment-to-work situations if they depend entirely on the orientation provided by their informal organizations?

Neither would I, but my assurance has been shaken recently by the conclusions from two unpublished Master's theses[1] investigating the effectiveness of orientation programs in a variety of organizations, both profit and non-profit, in a large Western metropolitan area. These two questionnaire-interview studies compared the goals of orientation programs as articulated by management officials with terminal knowledge, feelings, and attitudes of new employees, some four to six months after their formal induction.

Discounting the fact that sample size, less than 50 companies, and that the precision of the methods used could be questioned, the probability exists that this phase of the employment process is of questionable value. Orientation has been subjected to little critical analysis. To verify this statement concerning lack of scholarly or practical attention, check the number of analytical or research articles regarding orientation in personnel periodicals during the past twenty years. I did and there are amazingly few, and most of these are descriptive.

Some time ago I related these criticisms, including preliminary results from the two studies, to a group of personnel executives. Recently, one of these officials, a personnel manager in a large bank, called to tell me that he so agreed with my concerns that he had tried his own experiment. He excised the remainder of his formal orientation program following an initial interaction mainly concerned with obtaining basic personnel data. And after six months follow-up, just completed, he informed me, turnover during this critical period was no higher than formerly, and as far as he could determine, employee adjustment to work and attitudes toward the bank were, if anything, more positive. He was doubly pleased since he was applying the amount saved on orientation to improving other personnel systems.

This reaction is certainly extreme. I recount it merely as an illustration of what not to do. Despite the two negative studies and my friend's rash action, I intend to make a case for the proposition that orientation can pay off well, if the process of attitude formation and the adjustment process are understood in depth, and when the technical system is carefully programmed.

TYPICAL ORIENTATION

According to a fairly recent descriptive study,[2] most formal orientation processes start on the first day of employment. Some 39 percent of the reporting companies have formal programs, typically between four and ten hours in length. The program content appears to be largely informational and fairly standardized, comprised of verbal presenta-

Article—A systems approach to Orientation pg. 124

[1]Suzanne Gill, *A Study of Employee Satisfaction and Dissatisfaction Related to an Induction Program* (Unpublished Masters Thesis, Graduate School, University of Colorado, 1964) and Roger Sweeney, *A Study of Negative and Positive Effects of Orientation Programs,* Graduate School, University of Colorado (Unpublished Masters Thesis, 1968).

[2]*Orientation of New Employees,* Bureau of National Affairs, Personnel Policy Forum, 1964.

tions concerning company rules and regulations, employee benefits and services, physical layout (accompanied by a plant tour), introduction to peers and supervisors. An employee handbook[3] is usually provided and in the instance of unionized companies, information relative to collective bargaining and the contract are included.

OPTIMAL CRITERIA

How does the foregoing orientation pattern measure up to the guidelines which a National Industrial Conference Board study[4] has suggested as optimal criteria? In the study, William Mussman contends that orientation should be designed to: (1) Create favorable impressions and attitudes toward the company and work; (2) foster a sense of belonging; (3) facilitate learning and integration into the work group; (4) reduce adjustment problems involved in the awkwardness and ignorance of the new environment; (5) create a sense of security and confidence so that the training process can be facilitated. To attain the above goals, orientation must produce more of a depth experience than the mere collection of information dispensing devices is capable of developing.

THE PSYCHOLOGICAL CONTRACT

The primary focus in orientation relates to the very nature of the employment relationship. For example, the fact of employment conveys an implicit, psychological contract in which each party pledges to contribute something to the other for which each will receive something.[5] An organization is limited in its freedom to call on all of an individual's repertoire of behaviors relative to what is expected. Attention should be given to the notion that most people have dichotomous attitudes toward "expected behavior"—a zone of indifference and a zone of acceptance. In the former, responses are largely reflexive involving a minimal value factor. For example, most employees accept the right of management to set the hours of work, rest breaks and the like.

In the acceptance area involving motivation, company identification, and relations with peers while on the job, responses have a high sensitivity content and are psychologically important to the respondents, requiring consensus if behavior is to be effective in an organizational sense. Superficial informational orientation programs may score in the zone of indifference, limited by the law of foregetting, while completely missing the goal in the far more crucial zone of acceptance.

COGNITIVE DISSONANCE

Probably nothing is more inhibiting in the zone of acceptance than cognitive dissonance[6]—that state of mind conditioned by two contradictory or incompatible sets of information. A person experiencing cognitive dissonance feels compelled to reduce it by changing one of the two incompatible elements. When the formal and informal orientation systems convey different concepts relative to how one is rewarded or punished, cognitive dissonance is present.

---

[3]A recent study by Keith Davis, "Readability in Employee Handbooks of Identical Companies During a Fifteen Year Period," *Personnel Psychology,* **21** (4), (Winter, 1968), questions the value of employee handbooks in the orientation process—"The handbook is often the first organizational publication a new employee receives . . . Since it is a first impression, it needs to set a communication tone with the employee . . . If he does not get certain information from the handbook, he may be without it in the short run, and, consequently, handicap his adjustment to his new job." And the study concludes—"most employee handbooks are not yet adequately readable for the audience for which they are intended."

[4]William Mussman, "Employee Induction," *Studies in Personnel Policy* (No. 131, National Industrial Conference Board, 1953).

[5]For an excellent expansion of this concept see James D. Thompson, *Organizations in Action* (New York: McGraw-Hill, 1967), pp. 105-107.

[6]Leon Festinger, *A Theory of Cognitive Dissonance* (Stanford, California: Stanford University Press, 1957).

For example, when the formal "word" indicates that a new employee will receive extra pay for extra effort expended, and the informal "word" denies this by contending that extra effort produces no tangible pay off, employees undergo disturbing cognitive dissonance.[7] Furthermore, the incompatible element more likely to be identified is what management says rather than the "word" from his peer group, thus contributing to the classic credibility gap between management and employees. Consequently it is imperative that officials minimize such dissonance in orientation by carefully presenting content that is likely to produce incongruity. Means for resolving unavoidable conflict must be built into the system through feedback which identifies the presence and nature of dissonance early in the process. Sequenced group opportunities for employees to ventilate their concerns to those who really listen and have authority to change things, after the truncated formal orientation experience, promise far greater returns (preventative) than suggestion systems and attitude surveys (remedial).

ORIENTATION PROPOSITIONS

Now, within this deeper frame of reference, let me advance a number of propositions concerning the orientation process:

1. New employees will receive orientation of some kind—the only questions to be answered are when, where, by whom, what content, and how.

2. The informal organization has a personalized system and its content credibility for the new employee is usually higher than that attributed to the formal system.

3. The most influential persons in the ori-

entation process are the peer group and the direct supervisor in that order.

4. The new employee has a hierarchy of concerns that need to be met on a priority basis using media that relate directly to the nature of communication problems, sequenced over time.

5. There are certain informational items that the new employee needs to know (rules, regulations) that he may not feel a need to know.

6. The impression a new employee receives at this stage of the employment process will condition his organizational behavior in present and future organizations of which he is a member, will structure his perceptions of his employment experiences, and will be a significant factor in potential termination, or may inhibit or enhance positive motivation if he remains.

OPTIMAL ORIENTATION SYSTEM

In the context of these propositions, consider an optimal orientation system based on the following guidelines:

1. Examination of what employees want to know and what the company wishes them to know. Someone has said "all the new employee wants to know is can I 'cut the mustard' and where's the 'john?'" Obviously an over-simplification, but it suggests that much of what the company beams at the new employee in the way of information will not be remembered or even heard—the law of readiness is not operant. Three lessons should be apparent:

One, give the employee a liberal infusion of confidence that he can succeed on the job.

Two, identify the critical, minimal items that the company wishes him to know, sequencing the remaining content into the future.

Three, use the law of effect in organizing and presenting information. Information will be heard and remembered which is perceived

---

[7]For a provocative extension of other implications of the "effort-reward expectations" belief see Lyman W. Porter and Edward Fowler, III, "What Job Attitudes Tell About Motivation," *Harvard Business Review,* pp. 118-126 (January-February 1968).

to be directly related to success or failure on the job.

2. Identification of the communication problems involved in the learning process and selection of the most appropriate methodology. Orientation methods appear to be so standardized that it is doubtful that much, if any, attention has been given to relating method to the nature of specific communication problems. It is easy to forget that method is simply the means for improving communications when matching subject matter content with human capacities for learning and retention.

3. Articulation of work norms reinforced by their consistent transmission, reward, and punishment. Most organizations try to state employee behavior expectations in employee handbooks and work standards. But there is substantial question about whether the statements are articulated clearly in terms of the employees' ability to understand or his perception of reasonableness of their attainment. Unless such norms, even when properly understood and accepted, are conveyed consistently by all levels of management, and the reward for performance is perceived as equitable, they are meaningless and serve to prejudice the trust relationship. Consistency is so important, for example, subjective variances between supervisors in evaluating employee performance, using the same work standards, often compromise the validity of criteria espoused by higher management as the basis for monetary rewards.

4. Identification of content falling in individual zones of indifference and acceptance and the selection of appropriate means for generating attitudes conducive to self-discipline and shared goals. Since research indicates the presence of these two zones, they need to be identified for various work situations and levels of work because they vary with experience, education, attitudes, and according to the degree of trust present in a given work situation. To illustrate, punching a time clock may be within the zone of indifference for a blue collar worker but in the acceptance zone for a white collar worker.

5. Use of the informal orientation process to reinforce and amplify formal orientation content. Initial assignment of new personnel to work groups whose attitudes are positive, utilization of informal communication channels (peer group members with high earned status) for dissemination of orientation content, and continual monitoring (with free feedback) of all channels to minimize dissonance are means of implementing this guideline.

6. Provision of supervisory training in orientation and stimuli for supervisors to develop their own continuing orientation processes. It is questionable that supervisors recognize personal responsibility for orientation, probably because higher management seems to place little emphasis on it. Nor does management stimulate assumption of responsibility by supervisors through evaluation of their new employees' adjustment to work. Lack of supervisory concern is further reinforced by the willingness of personnel departments to assume complete authority for the process.

7. Opportunities in employee feedback for resolving dissonance. This aspect of orientation is such a cornerstone for effective employee relations that to mention it may seem unnecessary. But the one way, verbal flow prevalent in most programs and lack of feedback opportunities during the employment relationship could lead one to the conclusion that management is either too busy to bother with dissonance, or considers it a passing passion that will vanish with time.

The normative orientation schematic in Figure 3.1 emphasizes vital input items in the planning phase which, when omitted, usually produces the perfunctory, copy-cat, indoctrinaire orientation programs so typical in present-day organizations. The emphasis on validation of content, fitting method to the nature of specific communication problems, supervisory involvement in planning, training

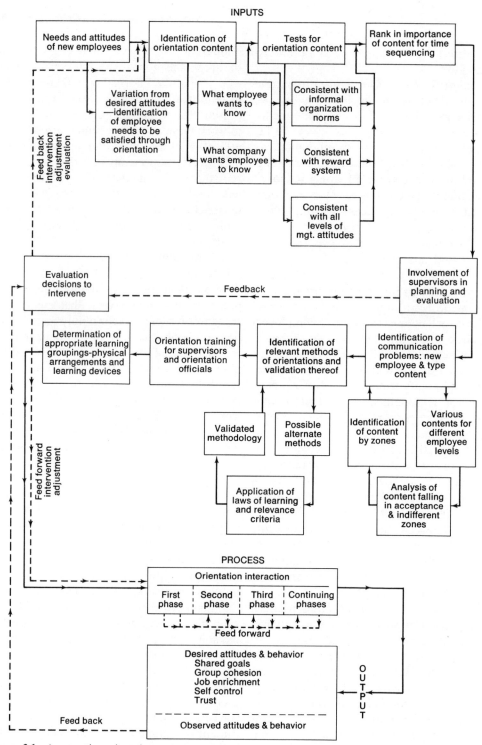

Figure 3.1 A normative orientation system.

for, and implementation of the process extended over time are particularly critical. The activity flow attempts to link the ideas contained in this paper into a systems approach to orientation.

EXPERIMENTAL ORIENTATION PROGRAM

An approach which embodies many of the foregoing concepts has recently been applied and researched in a large company with women who perform a bonding operation on an assembly line.[8] In a controlled experiment, one group of new recruits was given the traditional orientation treatment while a matched group was involved in a new program. Highly encouraging organizational behavior was obtained in the latter. The new program was based on interview data which revealed that: (1) the first days on the job were anxious and uncertain ones; (2) new employee initiation practices by peers intensified anxiety; (3) such anxiety interfered with the training process. The researchers found that when anxiety is minimized, learning increases almost as a straight line function of time.

The experimental process involved an entire day during which the new employees had no contact with their peer work group but had unlimited opportunities to talk with each other and to question those making informal presentations. The process stressed: (1) opportunities for success are good; (2) cautions relative to the validity of "hall talk"; (3) taking the initiative in communicating; (4) getting to know supervisors by aggressively asking them questions. Although no supervisory training accompanied the program, supervisors were apprised of the new process and alerted to their responsibility. It is apparent, when the four items above are analyzed, that the primary focus is on minimizing cognitive dissonance.

The researchers found, as a result of reduction in anxiety and dissonance in the experimental group, that: (1) training time, training costs, absenteeism, and tardiness were lowered one-half, one-third, and one-half respectively; (2) waste and rejects were reduced to one-fifth previous levels; (3) operational costs were cut as much as 15 to 30 percent. And an improvement in performance of the experimental group compared with the control group of 50 percent was measured, representing a net first year saving of at least $50,000. With reduced turnover, absenteeism, and training time, additional annual savings of $35,000 were estimated.

Interesting by-products included the effect of the positive attitudes of the experimental group members on their new work groups, an enthusiastic, in depth interest by supervisors relative to the causes of attitude change, a more challenging work environment, and involvement of supervisors in anxiety reduction resulting in still more responsible and creative behavior of employees.

SUMMARY

The waste of the investment in recruitment, selection, and training, when employee orientation is faulty, is quite apparent. Not so apparent are the even higher hidden costs involved in the loss of manpower, during the critical first months of employment, before the break-even point between wages and productivity is reached. Regardless of the type of cost assessment applied, there is little doubt that dollar losses from poor orientation run into the countless millions annually.

Since orientation connotes the process of pointing toward shared values of dignity, viability, creativity, and productivity with far less reliance on organizational structure, I have used the term "orientation" throughout rather than "induction." Furthermore, orien-

[8]E. Gomersall and M. Scott Myers, "Breakthrough in On-The-Job Training," *Harvard Business Review,* pp. 64-72 (July-August 1966).

Figure 3.2   Focal points in the orientation process.

tation implies a "feedforward process"[9] incorporating the ideas presented herein. Its focal points may be depicted by Figure 3.2.[10]

Formal orientation systems can be designed to provide the new recruit with a consistent, initial impression, reinforced and supplemented over time, centered around the job-personal growth nexus, consistent with

informal organizational norms and even supported by the informal social system in an anxiety-reduced work context. Complex? Yes! Difficult to implement? Of course! Worth it? Only if you are interested in profits or wish to provide services at the lowest possible cost. Test some of these ideas. They work!

[9]"Feedforward" has been defined by I. A. Richards in "The Secret of Feedforward," *Saturday Review*, February 3, 1967, pp. 14-16, as the reciprocal of feedback. He amplifies—"Whatever we may be doing, some sort of preparation for, some design for one sort of outcome rather than another is part of our activity. This may be conscious, as an expectancy . . . or unconscious, as a mere assumption. At one end of the scale, it can be a highly articulate examination process . . . at the other, it may be hardly cognized or embodied at all, even in the vaguest schematic image." And where feedback is characterized by status quo and remedy, feedforward is dynamic and preventative.

[10]For a provocative extension of these ideas to a total organizational context see Mason Haire, "A Human Group Model of Organization," in George Fisk, ed., *The Psychology of Management Decision* (Lund, Sweden: C. W. K. Gleerup Publishers, 1967), pp. 33-43.

THE APPLICATION OF BEHAVIORAL SCIENCE THEORY TO PROFESSIONAL DEVELOPMENT

George P. Huber

INTRODUCTION

This paper has as its purpose the exploration and categorization of some of the ideas resulting from the work of behavioral scientists which appear applicable to on-the-job development of professional managers and professional specialists. It is an attempt to present scientific findings in a form which might be useful to the administrator of a professional development system.

In the context of this paper, it will be useful to regard development as the directed process by which the attitudes and abilities of organizational members are altered to the advantage of the organization.[1]

The attitudes and abilities to be considered were chosen and categorized as general motivation, specific motivation, interpersonal competence, and professional competence. For each of these concepts a set of propositions has been abstracted, either directly or indirectly, from the work of the behavioral scientists. Consideration of these propositions would appear to be useful to the administrator of a professional development system. If their probable consequences are viewed as organizationally desirable, the administrator

From George P. Huber, "The Application of Behavioral Science Theory to Professional Development," Academy of Management Journal 10 (3), 275–286 (1967). Reprinted by permission.

[1]This is not to say that development would not otherwise take place. We are concerned here with a formal administrative effort.

would likely select strategies and tactics with which to operationalize the propositions. The paper includes for each proposition one or more strategies, but for the sake of brevity does not include tactics.

Depending upon the circumstances surrounding the strategy implementation, there may occur a great many possible functional and dysfunctional consequences. Some of these possible consequences are given for each of the strategies.

As might be expected, some strategies were applicable to more than one proposition and some consequences were applicable to more than one strategy. Although an attempt to avoid such duplication was made, there were instances where elimination of a strategy or consequence would have been unrealistic.

MOTIVATION

Motivation may be defined as the inclination to satisfy a need. This paper is primarily concerned with the self-esteem and self-actualization needs (Maslow, 1943), since it is assumed (1) that these needs are characteristic sources of motivation for professionals and (2) that the administrator of the development system has the power necessary to aid the professional in at least partially satisfying these needs through the organization. It is assumed in the following pages that motivation is positively correlated with the concepts of (1) level of aspiration, (2) degree of commitment, and (3) inclination toward action. An investigation into the exact relationships among these three concepts is an undertaking beyond the scope of this paper.

The directness of the relationship between a person's actions and environmental reward may be used to scale a continuum of motivation. At the left end of the continuum are those persons who always attempt to do well in any undertaking, seeming somehow to achieve sufficient satisfaction from conquering the problem and requiring very little in the way of direct incentives. At the right end of the continuum are those persons who attempt to do well in only those undertakings which seem to be directly and rather immediately related to the satisfaction of some well-defined goal.

The left end of this continuum characterizes an attitude described as "a latent disposition to strive for a particular goal-state or aim, e.g. achievement, affiliation, power" (Atkinson & Reitman, 1956). This attitude of "general motivation" is of value to the organization in that it results in a restlessness, a dissatisfaction with the status quo, which under the proper circumstances will result in the innovations and creations generally expected of professionals and in a tendency to attempt the "self-development" so often referred to by management practitioners.

The right end of the continuum characterizes an attitude described as an inclination to strive for a particular goal, e.g., a promotion, a salary increase, a publication. This attitude of "specific motivation" is of value to the organization for at least two reasons. The first is that under the proper circumstances it can result in the accomplishment of the specific tasks which the organization requires. The second, to be emphasized in this paper, is that under the proper circumstances this attitude can be used to direct the professional development of individual organizational members.

1000 General Motivation, an Attitude

General motivation is in part a function of the professional's previous experiences which have shaped the hierarchy and intensity of his needs and the perception he has of his ability to satisfy these needs. It may be that by the time a person enters the professional ranks his need pattern and perception of his abilities are so well established that it is prohibitively difficult to intensify his general motivation. This paper rejects this assumption and proceeds on the assumption that the level of a person's general motivation can

be increased by manipulating his experiences over an extended period of time.

1100 Proposition 1: People establish their goals in light of their past performance. A record of meeting or surpassing other than trivial goals will result in a higher level of aspiration and a greater degree of commitment resulting from increased confidence.

1110 Strategy: The administrator forces the professional's explicit goals to be well within the range of expected performance, but non-trivial.

1111 Possible functional consequence: If they achieve or surpass the goals, the professionals may acquire a higher level of aspiration (Stedry, 1960) and a greater degree of commitment. This in turn may cause them to be more highly motivated and more interpersonally competent (Argyris) in that they may be less defensive.

1112 Possible functional consequence: If they perceive success early in their tenure, the professionals may use their excess time and energy in a functionally innovative or exploratory manner and consequently may benefit their own development and organizational operations.

1113 Possible dysfunctional consequence: If they feel unchallenged or under-valued, the professionals may withdraw psychologically or physically from the organization. In some cases they may seek on-the-job challenges that may not be in accordance with the organization's interests (Argyris, 1957).

1200 Proposition 2: People establish higher goals if the cost of failure to achieve them is small.

1210 Strategy 1: The administrator provides a supportive, generally approving relationship for the professionals.

1211 Possible functional consequence: If they perceive that the cost of failure is low, the professionals may establish higher goals (Stedry, 1960) and feel free to explore and innovate (Argyris, 1957), thus exposing themselves to more development-enhancing, problem-solving experiences.

1212 Possible functional consequence: The administrator-professional relationship may be characterized by more cooperation and trust (Deutsch, 1962). This may result in less defensive behavior and consequently greater interpersonal competence.

1213 Possible functional consequence: The professionals may achieve a higher state of psychological health in that they may become less defensive and less anxious (Cantor, 1958, Chap. 4; Argyris, 1964, Chap. 2; Kahn *et al.*, 1964, Chap. 14). These conditions may in turn result in greater interpersonal competence and a greater exposure to problem-solving experiences.

1214 Possible functional consequence: Perhaps as a function of the interaction of the previously named consequences, or aside from them, the productivity of the professionals may be increased (Likert, 1961, p. 119).

1215 Possible dysfunctional consequence: As a result of losing a critical but objective reference standard, the professionals may be less able to evaluate themselves effectively (Festinger, 1961) and thus not be aware of the inadequacies which hinder their development.

1216 Possible dysfunctional consequence: If the generally-approving relationship is strongly reciprocated or bargained for, the organization may be faced with the pathologies of favoritism or vested interest (Deutsch, 1962; Dalton, 1959).

1220 Strategy 2: The administrator disguises the disciplinary and corrective actions applied to the professionals.

1221 Possible functional consequence: The professionals will not be faced with the high stresses resulting from demotions or reprimands and may not be as prone to withdraw psychologically or physically from the organization or to become so anxiety-laden that

they are less effective (Dalton, 1959; Kahn *et al.*, 1964, Chap. 14).

1222 Possible functional consequence: The sponsors of the professionals will not be exposed as having made faulty judgments. This in turn will cause them to be neither defensive (never recommending a professional) nor anxiety-laden (never facing up to having to evaluate a professional) (Dalton, 1959).

1223 Possible dysfunctional consequence: The evaluative ability of the professional, his peers, and any others observing the reward and penalty structure of the organization may become less effective in that a potentially useful reference standard will have been removed. This in turn will make them less aware of their own inadequacies and retard their development (Festinger, 1961).

2000 Specific Motivation, an Attitude

The organization requires results from its members which may not be in keeping with the professional's immediate goals. In order to arouse and direct the efforts toward organizational goals, which may be the professional's increased professional or interpersonal competence, the organization attempts to produce specific motivations in him. The paper proceeds on the assumption that specific motivations can be created and intensified in professionals by manipulating the measurement, evaluation, and payoff system.

2100 Proposition 1: The magnitude and distribution of the efforts of a professional will be affected by the structure of the measurement and evaluation system.

2110 Strategy 1: The administrator makes known to the professionals the details of the explicit measurement and evaluation system in use.

2111 Possible functional consequence: The professionals' motivation applicable to the evaluated tasks may be increased. If the accomplishment of the evaluated task is a potential learning experience, then more learning and development will take place (Zalesnik, 1958; Bennis, 1958).

2112   Possible functional consequence: The professionals may become task-oriented rather than administrator-oriented, thus increasing performance on the task under scrutiny.

2113   Possible dysfunctional consequence: The professionals may become so task-oriented that they neglect the question of "why" for "how," quickly accept symptomatic rather than causative relief from task problems, and in general neglect the future in favor of the present.

2114   Possible dysfunctional consequence: The professionals may seek to influence their score by other than legitimate means, thus perhaps adversely affecting the organization (Dalton, 1959; Ridgway, 1960; Blau, 1955).

2120   Strategy 2: The administrator makes known to the professional that a stated single index of performance is under scrutiny.

2121   Possible functional consequence: The professionals may focus their efforts on the measured aspect and, if that aspect contains a potential learning experience for them, increase their professional competence.

2122   Possible dysfunctional consequence: The professionals may neglect other aspects of their tasks (Blau, 1955; Ridgway, 1960).

2130   Strategy 3: The administrator makes known to the professional that several indexes of performance with undetermined weightings are under scrutiny which in total cover the position.

2131   Possible functional consequence: The professionals may adopt a broader, organizational viewpoint as opposed to a narrower, self-interest viewpoint, thus increasing their professional competence and organizational usefulness (Leavitt, 1958).

2132   Possible functional consequence: The professionals may be less prone to neglect frustrating or undesirable aspects of their tasks (Blau, 1955).

2133   Possible dysfunctional consequence: The professionals may incorrectly weight the performance indexes as they imagine them to be weighted and so misdirect their efforts (Blau, 1955; Ridgway, 1960).

2134   Possible dysfunctional consequence: The professional may become insecure as a result of this ambiguity and become overly administrator-oriented (Kahn *et al.*, 1964, Chap. 14).

2200   Proposition 2: People put forth more effort toward the attainment of implicit goals as opposed to explicit goals.

2210   Strategy 1: The administrator causes only implicit goals to be established.

2211   Possible functional consequence: The professionals may exert more effort than with explicit goals (Stedry, 1960) because they may not realize that they have satisfied the minimum organizational requirements. As a result of the increased effort they may become more professionally competent and more productive.

2212   Possible dysfunctional consequence: Because a useful reference standard has been eliminated, the professionals may acquire an unrealistically high or low evaluation of their achievements, thus reducing the possibility of recognizing and eliminating their inadequacies.

2300   Proposition 3: People direct more effort toward those goals which they have partially or completely established.

2310   Strategy: The administrator causes the professionals to participate in the establishment of their goals.

2311   Possible functional consequence: The professionals will be more highly motivated to achieve the established goals (Tannenbaum and Massarik, 1950, pp. 408-418; Stedry, 1960), and if achievement of the goal results in learning, they will achieve a higher state of development.

2312   Possible dysfunctional consequence: If participation in goal-setting becomes accepted as a norm, the professional may resist any externally imposed organizational goals.

2400   Proposition 4: People increase the range and strength of their coping efforts if their role requirements are great.

2410   Strategy 1: The administrator assigns the professionals to positions which have future requirements beyond their immediate abilities.

2411   Possible functional consequence: The professionals may search for and find new facts and behavior patterns which will enable them to meet the future position requirements (Argyris, 1964; Kahn, *et al.,* 1964).

2412   Possible dysfunctional consequence: If the future requirements of the position are perceived as excessive, the professionals may undergo a neuroses-producing experience which may result in permanent damage to their organizational utility (Kahn, *et al.,* 1964, p. 261).

2420   Strategy 2: The administrator assigns professionals to membership in an undermanned group in which each member is evaluated on the basis of the group's performance. Argyris (1964, p. 228) points out that "An undermanned organization will have its predicted effects (1) *if* the tasks available permit individuals to use their important abilities, (2) *if* the employees believe that the undermannedness is legitimate, and (3) *if* they are sharing in the increased fruits of production." To this should be added a condition to the effect that the group must be "facilitatively interdependent" (Thomas, 1962).

2421   Possible functional consequence: The professionals may acquire stronger responsibility forces (Thomas, 1962) and may exert greater effort toward the accomplishment of their tasks (Argyris, 1964, pp. 221-228; Berkowitz, 1957).

2422   Possible dysfunctional consequence: Same as 2412.

COMPETENCE

Competence may be defined as the ability to perform tasks in a satisfactory manner. For professionals the tasks are generally problem-solving in nature, and for this task type Argyris (1964, p. 24) offers the following qualitative statement: "Competence may be hypothesized to increase (1) as one's awareness of problems increases; (2) as the problems are solved in such a way that they remain solved; and (3) with minimal expenditure of energy and disruption to the problem-solving process (within or between individuals)."

For analytical purposes, problem-solving competence may be categorized as being either professional or interpersonal. Interpersonal competence is concerned with the ability to solve the problems arising between oneself and others. Professional competence is concerned with all of the abilities related to one's profession, and in most professions would include interpersonal competence. This overlap will be disregarded in this paper in that the intellective, rational, technical abilities will be those referred to under the discussion of professional competence.

Interpersonal competence is of value to the organization for at least two reasons. The first is that it facilitates formal and informal communication within and at the periphery of the organization. The second reason, especially applicable to this paper, is that professional competence can be enhanced by feedback to the professional concerning the results of his efforts. Some of this feedback will come from others and will be more useful to the professional if he is interpersonally competent.

Professional competence is of value to the organization because it is a necessary ingredient in the solution of the unprogrammed problems of the organization.

3000   Interpersonal Competence, an Ability

Two factors contributing to interpersonal

competence are self-awareness and self-esteem—self-awareness because we are more receptive to communications about ourselves which are consonant with our self-concept, and self-esteem because it enables us to be less defensive and more able to minimize the defensiveness of the communicator. A decrease in the defensiveness of either the sender or receiver of a communication not only results in less distortion of the message but also tends to decrease the defensiveness of the other (Argyris, 1964). The paper proceeds on the assumption that interpersonal competence of a professional can be increased by increasing his self-awareness and self-esteem.

3100   Proposition 1: An increase in self-awareness leads to an increase in interpersonal competence.

3110   Strategy: The administrator creates an organizational situation in which candidates are exposed to a large amount of descriptive, nonevaluative feedback in a generally supportive climate. This strategy attempts to provide more information in a form which is more likely to pass through the individual's "filter mechanism."

3111   Possible functional consequence: The professionals may become more aware of themselves and their effect on others and consequently will become more effective communicators. As a result they may receive feedback that destroys their incorrect self-image and results in positive coping procedures (Argyris, 1962, p. 18; Leavitt, 1958, p. 97).

3112   Possible dysfunctional consequence: The professionals may not be stable enough to accept the feedback and may develop dysfunctional neuroses (Kahn *et al.,* 1964, Chap. 14).

3200   Proposition 2: An increase in self-esteem leads to an increase in interpersonal competence in that it minimizes the necessity for the distortion needed to defend oneself against adverse communication about oneself.

3210   Strategy: The administrator creates an organizational situation in which the professionals are able to define their own realistic, valued goals and the paths to these goals, and to receive feedback about their progress in achieving these goals. Limited by the constraint that the professionals must be able to assign the solution of the problem to themselves, the administrator provides the reasonable and necessary resources.

3211   Possible functional consequence: If the professionals attain their goals and achieve a higher self-esteem, they may be able to receive with less distortion the communications of others (Argyris, 1964).

3212   Possible consequence: The professionals may not attain their goals and may consequently decrease their self-esteem.

3213   Possible dysfunctional consequence: If the professionals attain their goals, they, if not fully aware of themselves, may so generalize their success as to distort to a greater degree the communication of others about themselves.

4000   Professional Competence, an Ability

Ability is a function of, among other things, learning experiences. How much can be learned is a function of several factors which may be categorized as follows:

The first factor is the amount of relevant material available with which to associate the new material (Underwood, 1964). The process of selection, not part of this paper, supposedly provides the administrator with only those persons who possess sufficient mental inventories to allow them to profit from those aspects of the developmental program designed to increase their professional competence.

The second factor which influences learning is the potential learning rate of the individual. This factor is a function of his cognizance of his social environment (Argyris, 1964), his cognizance of his physical environment (Leavitt, 1958), and his ability to usefully assimilate inputs from his environment (Bereison & Steiner, 1964). Cognizance of social environment was discussed in the preceding section on interpersonal competence. Cognizance of physical environment is a function of the individual's sensory mechanism, his stimuli filtering system, and his response schemata (Abercrombie, 1960). These attributes are assumed to be present to a sufficient degree as a result of the selection process. Likewise the ability to usefully assimilate inputs, roughly represented by the intelligence quotient, is assumed sufficient as a result of the selection process.

The third factor which influences learning is the effort put forth by the professional. This factor has been explored in the preceding sections on motivation.

The fourth factor which influences learning is the amount and form of information presented to the candidate. It is this factor with which this section of the paper deals. Unfortunately, behavioral scientists have not provided the practitioner with much theory concerning the amount and form of information which should be used in complex learning situations. As a result some of the material of this section comes from the empirical observation and penetrating insight of outstanding practitioners and observers of the managerial function.

The paper proceeds on the assumption that professional competence can be increased by properly manipulating the amount and form of information to which the professional is exposed.

4100   Proposition 1: Persons assigned to professional oriented "task force" organizations, where roles are only moderately structured and communication requirements are high, will become more professionally competent than those who are restricted to highly structured positions with low communication requirements. This is not to say

that this is the "best" form of professional development, but it does imply that task force assignments have some unique, desirable characteristics.

4110   Strategy: The administrator assigns the professionals to participation roles in such groups as review boards, problem-solving teams, or investigating committees.

4111   Possible functional consequence: Problem-solving ability may increase in that exposure to knowledgeable persons of varied backgrounds will likely increase the candidate's awareness of (1) the nature of various problems and their significance, (2) the possible consequences of recognized alternatives, and (3) the available and appropriate resources in the organization. (Bakke, 1959; Craf, 1958; Abercrombie, 1960).

4112   Possible functional consequence: The professionals may achieve high motivation and satisfaction from this type of role and group assignment (Berkowitz, 1957; Thomas, 1962).

4113   Possible functional consequence: If a large enough group exists, the administrator may have a better opportunity to observe leadership behavior (Hare, 1962, Chap. 8).

4114   Possible dysfunctional consequence: The professionals may become so group-oriented that they develop too great a conformance to group opinions and behavior patterns (Berkowitz, 1957; Deutsch, 1962).

4115   Possible dysfunctional consequence: Over a long period of such assignments, the professionals may lose their specialized competences.

4200   Proposition 2: People who are exposed to feedback about their performance will tend to improve their performance.

4210   Strategy: The administrator arranges for the professionals to be counseled with regard to their progress.

4211   Possible functional consequence: The professionals may receive more realistic feedback and consequently may be able to positively alter their behavior pattern.

4212   Possible functional consequence: The candidate may feel more secure and consequently may feel freer to engage in exploratory learning behavior (Kahn *et al.,* 1964).

4213   Possible dysfunctional consequence: The candidate may become overly counselor-oriented and the organization may become faced with the pathology of favoritism (Deutsch, 1962).

4300   Proposition 3: People who are exposed to many varied experiences generally become more competent in that they have more alternatives from which to choose and more effective schemata with which to perceive their environment.

4310   Strategy: The administrator arranges for the professionals to proceed through a sequence of varied job assignments.

4311   Possible functional consequence: The professionals acquire and have at their disposal expanded sets of alternatives and schemata (Abercrombie, 1960).

4312   Possible dysfunctional consequence: If the professionals perceive their sequential assignments as less than satisfactory experiences, they may develop low morale (Chowdry and Pal, 1960, p. 188).

4400   Proposition 4: People who are exposed to stress become more highly motivated and develop methods of coping with the stress.

4410   Strategy: The administrator places the professionals in stress-producing environments.

4411   Possible functional consequence: The professionals may become more highly motivated, thereby enhancing the possibility of their growth and organizational accomplishment (Hare, 1962, Chap. 9).

4412   Possible functional consequence: The professionals may search for and find new means of solving the stress-producing problems (Kahn *et al.,* 1964).

4413   Possible dysfunctional consequence: If the professionals experience too great a degree of stress they may collapse and lose some of their organizational utility (Hare, 1962, Chap. 9; Kahn *et al.,* 1964, Chap. 14).

SUMMARY

To date the basis for the design of professional development programs has been almost exclusively the experience and observation of practicing professionals. This paper suggests that theory stemming from the behavioral sciences may be useful in the design of such programs. Weight is added to the argument by the fact that many of the administrative strategies derived from the examined behavioral science theories are commonly found in the more progressive programs.

REFERENCES

ABERCROMBIE, M. L. J. *The Anatomy of Judgment* (New York: Basic Books, 1960).

ARGYRIS, C. *Personality and Organization* (New York: Harper, 1957).

ARGYRIS, C. *Interpersonal Competence and Organizational Effectiveness* (Homewood: Irwin-Dorsey, 1962).

ARGYRIS, C. *Integrating the Individual and the Organization* (New York: Wiley, 1964).

ATKINSON, J. W. and REITMAN, A. "Performance as a Function of Motive Strength and Expectancy of Goal-Attainment," in Atkinson, ed., *Motives in Fantasy, Action, and Society* (Princeton: Van Nostrand, 1958).

BAKKE, E. W. "Concept of the Social Organization," in Haire, M. *Modern Organization Theory* (New York: Wiley, 1959).

BENNETT, W. E. *Manager Selection, Education and Training* (New York: McGraw-Hill, 1959).

BENNIS, A., *et al,* "Authority, Power, and the Ability to Influence," *Human Relations,* 143-155 (1958).

BERELSON, B. and STEINER, G. A. *Human Behavior* (New York: Harcourt, 1964).

BERKOWITZ, A. "Effects of Perceived Dependency Relationships upon Conformity to Group

Expectations," *Journal of Abnormal Social Psychology* **XLV** 350-354 (1957).

BLAU, P. M. *The Dynamics of Bureaucracy* (Chicago: University of Chicago Press, 1955).

CANTOR, N. *The Learning Process for Managers* (New York: Harper, 1957).

CHOWDRY, K. and PAL, A. K. "Production Planning and Organizational Morale," in Rubenstein and Haberstroh, etd., *Some Theories of Organization* (Homewood: Irwin-Dorsey, 1960).

CRAF, J. R. *Junior Boards of Executives* (New York: Harper, 1958).

DALTON, M. *Men Who Manage* (New York: Wiley, 1959).

DEUTSCH, M. "Cooperation and Trust: Some Theoretical Notes," in *1962 Nebraska Symposium on Motivation* (Lincoln: University of Nebraska Press, 1962).

FESTINGER, L. "A Theory of Social Comparison Processes," in Hare, *et al.,* eds., *Small Groups* (New York: Knopf, 1961).

HARE, A. P. *Handbook of Small Group Research* (Glencoe: Free Press, 1962).

KAHN, A., *et al., Organizational Stress: Studies in Role Conflict and Ambiguity* (New York: Wiley, 1964).

LEAVITT, H. J. *Managerial Psychology* (Chicago: University of Chicago Press, 1958).

LIKERT, R. *New Patterns of Management* (New York: McGraw-Hill, 1961).

MASLOW, A. H. "A Theory of Human Motivation," *Psychological Review* **XL** 370-396 (1943).

RIDGWAY, V. F. "Dysfunctional Consequences of Performance Measurements," in Rubenstein and Haberstroh, eds., *Some Theories of Organization* (Homewood: Irwin-Dorsey, 1960).

STEDRY, A. C. *Budget Control and Cost Behavior* (Englewood Cliffs: Prentice-Hall, 1960).

TANNENBAUM, R. and MASSARIK, F. "Participation by Subordinates in the Managerial Decision-Making Process," *Canadian Journal of Economics and Political Science* (1950).

THOMAS, E. J. "Effects of Facilitative Role Interdependence on Group Functioning," in Cartwright and Zander, eds., *Group Dynamics* (Evanston: Row, Peterson, 1962).

UNDERWOOD, B. J. "Forgetting," *Scientific American* (March, 1964).

ZALESNIK, A., *et al. The Motivation, Productivity, and Satisfaction of Workers* (Norwood: Plimpton Press, 1958).

MANAGEMENT DEVELOPMENT: A SYSTEMS VIEW

Paul S. Greenlaw

Before discussing managerial development in systems terms, it will be useful to present a systems view of the manager's role as an organizational member. Central to such a conception are two basic notions. The first of these is that the basic activity performed by the manager in any organization is that of decision making. Developing organizational policies, rules, procedures and methods, handling human problems, organization structuring, communicating information to subordinates—all involve managerial decision making in one way or another.

The second notion of central interest to our discussion is that his managerial decision-making process takes place within an organizational information-decision system. The organization, viewed as such a system, is comprised of six different kinds of systems *elements:* input, transformation, output, feedback, memory and control. Let us now examine briefly the manager's role in the organization in terms of each of these.

What the manager essentially does as a decision maker is to transform information relative to his operations into specified courses of action to be taken by himself and/or other members of the organization. For example, when a first line production supervisor observes one of his men violating the plant's no smoking rule, he may decide to discipline the man. In systems terms, this decision represents the *transformation* of an

From Paul S. Greenlaw, "Management Development: A Systems View," Personnel Journal 43 (4), 205–11 (1964). Reprinted by permission.

informational *input* (knowledge of the rule violation) by the supervisor into a performance *output* (the disciplinary action undertaken).

Two further observations are in order concerning the nature of system inputs and outputs. First, many elements of organizational behavior may be considered as representing either inputs or outputs, depending upon the vantage point from which they are viewed. Looking at the events described in the previous illustration from the point of view of the disciplined subordinate, rather than his supervisor, for example:

1. The rule violation would be considered as a performance output; and
2. The supervisor's communication of his disciplinary decision would represent an informational input to the subordinate.

What this observation points up is that the total organizational system is, in effect, comprised of a number of interdependent sub-systems (and sub-sub-systems), with the outputs of some serving as inputs to others. Whether one wishes to consider the individual members of an organization as constituting its sub-systems (as above); to view the organization's departments as sub-systems, and their members as sub-sub-systems; or to focus attention on still other sub-organizational elements, will depend upon the purposes of his analysis.

Second, the input elements of the organizational system (or any of its sub-systems) may assume any one of at least four different forms:

1. A message communicated orally to a member of the organization,
2. A message communicated in written form to a member of the organization,
3. Human behavior observed by an organizational member—e.g., the rule violation in our above example, or
4. A non-human event or process observed by an organizational member, as when a

foreman sees that a machine in his department has broken down.

All of these input types represent messages which may help provide the basis for making managerial decision transformations.

The manager's decision transformations also influence and are influenced by the other three types of systems elements indicated previously. In making decisions, the manager:

1. Draws on information about previous happenings as stored either (a) in his own human memory, or (b) in some external memory system—e.g., organizational data recorded in files, on punched cards, etc.,

2. Receives *feedback* as to the appropriateness of his behavior aimed at its improvement in the future, as when a manager's performance is appraised by his superior, and

3. Is guided by certain *control* elements within the organizational system. The control elements include those policies, objectives, models, procedures, decision rules, etc., which specify for the manager what shall be done with the input, memory and feedback in order to produce the output required.

These six types of systems elements and some of their interrelationships with respect to the managerial decision-making process are illustrated in Figure I.

Drawing on the above discussion, several further observations are now in order to provide a basis for an examination of management development in systems terms. First, a major value of the systems approach is that it permits us to sharpen our analysis of the decision making process by breaking it down into its basic elements and examining each in relationship to the others rather than simply viewing this process as a gross phenomenon. Second, the ultimate objective of all managerial endeavor, including management development efforts, ought to be, in systems terms, that of improving the quality of the organization's *outputs*—i.e., arriving at more effective courses of action in terms of attaining organizational objectives. Third, the quality of any organizational output is conditioned by the quality of all other relevant systems elements—input, memory, transformation, control and feed-back—and, hence if any of these other elements is inadequate, output too, will not be adequate. For example, some courses of action chosen by a manager may be ineffective largely because his *transformational abilities* are weak—i.e., he lacks skill in making decisions. In other cases, however, inadequate output may be generated primarily because the manager is not able to obtain the information needed to make an effective decision, or because the courses of action which he is permitted to choose are circumscribed by poorly programmed control elements—policies, rules, procedures or methods. Fourth, from the above it follows that if managerial development efforts are to be effective in improving the quality of the outputs produced by the manager as a decision maker, they must take into consideration *all* systems elements relevant to his performance within the organization.

Let us now turn to the question: "To what extent have those responsible for managerial training and development taken such a systems view?"

MANAGEMENT DEVELOPMENT: A SYSTEMS VIEW

In attempting to answer this question, it will not be possible to give specific consideration to all of the many different kinds of managerial training and development programs being carried out by business (and other) organizations. Rather, the ensuing discussion will center around some observations about one major type of management development approach in wide use today—off the job training. Included in this category are in-company conferences, university executive development programs, and institutes and seminars sponsored by professional associations. Although the objectives and content of different programs of this type vary considerably, all are similar in that they take the executive away from the organizational system in which he normally functions, and attempt to induce improvement in his managerial abilities in one way or another—utilizing such approaches as the lecture or discussion methods, case studies, role playing, business gaming, etc.

of a supervisor in a mock performance appraisal interview, or playing a business game.

On the other hand, it would appear that in the design of many off-the-job training programs, inadequate consideration is given to the other systems elements which have an important bearing on the outputs of those managers whom the organization is attempting to develop—i.e., *organizational* memory, input, control and feedback. As a number

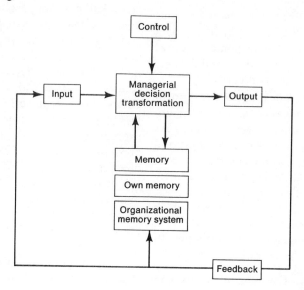

Figure 3.3 Elements in the organizational information-decision system.

In terms of our system view, these off-the-job programs generally focus primary attention on further developing either the manager's own *memory element* and/or his *transformational skills,* both in which, of course, are interrelated facets of the same personality system. That is, the manager:

1. May be furnished with information which hopefully will be stored in his mind for future utilization in making decisions—e.g., being familiarized with the company's new contract with its union, or

2. May be provided in the training conference with some form of synthetic experience in actually transforming certain types of inputs into outputs—e.g., assuming the role

of observers have noted, certain kinds of human relations problems in the business firm seem to occur more because of the existence of stress situations which are largely a function of organizational design—work flow inputs on the job, types of interaction patterns required, etc.—than because of any major inadequacies in the human skills of the organizational members so involved. For example:

1. Chapple and Sayles in their book *The Measure of Management* have cited a case in which repeated arguments between a firm's sales manager and credit manager although "interpreted by management as a clash of personalities," were basically due to

the fact the flow of certain work in the organization "was divided into separate pieces on the basis of functional similarities."[1]

2. In his "Parable of the Spindle," Elias Porter has indicated how a number of human problems existing in a restaurant operation were largely overcome when through the introduction of a spindle, it was no longer necessary for waitresses to give their orders verbally to the cook.[2]

Yet in designing, and in deciding on which managers are to participate in, many so-called "human relations" courses in industry today, concern is often given only to the modification of the human skills (transformational abilities) of the manager, without consideration of the impact that such other organizational system elements may be having on his performance output. For example:

The training director of one industrial concern was asked by the firm's plant manager to recommend a human relations training program for an industrial engineer who apparently was experiencing some difficulties in "getting along" with some of his colleagues in certain types of situations. In the discussion which ensued, sole consideration was given to which available program could best help the engineer more fully develop his interpersonal skills. No attention at all was given to the possibility that his human skills might have been quite adequate, and that the problem which existed might have been due largely to stresses created by inadequacies in other systems elements relevant to his job—e.g., his being required to follow certain organizational rules and procedures (control elements) which made it necessary for him to create unnecessary problems for his colleagues.

[1]Eliot D. Chapple and Leonard R. Sayles, *The Measure of Management* (New York: McGraw-Hill Book Co., Inc., 1961), pp. 23, 25.
[2]Elias H. Porter, "The Parable of the Spindle," *Harvard Business Review* **40**, 58-66 (May-June, 1962). The spindle, upon which the waitresses could place their *written* orders helped relieve tensions in a number of ways. For example: (1) serving as a memory element, it obviated the cook's need to remember the orders given him by the waitresses, and (2) as a queuing device it relieved the waitresses from the necessity of standing in line in order to give their orders to the cook.

Further, the question may be raised: "In light of the considerable difficulty usually encountered in attempting to change the individual's basic personality structure once he has reached adulthood, might not it often be easier to improve the manager's output by modifying the organizational inputs, feedback and controls which affect his performance, rather than his own memory system and transformational skills?" As Chapple and Sayles have pointed out, considerable attention to managerial development has been devoted to the so-called "conversion" approach,

changing people through efforts to modify their attitudes, values, and feelings, that is, by "working on their personalities" . . . individual personalities can be changed only with the greatest difficulty, if at all . . . with rare exception . . . the most efficient way of accomplishing change is to modify the organization itself: the technology, systems and procedures, layout, controls, and the positioning of individual personalities within the organizational structure.[3]

These observers suggest, for example that:

If Supervisor A has a tantrum whenever situation X occurs, his job can be changed so the behavior that is difficult for him is not required. It is unlikely that he will ever learn to tolerate situation X.[4]

Or, to restate this suggestion, in systems terms: if information input X is consistently transformed into an inappropriate emotionally traumatic behavioral output by Supervisor A, it is much easier to modify the input element than the transformation element.

One should, of course, not infer from this suggestion that all attempts to develop the manager's transformational skills be abandoned, for within the constraints of his personality structure, these skills may often be improved considerably. Moreover, it is obviously not always possible to restructure the organization's input, feedback, memory and control elements to suit the personalities of

[3]Chapple and Sayles, *op. cit.,* p. 191.
[4]*Ibid.,* p. 202.

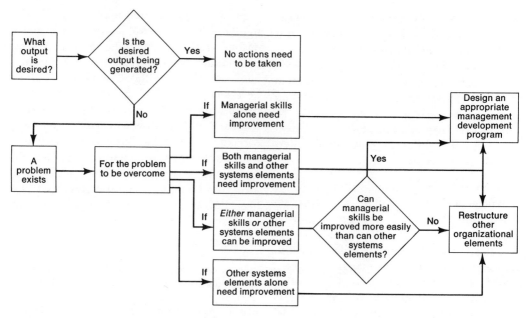

Figure 3.4   Management development: a systems view.

its members. Rather, the view just described simply suggests that in attempting to improve managerial output, all systems elements be considered with the question in mind: "'Which elements may be most easily modified so as to meet organizational objectives?"

Another point that seems to be of importance in viewing management development efforts is that in many cases if the manager's transformational skills are to be improved so also must certain other systems elements be modified. Evidence suggests that managers exposed to off-the-job development may fail to apply the knowledge and skills learned in such training when they return to their own jobs largely because the changes which they attempt to make in their own behavior are *not supported* by their own supervisors.[5] For instance, a manager who comes to the conclusion, through exposure to a human

relations course, that he ought to be more "permissive" in his leadership style may find that any attempts taken to these ends will be ridiculed by his own boss. Or, in systems terms, he may fail to modify his transformational skills largely because of inappropriate *feedback* from his supervisor rather than because of any major inadequacies in the training program inputs or in his willingness to try out new patterns of behavior.

In recognition of this need to modify the supervisory feedback element as well as the trainees' own memory and transformational and training program input elements, a number of companies have followed the approach of exposing their management groups to various forms of training "from the top down." In one manufacturing plant with which this author is familiar, for example, the plant manager and general foremen were

[5]For example, in a study of the effects of training in two divisions of the Detroit Edison Company, "it was found that there had been a loss of ground in one division, which was more than compensated for by gain in the other. . . . The researchers found that in the division where progress had been made, the foremen were led by a higher management which supervised them very

much in line with the principles developed in the course. On the other hand, in the division which lost ground, the foremen were under supervisors who directed them in a manner which was entirely out of harmony with the program." William F. Whyte, *Men at Work* (Homewood, Ill.: The Dorsey Press, Inc., and Richard D. Irwin, Inc., 1961), p. 12.

given courses in creative thinking and employment interviewing before these programs were instituted for the first line supervisors. Having been exposed first themselves to the new skills and concepts taught, the general foremen seemed to be more receptive to and to give more support to attempts by their subordinates—the supervisors—in trying out new patterns of behavior on the job than when such an approach was not followed.

A BROADER ROLE FOR THE TRAINING DIRECTOR

Now that a number of observations have been made about off-the-job training programs in systems terms, some concluding observations about the role of the training director with respect to these programs are in order.

In spite of the many millions of dollars being spent each year on off-the-job developmental programs, an uncomfortably large number of these efforts seem not to have been as successful as hoped in effecting significant improvements in managerial output. In some cases, this probably has been due more to the utilization of inappropriate educational methodologies than to anything else—e.g., employing the lecture method to try to improve the manager's interpersonal skills. In many other cases, however, even developmental programs based on sound learning theory have not enjoyed the success which their designers had intended.

A central thesis of this article is that the effectiveness of off-the-job training programs has in many cases been limited because their designers—by conceiving of their role primarily as *educators* interested in improving the manager's memory and transformational abilities—have not given adequate consideration to the impact of other systems elements on performance output. The systems view suggests that for more effective developmental efforts the training director must conceive of his role more broadly—both as an educator and as a systems analyst.[6] In doing so, he must focus attention on a number of questions such as those indicated in Figure 2, concerning the need and feasibility of improving all types of systems elements relative to managerial performance. Only in this way can those responsible for managerial development contribute significantly to the betterment of organizational output.

[6]It should be noted that such a broader view of organizational learning has been taken by such enterprises as the RAND Corporation and the System Development Corporation with respect to military-oriented training. For numerous references to this type of endeavor, see: Robert M. Gagne, ed., *Psychological Principles in System Development* (New York: Holt, Rinehart and Winston, 1962).

GUIDELINES FOR THE DESIGN OF NEW CAREERS

Sidney Fine

INTRODUCTION

Two men working side by side may be performing the same simple tasks, yet for one the activity is merely a job and for the other it is a step in a career ladder. The first worker feels "used," unvalued, disposable; the second feels involved, valued, committed.

There is a sound basis for these differences in feeling, although not apparent from superficial job analysis. The differences may start with the job title—one worker is called a "laborer," the other a "trainee." One worker is told nearly everything he must do, and everything he must do is simple and unchallenging. The other worker has the same assignment, but he has been given leeway to act on his own in certain aspects of procedure. He is not so closely supervised.

If something unexpected occurs for the first worker and he handles it badly, he is likely to be fired; for the second worker, a similar incident may be the occasion for special on-the-job coaching. The first worker has no basis for feeling that what he happens to learn is part of an accumulating trade or craft knowledge on which he can build; the second worker believes that everything he learns, even on a low functional level, may ultimately pay off since he is "learning the business." This worker feels relatively secure because he is accepted and has a stake in what he is doing. The first worker feels insecure and knows he will last on the job only so long as there is more of the same work to be done; he may see himself caught in a "dead end." The second worker believes he is going somewhere.[1]

These differences emerge only after intensive probing. When one inquires "Why?" one finds that the reasons range from shortsighted economics to rationalizations having varying degrees of substance and citing prejudice (racial, national, or religious), nepotism, favoritism, and social class. Still further probing reveals waste of human resources in worker selection and assignment, inefficiency in labor utilization and performance, and worse still, corruption of the personal values on which motivation and achievement depend. For a highly technological and dynamic society which is experiencing skill shortages and which stresses the importance of the individual, these failures represent an intolerable dissonance—an exceedingly costly indulgence. Worse still, these failures make a mockery of the objectives of our educational system. All teaching and vocational counseling provide implicit assurance that education is worthwhile because it enables one to make the most of opportunities when they occur, and because of the higher payoff in wages and job satisfaction. In fact, we are today seeking ever better ways to inculcate this notion in every student in order to stimulate his achievement and competence motivation. But to what avail will this effort be if our employment system continues to reward people irrelevantly for accidental factors of being or of family relationship rather than for performance and competence? A vicious circle will be intensified, whereby irrelevant status factors continue to gain ascendance over performance factors.

One vital way of reaffirming the goals of our educational system is to put forth greater effort to realize the concept of opportunity

From Sidney Fine, "Guidelines for the Design of New Careers." Reprinted by permission of the W. E. Upjohn Institute for Employment Research.

[1] This contrasting situation is not, of course, universal. It is relative to the individuals involved, but reflects a common enough situation.

for all in the area of work. This can be done by designing all jobs as rungs on career ladders. Thus, all workers would have the door open to develop their potential to the extent that they are willing and able. This calls for commitment on the part of the employers—the first and most essential step in the development of new careers.

In general, employers may indicate their commitment to a career concept in one of three ways:

1. Acceptance of the longevity principle (tenure plus grade increments) either as part of collective bargaining agreements or as a matter of company policy.
2. Specific contractual agreement, as in apprenticeship.
3. Informal acceptance of individuals into specified and career-titled ports of entry.

This commitment should be extended and amplified to encompass all jobs.

Is this aim of equal opportunity unrealistic because of limited "room at the top"—that is, the limited number of better jobs? Is it unrealistic only if it is interpreted as requiring promotion for all regardless of individual differences in potential and performance. If the fact of individual differences in potential, motivation, and performance is accepted, the principles of competition and equal opportunity can go a long way toward enabling people to find the jobs that suit and satisfy them. Surely, our implicit faith in the inexhaustibility of job opportunities as a result of evolving technology (a concept always challenged) should be coupled with faith that people will sort themselves out when opportunity is universally available. While it may be human to seek advantage on the basis of prejudice, discrimination, etc., against others, it is just as human to compete and to accept the rule of merit where conditions of fair competition apply. In any case, we must increasingly recognize the fact that job content is less and less likely to be a source of satisfaction in the sense of self-realization

for most people, and that, more and more, satisfaction will need to come from the overall employment situation and leisure-time activities.

Once employer commitment to the career concept of employment is established, it is then practical to apply additional guidelines of a technical and strategic nature. Technical guidelines are intrinsically concerned with tasks, jobs, and the work itself. They relate to the specific conditions suggested above that make a worker feel he is in a job that leads somewhere. Strategic guidelines are of an extrinsic nature, concerned with introducing careers as a realistic program in the working world as we find it. The remainder of this paper concerns these two guidelines.

TECHNICAL GUIDELINES

As noted earlier, it is necessary to look beneath the surface of task performance to see the difference between jobs and careers. We must penetrate to those attitudes, policies, structures, and behaviors of organizations that invest a job-worker situation with "career characteristics." These are the "technical" matters which ultimately must be considered in the design of new careers. They include the titling of the job, selection procedures, structuring and specification of the tasks, supervision and performance evaluation, pay and fringe benefits, and training.

Titling

Certain terms used in titles immediately signal the status of the job as entry onto a career ladder. Among these terms are "learner," "trainee," "apprentice," "junior," "aide," and "assistant." Certain other terms like "helper," "laborer," or "hand" carry a different connotation; namely, that of someone employed only to perform certain limited tasks. Where the first set of terms is used, the concept of career ladder is reinforced by references to subsequent stages of the career as "journeyman/master" and "associate/senior."

In some situations where the original title carries a strong low-status noncareer connotation, employers (and workers) are impelled to devise entirely new titles and terms to suggest that the jobs are more than meet the eye and are actually career situations. Helpers become "first" and "second" helpers; janitors become "building superintendents"; mechanics become "motor analysts"; salesmen become "sales consultants"; etc.

Thus, in the design of new careers the title is extremely important. It is symbolic of the employer's commitment to the career concept and of the worker's choice of a career rather than a job. Using such titles would be especially necessary for situations where jobs formerly did not have career status and are being included in such a context. An obvious example is that of busboy, which could be retitled "waiter assistant" or "food service aide."

Selection Procedures

When workers are hired as "hands" for jobs, selection is typically limited to a physical appraisal. This can be quite perfunctory as in the case of hiring men for day labor, or it can involve a physical examination when hiring laborers in plants where life and disability insurance are in force. In these job situations, employers have in mind certain specific physical tasks that need to be done on a temporary or continuing basis. There is little interest in the individual and no commitment to provide opportunities for growth and development.

However, where commitment has been made, selection standards and procedures are usually introduced. Typical of the selection methods used, in addition to physical examinations, are tests of general aptitude and language skills, minimum educational requirements such as high school graduation or equivalence, and background requirements such as a "clean record." Such qualifications, plus a probationary work period, usually suffice where only longevity considerations obtain. Presumably such selection procedures are intended to ensure some degree of adaptability in the employee to changing technological and employment conditions.

In the case of apprenticeship and ports of entry, selection can and frequently does become much more specific to ensure interest and temperamental characteristics believed to be appropriate to the career in question. Tests are used for this purpose, but in addition a much more intensive evaluation will be made of the background information (e.g., courses studied or leisure pursuits) obtained in the interview. References will be required. While few of these techniques are adequately validated for the particular careers in question, they are, nevertheless, very widely used. Perhaps the best that can be said for them is that they tend to eliminate highly improbable candidates. Most of all, they are indicative of the employer's commitment.

There is little doubt that selection procedures have been used to discriminate against, eliminate, and reject low-status, disadvantaged minority group applicants in favor of white middle-class types. However, when these same procedures are employed within the context of using indigenous individuals for careers within the community, they can be regarded as a sign of commitment and sincerity. After all, it is to no one's advantage to employ people for careers for which they are not suited by aptitude and personal preference. This, in effect, abrogates the possibility of growth which is central to the career concept. In this connection it should be noted that the Lincoln Hospital Project in New York made an extremely careful effort in selecting community service aides.[2]

---

[2]*Progress Report to U.S. Office of Economic Opportunity on the South Bronx Neighborhood Service Center Program* (New York: Albert Einstein College of Medicine, November 1966).

Structuring and Specification of Tasks

We have a better understanding today than formerly of the nature of the "ladder" and of how we must organize tasks into jobs in a career hierarchy to effect the career concept. Thus, we now know that the tasks of entry jobs must be largely prescribed, and that as the worker gains experience he must be granted more discretionary duties. This is what increases his value to the organization. This can be done by making use of the functional concepts included in functional job analysis, and by recognizing the role of critical incidents in jobs as indicators of potential. We now turn to a consideration of the role of these complementary concepts in the design of careers.

Prescribed and Discretionary Content. According to Brown[3] and Jaques,[4] the *prescribed content* of a job consists of those elements about which the worker has no authorized choice. The prescribed elements are of two kinds: (1) the results expected, and (2) the limits set on the means by which the work can be done. The results of a job are nearly always prescribed in the sense that the object of a person's work is set by the manager and/or supervisor and not by himself. As far as methods of work are concerned, some are prescribed and some are discretionary. The prescribed methods are determined by the equipment available, the physical limits of the job situation, the routines, and general policies governing the methods to be used in pursuing results.

The discretionary content of work consists of all those elements in which choice of how to do a job is left to the person doing it. Here a worker is authorized and expected to use discretion and judgment as he proceeds with his work, overcoming obstacles by picking what he considers the best of the alternative courses available at each stage, and pursuing the course he has chosen.

Here we see just what the contribution of education, training, and experience means to a career and why these are essential. In effect, they provide the knowledge about alternative methods and their consequences as they relate to achieving the results of work. The individual first entering upon a career, on the whole, lacks knowledge and experience about specific results and methods, and hence his performance must be largely prescribed. By the same token, employers providing career opportunities must be in a position to distinguish, specify, and scale prescribed and discretionary duties carefully so that the job experiences and related training together contribute to the growth process, the gradual development of discretionary duties, and the assumption by the worker of the coincidentally increased responsibility.

It is important to note that the tasks themselves do not have absolute prescribed or discretionary content. The task of sweeping the floor with a broom may have been prescribed for one worker and may be the result of discretionary responsibility for another. This fact calls attention to how even the simplest tasks can be structured as parts of jobs or careers. In jobs for "hands," tasks are largely prescribed to be done in a specified way to achieve a particular result. In careers, tasks are designed with significant discretionary content so that an individual is trained in various options and is increasingly authorized to use his judgment in selecting one or another way to achieve the specified result. In their work, Brown and Jaques point out that they have never found a job in which both prescribed and discretionary aspects were not present in some degree.

One other aspect should be clear about these two different types of elements, and that is that discretionary elements are not immediately apparent. To the superficial observer, all that he sees may seem to be

[3]W. Brown, *Exploration in Management* (New York: Wiley, 1960), Chap. 2.

[4]E. Jaques, *Measurement of Responsibility* (Cambridge, Massachusetts: Harvard University Press, 1956), Chap. 3.

prescribed because work done properly and effectively is a smooth, rhythmic, directed performance in which options concerning alternatives have long since been decided, either by management or by the worker. However, if the options are determined by the worker with the authorization of management, the performance will be the result of his discretion.

This general framework for understanding the design of tasks and their organization into jobs and careers is further illuminated by the concepts of functional job analysis.

Functional Job Analysis (FJA),[5] Functional Job Analysis distinguishes between *what gets done*—the what/how of technology concerned with machines, tools, techniques, processes, and end results—and *what the worker does*—the what/how of the worker's physical, mental, and interpersonal activity. "What gets done" categories are referred to as work fields; "what the worker does" categories are referred to as worker functions. Two examples should help make this distinction clear.

In urban development work, sites get surveyed and laid out and plans get drafted. The surveying, laying out, engineering and drafting are technological activities (work fields) referring to what gets done. Many different workers contribute in different ways to getting this work done. These different ways (worker functions) include handling, manipulating, and/or precision working in relation to things (tools, equipment, materials); computing, compiling, analyzing and/or coordinating in relation to data; and taking instructions, exchanging information, consulting, and supervising in relation to people.

In urban development work also, sometimes opinion and attitude surveys need to be made to generate information concerning slum clearance or a new expressway. The opinion survey or investigation is what gets done. But, this can be done in different ways; for example, by mail questionnaire, by telephone, by door-to-door questionnaire completed with pencil and paper, or by door-to-door questionnaire using a tape recorder. In each instance the worker functions somewhat differently, calling on different combinations of skills.

As is perhaps evident from these examples, two different vocabularies are involved which, because of common usage, are sometimes difficult to shred apart. However, despite the intimate relationship—two sides of the same coin, so to speak—the distinction is fundamental because it provides a framework for understanding the structure of tasks in jobs regardless of whether they are prescribed or discretionary.[6]

The worker functions are the ones that primarily concern us here, since they represent the range of ways in which workers perform in all jobs, the molds according to which their tasks are cast, and hence, the elements of the job design.[7] What workers do (worker functions) in the appendix chart are arranged in three hierarchies. The particular functions in each hierarchy are unique to it and proceed from the simple to the complex; that is to say, from those in which the prescribed duties are relatively few and dominate the job content to those in which the prescribed duties can be quite numerous, but are nevertheless overshadowed by the discretionary job content. They are, in effect, basic building blocks or modules; and, because they range from the simple to the

---

[5]FJA is an outgrowth of research directed by the author at the United States Employment Service, 1948-1959. One result is the revised occupational classification system of the Third Edition (1965) of the *Dictionary of Occupational Titles.* [See also: S. A. Fine, "The Structure of Worker Functions," *Personnel and Guidance Journal,* pp. 34, 66-73 (1955); and S. A. Fine, "Functional Job Analysis," *Personnel Administration and Industrial Relations* (Spring, 1955).]

[6]The distinction has been formalized in the codes of the new occupational classification system of the *Dictionary of Occupational Titles,* where the first three digits of the six-digit code refer to what gets done (work fields) and the last three to what workers do (worker functions).

[7]See Appendix to this paper.

complex, the direction of career growth is implicit in them.

The focus of the functions upon things, data, and people corresponds to the potential of a worker as represented by his interacting systems—physical, mental, and interpersonal. His potential to master the prescribed and discretionary content inheres in these systems and in the adequacy of his education and training.

Critical Incidents. In addition to defining the functions of a job in a career ladder, it is necessary to recognize effective and ineffective performance, particularly as such performance relates to discretionary duties. Workers interact with job demands, moving between the prescribed and discretionary duties of their jobs and between levels of functioning. Their potential tends to be evidenced by the effectiveness or ineffectiveness of their discretionary performance. These are critical incidents. They often reflect the unexpected, unspecified events.

Flanagan has pointed out that a listing of the duties and responsibilities connected with a job, even though the list seems complete, may leave out requirements which are of a critical nature.[8] For example, the primary duties of a bottle-capping machine operator would be stated as "Insert bottles one at a time into the capping machine, depress capping lever, remove bottle, and examine for security of the cap." A worker on this job would more likely be considered outstanding and show his potential if he seldom caused a work stoppage on the production line by permitting his machine to run out of caps than if he capped bottles at a very high rate.

As Ghiselli and Brown have noted, "There are some kinds of behavior that are especially critical in the sense that they are much more likely to lead to administrative actions or judgments concerning the worker than is the goodness or poorness which characterizes his performance of the prescribed duties and responsibilities."[9]

Out of these critical incidents, then, a job may develop and a worker may grow. The observation of such critical incidents becomes the basis for evaluating performance (whether done systematically or not), indicating the worker's capacity to meet the challenges of the job, whether he is in need of help or performing beyond normal expectations.

Supervision and Performance Evaluation

The emphasis in supervision is usually upon the attainment of production standards. However, it is equally important, perhaps more so, for supervision to recognize the potential of workers and aid and abet their growth and careers. Some observers even argue that if supervisors paid more attention to their human function—"growing people" —"getting the work out" might well take care of itself. Certainly, there is some truth in this position, even if it is too strongly stated as a generality.

Here are some of the specific roles of supervision that need to be recognized as crucial to the proper development of a career:

A. The supervisor is the human embodiment of management's commitment. Regardless of what management *has said* about the job, it is what the supervisor *does* that will convey the message.

B. The supervisor must be clear and specific concerning prescribed and discretionary content of assignments. These must be consistent with the functional definition of the job and the expectations of the worker. On this basis the supervisor can make preliminary evaluations of how well suited the worker is to the job demands.

C. The supervisor must be able to expect

[8]J. C. Flanagan, "Critical Requirements: A New Approach to Employee Evaluation," *Personnel Psychology* **2**, 419-425 (1949).

[9]E. E. Ghiselli and C. W. Brown, *Personnel and Industrial Psychology* (New York: McGraw-Hill, 1955), p. 37.

the unexpected and observe and report the critical incidents which suggest performance below or beyond expectations.

D. All of the above must show up in an interest in the worker as much as an interest in the work. Such an interest will be sensitive to the need to change from close to general supervision within the framework of the functional requirements of the job.

Pay and Fringe Benefits

The career situation defines from the very outset a gradual and reasonable rise in pay, both within a given position in the career ladder and for each step upward. The increments may be small relative to the number of steps in the ladder, the nature of the work, the type and prosperity of the industry, etc., but they are definite and spelled out in advance. The time to be spent in each position may be made equally explicit, although this may be stated in terms of ranges to accommodate differences of ability and turnover.

A probationary period may be specified for the entry position. This may be an anxious period, but it is, nevertheless, quite legitimate. After all, the worker is free and may want to quit if he doesn't find the situation suitable. The fact that the employer establishes a probationary period is an additional sign of his commitment to the worker if he turns out to be suitable. Usually, the probationary period is concluded with the first pay increment.

Some of the other compensation devices usually characteristic of a career and not of a job are: health insurance (usually partially paid by the worker); sick and annual leave (the latter increasing to a maximum with years of service); investment in a pension plan; participation in credit unions; stock sharing; and end-of-year bonus payment.

Training

A career implies development of one's potentialities, and therefore opportunities for education and/or training. For many jobs this may be entirely limited to on-the-job training provided either by a more experienced worker and/or the supervisor. For more and more jobs such training includes some off-the-job classroom training, either in the plant or in some special school outside the plant. These latter situations tend to be relatively common for technical and professional jobs. However, as technology becomes more complex and installations more costly, even machine production employees are being given periods of from one day to two weeks of intensive training on the new equipment off the job. This, of course, is done with a continuation of regular pay.

The commitment of employers to careers for their employees sometimes extends beyond training in job content. Some employers, for example, are providing literacy training on the grounds that better educated employees make better all-around employees with greater potential for promotion.[10]

With the commitment to training, the employer must also define positions in the career ladder that provide for upward mobility. Clearly, this is self-insurance for the employer so that he is first in line to reap the benefits of the training. Otherwise, the increased employability resulting from the training will lead the worker to job opportunities in other establishments. It is fear that they will not directly benefit that discourages many employers from providing training.

If possible, training programs and their timing should be included in the description of a program of career development so that a worker may see the growth possibilities in his situation right from the start. Along with the commitment of the employer, it would be desirable for workers to commit themselves to continuing education. However, in view of the infinite variety of conditions and capabilities of workers, it is idle to assume

[10]"Dropouts Go Back to School at Work," *The Milwaukee Journal,* May 4, 1967.

that this commitment can be on an equal basis. The best that can be expected is a positive response if the facilities and opportunities are clearly defined.

STRATEGIC GUIDELINES

Whereas technical guidelines are concerned with the methods and procedures of comprehending and organizing the content of tasks, jobs, and training, the strategic guidelines are concerned with the disposition of time, money, and effort in introducing and achieving acceptance of careers into the world of work. They involve both immediate and long-term considerations. They are also concerned with understanding people and leaders so that the tactics used to achieve recognition help rather than hinder the development of new careers. Specifically, the focus of strategic guidelines is on *who* (the most immediate beneficiaries of new careers), *what* (the target work fields for which new careers will be designed), and *how* (approaches to be used in defining and winning acceptance for new careers).

Who Are the Beneficiaries?

Who will be the beneficiaries for whom new careers should be developed at this point in time? While the obvious answer that follows from the guideline of commitment to equal opportunity for all is, "everyone without discrimination," this ignores the fact that the immediate stimuli for the new careers movement are the disadvantaged and the poor who have in the past been excluded from involvement in careers. After all, the career idea is not new for the middle class or even the upper levels of the working class. Apprenticeships and attendance at technical schools, business colleges, and academic colleges has been a normal, everyday part of their existence. However imperfectly it has operated, entering upon and following a work career has been common for this large majority of

our population. In fact, that this has been so is an important basis for affluence in our society. Obviously, if the advantaged are to compete on an equal basis for new careers with the disadvantaged, the latter will continue to be excluded. Hence, the poor and disadvantaged should be given primary consideration and extra assistance, particularly in those new careers which are oriented to community services in the area where they live.

It is, of course, argued that such emphasis is a waste of time because the poor and disadvantaged are not motivated to better themselves and, in fact, that is why they are poor. This is an old generalization and until recently it even had the aura of truth. However, as the result of the experiences of the antipoverty programs, it is a rationalization that will no longer hold up completely. The following item reporting on the current Congressional Senate Committee hearing discussing the pros and cons of continuing the poverty program summarizes what is now known and believed by responsible people:

> The poor have shattered at least two stereotypes. First, that they lack motivation, and secondly, that they do not have sufficient knowledge or know-how to run their own programs. The success of a number of indigenous groups in drawing up meaningful programs and subsequent ability to reach the community tends to belie these arguments.[11]

Article after article in the daily press, reporting programs sponsored by the Office of Economic Opportunity and the Department of Labor, attest to the initiative and motivation of even the hard-core disadvantaged. Certainly failures can be found among them, but a closer examination of many of the failures has revealed, along with personal inadequacy, insincere and superficial programs sponsored by the middle-class community which, in effect, have attempted to

[11]"Jobs Due to Cool N.Y. Summer," *Christian Science Monitor,* June 2, 1967.

lead the poor back to dead-end jobs. Many poor no longer want such jobs. These jobs barely provide them with subsistence; from an economic point of view, the jobs are little, if any, better than welfare. Like welfare, they rob the poor of their dignity as effective human beings.

Thus, while the poor and disadvantaged have shown that they can accept and meet the challenges of opportunity despite much reason for distrust, it is not at all clear that middle-class society is ready and willing to provide and sustain opportunities for challenging work and upward mobility for the disadvantaged.

What Work Fields?

There is no need to be dogmatic or academic about this question. After all, if career orientation of jobs helps solve manpower shortages and pays off in development of human resources, then all work fields should be included and, in time, undoubtedly will be. However, at this point in time, the poor and disadvantaged are justifiably suspicious of enticement back into restaurants, laundries, dry cleaning establishments, and the like where so many jobs are going begging. Traditionally, these have been the dead-end jobs in which they have been ruthlessly exploited.[12]

More fruitful fields of work for career development would seem to be the newly emerging community services fields. These include health services in traditional settings such as hospitals and in the new mental health and maternity centers; community relations, both in traditional welfare settings and in neighborhood storefronts; urban planning, including site surveying, drafting,

and opinion gathering; teaching (as aides and assistants); recreation; and libraries. In the first place, these are relatively new areas with new jobs and new careers emerging, requiring a whole range of skills and training from the simple to the complex. They do not have the onus associated with jobs in restaurants and the like. Second, many of the poor and disadvantaged seem to have an adaptive skill base more suitable for dealing with people, particularly those people who have similar problems and aspirations. A third reason is that there are tremendous shortages in these fields of work with few trained people to step into the emerging jobs. Finally, through jobs in these work fields, the disadvantaged are, in effect, helping themselves.

How Initiate Careers?

Essentially, there are two models for initiating new careers, both having their origins in the way careers emerge more or less naturally in the world of work. The first is the result of breaking down existing professional or skilled jobs and generally separating out the simpler tasks.[13] The second is a developmental approach starting with the definition of public and/or technological needs, and followed by the design of tasks to meet those needs. Depending upon circumstances and pressures, there would seem to be a place for both approaches to be followed.

On the whole, the first approach might be

---

[12]It should be pointed out that enlightened managements of some large chains like Hot Shoppes, McDonald's, Horn & Hardart Co., and Hilton and Sheraton Hotels have been making sincere efforts to organize their jobs into career systems with some success in attracting and holding employees, as compared to other similar establishments that have not done so.

[13]This model is exemplified by an item in the Labor Letter of *The Wall Street Journal,* May 9, 1967, describing it as a way in which employers are dealing with manpower shortages:

The aim is to remove from professional and skilled workers' jobs routine tasks that less skilled employees can do. A Dallas electronics concern created a new position of "non-degree engineer" to handle technical tasks. Foxboro Company in Massachusetts frees highly trained technicians for more sophisticated tasks by training others to build electronic circuit boards. Massachusetts General Hospital begins using technicians rather than doctors or nurses to operate oxygen pumps during operations. Cleveland area welfare officials seek to hire 80 Welfare Aides to handle paperwork for overburdened social workers.

more suitable for craft and technician jobs, since in these areas there is a healthy tradition of giving credit for experience and for performance ability to be recognized for its own sake.[14] It is likely to be a less fruitful approach in the case of the professions. Since much thought and effort are being expended on the development of *nonprofessional* or *subprofessional* careers, it is useful to examine some of the assumptions made in these areas that are quite debatable.[15] Five such assumptions will be considered here:

1. *Existing professions fully meet public needs at which they are aimed.* It follows, then, that since the need is "covered," so to speak, there is no room for a new career and that tasks must indeed be separated out from existing careers to constitute new jobs. The developmental approach assumes that needs are broader than professions that presume to cover them, and that from time to time such needs and their coverage are amenable to reassessment. Thus, on the basis of the first approach, the nurse's aide emerged as a job, but, on the basis of the second, physical and occupational therapists emerged as professions alongside the registered nurse.

2. *Professionals recognize their limitations and actively seek and welcome nonprofessional careerists to help them meet public needs.* This assumption is often verified in individual conversation with dedicated careerists seeking to fulfill the objectives of their profession. It may even be true of groups of professionals in certain localities. Thus, in some communities teachers have welcomed teacher aides. However, by and large, for professions as a whole, the opposite attitude is probably more common. And this is natural since all professions have achieved their identity by being exclusive and by raising and tightening requirements. This has been well documented, especially during the past generation, and is as true for organized skilled craftsmen as it is for professionals. This negative attitude of exclusion is generally justified on the basis of maintaining high standards of performance and minimizing charlatanism. Even where a lower level of personnel has been allowed into a profession (for example, occupational therapy), the senior professionals make every attempt to restrict it and keep it in its place. The job that has been created is not a rung in a ladder. No amount of experience as an occupational therapy assistant is recognized as a substitute for the four to five years of college training necessary to certify as an occupational therapist. Other professions (for example, physical therapy) will not even permit a category of subprofessional, regardless of need and socio-economic pressure.

3. *There are professional and nonprofessional tasks; this is what distinguishes between professionals and nonprofessionals.* Presumably simpler tasks are nonprofessional and more complex ones professional. Thus the simpler tasks being performed by a professional are fair game for separation out into so-called nonprofessional or subprofessional jobs, and these can serve as first steps in achieving professionalism. But this is not the way it is. The simpler tasks are not the first step toward professionalism. In fact, even the performance of the more complex tasks does not make one a professional. Task performance is not the heart of the matter: what matters are the rites of passage—the commitment to training, to attendance at authorized schools, to securing credentials, to memberships in professional organizations, to subscription to a code of ethics, etc. In fact, doing

---

[14] Once having attained the ability, however, the worker may need to maintain his status in order to obtain work by membership in a union, or similar group, and/or by periodic license renewal.

[15] The writer does not favor the use of the terms "nonprofessional" and "subprofessional" because of their degrading, subordinate implications, despite their inclusion of the word "professional." However, for the moment, they are the terms in use, and at least have the virtue of being commonly understood. An important task faced by designers of new careers is to eliminate these terms and to substitute for them expressions more descriptive of the work functions performed.

all of these things and not performing the tasks at all can still make one a professional, but performing the tasks without submitting to the rites of passage rarely makes one a professional. Even a "grandfather" provision (certification as a professional on the basis of long experience attained prior to the existence of formal professional preparation) is fast disappearing.

4. *Professionals want to work at the most difficult and "professional" tasks at all times.* They therefore welcome giving up simpler tasks. This may be true for some individuals, but not for all—probably not for the majority. The present writer has interviewed hundreds of professionals: engineers, bioscientists, psychologists, counselors, and others, and in general has found that most professionals want to range over the continuum of difficulty. This includes doing such "menial" things as washing test tubes, sketching graphs, computing statistics, compiling bibliographies, and typing reports. Not that they don't welcome help at times—rather it's a matter of pacing, variety, conservation of energy, and time to think. Few professionals want to be stretched to their limits at all times. Furthermore, having others perform these tasks frequently breaks up the continuity of a professional's activity, and requires him to supervise, a task he does not ordinarily relish.

5. *Putting together simple "nonprofessional" tasks constitutes a first step in a career ladder.* Unfortunately, this is rarely the case, regardless of how it is made to look. What is thus constituted is a job, and more often than not, it is a "servant" job. There is no on-the-job provision (training and/or credit for experience) to attain higher rungs in the professional ladder, although in many instances the longevity commitment is made. For example, nurses' aides can only obtain the status of registered nurse by leaving their jobs and going into nurses' training school. On the other hand, they can receive tenure, in-grade increments, and the like. Mere

proximity to professionals does not result in professional careers. Unless conceived in a career context, aide or assistant positions may turn out to be low-paying, dead-end jobs which frustrate the workers.

The examination of the above assumptions involved in the initiation of nonprofessional careers suggests how easy it can be to confuse technique and strategy. For example, as a short-term strategy, it may be wise to constitute jobs out of low functional level tasks found in professional jobs in some of the new work fields discussed above. The virtue of this strategy is that it can alleviate manpower shortages and provide quick employment where this is a pressing need. But unless this strategic move is immediately followed up with the technical considerations outlined above, it can fail to build nonprofessional careers.

In the long run, the developmental strategy probably provides a sounder basis for initiating new careers in the professional work fields. Using this strategy, the first step is to determine what needs to be done to achieve a particular objective—let us say, urban planning. This is followed by an examination of the states-of-the-arts involved to establish the technologies and various alternatives available to get the work done. On this basis, it is then possible to move directly into the technical considerations described above, whereby: (1) the work that needs to be done to achieve objectives is clearly delineated: (2) the optional ways in which workers can perform the work are explored; (3) the functional performances of the workers are decided upon in relation to the technologies to be used; (4) the functional performances are then organized into jobs; (5) the jobs are related to each other by delineating experiences which lead to higher functional performance; and (6) curricula are developed that lead to achievement of competencies necessary to promote to each higher functional level.

Since this approach starts with needs rather than with existing professions, it can lead to proposals to realign certain tasks already being performed by some professionals. Needless to say, it is therefore absolutely essential that this approach have the cooperation of incumbent professionals, particularly those specializing in curriculum and certification in specific work fields.

This will not be easy, since the professionals will need to resolve the inherent conflicts between professional identity and dedication to achieve objectives. However, short term or long term, sooner or later, every profession must face this problem and reassess itself in terms of available criteria, changing states of the relevant arts, and its ability to supply manpower in its area of specialization.

At the very least, the longer term developmental strategy lays open the sensitive areas and provides the criteria and reference points with which the shorter term strategy must eventually be concerned. Clearly distinguishing between strategy and technique has the effect of establishing the proper place for the guidelines appropriate to each, and of freeing the effort expended from the kinds of rationalization that, in effect, substitute strategy for technique.

A Suggested Application

How can these guidelines be effectively brought together in a model approach to the problem? Needless to say, there are probably as many models possible as there are varying circumstances. The one to be suggested here is for the purpose of providing a focus for support monies, should they be available to make a substantial attack upon the problem. It is also conceived in terms of conditions that need to be faced and coped with and that might be generalizable to other situations.

It is proposed that most of the money available for exploring the implementation of a new careers program be concentrated in a single city of about one million people containing an effective municipal civil service willing to commit itself wholeheartedly to pursue the implementation of a new careers program. The following are the reasons for the selection of such a site.

1. A city this size faces the range of problems of both larger cities and cities half its size. Experience in such a context would appear to have wide applicability.

2. Municipal civil services have a history and tradition of recognizing experience as a substitute for education, and of qualifying persons for entry and promotion in career ladders.

3. Municipal civil services have a primary concern with the labor shortages and skill training problems associated with emerging work fields, such as health services, education, social welfare and rehabilitation, public safety and law enforcement, housing, etc.

4. These work fields present varying types of career ladders, contain both old and new job classifications, and involve various degrees of professionalization. They therefore offer the opportunity for designing and negotiating career ladders appropriate to many different kinds of conditions.

5. A municipal civil service may well become the employer of last resort in dealing with hard-core unemployed. It will therefore be impelled to deal with its employment and training problems in the most constructive way possible.

6. Because of size and prestige, it is in a position to establish precedents that could spread to related agencies in the private sector. In any case, it will have to deal with employee groups that relate to both the civil service and the private sector.

7. By focusing on the several services of a single community, no one professional organization, union, or other employee organization needs to feel picked on in the sense of having to make sacrifices and set precedents that will be embarrassing.

8. This could be coordinated with a "model cities" planning program which is likely to be moving in the same direction and to be motivated highly to obtain the kinds of personnel indicated.

In carrying out this feasibility study, several problem areas should receive special attention:

1. *Determining Methods for Qualifying Hard-Core Unemployed and Disadvantaged on the Basis of Adaptive Skills Alone for Entry into Jobs, if Necessary.* Here the initiative of the federal civil service might well be followed. It has designed an experimental procedure to qualify people for its "A" level jobs on the basis of background information concerning:

Reliability and dependability.
Job readiness (willingness to come to work).
Willingness to do uncomfortable work.
Ability to work safely without harming oneself.
Willingness to follow direct orders.
Interest and motivation to work at "A" level.

The last factor is given the heaviest weight in arriving at a rating, assuming that applicants meet the requirements of the first screen-out element. A further step might be to assign functional levels to basic job tasks, and establish time periods to be spent at these tasks which could be considered as qualifying for the next higher step on a ladder. The relative merits of examinations, work sample tests, performance ratings, and time periods could be explored for certifying purposes.

2. *Exploring Procedures Suitable for Dealing with Institutional Rigidities.* As indicated, several different kinds of professional organizations will need to be dealt with for the work fields listed above. They are likely to have tackled the problem of nonprofessional support in different ways, and to have expressed more or less resistance in accepting and ex-

tending career ladders from the bottom to the top. Faced with the immediacy of manpower and skill shortages, recruitment and turnover problems, etc., and the commitment of a powerful civil service to deal positively and constructively with these problems, they will no doubt be disposed to cooperate (but with varying types of assurance) to maintain their standards and integrity. The thorough documentation of approaches and resolutions of such negotiations could be an important input to other communities and to state and national levels of the respective professional organizations. We need to know the varying impact of different national groups upon a local branch, and also how the circumstances of a community might affect one or another of these organizations. It may even be feasible to allocate funds to one or more of such local professional organizations to establish their own initiative toward subprofessional careers within the context of the same community.

3. *Determining Job Analysis Methods Suitable for Defining Career Ladders.* The use of several approaches has been indicated, but not enough is known concerning their large-scale use and their relative acceptability to civil service, professional, and union groups. We need to have the experience of training task forces from these organizations in the methods of designing career ladders and then learn how comfortable these task forces are working with the methods.

4. *Determining the Relative Usefulness of the "Breakdown" and Developmental Approaches in Designing New Careers and the Time Factors Involved in Each.*

A. Does the breakdown approach really save time? Is the time saved spent later in dealing with many unresolved problems?

B. Is the developmental approach feasible? Practical? Does the lack of existing structure create too much anxiety? Does an open-ended attack upon needs create too many "crosswinds"—cross too many "professional" or "craft" lines?

C. Are there other approaches that might prove to be more practical?

5. *Exploring Various Methods Which Would Allow for Continuing Education.* To what extent should both worker and agency contribute time and training costs? Should the level of the job on the career ladder affect these decisions? To what extent should training be given on the job? Off the job in the agency? Off the job in a technical school, community college, etc.? How will training times be coordinated with work operations?

By studying all of these problems in a single community, the conditions under which solutions can be worked out will be kept constant and the possible facilitating aspects of interaction effects can be observed.

SUMMARY

The design of new careers involves technical and strategic considerations but, above all, employer and community commitment. It is commitment on the part of employers that transforms dead-end jobs into opportunities for growth. This is fundamental. Once com-

mitment is established, then technical and strategic guidelines become relevant.

Technical guidelines include:
Titling to reflect the commitment to a career.

Selection procedures that recognize the range and development of potential, and do not exclude on the basis of irrelevant and unnecessarily high criteria.

Structuring of tasks to allow for higher functional attainment and increase of discretionary functioning.

Supervision that implements the growing of people, as well as the achievement of production standards.

Provision of regular increases in compensation to correspond with increased experience and competence.

Provision of training and growth opportunities for those who can and need to achieve higher functional performance.

Strategic guidelines include:
Directing opportunities for new careers primarily at the poor and disadvantaged.

Developing new careers primarily in the newly emerging community and health services work fields.

APPENDIX

What Workers Do.[16] *(Worker Functions)*

THINGS	DATA	PEOPLE
Precision working	Synthesizing	Monitoring
Setting up	Coordinating	Negotiating
Manipulating	Analyzing	Supervising
Operating-controlling	Compiling	Consulting, instructing, treating
Driving-controlling	Computing	Persuading, diverting
Handling	Copying	Exchanging information
Tending	Comparing	Serving
Feeding		Taking instructions-helping
Learning	Learning	Learning
Observing	Observing	Observing

[16]See *Dictionary of Occupational Titles,* 3rd Edition, Vol. II, 1965, pp. 649-650, for the worker-function array in use by the U.S. Employment Service in its present coding system. There are some minor differences between it and the one illustrated here.

Initiating new careers by resorting to both short- and long-term approaches, and especially avoiding assumptions that ignore the realities of professionalization.

It is important to keep the technical and strategic considerations separate so that the various people and groups that are inevitably involved in designing new careers may see where they stand and assume an appropriate stance with regard to their occupational identities and professional objectives.

Note: Each successive function reading down usually or typically involves all those that follow it.

Feeding, tending, driving-controlling, operating-controlling, and setting up are special cases involving machines and equipment of handling, manipulating, and precision working respectively, and hence are indented under them.

The hyphenated functions: operating-controlling, driving-controlling, and taking instructions-helping are single functions.

The functions separated by a comma are separate functions on the same level, separately defined. They are on the same level because empirical evidence does not make a hierarchical distinction clear.

Learning and observing are adaptive functions basic to functioning in all three areas.

SET: A SKILL-ELEMENT APPROACH TO JOB TRAINING UNDER UNCERTAINTY

Raymond C. Helwig

The paradox of our present employment situation is that we have jobs unfilled because of lack of skilled applicants, yet we have people unemployed because they lack the necessary skills.[1] The answer to this riddle may seem obvious—qualify some of the unemployed and potentially unemployed to fill some of the available jobs. However, the implementation of this answer presents a challenge to the ingenuity, the ability to co-ordinate, and the cooperativeness of the four main segments of our economy concerned with this problem: business, labor, government, and education.

The purpose of this paper is to explore the problems of planning job training and to propose an approach for handling these problems. The proposed approach—SET (Skill-Element Training)—involves six main steps:

(1) Analyze the skill requirements of occupations, breaking the skills down into elements.

(2) Find common patterns of skill-elements among groups of occupations.

(3) Forecast the numbers of workers who will be required and available for each of these groups of occupations.

(4) Establish training programs for the

From Raymond C. Helwig, "SET: A Skill-Element Approach to Job Training under Uncertainty," Personnel Journal 45 (11), 656–661, 695 (1966). Reprinted by permission.

[1] *U.S., Manpower Report of the President—March 1966*, p. xii.

skill elements which the forecasts predict will be in short supply.

(5) Make available to a trainee a combination of skill-element training courses which will give him preparation for a group of occupations.

(6) Supplement skill-element training with sufficient occupational training to show the trainee how he can use the skill elements in various occupations.

The important questions of where job training should be conducted and who should pay for it are not considered in this paper. It is believed that SET is applicable to a variety of training situations, including both institutional and on-the-job training.

Before examining SET further, however, the problems common to any planning of job training must be considered, along with possible solutions.

DIFFICULTIES OF FORECASTING

Forecasting is required for any planning of job training, and appears to be a weak link in a great deal of such planning. Forecasts must be made of the numbers and types of workers who will be required and available in the future, in order to be able to plan the types of job training that will be needed. It is the difference between the number required and the number available which is of most interest for planning purposes.

Forecasting is made more difficult by the partial geographic mobility of labor. If labor were completely *immobile* geographically, we could simply forecast separately the training needs of any labor market area, without worrying about other areas.

If labor were completely *mobile* geographically, we would need only one aggregate forecast for the whole country. We would not have to concern ourselves with the geographic breakdown of where workers are required, where they are available, or where training facilities are needed.

Partial geographic *mobility* of labor requires a forecast of the needs and availabilities *within* each labor market area, plus forecasts of mobility *between* labor market areas. The large number of occupations and labor market areas makes any attempt at thorough forecasting a Herculean task. As a hypothetical example of one small part of such a forecast, assume that there are only two labor market areas, Chicago and Detroit, and that we are concerned with only one occupation: automobile mechanics. Assume that our forecast shows that the number of mechanics needed in Detroit will exceed the number available locally, but that Chicago will have a surplus. Should facilities be established in Detroit to train mechanics? The answer depends on the geographic mobility of automobile mechanics: how many of the mechanics in Chicago will go to Detroit where the jobs are? If such mobility is high, additional training facilities in Detroit may be unnecessary.

UNCERTAINTIES OF FORECASTING

In addition to the problem of *difficulties* of forecasting, there is also the problem of *uncertainties* of forecasting: we are not sure that the forecasts will turn out to be correct. These uncertainties are due to two main causes: assumptions which must be made, and limitations of occupational data.

Assumptions must be made for both the demand and supply forecasts. Demand forecasts (of the numbers and types of workers who will be *required*) involve predictions as to type of products or services to be sold, volume of sales, methods of manufacturing or providing products or services, and location of plant facilities. These predicted variables may be affected by many factors, as shown in Figure 3.6, about which assumptions must be made, which may turn out to be incorrect.

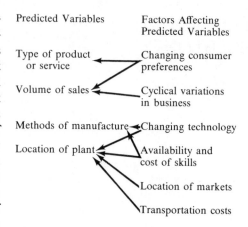

Figure 3.6 Factors affecting predicted variables in forecasts of number and type of workers who will be *required*.

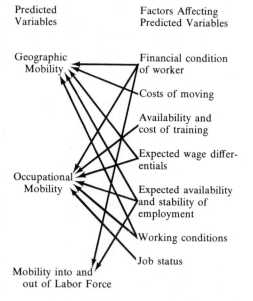

Figure 3.7 Factors affecting predicted variables in forecasts of number and type of workers who will be *available*.

Supply forecasts (of the numbers and types of workers who will be *available*) involve predictions as to three types of mobility:

(1) Geographic mobility; i.e., movement from one labor market area to another.

(2) Occupational mobility; i.e., movement from one occupation to another.

(3) Mobility into and out of the labor force; i.e., movement between the status of "in the labor force" (employed or seeking work) and *"not* in the labor force" (not working and not seeking work).

These predicted variables may be affected by many factors, as shown in Figure 3.7, about which assumptions must be made, which may turn out to be incorrect.

Forecasts of both supply and demand for a skill are hampered by limitations of occupational data. Present census data on occupations are neither designed nor useful for describing the jobs in our economy. Neither the industrial nor social-economic breakdowns used are intended or suitable for this purpose. The new 3rd edition of *Dictionary of Occupational Titles* has more suitable classifications. However, its purpose is not to give aggregate estimates of the various types of jobs in the country.[2]

What are the implications of these skill forecasting uncertainties? Uncertainty in planning has two aspects: (1) we may be wrong; (2) there may be a penalty attached to being wrong. Consequently, there are two possible methods for coping with these uncertainties. First, we can try to reduce the probability of being wrong. Second, we can try to reduce the penalty for being wrong.

REDUCING THE PROBABILITY OF BEING WRONG

Two possible avenues are open for reducing the probability of being wrong: (1) we can try to improve the forecasting methods, and (2) we can keep the length of the forecast short.

Because of the forecasting difficulties, obtaining substantial refinement of the oc-cupational forecasts would be a mammoth undertaking.[3]

The second avenue, keeping the length of the forecast short, seems justified. Long-range forecasts have value in that they enable us to plan the training for the lifetime in which it may potentially be used. However, the further we try to look into the future, the greater the uncertainties become. The short-run forecast is more concerned with immediate needs. However, if it is too short, the risk of obsolescence of skills is obvious: the training may be for occupations being eliminated. The short-run forecast should be a compromise. A five-year period, as is used in area skill surveys made by various state employment agencies,[4] appears to be reasonable.

Emphasis on such relatively near-term job skills seems justified for a number of reasons:

(1) the desire to reduce unemployment among the unskilled as rapidly as practicable;[5]

(2) the desire to remedy current shortages of certain skills;[6]

(3) the time value of money: a dollar to be earned two years from now has a greater present value than a dollar to be earned twenty years from now;

(4) Once an employee is given an entry skill which will enable him to get and hold a job, he will have continued opportunities for further training;

(5) many skills have a short life due to technological change. Of 24,000 jobs listed in the 1949 edition of *Dictionary of Occupational Titles* over 8,000 have been deleted or combined with other jobs in the 1965 edition;[7]

[2]James Scoville. "The Development and Relevance of U.S. Occupational Data," *Industrial and Labor Relations Review* **IXX** (1), 70-9 (October, 1965).

[3]For a discussion of occupational forecasts made and planned see Vladimir D. Chavrid. "Occupational Information Needs Expanding," *Employment Service Review,* pp. 29-32 (August 1965).

[4]*Ibid.*

[5]*U.S., Manpower Report of the President—March 1966,* pp. xi-xix, 1-2, 67-68, 77-85.

[6]*Ibid.,* pp. xiii-xv, 4, 31-35.

[7]U.S. Department of Labor, *Manpower Research and Training,* p. 87 (1966).

(6) many workers will remain in their entry occupations a relatively short time.[8]

REDUCING THE PENALTY FOR BEING WRONG

The second method is to reduce the *penalty* for being wrong. What is the penalty for an incorrect skill-need forecast which results in the wrong type of training being given? The answer depends largely on how much benefit the training will have for a job other than the one trained for—that is, on the transferability of the skill. It is helpful in this regard to describe job training as general or specific, although most job training is a combination of the two. General training may be defined as that which is useful to many employers in various industries. Specific training is that which is of use only to one employer.

In order to reduce the *penalty* for being wrong, the training should be made *more* general. How general will depend partly on our attitude toward risk. If we wish to mini-

[8]The limitations of occupational data referred to by Scoville (note 2) are exemplified by an attempt to find data on occupational mobility. For a study of occupational mobility by census occupational category see A. J. Jaffe and R. O. Carleton, *Occupational Mobility in the United States 1930-1960* (New York: King's Crown Press, Columbia University, 1954). They estimated that only about 20% of employees who started work in the category of "operatives and kindred workers" would remain in that occupational category their entire lives. For those under age 25 in the occupational category "craftsmen, foremen and kindred workers" one-third were expected to remain in it. A more recent study examined mobility among employers: Harvey R. Hamel, "Job Tenure of American Workers, January 1963." *Monthly Labor Review*, LXXXVI, No. 10 (October 1963) 1145-52. He found that as of January 1963 the median number of years continuous employment with present employer was 5.7 for all employed men. As would be expected, this figure increases with the age of the men: it is 7.6 years in the 35 to 44 age bracket, and 12.8 years for age 45 years and over. While the occupational mobility figures may understate frequency of changes in skills used, the figures on mobility among employers probably overstate them. A worker may use the same skills in jobs with different employers. He may have multiple jobs requiring different skills within the same broad census occupational category.

mize the penalty for being wrong by making job training completely general, we also tend to reduce the reward for being right. The training might be so general as to have very little value to any employer and consequently, very little value to the trainee.

This specialization-versus-generalization dilemma is a problem of all training, including higher education, and has long been recognized. In higher education, the length of the training period and its cost are much greater than for job-skill training. Obsolescence of the skills learned in higher education would, therefore, be an even greater economic tragedy. Higher education has handled this problem by trying to make the training general enough to provide a foundation for life-long development, but still sufficiently specific to enable the graduate to obtain and perform well in an entry job.

SKILL-ELEMENT TRAINING (SET)

How can we best handle this dilemma of specific versus general training at the job-skill level? How can we reap the reward of a correct skill-need forecast without incurring an excessive penalty if we are wrong? The answer appears to be to make the training relatively general, making it only specific enough to impart specific entry skill for the trainee to get and hold a job. Of what, then, should the training consist?

SET, which is proposed as an approach for planning job training, consists of six steps:

(1) Analyze the skill requirements of occupations, breaking the skills down into elements. For example, we may find that the knowledge needed by an automobile mechanic includes a knowledge of basic electricity.

(2) Find common patterns of skill-elements among groups of occupations. For example, a knowledge of basic electricity might be an essential skill element in many diverse occupations in many industries. Isn't

some knowledge of electricity necessary for such occupations as construction electrician, power station operator, communications and utility repairman, electrical-instrument repairman, and maintenance electrician, as well as automobile mechanic?

What other skill elements might these particular occupations have in common? What about the use of fastening techniques, such as soldering or splicing?

(3) Forecast the numbers of workers who will be required and available for each of these groups of occupations. Occupational forecasts presently being made, such as the area skill surveys, could be used for this purpose. The forecasts of individual occupations such as automobile mechanic, and electrical-instrument repairman would be combined to get a forecast of a group of occupations which might be called "Basic electricity-oriented occupations."

These forecasts would involve the uncertainties previously discussed, which, however, would be reduced by keeping the length of the forecast short, and by combining occupational forecasts into forecasts for groups of occupations. This grouping should particularly reduce the uncertainty attributable to occupational mobility, because many occupational changes are made between occupations requiring similar skills. For example, in planning for training in the skill-element of basic electricity, we would not need to worry about occupational mobility between two occupations which both require this skill.

(4) Establish training programs for the skill-elements which the forecasts predict will be in short supply. One such training program might be in basic electricity, another in fastening techniques.

(5) Make available to a trainee a combination of skill-element training courses which will give him preparation for a group of occupations selected in an area or areas in which he has aptitude, interest, and an opportunity for entry.

(6) Supplement skill-element training with

sufficient occupational training to show the trainee how he can use the skill elements in various occupations.

SET could also be used for that part of preparation for jobs which is now lumped under the titles of literacy training or basic education.[9] It could also be used to find common patterns of such skills required by groups of occupations. For example, many occupations would be found to require ability to communicate orally, to communicate in writing, to read and comprehend numerically-calibrated dials, and to make arithmetic computations. In planning job training, these skill-elements could be incorporated with the remainder of the job training, where they could be taught in a way that would be relevant to jobs and meaningful to the trainees.

What would be the advantages of SET as opposed to training purely by occupation? First, the training can be more general—that is, having more chance of use in another occupation and thus reducing the penalty for a wrong occupational forecast. Second, economies of scale can be achieved by grouping of people preparing for diverse occupations into the same training classes. Training could thereby be offered in small-to-medium-size cities which might not have enough trainees to warrant training by occupation. Third, the training of instructors should be facilitated because each instructor could be somewhat specialized. Fourth, the need for early specific job choice by the trainee would be eliminated, and the need for early intensive individual counseling reduced.

The possible disadvantages of SET do not seem serious, but they need to be recognized so that steps can be taken to minimize their effects. First, a tendency for the skill-elements

[9]Increasing emphasis on this aspect of job preparation in government-sponsored programs under the Manpower Development and Training Act is discussed in U.S., *Manpower Report of the President—March 1966*, pp. 3, 79, 97. Also see U.S. Department of Labor, *Manpower Research and Training—1966*, pp. 14-15.

not to be meshed in a way meaningful to the trainee. This disadvantage in itself would probably militate against complete dependence on SET. SET would include supplementary occupational-training which would show the trainee how he can use the skill-elements in various occupations. Second, it is possible that a skill-element, such as electricity, should be taught in a different way for different occupations, such as power-station operator and electrical-instrument repairman. However, this disadvantage seems merely to limit the degree to which occupations can be grouped. It should still be possible to find groups of occupations with similar patterns of skill-elements.

DOT—A STEP TOWARD SET

A major step in the direction of analyzing skill requirements of groups of occupations has been taken with the publication of the 3rd edition of the *Dictionary of Occupational Titles* (DOT). Volume I is titled "Definitions of Titles." It lists, for each of 21,741 jobs, titles and definitions of duties, plus a numerical code. Volume II is titled "Occupational Classification." It contains job titles arranged by worker trait groups, with a qualifications profile for each group. Worker trait groups are groups of jobs requiring similar combinations of general education development, specific vocational preparation, and other characteristics.[10]

These volumes contain much data which could be utilized for the SET approach. For example, under the listing "automobile mechanic" in Volume I are found several duties, one of which is "disassembles unit and inspects parts for wear, using micrometers, calipers, and thickness gauges." The occupational code is 620.281. The first digit shows that it is in the broad category of "machine

trades occupations." The first three digits together show that it is in the narrower occupational category of "Motorized vehicle and engineering equipment mechanics and repairmen." The last three digits (following the decimal) show the job's relationship to data (4th digit), people (5th digit) and things (6th digit). The digits 281 show that the job involves analyzing data, no significant relationship with people, and precision working with things.[11]

Each of these terms is defined in Appendix A to Volume II. Within each of the last three digits, the number (from 0 to 8) indicates the highest level of complexity at which the worker must perform. Relationships with regard to data range from "comparing" at the bottom to "synthesizing" at the top. With regard to people, the range is from "serving" to "mentoring." With regard to things, the range is from "handling" to "setting-up."[12]

Other information on skills required is included in DOT Volume II in the qualifications profile for each group of jobs having similar requirements. The qualifications profile is expressed in numerical codes which are defined in Appendix B. Two parts of this profile are of interest as a step toward SET: general education development and specific vocational preparation. General educational development is divided into three areas: reasoning development, mathematical development, and language development. Within each of these three areas are several levels, each of which is defined. Specific vocational preparation is coded in terms of the amount of time required to develop average performance. In addition to the coded qualifications profile, other information on skill requirements is contained in the Volume I job definitions and the discussions on the same pages as the qualifications profiles in Volume II.[13]

---

[10]U.S. Department of Labor, *Dictionary of Occupational Titles* (Washington, D.C.: U.S. Printing Office, 1965), 3rd ed., Vols. I and II.

[11]*Ibid.*

[13]*Ibid.*

[13]*Ibid.*

SUMMARY

Forecasts of demand and supply for specific occupations are hampered by limitations of data and are cloaked in uncertainty. The penalty for a wrong occupational forecast can be reduced by making the training relatively general—useful for numerous occupations, but still specific enough to be useful. SET (Skill-Element Training) is proposed as a method of approaching this problem. SET involves six steps: (1) Analyze the skill requirements of occupations, breaking the skills down into elements; (2) Find common patterns of skill-elements among groups of occupations; (3) Forecast the numbers of workers who will be required and available for each of these groups of occupations; (4) Establish training programs for the skill elements which the forecasts predict will be in short supply; (5) make available to a trainee a combination of skill-element training courses which will give him preparation for a group of occupations; (6) Supplement skill-element training with sufficient occupational training to show the trainee how he can use the skill elements in various occupations. The third edition of the *Dictionary of Occupational Titles* is an important step toward availability of occupational information and classifications required for the SET approach.

PART FOUR

PERFORMANCE MONITORING PROCESSES

After successful selection and development of manpower, performance must become the next focal point. While every component of the personnel management system affects performance directly or indirectly, our concern in this part relates to performance monitoring, i.e., appraisal and evaluation of employee performance.

Monitoring is a vital part of virtually any operation flow, for only through monitoring can it be insured that the process in question is functioning properly. Although all aspects of every process require such monitoring, perhaps it is most important in the personnel process where employee performance is critically interrelated with the attainment of the organization's objectives.

The articles in this part deal with the problems of, and procedures for, effective performance monitoring. The first article, "A Study of Factors Relating to the Effectiveness of a Performance Appraisal Program," is particularly important and somewhat different in orientation from the remaining selections. This article highlights the importance of well-conceived and implemented research programs and describes a study which investigated the effectiveness of one company's appraisal program. The results suggest that only if performance monitoring procedures themselves are monitored, will program effectiveness be maximized.

The second article, "Assessing the Performance of Key Managers," addresses itself to the historically difficult problem of evaluating managerial performance. Note the futility of attempting to assess performance without a clear conception of what effective performance is as it relates to the organization's goals.

Implied in any type of assessment attempt is the existence of a criterion or standard against which the assessed can be compared. Many times the failure of what seems to be a carefully designed and implemented assessment program can be traced to the lack of an adequate standard. The final article, "The Dollar Criterion—Applying the Cost Accounting Concept to Criterion Construction," deals with the problem of constructing an adequate standard. A rationale for criterion construction is presented and critically examined.

A STUDY OF FACTORS RELATING TO THE EFFECTIVENESS OF A PERFORMANCE APPRAISAL PROGRAM

Herbert H. Meyer
William B. Walker

INTRODUCTION

Performance appraisal is a widely practiced personnel activity which has seldom been subjected to systematic study. The premise on which the application of a formal appraisal program is based—namely, that to know where one stands with his boss and to be apprised of his shortcomings will help him to improve his performance—seems to have so much obvious validity that personnel people are apt to feel it is unnecessary to conduct formal studies of the effectiveness of this program. While some writers have recently questioned the value of formal appraisal programs, or at least of certain approaches to appraisal, few research studies have been focused on the conditions associated with the success or failure of the program.

In the course of gathering data for another study, an opportunity was provided to obtain data relating to reactions of "middle management" employees in a large manufacturing company to the performance appraisal program. While this side exploration does not by any means provide a definitive answer to the question of what factors contribute to the effectiveness of the performance ap-

From Herbert H. Meyer and William B. Walker, "A Study of Factors Relating to the Effectiveness of a Performance Appraisal Program," Personnel Psychology 14 (3), 241–298 (1961). Reprinted by permission.

praisal program, it does throw some light on the subject.

DESIGN OF THE STUDY

The major study[1] of which this investigation was a part was aimed at identifying some of the correlates of certain measures of achievement motivation. One of the hypotheses investigated was that high achievement motivation would be associated with positive reactions to the performance appraisal program. The subjects for testing this hypothesis consisted of 31 managers in several manufacturing components of the General Electric Company and 31 specialists whose status (position levels) in the organizations was approximately the same as the managers. These 62 men were given a thematic apperceptive measure designed to be scored for "need for achievement" and a Risk Preference Questionnaire which presented situations involving risk and required the subject to choose between low, intermediate, and high risk options. The use of this risk questionnaire as an index of achievement motivation was based on the theoretical model presented by Atkinson,[2] in which he demonstrated that the person with high achievement motivation will prefer intermediate risks (approximately 50/50 odds) whereas the person with high fear of failure motivation will prefer either safer odds or higher risk odds where failure is excusable.

All the Company components included in the study had formal performance appraisal programs. One of the primary purposes of these programs was to provide the measure of "merit" for determining pay level under a merit-pay type of salary plan. Appraisals

[1]H. H. Meyer and W. B. Walker, "Need for Achievement and Risk Preferences as They Relate to Attitudes toward Reward Systems and Performance Appraisal in an Industrial Setting." *Journal of Applied Psychology* (1961).

[2]J. W. Atkinson, "Motivational Determinants of Risk-Taking Behavior." *Psychological Review* LXIV, 359-372 (1957).

were generally based on the responsibilities assigned to each individual as described in his "Position Guide." The appraisal forms used also included sections for identifying development needs and for suggesting remedial actions.

During the interviews conducted as a part of this research study, each subject was questioned about his experience with the performance appraisal program and was asked to give an especially detailed description of the last performance appraisal discussion he had had with his manager. Based on each subject's report, the interviewer rated the following items:

1. How faithfully did the manager follow the performance appraisal procedure?
2. How skillfully did the manager handle the feedback discussion?
(Note that this was the interviewer's evaluation, based on the subject's description of the discussion, not the subject's evaluation of the discussion his boss had held with him.)
3. How favorable was the respondent's attitude toward the performance appraisal program?
4. How favorable was the respondent's attitude toward the "merit-pay" plan?
5. Did the man being interviewed report that he had taken some specific action to improve his performance based on the performance appraisal discussion?

The last item was categorized simply on a "yes-no" basis by the interviewer. The man's response was coded "yes" if he could cite some specific action he had taken based on items discussed or suggestions made during the interview. He might have indicated, for example, that he had enrolled in a "Human Relations" training course at the suggestion of his supervisor, or that he had reorganized his method for keeping scrap records so that he could get an earlier indication of needed corrections, or that he had

made a special effort to get reports in on time since this was mentioned by the manager as an item which needed improvement.

This latter variable, the respondent's report of whether or not he had taken constructive action to improve performance based on his last performance appraisal discussion, was used as the criterion of the success of the performance appraisal program for purposes of this study. The analysis of data was carried out by computing correlations between this criterion variable and other measures obtained in the investigation.

RESULTS

Of the 62 men interviewed in this study, 49 (23 of the managers and 26 of the specialists) reported that they had had performance appraisal discussions with their managers within the last year or two, which they could describe in some detail. Of the 49, 21 (12 managers and 9 specialists) reported that they had taken some specific constructive action to improve performance, based on suggestions made or topics discussed in the feed-back interview.

Table 1 presents correlations between the dependent variable, "constructive action taken based on last performance appraisal discussion," and the independent variables obtained in the study. It can be seen that the best predictor of whether or not the subject took constructive action based on his performance appraisal was how well his manager had handled the appraisal feedback discussion. Of the measures designed to assess motivation, the thematic apperceptive measure of "need for achievement" showed only a low correlation, not statistically significant, with the criterion variable, while preference for intermediate level risks as an index of achievement motivation was found to be highly correlated with the criterion.

TABLE 1. **CORRELATES OF THE VARIABLE "CONSTRUCTIVE ACTION TAKEN BASED ON LAST PERFORMANCE APPRAISAL DISCUSSION"**

	MANAGERS (N = 23)	SPECIALISTS (N = 26)	TOTAL (N = 49)
1. How well manager handled appraisal discussion	75**	55**	63**
2. Thematic apperceptive measure of "need for achievement"	04	32	21
3. Preference for intermediate level risks	48*	68**	63**
4. Attitude toward Merit Pay plan	35	60*	50*
5. Attitude toward Performance Appraisal program	05	38	30
6. Age	–46*	–48*	–48*
7. Education	–18	–38	–26

*Significant at 5% level of confidence.
**Significant at 1% level of confidence.

It is interesting to note that attitude toward the merit-pay salary plan is significantly correlated with the report of taking constructive action, whereas attitude toward the performance appraisal program itself does not correlate with the same variable at a significant level. Age shows negative correlations, as might be expected, indicating that the younger men were more likely to take constructive action to improve performance than were the older men. Education also shows negative correlations with the criterion, although these correlations are not significant. These negative correlations would indicate, however, that in this sample there was some tendency for the less well educated men to be more likely to take constructive action than was true for the better educated men.

Additional analysis, not reported in the table, showed that the first variable, "How well the discussion was handled," was significantly correlated with the participants' attitudes toward the merit-pay salary plan (.45). As an interesting sidelight, it was also noted that the interviewers' ratings of the participants' "level of understanding of the salary plan philosophy" was significantly correlated

(.42) with attitudes toward the merit-pay system. In other words, those who demonstrated a better understanding of the philosophy on which the salary plan is based expressed more favorable attitudes toward the plan. (It is important to keep in mind, of course, that both of these ratings were made by the same interviewer, and therefore it is possible that the interviewer's rating of one variable could have biased his rating of the other.)

A multiple correlation for predicting action based on the appraisal discussion, from the three variables in Table 1 which show the highest correlations, would indicate that theoretically this prediction should be perfect. Figure 1 illustrates the results of combining these three variables in a crude manner to predict action based on the appraisal. It will be noted, for example, that seven out of eight of the men who were (1) below the average age for the group, (2) expressed preference for intermediate risks, and (3) whose managers had done an above-average job in handling the appraisal discussion, took some constructive action to improve performance on the basis of the discussion. At the other end of the scale, it will be noted that none of the men who scored below average on these three variables took constructive action based on their appraisal discussions. This prediction would be equally good if the multiple correlation were computed for either one of the groups and then "cross-validated" on the other group. Needless to say, this kind of check at this stage of the data analysis cannot be accepted as a legitimate cross-validation of the findings.

individual took constructive action based on performance appraisal. (This latter correlation could also be accounted for by the fact that both variables involved were highly correlated with "how well the appraisal discussion was handled.")

The high correlation found between preference for intermediate level risks and the subjects' reports of whether or not they took constructive action based on the performance appraisal discussion provides evidence to

Figure 4.1   Predicting constructive action based on the performance appraisal from scores on three variables.

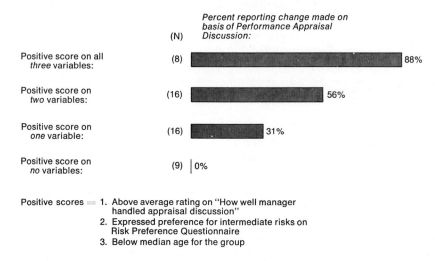

Positive scores = 1. Above average rating on "How well manager handled appraisal discussion"
2. Expressed preference for intermediate risks on Risk Preference Questionnaire
3. Below median age for the group

DISCUSSION

The results of this study suggest that the skill with which a supervisor handles the appraisal feedback discussion with his subordinates is a key factor in determining whether or not the performance appraisal program is effective in motivating behavioral changes. It would also appear that the skill with which the supervisor handles the appraisal discussion might have an important influence on the degree to which a subordinate understands the philosophy on which the pay-for-performance salary plan is based, and this in turn might influence his attitude toward the plan. Moreover, a favorable attitude toward the salary plan was found to be significantly correlated with whether or not the

support the hypothesis that this measure is assessing some aspect of achievement motivation.[3] It is not necessary, however, to interpret this result as indicating only that the aspect of motivation measured is a positive, success-oriented type. While this measure was scored by comparing the number of intermediate level risk choices to choices for extreme risks, whether high or low, a more detailed analysis of the results showed that preference for *low risk* alternatives actually generated the correlations found between this measure and the criterion. In other words, if preference for high level risks was lumped together with preference for intermediate level risks, and these compared with pre-

[3] *Ibid.*

ference for low risks, the correlations found between this measure and the criterion were not affected. Thus, the preference for safe bets, or the avoidance of risk, appears to be the critical behavior tapped by this measure. This may indicate a negative, fear-of-failure type of motivation.

According to the motivation theory model presented by Atkinson, one might predict that the men who show preference for safe bets would also be less likely to take constructive action based on the performance appraisal. The fact that an individual took action based on the appraisal feedback discussion must have meant that the manager discussed an area of needed improvement. This might be interpreted by the individual as a *failure* on his part in some aspect of job performance. Atkinson demonstrates that the effect of failure on the person with a high

level of anxiety about failing is to decrease his motivation and cause him to avoid the situation. He also cites research evidence to support his theory.

The findings of this study with the most immediate practical implications are probably those relating to the skill with which appraisal feedback discussions were handled. The fact that this variable was found to be highly correlated, not only with the tendency to take constructive action based on a performance appraisal discussion, but also with attitudes toward the salary plan and performance appraisal would indicate that any steps taken to upgrade the quality of these appraisal interviews would have a decided impact on the success of the merit-pay salary plan, and especially on the performance appraisal program as an integral part of the plan.

ASSESSING THE PERFORMANCE OF KEY MANAGERS

Charles L. Hughes

No jobs and no persons should exist in any organization except in pursuit of company goals. The jobs of managers are among the clearer examples of the relationship between individual performance and the achievement of the enterprise. There is, nevertheless, much witchcraft related to the evaluation of individual job performance. Managers will discuss company plans, marketing objectives, production goals, cost effectiveness, gross profit margins, and other criteria for assessing organizational performance, and then make a 180 degree about-face and assess the performance of the people responsible for accomplishing organizational goals with an entirely different set of criteria. If a manager's job exists to carry out certain objectives and strategies of the organization, it is reasonable to assess his performance effectiveness, value to the company, and personal rewards in terms of how well these organizational goals have been achieved. An effective manager is one who accomplishes the organization's goals.

ORGANIZATIONAL GOAL SETTING

Goal setting is a forward-looking process that establishes objectives and strategies for their accomplishment for the time period ahead. Obviously, unless goals have been set in the past they cannot be used today as yardsticks for evaluating job performance. In other

From Charles L. Hughes, "Assessing the Performance of Key Managers," Personnel 45 (1), 38–43 (January-February, 1968). Reprinted by permission of the American Management Association.

words, an organization without goals cannot expect the members of the organization to be goal-seeking.

Goal setting is a management system for setting objectives to be accomplished and defining strategies and plans for achieving those objectives. When the goals of any manager or group support the objectives at the next highest level of organization, the structure of the organization and the content of any manager's job responsibiility become interrelated in a pattern that is highly motivational and identifies criteria that can be used to assess both individual and organizational effectiveness. The goal system brings the responsibility for planning and control into the job of the person who manages a team of key people—which is where these belong, rather than with a staff planning group or exclusively with the top executives.

The process of evaluating managers begins with the establishment of company objectives and with definition of the purposes of the organization. When company objectives have been identified, reviewed, and approved at several levels of management, then the executive in charge of a team of managers can begin to set business goals. If the goal of the department is to have any relationship to the overall goals of the company, the department team must have made an input to the top-level company planning. This will permit a linking between the goals of the marketing, manufacturing, or engineering organization and the overall objectives of the company. The longer-range company objectives must be established by top management with the full and responsive involvement of other levels of management. Next, division or department objectives are created as subgoals to the overall company goals. These define specific things to be accomplished and results to be achieved by that business unit. If managers set their own goals in support of company objectives, they can be expected to be more realistic and to have more motivational power for individuals.

A well-set goal defines the yardsticks that can be used at any point in time to assess progress and degree of goal accomplishment. For example, a poor statement of a goal would be, "Continue the present rate of sales increase"; a better goal statement might read, "Secure X per cent of the market for product Z during the next year." The first statement fails to meet the rule-of-thumb test of a good goal: Any statement that can be reasonably followed by the phrase, "and more of the same next time," is a nebulous and fuzzy goal. The end result for a time period requires a clear target with a sharp focus. In other words, for a business goal to be useful to managers in motivating them to high levels of performance, it must be meaningful to the man who is responsible for accomplishing the goal and whose performance will be measured against it. A meaningful goal is one that is understandable, desirable, obtainable, meets personal needs, and has been influenced by the person responsible for its accomplishment.

OBSOLETE APPROACHES

The problem of evaluation of key managers is the same that is found in any other functional specialty in today's modern organization. The traditional organization pyramid and its chain of command structure is usually known as bureaucracy. The bureaucratic, that is, functionally specialized, form of organization is obsolete. This mechanistic approach to management may have been useful at one time to prevent capricious and whimsical management and in response to the increasing complexities of management technology. However, a new approach to management is coming into being, and management styles must change once again. Performance evaluation is a critical problem that arises from traditional management practices. When any person's job is circumscribed and programmed to such a degree that the man's responsibilities are primarily to carry out a sequence of tasks instead of accomplishing specific performance objectives related to the company's goals, then there are many opportunities for evaluation of performance with irrelevant criteria.

To assess individuals according to personality traits and Boy Scout oaths is to ignore the accomplishment of organizational objectives. Individual characteristics may have some bearing on how well the job is performed, but they are peripheral to the job itself and have no direct bearing on the accomplishments of the individual.

Another misleading and sometimes harmful criterion is the job description. An advertising manager may have a job description on file in the personnel department deeply buried somewhere in his desk drawer, but he probably views it as a shoddy piece of fiction that bears no realistic relationship to what he does and what he feels to be important in his job. Job descriptions often exist because the personnel manager needs to think he is making a contribution to the corporation's success. They may be useful analytic tools for the purpose of establishing compensation base lines, but they are seldom accurate statements of the things to be accomplished in the job. Job descriptions are intentionally written in general terms, and they are static abstractions rather than dynamic documentation of the important business to be accomplished by a person. It is the job that motivates, not the job description. Responsibility for establishing plans and controls in one's work forms the basis for motivation and also provides meaningful criteria for the assessment of performance. Performance should be measured only against the accomplishment of established organizational goals.

NEW ORGANIZATIONAL STYLES

As the tasks and goals of the organization become more complicated and technologically oriented, collaboration and consensus will be required among various vertical and lateral relationships of the organization. Because professional managers in the goal-oriented organization will identify with the objectives of their organizational unit or their own job, the linking of various groups together through the goal-setting structure will be increasingly important. People will be evaluated not simply according to how "important" or how highly ranked the job is, but according to demonstrated ability to accomplish organizational objectives. Organization charts will be designed to reflect the hierarchy of goals rather than a pyramid of functional specialties. Performance assessment is difficult today for many organizations because there is no adequate system for establishing objectives and strategies—that is, for linking managers together in a unified network of goals and plans.

Job goals for key personnel must be interrelated with the goals of other units, since managers will not be able to achieve their job goals without the active involvement and support of people in other functions. Managers may be acting as entrepreneurs selling service to the organization in return for rewards and opportunities; narrow specialization and compartmentalization are already obsolete.

A system of collaborative goal-setting for the management team will permit the top executives to realistically assess the performance of the individual managers. For example, engineers are a specialized breed today who often feel as much allegiance to their profession as they do to the organization. How can the performance of a research director be evaluated? He must establish goals, then establish check points that will indicate what he expects to accomplish by certain time periods. Activities are meaningless without a goal to shoot for; they are useful steps in a strategy for achieving a goal, but the goal is to accomplish a measurable business objective.

NEW METHODS OF ASSESSMENT

How can a manager apply goal accomplishment as a criterion? Goal-setting is the first step in the process, and the second step is the evaluation of the goals themselves in order of relative importance; the goals of one department might be much more significant than the goals of another, and if both achieve their goals equally, the one whose goals are relatively more important has contributed more to the success of the organization and has earned a higher evaluation and reward. For example, a manager (in conjunction with his boss and his immediate team of managers) can rank order the goals of each organizational unit on the basis of which will contribute the most to reaching company goals. There is no substitute for the good judgment of interested and involved people in bringing a consensus of goal ranking. Obviously, there may be many factors used for rank ordering: amount of sales billing generated, percentage of market served, value in improving customer service, and so on. The company objective is a guide for the goals of the department. The goals are the targets of the individuals responsible. There must be an organized system of goals and measurements organized around individual profit centers.

For the third step, the assessment of the individual managers against their own job goals, an evaluation system or tool is needed. Many approaches have been devised for measuring performance; scales with assorted adjectives and numerals have been devised and revised many times, but they all have problems and are sources of management discontent. The simplest form of scaling may be the most effective, because it avoids many quantifying and semantic difficulties. A simple rank ordering from the "most effective" to the "least effective" is relatively easy and does not require the design of elaborate yardsticks. Under this system, top management would review the goal achievement of key managers using a criterion of "contribution to the achievement of the goals of the organization." The person who is judged to have done the most is ranked in the "first" position, the second highest contributor is rated "second," and so on down to the last man. Additional management judgments must be brought in for review and integration of rank orders; the judgments of several knowledgeable people can be combined. This obviously is a tedious and time-consuming process, but if managers are interested in a method of evaluating key people that will increase motivation to achieve company goals and will permit an assessment of their performance on a meaningful basis, they must invest the time in order to get the return.

The fourth step (after the rank ordering of performance on the goal-achievement criterion) is a comparison of the rank order of the goals against the rank order of the individuals. A useful technique is to prepare a scattergram in which the vertical axis is a rank ordering of the individuals and the horizontal axis is a rank ordering of the goals. We can then plot a point on the chart for the performance of a man compared to the goals for which he is responsible. These points then help us determine anomalies, cases where the importance of goals and judged performance do not appear to be logically related. For example, we might find a highly evaluated man whose goals are ranked low, or a man ranked low whose goal is ranked very high. Other scattergram comparisons can also be useful in assessing performance: rank order of performance versus present salary, length of service versus job performance, age versus performance, goals versus salary, and level in the organization versus performance. Much information potentially useful to management may be revealed, such as the individuals who show great potential for the future, and the converse, the individuals who are highly paid and high in the organization whose performance is low. Managers may find clues for job reassignment, promotion, demotion, the development of new managers, and areas where replacements will be needed for key positions.

THE BASIC CONCEPTS

In a goal-oriented company, key people will be evaluated against their part in achieving company objectives. To do this there must be a management system for organizational goal-setting that involves the manager and builds criteria and checkpoints into the plans. With such a system, managers can use the same criteria and system for evaluating its key personnel as are used for assessing organizational effectiveness. Jobs that do not have clear goals do not motivate, and an organization runs on motivation. A job with meaningful goals is more motivational than one in which the objectives are fuzzy or nonexistent. The greatest mistake in evaluating individual job performance is to use things that are readily available, whether or not they bear any relationship to the purpose of the job and the reason for its existence. No job should exist except to achieve organizational objectives. There is no satisfactory alternative, therefore, to the assessment of people in terms of their accomplishment of their job objectives.

THE DOLLAR CRITERION—APPLYING THE COST ACCOUNTING CONCEPT TO CRITERION CONSTRUCTION

H. E. Brogden
E. K. Taylor

SUMMARY

A rationale for the construction of an overall measure of worker effectiveness is proposed and discussed in the light of some of the major problems of criterion construction.

As a result of the proposed approach, the criterion evaluations for the validation study may be selected with assurance that variables rejected have minimal effect on the efficiency of operation of the organization and that those retained provide an accurate estimate of the effect of the individual worker on efficiency of operation of the organization.

The rationale proposed involves converting production units, errors, time of other personnel consumed, etc., into dollar units. In so doing we give direct face validity to the individual criterion scales; that is, we show that each scale is directly oriented toward the objective of the organization and insure that validation analysis can be interpreted as estimates of the degree to which predictors contribute to this objective.

In addition, the criterion scales are converted to units equal at all points in each individual scale and comparable from scale to scale. Scales may then be combined into a direct unweighted sum with rational basis for such combination. The criterion constructed according to the proposed rationale should satisfy in all cases Bellows' requirement of acceptability to the sponsor of the study.[1]

The usefulness of the rationale proposed in the solution of related problems in selection and classification is stressed.

I. INTRODUCTION

It is generally agreed that the most important problem facing the industrial psychologist interested in test validation is devising adequate criteria of industrial efficiency. In spite of this, little effort is usually expended in criterion development. The criteria used are too frequently those most immediately available rather than those which would be most desirable.

This paper emphasizes the need for a common metric for sub-criterion variables, such that the measures obtained reflect the contribution of the individual to the objectives (or, usually to the overall efficiency) of the hiring organization. The principles to be discussed are pertinent to a number of possible common metrics. It is proposed in particular, however, that dollar units, determined on a cost accounting basis, will be found the most desirable units for many criterion purposes. For convenience this discussion will be confined to such monetary units—since the authors believe these to be most generally useful for criterion purposes. In addition, it is their opinion that the cost accounting criterion makes possible a more definitive solution of related problems in the area of personnel selection and differential placement.

The criterion problem under discussion in this paper is the development of an overall index of an employee's value to the hiring organization. The authors are not here concerned with the criterion problems arising in the choice or development of part criteria

From H. E. Brogden and E. K. Taylor, "The Dollar Criterion—Applying the Cost Accounting Concept to Criterion Construction," Personnel Psychology 3, 133–54 (1950). Reprinted by permission.

[1] R. M. Bellows, "Procedures for evaluating vocational criteria," *Journal of Applied Psychology* **25**, 499-516 (1941).

to be used in validation of predictors devised for measurement of particular job elements.

The Major Criterion Problems

To provide background for the discussion to follow, we will consider, briefly, some of the major criterion problems and indicate the relationship between these problems and the concept we are proposing. The principal problems encountered in criterion construction are, we believe, included in the following discussion.

1. *Definition of the Job.* Before any type of criterion construction can be undertaken, the job involved must be defined in order to identify a group of workers homogeneous with respect to their job duties. The cost accounting concept may sometimes be relevant in shedding light on discrepancies between apparently similar jobs. This is particularly true where two jobs have common elements but where the relative importance of these elements are quite different in terms of their value to the organization.

2. *"What it Is" that Criterion Elements Should Measure.* Definition of the nature of criterion elements is one of the basic problems in criterion construction. The solution to this problem is intimately related to the underlying logic of the cost accounting concept.

3. *Isolation of all Essential Sub-Criterion Elements.* There is probably no practical means of securing a criterion which will take *all* criterion elements into consideration. The writers believe that the cost accounting criterion procedures aid in judging which of the job elements are most essential.

4. *Devising Means of Measuring the Sub-Criterion Variables' Reliability.* The cost accounting concept proposed offers no solution to the problem of reliability.

5. *Avoiding Inclusion of Irrelevant Factors (Criterion Contamination).* The approach under consideration bears indirectly on certain types of criterion contamination.

6. *Developing a Procedure for Combining Sub-Criterion Measures.* This is the area in which the cost accounting criterion makes its major contribution.

7. *Developing Equal Scale Units.* The procedure proposed aids in the solution of this problem.

8. *Meaningful Units.* A direct solution to this problem is provided.

9. *Sponsor Acceptability.* The procedure by its very nature should yield a criterion that is meaningful and fully acceptable to management.

10. *Demonstrable Significance.* In addition to the foregoing the authors feel that a full consideration of criterion problems requires the introduction and discussion of the requirement that the criterion composite and its individual elements possess *demonstrable significance.*

In constructing predictor variables, the research investigator need not directly justify the use of any type of measure, since the responsibility for determining usefulness of the predictors rests on the criterion, and, of course, on the design of the research study.

In constructing criterion variables, however, it must be possible to demonstrate (by means other than the usual correlational techniques of validation studies) that the on-the-job behaviors measured do contribute to the objective of the sponsoring organization. If use of a criterion is justified only by showing its relationship to a better established criterion, the essential criterion problem will not have been solved. Justification of the second criterion is then required. This shift of responsibility cannot become an infinite regress. The criterion must, in the last analysis, be directly justifiable on logical grounds. To solve the criterion problem, it must be possible to show, as the authors would phrase it, that the criterion possesses demonstrable significance or, if you wish, "logical validity."

II. THE THEORETICAL SIGNIFICANCE OF COST ACCOUNTING UNITS TO THE SOLUTION OF THE CRITERION PROBLEM

In discussing the theoretical significance of cost accounting units, two approaches are possible. It will be profitable, we believe, to consider both.

The first grew out of a search for a common denominator or a common metric for combining various sub-criterion measures which are apparently quite different in nature. Suppose that for a typing job, the number of pages of typed copy produced is one sub-criterion variable and number of errors is a second criterion element. How can these two be combined to give an overall measure of typing proficiency suited to the needs of a particular hiring organization? One possible solution was suggested by Otis in the handling of two corresponding criterion elements obtained on keypunch operators.[2] In the given work situation, errors were found and corrected by a verifier. The total number of correctly punched cards could not be directly obtained. It was discovered, however, that something over 13 cards could be punched by the keypunch operator while the verifier corrected a single error. To obtain an overall criterion measure, 13 times the number of erroneous cards was subtracted from the total number of cards punched.

In this instance the *time* required for two different work units was employed as a means of expressing both measures in comparable units. The time required to correct an error was found to be 13 times that required to punch an original card. The implicit and

[2] Jay Otis in Stead, Shartle, et al., *Occupational Counseling Techniques* (New York: American Book Co., 1940).

obvious assumption in this combining procedure is that man-hours required for a given production unit is a fundamental measure of the degree of contribution to the efficiency of the organization. If the principle illustrated in this example is carried further, the possibility of converting man-hours required into the cost of punching a card or correcting an error becomes obvious. Without taking the time to elaborate too far at this point, the reader will note that with conversion to monetary units it would be possible to make allowance for possible differences in salary between keypunch operators and verifiers. While in this example such salary differences would probably be small, other cases could be cited where salary differences are greater and assume considerable importance. It would also be possible, for example, to obtain as a criterion measure the amount of supervisory time required by different workers in a given job assignment. Here, man-hours used as a common denominator would obviously fail properly to weight card punching, errors in punching, and supervisory time required into a composite defensible as a measure of the effect of workers in that job on the overall efficiency of the organization.

It should also be apparent that monetary units allow the expression of a considerable variety of additional factors in the same metric. Material wastage, accidents, overhead, etc., can, where they are important factors, be expressed in dollar units and combined to give an overall evaluation. A logical basis is thus obtained for combining elements which were originally expressed in units having no obvious relation to each other.

The second approach to the cost accounting criterion grew out of the previously mentioned close relationship between this concept and the criterion problem, "What is it that the criterion should measure?" The authors believe that a definition of "what it is that the criterion should measure" must stress that the only functions of the criterion are (1) to establish the basis for choosing the "best" battery from the experimental predictors, and (2) to provide an estimate of the validity of that battery. Logically, then, the question of "what it is that the criterion should measure" is subsidiary to the question of "what it is that the predictors should predict." Since, in practice, the predictors operate as selection instruments, the question can be rephrased again to ask "what is it that the selection process should accomplish?"[3]

Since the selection instruments determine which of a group of applicants will be admitted to an organization, the characteristics measured by the instruments must be related to the general objective of that organization. The instruments contribute to that objective to the degree that they select those applicants who will contribute most to the general objective of the organization.

In statistical processing, a battery of selection instruments is chosen through validation data to provide numerical scores having as close agreement with the criterion scores as possible. The battery is evaluated according to the degree of that relationship. A perfect relationship indicates perfect validity. Disregarding considerations such as time and expense, the criterion should, then, constitute the most perfect predictor obtainable and should, theoretically at least, be capable of effecting selection of those applicants who would contribute most to the general objective of the organization.

This line of reasoning leads in the authors' opinion to a definite answer to the question of "what it is that the criterion should measure." *The criterion should measure the con-*

tribution of the individual to the overall efficiency of the organization.

To say that the criterion should measure the contribution of the individual to the overall efficiency of the organization leads next to a definition of the objectives of the organization. The general objective of industrial firms is to make money. This statement carries no implication of an undesirable materialistic attitude. Even in the case of governmental agencies, and nonprofit organizations, it is desired to render service as efficiently as possible—and efficiency is measured in terms of monetary outlay. Monetary saving, being the objective of the organization, is the logical measure of the degree to which on-the-job activity of the individual contributes to or detracts from this overall objective. Only after we have succeeded in evaluating on-the-job performance in these terms can we be sure that our criterion measures conform to the objectives of the organization. It seems apparent that examination of the way in which a given employee affects overall efficiency requires that we determine the way in which his on-the-job activities produce objects or services of monetary value and the ways in which his errors, accidents, spoilage of materials, etc., result in monetary outlay.

While this paper is not primarily concerned with the nature of or techniques required to identify the component variables of a composite criterion, it might be noted that cost-accounting weights may be applied only to certain types of variables. Such variables must be expressed in units that can be evaluated in dollar terms. An object produced, an error or an accident can be evaluated in dollar terms; units of rating scales (as ordinarily constructed) cannot be so evaluated. It is believed, however, that unless criterion elements are of such a nature that they can be expressed in dollar units, their use as criterion measures cannot be directly justified and do not satisfy the requirement of logical face validity previously discussed.

[3]This may appear paradoxical in that the predictors are generally considered subsidiary to the criterion. The paradox is easily resolved, however, if the reader will bear in mind the distinction between the problem of establishing content of the predictor battery and that of understanding the objectives of the validation process. In establishing content, predictors are in practice subsidiary to the criterion. In relation to the objectives of the predictors and the criterion, understanding of the objectives of the criterion is subsidiary to understanding of the objectives of the predictors and of the selection process.

This does not mean that the authors propose to leave important areas of job success unmeasured. In practice it is better to employ scales of questionable validity and approximate weighting than to ignore an important area of job success entirely.

III. THE RELATIONSHIP BETWEEN THE COST ACCOUNTING CONCEPT AND TECHNIQUES OF CRITERION CONSTRUCTION

With this overall justification of the cost accounting concept, we will proceed to relate the general concept to techniques of criterion construction. In showing the relationship to these techniques, the concept can be further clarified. Techniques deriving from the cost accounting concept will be introduced in the course of this discussion.

As in the case of all criteria, the variables of a cost accounting criterion must be identified by means of some form of job analysis. In the development of cost accounting criteria, however, it is necessary in the analysis of the job to go beyond the mere identification of the component criterion variables and to determine the manner and extent to which the products or behaviors measured affect the efficiency of the organization. In this additional process, information basic to the construction of cost accounting criteria is obtained. Considerable attention will consequently be devoted to discussion of this phase of criterion construction.

Before proceeding to a discussion of this additional process, we should like to stress one point important in use of job analysis for identification of component criterion variables.

In job analysis for criterion purposes we believe that a clearcut distinction must be made between the end products of a given job and the job processes that lead to these end products. It may be pertinent to such other legitimate objectives of job analysis as training or position classification, to study the exact sequence of operations in the production of the finished product. The skills needed, the tools used, and the methods employed may all be needed for this purpose. Such information does not, however, give a direct answer to the major question, "how much does the employee produce and how good is it?" The criterion problem centers primarily in the quantity, quality and cost of the finished product. While work sequences and such factors as skill undoubtedly do indirectly affect efficiency of the organization, any attempt to demonstrate such effect will lead, first of all, to a demonstration of the way in which skill affects productivity and finally to a *tracing out* of the effect of the objects produced to determine what happens in the organization as a consequence of the production of errors, accidents or finished products. Such factors as skill are latent; their effect is realized in the end product. They do not satisfy the logical requirements of an adequate criterion.[4]

A tracing out of the exact nature and importance of the *effect* of each sub-criterion variable on the efficiency of the organization is the essential step which differentiates the dollar criterion from the more conventional techniques. This technique will, in our opinion, be found useful to the technician in the early stages of criterion construction in which job analysis is ordinarily employed. Its usefulness lies in the possibility provided of obtaining an early estimate of the relative importance of the various criterion elements, and a selection of those elements of most importance in arriving at a practicable approximation to a measure of the total effect of the individual on the efficiency of the organization. Evaluation in dollar units is one

[4]It is recognized that the relationship between job-process and job-product vary widely from job to job. There are, thus, some situations in which, after establishing the existence of a high correlation, job processes (because they may be easier to observe than job products) may be substituted as a criterion. They satisfy the logical requirement of criterion variables, however, only because of their demonstrated relationship to job products.

of the two variables determining the importance of the given criterion element to overall value to the organization. The second variable is the standard deviation of the given component criterion measures. From cost accounting evaluation and such rough estimates of the standard deviation as can be made before actual criterion measurement, the relative importance of the various possible sub-variables can be estimated. On this basis an intelligent and more exact judgment can be made as to which elements it is necessary to evaluate in constructing the criterion for the actual validation study.

Let us illustrate the tracing out process by taking as an example the criterion variables resulting from actual analysis of the job of a carpenter laying underflooring. We will assume that the criterion variables isolated are: (1) square feet of lumber wasted, (2) damage to equipment, (3) time of other personnel consumed, (4) accidents, (5) quality of finished product, (6) errors in finished product and (7) square feet of underflooring laid for a given time unit.

To trace out the effect of square feet of lumber wasted on the efficiency of the organization, we need only determine the cost of lumber. Records might be kept or supervisors might be questioned regarding individual differences in wastage and the value of the lumber wasted. These estimates will provide a basis for deciding whether or not to include lumber usage as a sub-criterion variable. If it were found that the cost of lumber used varied considerably from carpenter to carpenter, the variable would be included as a criterion element. If the cost of lumber were so little as to be of no consequence or if the amount wasted were practically the same for all carpenters, no measures of this variable would need to be obtained in the actual validation study.

If the equipment were supplied by the company, it would be necessary to determine the cost of repair and replacement. If this amount were significant, it would then be

necessary to estimate the extent of individual differences in such costs. The magnitude of these two factors would determine whether or not to include this as a criterion element.

In tracing out the effect of "time of other personnel consumed" we need only determine the salaries of the various individuals concerned. The actual component criterion variable, weighted in dollar terms, would be the total salary of all individuals concerned for the total amount of time wasted by the individual whose criterion is being computed. Such a variable would, of course, receive negative weighting.

It is realized that some difficulties may arise in assigning responsibility for time consumed. It may also be true in the case of supervisors that their sole function is supervision and that their time can be utilized for no other useful purpose. No general rule can be given for handling problems such as these.

If overhead is an appreciable factor in the total cost of the product it should be considered in evaluating the dollar value of the contributions of the subjects of the criterion study. Overhead costs, it should be stressed, are not properly prorated equally to each subject. The overhead cost per object produced is much less for an efficient worker than for an inefficient worker.

To trace out the effects of accidents, an evaluation of the cost of repairing the resulting damage would be required. Time of other personnel lost because of the accident, damage paid by the company because of personal injury, etc., would also enter into the cost accounting evaluation. Individual differences in frequency of accidents may, however, be found to be too small to warrant its consideration as a criterion variable in the case of carpenters. In this particular instance, also, the reliability of any possible criterion variable would bear close inspection.

Evaluation of quality and errors in the finished product would require the most laborious "tracing out." Here it would be necessary to determine by observation of, or interviews with, follow-up workers, the additional amount of their time required because of errors or deficiencies in quality. Such a follow-up, if made with complete thoroughness, might involve a large number of different types of subsequent workers and might even lead to the effect of such errors or variations in quality on the final evaluation of the finished structure. In any event the errors, etc., would be classified, and the average additional labor entailed as their consequence, determined. It would be neither feasible nor theoretically desirable to trace the effect of each individual error, since in doing so we would be allowing individual differences in efficiency of follow-up workers differentially to influence the criterion estimates of different subjects of the validation study. It can be seen that such tracing out may become complex since inadequacies in laying the underflooring may not only increase the time requirements for subsequent operations but may cause inadequacies in these subsequent operations which would have to be evaluated in turn.

Deficiencies in the final structure would present a special problem involving salability of the structure and reputation of the construction company. Some overall arbitrary judgment would probably have to be made by the administrators with necessary background for such a judgment.

Square feet of underflooring completed within a given time unit can be converted to dollar units by determining units completed per time interval by all carpenters in that given job classification, and dividing this into total wages for the time involved. In effect, we thus determine the cost of laying a square foot of underflooring or its value to the organization.

Given the cost accounting evaluations of the individual criterion elements and the best available estimates as to individual differences, the importance of each criterion element can now be estimated as the product of these two figures. In the example under

discussion it would probably be found that effect of equipment damage is negligible. Thus, this variable may well have been eliminated at the outset or at least after interviewing a construction supervisor. Lumber wasted may also be found unimportant because all workers use about the same amount. Quality of the finished product might possibly have too little significance to justify its evaluation. Whether or not these variables were included, the number of production units would probably be found most important.

It is believed that the tracing out of possible sub-criteria to their end effect on the efficiency of the organization will often lead to results at considerable variance with judgmental evaluations that the technician or management might have made without benefit of this additional information. In the case of the correction of punch-card errors referred to above, it took over 13 times as long, it will be recalled, to correct an error as to punch an original card. It is doubtful if a technician constructing a composite criterion would have judged errors to be so costly.

If the effect of such errors were traced further, it would be found, probably, that the number of errors escaping all checks is a function of the number of initial errors made. Such errors may in some organizations be extremely costly. Some may require effort equivalent to redoing a complete accounting job in addition to their effects on other scheduled work and on the reputation and morale of the organization. If the cost of correcting an initial error by a bank teller, for example, is 50¢ and one in every two hundred errors escaped initial detection and cost $100 on the average to find and correct, the total dollar weighting for each error would be one dollar instead of 50¢. In other words, the weighting would, on the average, be doubled. Experience with the cost of errors in statistical analysis suggests that such a finding would not be unusual.

A single clerical error, to cite an extreme

example in another type of work, in the computation of the amount of lead ballast in a ship being sold by the government for scrap resulted in a loss of several hundred thousand dollars to the seller.

This general approach of evaluating importance, in cost accounting terms, leads to consideration of elements that are important to evaluation of overall efficiency but which would probably be generally ignored by usual methods. If, for example, a good IBM tabulator operator produced twice as many usable reports as a poor one, it should be noted that even if they are paid on a piece-work basis, the rental of the machine is the same in both cases. In a cost accounting criterion, this cost would be taken into account along with many other such items. In the usual rating element or production record criteria, this factor would usually be ignored.

It may be helpful to list factors which will probably have to receive consideration in the proposed cost accounting type of employee evaluation. The following listing of such factors is not intended to be all-inclusive; a careful analysis of each job in relation to the organization will undoubtedly disclose factors peculiar to each.

(1) Average value of production or service units.

(2) Quality of objects produced or services accomplished.

(3) Overhead—including rent, light, heat, cost depreciation or rental of machines and equipment.

(4) Errors, accidents, spoilage, wastage, damage to machines or equipment through unusual wear and tear, etc.

(5) Such factors as appearance, friendliness, poise, and general social effectiveness, where public relations are heavily involved. (Here, some approximate or arbitrary value would have to be assigned by an individual or individuals having the required responsibility and background.)

(6) The cost of the time of other personnel consumed. This would include not only the time of the supervisory personnel but also that of other workers.

So far, we have considered briefly the relation of job analysis to the isolation of criterion variables and have discussed in some detail the nature and importance of the "tracing out" process to the construction of the cost accounting criterion. Given the criterion elements and the dollar weights obtained as a result of the "tracing out" process, the problems of technique of measurement for each criterion element and of combination of the measured elements still remain.

Both of these problems need only very brief consideration. Problems of technique of measurement, while of general importance to the criterion problem, bear no intimate relation to the concept of criterion construction under consideration. As we have indicated earlier, the measurements obtained must be in production unit form for ready application of the cost accounting procedures. Possible adaptations to rating measurement will be discussed later. Other important problems in technique of measurement, such as that of eliminating bias and that of obtaining adequate reliability, would be approached in the same manner as in any criterion construction problem.

The problem of weighting needs only brief consideration because its solution has in effect already been presented. Given the cost of production units, errors, etc., with all criterion units translated into dollar terms, the weighting problem is solved. All variables are expressed in a common denominator and may be directly summed to obtain an overall composite.

In the opinion of the authors, the most significant contributions of the cost accounting approach to criterion construction emerge in the combining of the criterion elements to yield an overall measurement of the workers' contribution to the effectiveness of the organization. Two distinct advantages of the cost accounting technique may be identified: (1) all measures are made in or translated into a single, meaningful metric—the dollar contribution to or detraction from the overall objective of the sponsoring organization; and (2) the resultant determination of the importance of each element in terms of its standard deviation. These two characteristics of the cost accounting approach completely solve the problem of combining criterion elements. The cost accounting units common to all elements make them directly additive; the reflection of importance directly as the standard deviation makes possible appropriate weighting by merely adding of raw score values of the several elements.

IV. SIGNIFICANCE OF COST ACCOUNTING UNITS TO RELATED SELECTION AND CLASSIFICATION PROBLEMS

It has been stressed in the introduction to this paper that the cost accounting approach to the criterion problem makes its most significant contribution, not only in converting the criterion variables to units most meaningful and satisfactory to an industrial sponsor of validation research, but also in offering a sound theoretical solution to a number of important problems in this general area of selection and classification. The ways in which cost accounting units offer a solution to problems internal to criterion construction have already been considered.

An evident extension of the usefulness of dollar units in combining component criterion variables is suggested in obtaining an integration of training cost, turnover, and on-the-job productivity into a single index showing the total picture of the potential value of an applicant. In relating cost of training to other criterion measures, it is evident that the employee whose services are terminated during training represents a loss to the company equal to the cost of selection and training. For the remaining employees, cost of training would have to be prorated over the time spent in the assignments toward which the training was directed. Turnover or attrition assume importance, then, when selection and/or training is costly. Of course, efficiency during the on-the-job training or warm-up should be considered along with formal training.

In a follow-up study of applicants selected by a given battery of predictors, training, attrition and production on-the-job (expressed in dollar terms) could be readily and logically integrated into a single value showing the total value or loss to the organization for the entire period of employment of a given individual. Cost of training would simply be subtracted from the total dollar value of his productivity during the period of his employment.

Elsewhere, one of the authors has shown how various statistical constants lend themselves to interpretations which should greatly aid the psychologist in convincing the sponsor of research studies of the appropriateness and adequacy of the criterion measures and the value of the resulting selection procedures.[5] Thus, saving effected per selected individual is given by the mean of the criterion scores of the selected group minus the mean of the population of applicants. The coefficient $r_{xy}\sigma_y$ gives the increase in dollar saving per unit increase in standard (z) predictor scores. In this formula r_{xy} is the validity coefficient and σ_y is the standard deviation in dollar terms of the criterion.

The validity coefficient itself gives the ratio of dollars saved by use of the predictors to select a given number of workers to the saving that would have resulted if selection of the same number of workers could have been made on the criterion itself; that is, it gives the per cent of perfect prediction achieved by use of a given set of selector instruments.

[5]H. E. Brogden, "On the interpretation of the correlation coefficient as a measure of predictive efficiency," *Journal of Educational Psychology* **37**, 65-76 (1946).

Criterion measures expressed in dollar terms allow determination of the interrelations of the cost of testing, the selection ratio, the standard deviation of the dollar criterion and the validity coefficient. Equations and graphs showing these interrelations have been presented elsewhere.[6] When test administration is expensive, the advantage that is expected from a highly favorable selection ratio is sharply diminished. In general, the role of the selection ratio in saving effected by testing undergoes considerable reevaluation.

Possibly the most important of the several related problems to be considered in this section arises in connection with differential classification. Even though regression weights of members of a test battery for predicting success in several assignments have been adequately established, the relative importance of amount of production, number of errors, etc., in the several assignments must still be considered in deciding upon the disposition of any given applicant.

Even though an applicant's predicted criterion score is equally high in both of two assignments, it does not follow that his placement in either of the jobs will be equally profitable to the company. Obviously a man who could do equally well as a janitor or as a manager would contribute much more to the objectives of the organization in the latter capacity. If the criteria for these two jobs were expressed in dollar units, the monetary benefits of this placement would be accurately estimated. In general, the use of dollar units for the criteria of all jobs provides a common denominator which makes it possible to compare an applicant's potential contribution in each of the several positions for which he might be hired.

When the predicted dollar criterion scores taken as deviations from the mean of the applicant population are added for all selected individuals for a given job, this sum is an expression of the dollar saving realized as a result of the selection process.

The sum of such predicted criterion scores for the selected cases (when expressed as deviations from the mean of applicants) gives the total saving expected from one of the several jobs under consideration. Furthermore, sums obtained in this way for each of several assignments are in comparable units and are directly additive. Thus, a "sum of sums" will indicate the total saving resulting from differential placement into several assignments. If the total saving is divided by total assigned cases, the average saving per selected individual may be obtained. This index of average saving will serve to show advantages of differential placement and may be used as a basis for determining optimal differential placement procedures.

V. DISCUSSION

A number of investigators have published procedures for weighting sub-criterion variables into a composite. Horst and Edgerton-Kolbe both proposed weighting to give the most reliable and "most predictable" composite.[7] Such procedures are believed by the authors to be unjustifiable unless the criterion measures involve only a single factor. Neither group nor specific factors can be neglected. Since such procedures provide the first principal axis of the configuration of criterion variables, some aspects of the job will most certainly be neglected or minimized. It might be noted in addition that in those situations where the supposition of a single factor would appear reasonable, weighting to provide the first principal axis would afford too little improvement over an equally weighted composite to justify the labor entailed.

[6]H. E. Brogden, "When testing pays off," *Personnel Psychology* **2**, 171-183 (1949).

[7]H. A. Edgerton and L. E. Kolbe, "The method of minimum variation for the combination of criteria," *Psychometrika* **1**, 183-187 (1936); Paul Horst, "Obtaining a composite measure from a number of different measures of the same attribute," *Psychometrika* **1**, 53-60 (1936).

Richardson has proposed a weighting procedure which has since been used in combining the sub-criterion variables so that they contribute equally to the covariance of the overall composite.[8] His procedure provides an interesting contrast to the above maximum reliability procedure. By Richardson's procedure the weights are large if the given criterion variable has low average correlation with the remaining sub-criterion variables; by the maximum reliability procedure, the weights are relatively small under these conditions.

We might stress here that weighting according to effect on overall efficiency as in use of dollar units is quite independent of the degree of correlation between the criterion elements. *If it costs 13 times as much to correct an error in card punching as to punch a card, the weights should be 13 and one regardless of whether the correlation between them is high and positive, negligible or high and negative.* If the correlation between two variables is very high, it may be considered expedient to obtain measures of one only and to employ it as a substitute for or as a predictor of the sum. If this is done, however, the substitute for the sum should be made to have the same dollar unit standard deviation as would the sum.

Toops has proposed combining sub-criterion variables according to "guessed beta's" or evaluations by qualified judges of the importance of each sub-criterion variable to overall on-the-job efficiency.[9] His procedure attempts, in part at least, to achieve by pooled judgment the same end that would be achieved by cost accounting criteria—assignment to each element a weight proportionate to the extent of its contribution to overall efficiency. It is difficult, however, in requesting judgments as to importance of a criterion variable to overall efficiency to disentangle the effect of the standard deviation of the sub-criterion variables from the value or importance of a unit of production, an error or some other unit of measurement of a criterion variable. Guessed beta's, in addition, are dependent upon the judgment of the person(s) doing the guessing.

These arguments will not be pressed too strongly; they are mentioned to emphasize the point that the obtained judgments are subjective and are not buttressed by analysis demonstrating the nature and importance of the ultimate effect on the organization of the individual production units, errors, etc., which enter into the final composite. When ratings are employed as criteria, it is probable that judgments such as that provided by guessed beta's will offer the most practicable rational basis for criterion combination.

It is suggested, however, that the procedure might be improved by explaining to the persons providing the judgment, how overall efficiency is best defined in terms of the effect on efficiency of operation of the organization, illustrating with a few examples the way in which various sub-criterion variables have their effect. In effect, then, an estimate would be obtained of the outcome of a cost accounting analysis.

VI. IMPLICATIONS OF THE COST ACCOUNTING CONCEPT FOR USE OF RATINGS

Within the limited resources usually available for validation studies, it is doubtful that all phases of production, errors, accidents, etc., can be economically evaluated through direct observation. Limitations as to time of completion and the intangible nature of certain important sub-criterion variables may, together with the above consideration, require frequent use of ratings to evaluate a number of the sub-criterion variables involved.

Application of the cost accounting proce-

[8]M. W. Richardson, "The combination of measures," in Paul Horst, ed., *The Prediction of Personal Adjustment* (New York: Social Science Research Council, 1941), pp. 377-401.

[9]H. A. Toops, "The selection of graduate assistants," *The Personnel Journal* **6**, 457-172 (1928).

dure to ratings presents certain special problems. With current rating procedures, the significance of the mean and standard deviation of the obtained ratings is questionable. It is probably more desirable, however, to include a rating with inaccurate scale units and weighting than to exclude any important criterion variable for lack of more objective evaluation procedure, since to exclude it entirely would be tantamount to estimating its weight as zero.

In many validation studies, ratings may have to be employed in evaluating all aspects of performance on the job. It is believed that the basic rationale of the proposed procedure does have implications, as yet quite untested, for procedures and format of such criterion ratings. Briefly the reasoning is as follows. Criterion ratings are substitutes for direct observations of effectiveness expressed in dollar units. The adequacy of ratings is, consequently, a function of the accuracy with which they estimate the measures for which they are substitutes. An obvious approach to the problem would be to state explicitly the objectives in the directions to the raters and to have the ratings themselves made in terms of the monetary value of individual differences in the area being measured. The disadvantage of this approach is that it as-

signs two judgments to the rater: first, he must evaluate the performance of the employee on the behavior under consideration; and secondly, the rater must make a second judgment in assigning a monetary value on that behavior.

What appears to be a more promising technique is that of determining in the tracing out process the continuum on which critical behaviors in a given area occur and to have raters evaluate in terms of these behaviors. If the dollar value of these several steps had also been determined in the tracing out process, these values could then be centrally applied during statistical processing to the ratings. The latter would then put greater stress on recording of observations and less on value judgments on the part of the raters.

In the absence of research data on the effect of such a modification in rating format and procedure on reliability, intercorrelations, and ease of administration, no claim of advantage can be made. It would be desirable, where production records are to be obtained for validation purposes, to collect ratings by both the proposed and some conventional procedure in order that their comparative merits may be determined by showing the accuracy with which they predict the production records.

PART FIVE

REWARDS

People work for diverse reasons. All, however, expect rewards, especially material rewards—money, vacations, retirement benefits, medical insurance and so forth. Although all the parts of the personnel management function are inextricably interrelated and interdependent, the rewards process, in particular, has a definite effect on both the personnel function and on the larger organizational system. If hiring, training, and monitoring procedures fail to some extent, the organization can usually continue functioning, albeit somewhat inefficiently. However, if reward procedures fail, the entire organizational structure is likely to fail with it.

Because such a major portion of rewards involve dollars and cents (the major part of most company budgets go to meet payroll and related expenditures), and because dollar profit is so vital to any organization, the rewards process permeates virtually every aspect of the organization.

The first article in this part, "Toward a Behavioral Science Theory of Wages," advances a theory of wages built not solely on an economic base, but on a broadly conceived plan that considers behavioral factors as well.

"Wage Inequities, Productivity and Work Quality" focuses on the relationships between quantity and quality of employee productivity, and employee perceptions regarding inequities in the amount of rewards provided for this production. A theoretical framework for understanding wage inequities is advanced, and data are described which provide a basis for experimentally testing the theory.

"Perceptions Regarding Management Compensation" relates the results of another experimental study. Its focus is the psychological aspects of compensation. Attention is drawn to questions concerning the importance attached to their pay by managerial personnel: individual perceptions regarding the amount of pay received, satisfaction with that pay and the needs which pay satisfies for people.

The relationship between the rewards an organization offers and personnel commitment to that organization is the subject of the final article. The strength of a person's commitment to an organization is influenced by the rewards he has received from the organization and the kinds of experiences he has had to undergo in order to receive these rewards. The author concludes that the greater the obstacles the person has overcome in order to obtain the organization's rewards, the greater his commitment.

TOWARD A BEHAVIORAL SCIENCE THEORY OF WAGES

David W. Belcher

Economic wage theory is less than completely satisfactory. In traditional economic theory, the economy is seen as a system of mutually interacting parts in which all transactions are subject to the influence of maximization of personal gain pursued in a stern, impersonal market. Human behavior is held to be rigorously bound by the rules of market behavior. Labor economists point to the inaccuracy of this view when applied to buying and selling labor's services and stress the range of variables—political, psychological, social, and ethical—that impinge on wage determination. Vigorous attempts have been made to build an economic wage theory that accommodates observed wage determination processes and institutions.[1] The attempts have been most successful in explaining the general wage level of a firm, least successful in explaining the internal wage structure, and silent on the effectiveness of wages as motivation.

Meanwhile, behavioral scientists in their study of individuals, groups, and organizations have turned up numerous bits and pieces of evidence that hold promise of filling the gaps left in explanations of wage determination by both general economic theorists and labor economists. This article is an attempt to extract from behavioral science findings and analyses those that appear pertinent to wage theory.

The material has been selected and organized to attempt to fill the largest gaps in economic wage theory. Thus the topics covered are (1) the wage level of the firm, (2) the internal wage structure of the firm, and (3) money as motivation. Because the attention here is to behavioral factors, these factors are employed when an economic explanation would also serve. An explanation is accepted as behavioral (not economic) unless it can be reduced readily to cost-per-unit-of-output terms.[2]

THE WAGE LEVEL OF THE FIRM

The decision to participate in (join and stay with) an organization has been explained in terms of the inducements-contributions utility balance.[3] In this formulation, the decision to participate in the organization is a function of the balance between the utilities of inducements offered by the organization and contributions made by the participant. The components are (1) the perceived desirability of leaving, which is a function of (a) the individual's satisfaction with his present job, and (b) his perception of alternatives that do not involve his leaving, and (2) the perceived ease of leaving the organization, which is a function of the number of perceived alternatives outside the organization.

Another formulation conceives of labor markets as social institutions. Employers tend to pay what other employers pay in the community and industry. They rely on wage surveys and social pressures discourage paying much above what other employers are paying. Unions reinforce this tendency by insisting that employers who pay below what

From David W. Belcher, "Toward a Behavioral Science Theory of Wages," **Academy of Management Journal** 5 (2), 102–116 (1962). Reprinted by permission.

[1] George W. Taylor and Frank C. Pierson, eds., *New Concepts in Wage Determination* (New York: McGraw-Hill, 1957), is the most successful.

[2] It is recognized that this definition of economic factors is unduly restrictive for most purposes.

[3] James G. March and Herbert A. Simon, *Organizations* (New York: Wiley, 1958); C. I. Barnard, *The Functions of the Executive* (Cambridge, Mass.: Harvard University Press, 1938), Chap. 1.

other employers are paying raise their wages. These institutional forces lead employers to set wages in line with the community or industry.[4]

A third formulation emphasizes the power and influence of firms and unions. Large firms have influence because of their size, money, the influence of the "power elite."[5] "Wage leaders" have influence in labor markets. Unions are political institutions and exert power upon the labor market through their size, money, and the influence of their leaders.[6]

Once participants have joined the organization, it is possible to conceive of non-financial rewards as at least partial substitutes for financial rewards. Representative non-financial rewards are (1) job satisfaction, interest and involvement, (2) power pay (a job of greater importance, exclusive jurisdiction over the job), (3) authority pay (promotion, more authority), (4) status pay (giving the individual higher status), (5) privilege pay (giving subordinates opportunities for informal relationships with people of higher authority).[7] The possibility of substitution of non-financial rewards for financial rewards is limited, however, because status tends to equal financial reward in the long run.[8] Non-financial rewards may be more effective than financial rewards in keeping employees on the same job because automatic increases tend to destroy the incentive for stability and merit increases involve difficult administrative decisions.[9]

[4]Robert Dubin, *The World of Work* (Englewood Cliffs, N.J.: Prentice-Hall, 1958), pp. 229-230.

[5]Robert A. Dahl, in Robert A. Dahl, Mason Haire, and Paul F. Lazarsfeld, eds., *Social Science Research on Business: Product and Potential* (New York: Columbia University Press, 1959), pp. 25-26.

[6]Arthur M. Ross, *Trade Union Wage Policy* (Berkeley: University of California Press, 1948). Ross is a labor economist but his classic work on unions as political organizations is a behavioral analysis.

[7]Dubin, *op. cit.*, pp. 241-246.

[8]Delbert C. Miller and William H. Form, *Industrial Sociology* (New York: Harper & Brothers, 1951), p. 370.

[9]Dubin, *op. cit.*, p. 238.

INTERNAL WAGE STRUCTURE

Economic theory has perhaps had least success in explaining the internal wage structure of the firm. It is here where a behavioral science wage theory should find its greatest usefulness.

Social Norms

One formulation serving to account for occupational wage differentials emphasizes the force of tradition. The institutions of the community provide customs and traditions which are brought into the organization. The organization and groups within it develop customs and traditions. Some jobs are regarded as more important than others because tradition decrees that these jobs have more prestige. Occupational groups have customs and rituals that affect the position of the occupation in the structure.[10] Wage differential between jobs in the same plant are correlated with the degree of skill the jobs once possessed rather than the skill required today.[11]

Simon's social norms theory of executive compensation is similar. He postulates that executive salaries are determined by requirements of "internal consistency" of the salary scale with the formal organization and the norms of proportionality between salaries of executives and their subordinates (norms of span of control and ratio of executive's salary to that of his immediate subordinates). Simon described acceptance of the rate for junior executives paid by other employers as economic determination. In the terms used above even this could be called a social norm.[12]

The Just Price of medieval times, perhaps not unrelated to the "fair wage" of the crafts,

[10]Miller and Form, *op. cit.*, p. 370.

[11]W. L. Warner and J. O. Low, *The Social System of the Modern Factory: The Strike, a Social Analysis* (New Haven: Yale University Press, 1947).

[12]Herbert A. Simon, "The Compensation of Executives," *Sociometry*, pp. 32-35 (March, 1957).

provides a wage distribution established from a pre-established status distribution.[13]

Scott reports that there is a close relationship between total rewards and occupational status, but not a close relationship between earnings and occupational status.[14]

Single Factor Explanations

A number of factors have been suggested as explanations of occupational wage differentials. For example, Jeremy Bentham[15] suggested two criteria: (1) that wages of occupations should accord with the social utility of the function performed and (2) that they should accord with the disagreeableness of the occupation. Clark postulated that wages of occupations are correct when people of equal ability receive equal wages in all occupations.[16] Tawney suggested sufficient income to permit a man to perform his work, insisting that what a man is worth is a matter between his own soul and God.[17]

Jaques suggested freedom to act as a factor explaining occupational differentials. He suggested that pay for an occupation (at least at the executive level) be determined by the length of time during which the incumbent is free to act without checking with his superior.[18] "Behavior control" correlates highly with status according to Caplow.[19]

Sociology of Labor Markets

Sociological analysis of types of labor market indicates the variety of social forces impinging on occupational wages and how different forces govern the different markets. The fact that a given organization may be operating in several types of labor markets accounts for much of the difficulty in maintaining internal wage structures. The following analysis leans heavily on Caplow's *Sociology of Work.*[20]

The Bureaucratic Labor Market. A bureaucracy is an organized hierarchy of social positions complete in itself without reference to the character of individuals who occupy the positions. The key words which identify bureaucracy are rationality and impersonality. Perhaps all large complex organizations are bureaucratic. In a bureaucracy wages are assumed to be proportionate to status rather than vice versa.

The bureaucratic labor market is insulated from economic considerations by three factors. The labor supply problem is solved in large part because recruits enter at the bottom of the hierarchy and are moved up to positions structured in terms of qualifications. The crucial market situations involve promotion and transfer rather than recruiting. The main labor supply problem in a bureaucracy involves the individuals which the bureaucracy cannot train itself, e.g., accountants, engineers, physicians. Labor demand is largely to fill low level positions. In both demand and supply, the closed bureaucracy is largely a self-regulating system. A third insulator is the importance of non-financial incentives, the main one tenure.

In theory, wage determination in a bureaucracy is an administrative decision based upon rational principles. The wage rank order must follow the rank order of training and experience required by positions. Status and wage must be correlated perfectly. Both qualifications and pay for positions with similar work and responsibility must be equal.

[13]Theodore Caplow, *The Sociology of Work* (Minneapolis: University of Minnesota Press, 1954); John W. Baldwin, "The Medieval Theories of the Just Price," *Transactions of the American Philosophical Society* (New Series) **49** (4), (July, 1959).

[14]W. H. Scott, et al., *Technical Change and Industrial Relations* (Liverpool University Press, 1956).

[15]Jeremy Bentham, *A Table of the Springs of Action.*

[16]Harold F. Clark, *Economic Theory and Correct Occupational Distribution* (New York: Columbia University, 1931), p. 57.

[17]Richard H. Tawney, *The Acquisitive Society* (New York: Harcourt, Brace and Company, 1920).

[18]Elliott Jaques, *Measurement of Responsibility* (London: Tavistock Publications, 1951).

[19]Caplow, *op. cit.,* p. 55.

[20]*Ibid.,* pp. 142-176.

In practice, (1) the job classification system is superimposed on a pre-existing wage structure, (2) wages for particular occupations should correspond to community rates after allowing for non-financial rewards, (3) most bureaucracies have a pay range for each job.

Conflicts among the stated principles require frequent revision in wage structure. The wage survey creates problems because (1) some of the occupations are not found elsewhere in the community and some only in other bureaucracies (in the latter case, circularity exists), and (2) it brings to the supposedly rational structure inequities attributable to political pressure, occupational monopoly, or historical accident. The requirement that differences in qualifications be reflected by differences in pay creates conflicts between occupations with only a few subdivisions and those finely divided. Making distinctions between the occupations and keeping the parts in line is difficult.

These problems suggest that a bureaucratic wage structure can only operate with reasonable success in complete isolation or by steady expansion permitting a generous promotion policy. In a stable or declining organization, perhaps the only answer is a steady increase in non-financial rewards. The fact that few bureaucracies are completely closed creates further problems.

The Industrial Labor Market. This is the market for semiskilled labor. Labor supply depends in theory on the local labor force and competition for workers, but in practice is largely irrelevant for wage determination because of collective bargaining. The demand is fluctuating because of freedom of lay-off and the type of demand is determined by the employer.[21] The range of wages is the legal minimum (floor) and the "going wage" set by collective bargaining (ceiling). Semi-skilled factory labor can be hired at a wide range of prices.

Custom strongly affects these wages. Wage changes are determined with reference to wages previously paid for that kind of work. The higher the proportion of women and minority groups, the lower the average age of working force, the smaller the community, the lower the wage level even with unions. The larger the labor force, the farther north, the smaller the proportion of the population in industrial employment, the higher the wage level. Wage differentials between jobs in the same plant are also influenced by custom and are roughly correlated with the skill assumed necessary for the job. This is closer to skill once required than to skill required today. The occupational hierarchy operates on the assumption that variations in skill required are apparent and easily classified. The assumption is invalid. When a differential exists between two jobs, the holders of the more highly paid job assume it requires more skill and resist any alteration of the differential. Thus both management and union are hesitant to change differentials.

Wage differentials are changed by technological changes, rationalization, and group power struggles. But these changes are almost entirely independent of the market and usually of contract negotiation.

Within the industrial plant there is considerable mobility between departments and jobs, usually in the direction of higher wage rates. A consequence is that in many plants, the high paid jobs are held by high seniority workers, and the wage structure is more closely correlated with seniority than skill. In these cases, factory employment is tending toward bureaucracy expressed as high wages paid to those with greatest seniority. In fact, close analysis of the industrial labor market reveals several similarities to the bureaucratic labor market.

The Craft Labor Market. In theory, labor

---

[21]Robert L. Raimon, "The Indeterminateness of Wages of Semiskilled Workers," *Industrial and Labor Relations Review* pp. 180-194 (January, 1953).

supply of a craft is fixed and the demand variable. Identification is with the craft rather than the employer. Because fluctuating labor demand and fixed labor supply would mean fluctuating wages and cut-throat competition, the craft union operates like a monopolist selling a standardized product. The medieval solution was the "Just Price"; the modern slogan of the "fair wage" carries the same ethical implication.

The wage in prosperity may be the highest price consistent with full employment of the craft. The lowest wage in depression seeks to assure subsistence of all active craftsmen. Adjustment to changed wage rates requires craft control of the distribution of work.

The function of craft control over conditions of sale of craft labor is to preserve the system of selling labor in standardized units by preventing the employer from modifying either the system or the attractiveness of work. Craft markets are essentially local and craft controls operate locally.

These arrangements are inconsistent with both bureaucratic and industrial arrangements. Various compromises are worked out when craftsmen are employed under these systems. One approach is to pay craft wages but withhold all or part of the benefits available to other employees.

The Market for Professional Services. A large proportion of professionals are salaried employees of bureaucracies. Analysis of the market for free professionals not only illustrates the problems of salary determination of professionals in bureaucracies, but provides clues to markets for other types of individualized services.

The supply of professionals is fixed in the short run and tends to decrease with increased demand in that professional controls are tightened. Demand for professional services is highly variable.

The pricing of professional services is subject to a special ideology. Professionals, in theory, are perfectly non-interchangeable.

The value of a unit of work is theoretically unmeasurable and not convertible to money.

The fixed supply and varying demand permit the professionals, like the crafts, to fix the price but the professional ethic discourages attempts to standardize prices. Where the professional ethic prevails, the only remaining criterion of payment is what the market will bear, *i.e.,* ability to pay. Basing remuneration on the ability to pay of the client rather than upon the value of the service has been the chief feature of the market for professional services. Recently, however, a trend toward standardized prices in the professions has appeared. The principal concerns of the professional association are to establish minimum prices and to restrict price competition.

The Market for Common Labor. The supply of casual labor is highly variable. Demand is fairly constant in the long run but varies sharply in the short run. Both are highly elastic.

Although the conditions appear to approach the classical market, they do not. Public opinion opposes a continuous price range on ethical grounds and insists that prices be quoted in round figures. Nonmonetary considerations exist and preferences for certain prices. The going wage is a round figure and persists for long periods.

The market for domestic and farm labor is similar to the market for common labor in that the going wage tends to be a round figure and persists for long periods. Usually such workers are isolated and unorganized. Often remuneration is partially in kind. The employer-employee relationship may be close. Personal preferences may result in wages two or three times the going rate or almost zero. The market may go out of balance without reference to general economic conditions, resulting in zero supply or zero demand.

The market for laundry workers in large laundries and for migrant farm workers on large farms has similarities to the common labor market but also to the industrial labor market.

Other Types of Labor Market. The market for unique services (entertainment, sports, journalism, politics, advertising, and certain areas of management) is similar to the market for professionals in that supply is one individual and value of the service is difficult to measure. It is different from the professional market, however, in that the value of unique services is often speculative and is set by individual bargaining or bidding.

The market for commission salesmen and sales managers is another which may offer wages out of any proportion to the individual talent or skill. The strategic element may be the personal relations aspect of the salesman's activity. In most cases, however, salesmen appear to require knowledges and skills quite easily priced in a bureaucratic system.

This sociological analysis of various types of labor markets serves to emphasize the different factors operating in each. The typical large employer must reconcile the various forces operating in all or most of these markets in creating his internal wage structure.

The Employer As A
Wage-Setting Institution

Analysis of the various types of labor markets emphasizes the fact that wage determination is a decision-making process that must adapt to numerous, often conflicting influences. To accomplish the purposes of the organization, the employer graduates the pay scale to correspond with the ranking of the productive contribution of jobs. Jobs that are more important to the purposes of the organization are paid more money. This is done to see that work gets done and that employees have an incentive to move to more important jobs.[22]

Job evaluation systems provide a set of norms for classifying jobs. Although they tend to simulate economic reasoning in their quest of objectivity, they remain largely aids to decision-making.

Group Power Theory

Occupational differentials are derived at least in part from group pressures. The strengths and direction of group pressures are functions of (1) identification of individuals with the group, (2) uniformity of group opinion, (3) group control over the environment, (4) interaction within the group, (5) cohesiveness of the group, (6) the amount of intergroup competition, (7) the extent to which group pressures support organizational demands, (8) technology of the plant. Identification of the individual with the group is a function of (1) prestige of the group, (2) goals shared, (3) frequency of interaction, (4) number of needs satisfied by the group, (5) amount of competition among group members, (6) position of the group. The position of the group is a function of (1) success of the group, (2) average status level of members, (3) visibility of the group. Visibility of the group is a function of its (1) distinctiveness, (2) size, (3) rate of growth.[23]

The organization of the work contributes significantly to the behavior of work groups. Jobs in the middle range are most susceptible to successful group action. These are the semiskilled jobs discussed above as characterizing the industrial labor market. They are not well defined in the labor market. Uncertainty about the value of the job, ambiguity of status and skill make for successful group pressure.

These group pressures are an important force operating upon occupational differentials. The worker is occupationally oriented even when a semiskilled factory worker and behaves as if he belonged to a highly specific occupational group. Certain jobs are ranked as more important or desirable and are ex-

---

[22]Dubin, *op. cit.,* p. 233.

[23]March and Simon, *op. cit.,* pp. 59-61, 65-68.

pected to have higher pay. Over a period of time the action of groups perfects the correlation. The union as well as management is forced by these pressures.[24]

Status has become a group phenomenon and since income tends to be correlated with status, income tends to be based upon group membership rather than skill inherent in the job. All relations tend to become social relations. Social stratification ensues whenever groups have different social characteristics or functions. All groups tend to regard themselves as separate from and superior to other groups.[25]

MONEY AS MOTIVATION

Economic wage theory assumes maximization of personal gain as a prime mover of the system. Personal gain to labor is measured in wages. Behavioral scientists view this formulation as too narrow a view of motivation. A behavioral science theory of wages should specify the significance of wages as a motivator and the conditions under which wages are effective as motivation.

Definition

An idea of the complexity of motivation may be obtained from Lazarfeld's definition. He finds it necessary to employ a three-dimensional scheme involving (1) time (present only or including the future), (2) scope (specific or general), and (3) dynamics (passive or driving). Thus motivation is a disposition of general scope with the implication that it drives the bearer toward activities that bridge the present and future. This definition serves to distinguish motivation from preferences, attitudes, wants, expectations, tendencies, and intentions.[26]

Freudian Motivation Theory

Freudian motivation theory postulates the existence in human beings at least in advanced cultures a common hierarchy of needs—(1) physiological, (2) safety, (3) social, (4) esteem, (5) self-actualization. Higher order needs do not appear until the lower level needs are sufficiently satisfied to permit attention to the former. Satisfied needs do not motivate.[27]

Money may be postulated to purchase satisfaction of (1) physiological needs, (2) many safety needs, (3) esteem needs that may be satisfied off the job. By the same reasoning, money (1) only indirectly aids in satisfying social needs, and (2) can only help in satisfying self-actualization needs by removing obstacles. By implication, satisfaction of social, esteem, and self-actualization needs on the job requires satisfactions other than money.[28]

Self Theory

According to self theory, man lives in a universe of events and objects endowed with meanings by man himself through social definitions couched in language. The individual derives his plans of action from the roles he plays and the statuses he occupies in the groups with which he feels identified—his reference groups. His attitudes toward himself as an object are the best indices to these plans of action, and hence to the action itself, in that they are the anchoring points from which self-evaluations and other evaluations are made. These attitudes serve to guide him even in relatively unfamiliar situations.[29]

[24]Leonard R. Sayles, *Behavior of Industrial Work Groups* (New York: Wiley, 1958).

[25]Miller and Form, *op. cit.,* pp. 372, 161.

[26]Lazarsfeld, in Dahl, Haire and Lazarsfeld, eds., *op. cit.,* pp. 113-114.

[27]A. H. Maslow, *Motivation and Personality* (New York: Harper & Brothers, 1954); Douglas McGregor, *The Human Side of Enterprise* (New York: McGraw-Hill, 1960).

[28]Charles D. McDermid, "How Money Motivates Men," *Business Horizons,* pp. 93-100 (Winter, 1960).

[29]C. Addison Hickman, and Manford H. Kuhn, *Individuals, Groups, and Economic Behavior* (New York: The Dryden Press, 1956); George H. Meade, *Mind, Self, and Society* (Chicago: Chicago University Press, 1936).

Motivation according to self theory is imbedded in the attitudes, values, and roles of individuals in various groups. It becomes a matter of investigation whether the significance of the various motivators (including money) are similar for all groups in our culture[30] or differ between occupational groups.[31]

Social Channelling of Motivation

Motivation, according to this view, is built into the entire social system. It is regarded as highly appropriate to earn a living, "get ahead," provide financial and other security for one's family. By the time a person goes to work, he carries with him these fundamental motivations appropriate to being an employee. Thus every employee comes to a company perceiving the appropriate channels of motivation along which his behavior can be directed. These channels of motivation are the product of society and are given specific form in each business organization. Labor unions operate within the motivational system shared by all citizens and their goals are not concerned with changing the motivation system of society but with influencing management policy in effecting specific rewards for workers in the form of incentives for work. Incentives for work provide the visible rewards for staying within motivational channels—to join an organization, stay with it, and improve performance.[32]

Motivation is intimately tied up with institutional patterns of behavior of society. People behave the way they do in economic organizations because behavior patterns have become institutionalized in such organizations. It cannot be assumed that self-interest

means the same thing in different organizational contexts. The organization molds behavior.[33] The importance of money as a motivator apparently varies also by occupational group[34] and social group.[35]

Work Theory

Many factors outside the work place, some beyond the control of management, shape work conduct and the pattern of social relationships inside the work place—economic variables, social and cultural variables. To get at the meanings people assign to their work, it is necessary to know their group identifications—the groups whose norms and controls they take their cues from. This in turn leads to an analysis of the degree to which different groups embrace different cultural values that define the significance of work.[36]

Apparently most men in our culture will work if they have no need for money—for self-expression, for social relationships, to give meaning to life. There are, however, differences between occupational groups in reasons for working. Professional men cite interest in their field or sense of achievement. Managers and sales people cite keeping occupied and active. At lower levels, the job becomes more important as mere activity.[37]

Studies of non-literate societies report that people work because they must, because everyone else works, and because it is the tradition to work. As among ourselves, labor is performed by non-literate people for reward. But the rewards differ widely in different societies, both in the forms they take and

[30]Dubin, *op. cit.,* p. 228; Miller and Form, *op. cit.,* p. 382.

[31]Scott, et al, *op. cit.;* Talcott Parsons, "Motivation of Economic Activities," *Canadian Journal of Economics and Political Science,* pp. 187-200 (May, 1940).

[32]Robert Dubin, *Working Union-Management Relations* (Englewood Cliffs, N.J.: Prentice-Hall, 1958), p. 16.

[33]Robert Dubin, *Human Relations in Administration* (New York: Prentice-Hall, 1951), p. 27.

[34]Scott, et al., *op. cit.*

[35]W. Lloyd Werner, et al., *Social Class in America* (New York: Harper, 1949).

[36]Harold L. Wilensky, in *Research in Industrial Human Relations* (New York: Harper & Brothers, 1957), p. 45.

[37]Nancy C. Morse and Robert S. Weiss, "The Function and Meaning of Work and the Job," *American Sociological Review,* pp. 191-198 (April, 1955).

in the degree to which they act as drives. In non-industrial societies, the rewards are direct. Wages, where they exist, are usually paid in kind.

In a vast number of non-literate societies, as in our own, the drive for prestige constitutes a powerful psychological factor in determining behavior. The prestige that accrues to the hard worker, the fast worker, the careful worker, the competent worker, is a significant factor in motivating labor in most societies.[38]

Ego-Enhancement

According to Stagner, workers frequently are not conscious of their real motives. No single specific kind of satisfaction can be cited as the key to worker motivation. Workers want more of whatever is needed for satisfaction at any given time: pay, security, praise, recognition, self-expression. In the case of executives, ego-motivation rather than economic motivation is predominant—achievement, prestige, self-expression, power, recognition. Man is concerned about his status. He wants enough food, clothing, other material things to protect him from hardship, but beyond this, he is trying to keep or improve his standing in the community. How he compares with others, with his own ambition, are the crucial questions. Economic motives may in some cases be significant and not in others. Ego-satisfactions frequently have more attraction power for the worker and the executive alike.[39]

Argyris emphasizes self-actualization as the primary motivator. He defines self-actualization as growth toward independence through interaction with others.[40] This may or may not conflict with ego-enhancement.

Variety of Motives

To Brown, there are three motives for working, each related in varying degrees to the work itself: (1) the work may be done as an end in itself, (2) the work may be carried out willingly for other motives directly associated with the work situation (comradeship, status, power), (3) the work may be carried on for genuinely extrinsic motives (money for a variety of purposes).[41]

He takes the position that: (1) There is no one ideal incentive. Incentives vary from one culture to another, one firm to another, one individual to another. (2) The law of diminishing returns applies to all material incentives. (3) Incentives may conflict with other motives. (4) Money is of less significance than had been supposed. (5) But in our culture motives tend to become monetized. People have been taught that money is the key to satisfaction, so when they feel something is wrong with their lives they naturally ask for more money.[42]

Complexity

In motivation theory, the single motive and the monotonic function are objectionable. Two steps must be taken. Factor A must be shown to be effective. Then an increase in Factor A must be shown to produce an increment in the dependent variable. If piece-rate incentive plans are to be criticized because (1) they rely on a single motive, and (2) they assume "more reward—more performance," then the same conclusion must be reached about participation, communication, decentralization, and delegation until proven otherwise.[43]

Satisfiers vs. Dissatisfiers

The factors that make for job satisfaction

[38]Melville J. Herskovitz, *Economic Anthropology* (New York: Knopf, 1952), pp. 122-123.

[39]Ross Stagner, "Psychological Aspects of Industrial Conflict, Motivation," *Personnel Psychology*, pp. 1-15 (Spring, 1950).

[40]Chris Argyris, *Understanding Organizational Behavior* (Homewood, Illinois: The Dorsey Press, 1960), pp. 9-10.

[41]J. A. C. Brown, *The Social Psychology of Industry* (Pelican, 1954), p. 206.

[42]*Ibid.,* p. 202.

[43]Mason Haire, in Dahl, Haire and Lazarsfeld, eds., *op. cit.,* p. 84.

seem to be different from those that make for job dissatisfaction. The factors that make for job satisfaction are those related to the job, to events that indicate success in the performance of work, and to the possibility of growth. The factors that make for job dissatisfaction are, conditions that surround the job—supervision, interpersonal relations, physical working conditions, salary, company policy and practice, benefits, and job security. When these latter factors deteriorate, job dissatisfaction ensues and performance suffers—job dissatisfaction actually appears to *interfere* with work. But improving them does not provide job satisfaction, nor increase performance beyond the neutral point.

The job factors are the motivators. Improvement in them can increase performance beyond the neutral position. Money earned as a reward for outstanding performance becomes a reinforcement of recognition and achievement (motivators).[44]

Motivation As a Function of Organization

Much current work on organization theory suggests that organizations can be designed to foster motivation. Likert's modified theory of organization employs a "linking pin function" to tie group communication, influence, decision-making, and thus motivation to the goals of the organization.[45]

McGregor emphasizes arranging work so that people can accomplish their own goals by directing their own efforts toward organizational objectives. His "target approach" stresses the requirement of a commitment before motivation can be expected.[46] Bakke's fusion process appears to have the same basic

objective.[47] Drucker's management by objective approach seeks to achieve motivation by linking personal goals and organizational goals.[48]

Herzberg's study of motivation concludes that: (1) improving conditions surrounding work cannot motivate—they only encourage enjoyment away from work, (2) motivation requires: (a) jobs that demand performance and provide achievement, growth, and responsibility, (b) supervisors who can plan, evaluate, and reward good work, (c) selecting people who fit the work, (d) standards of performance that measure work, (e) rewards geared to performance.[49]

Also applicable here are studies of the geographic ecology of motivation. The structure of the group in the work situation in terms of possibility of interaction has an effect on motivation.[50]

Of equal applicability are the studies showing how individuals are compelled by the group to adopt common ways of behaving. The worker seeks to express his needs by attempting to pull the group in conformity with him. But the group possesses the power to compel the individual to conform. The conflict between individuals and the group under individual incentive plans observed by Whyte, Roy, Dalton, and Sayles is especially pertinent.[51] Methods suggested to resolve this

[44]Frederick Herzberg, et al., *The Motivation to Work* (New York: Wiley, 1959), 2nd ed.

[45]Rensis Likert, "A Motivational Approach to a Modified Theory of Organization and Management," in *Modern Organization Theory* (New York: Wiley, 1958), pp. 184-217.

[46]McGregor, *op. cit.*

[47]E. W. Bakke, *The Fusion Process* (New Haven: Yale University Labor and Management Center, 1953).

[48]Peter F. Drucker, *The Practice of Management* (New York: Harper and Brothers, 1954).

[49]Herzberg, et al., *op. cit.*

[50]C. R. Walker and R. H. Guest, *The Man On the Assembly Line* (Boston: Harvard, 1952); E. Jaques, *The Changing Culture of a Factory* (New York: Dryden Press, 1952).

[51]Melville Dalton, "Economic Incentives and Human Relations," in IRRA, *Industrial Productivity* (1951); Robert H. Roy, "Do Wage Incentives Reduce Costs," *Industrial and Labor Relations Review,* pp. 195-208 (January, 1952); Donald Roy, "Quota Restriction & Goldbricking in a Machine Shop," *American Journal of Sociology,* pp. 427-442 (March, 1952); Leonard R. Sayles, "The Impact of Incentives on Inter-Group Work Relations—A Management and Union Problem," *Personnel,* pp. 483-490 (May, 1957); William Foote Whyte, et al., *Money and Motivation* (New York: Harper, 1955).

conflict by increased personal involvement of group members do not consistently increase motivation.[52]

The modern tendency to treat organizations as social systems linking individuals to groups and groups to the organization would seem to hold major promise for motivation.

Goal Path Theory

Kahn offers a goal path theory of motivation. Motivation involves goals sought, paths for goal attainment perceived, and barriers which stand between the individual and the goal. Motive consists of two parts: (1) the *need* within the individual and, (2) the *goal*—an object in the environment seen as a source of need satisfaction. The approach the individual takes will depend upon what he sees as a *path* toward his goal and the *freedom* (absence of barriers) to take the path.

Thus if a worker sees high productivity as a path leading to attainment of one or more of his personal goals and is free to produce, he will be a high producer. If he sees low productivity as a path to his goals, he will be a low producer. Among workers with a high need for money and freedom to pursue it, 66 per cent of those who saw high productivity as instrumental to the goal of making more money were high producers. Among workers of equally high need for money and equal freedom, but who did not perceive high production as instrumental to their goals, only 22 per cent were high producers.[53]

March-Simon Motivation Thesis

In this formulation, motivation to produce is a function of (1) the character of the evoked set of alternatives, (2) the perceived consequences of evoked alternatives, and (3) the individual goals in terms of which alternatives are evoked. The evoked set of alternatives is a function of (1) the existence of other work alternatives, (2) supervisory practices, (3) the task, (4) the system of rewards, and (5) the work group. The perceived consequences are functions of (1) the perceived alternatives to participation, (2) characteristics of individuals, (3) group pressures, (4) dependence of rewards upon productivity, and (5) operationality of criteria for rewards. Individual goals are a function of (1) the individual's identification with groups, (2) the strength and direction of group pressures, (3) the extent group pressures support organizational demands, and (4) basic values derived from earlier experience.[54]

Non-Motivation

No discussion of motivation can ignore the areas where motivation appears impossible. Herzberg, for example, concludes his study of motivation by insisting that motivation is impossible on machine tending jobs and in bureaucracies and that further rationalization of work prevents motivation on many jobs.[55] It is possible that many clerical, retail sales, custodial, and domestic occupations where promotional possibilities are nonexistent fall into the same category. Wilensky believes we are headed toward an organization of work where only a small group in control will be work-committed and the mass will continue to retreat from work.[56] These conclusions appear to support the wisdom of the March-Simon formulation separating motivation to participate from motivation to produce.[57] If worker motivation becomes impossible on

---

[52]Robert Dubin, in Robert Tannenbaum, Irving R. Weschler, and Fred Massarik, *Leadership and Organization* (New York: McGraw-Hill, 1961), p. 412.

[53]Robert L. Kahn, "Human Relations on the Shop Floor," in E. M. Hugh-Jones, ed., *Human Relations and Modern Management* (Chicago: Quadrangle Books, 1959), pp. 43-74.

[54]March and Simon, *op. cit.,* Chapter 3.

[55]Herzberg, et al., *op. cit.*

[56]Harold L. Wilensky, "Work, Careers, and Social Integration," *International Social Science Journal,* pp. 543-560 (April, 1960).

[57]March and Simon, *op. cit.*

most jobs, motivation to participate in the organization acquires major pertinence.

CONCLUSION

An attempt has been made to select and organize behavioral science findings and analysis that bear on wage determination. A behavioral science theory of wages should fill gaps left by economic wage theory and institutional analysis. A behavioral science theory of wage level of the firm would include the following elements: (1) the inducements-contributions utility balance, (2) the labor market as a social institution, (3) unions and employers as holders of power and influence,[58] and (4) non-financial rewards as substitutes for financial rewards. A behavioral science theory of internal wage structure would consist of the following elements: (1) the force of social norms and tradition, (2) accommodation of sociologically diverse labor markets, (3) employers as wage-setting institutions, and (4) the force of group power on the internal wage structure. A behavioral science theory of wages as motivation would deal with: (1) basic motivations common to all individuals derived from basic individual needs and the common culture, (2) motives derived from reference groups and varying among the groups, (3) complexity of motivation in operation, *i.e.,* multi-factor, non-linearity in effect, the possibility that some factors are positive motivators and some others negative motivators, (4) perceived alternatives and their consequences, (5) motivation as a function of organization design, (6) non-motivated work.

Although at this stage model-building appears premature, some tentative models may be offered. In behavioral science terms, wage level influences may be postulated. The wage level of the firm will be higher, (1) the lower the level of job satisfaction, (2) the larger

the number of alternatives perceived by employees, (3) the more reliance is placed on wage surveys, (4) the more influence exerted by unions, (5) the more the firm desires to be a wage leader, (6) the less the firm substitutes non-financial rewards for financial rewards. Conversely, the wage level of the firm will be lower, (1) the higher the level of job satisfaction, (2) the smaller the number of alternatives perceived by employees, (3) the less reliance placed on wage surveys and the stronger the social pressure exerted by employers on each other, (4) the less influence exerted by unions, (5) the less the firm desires to be a wage leader, (6) the more the firm substitutes non-financial rewards for financial rewards.

Similarly, in behavioral science terms, influences on the internal wage structure of the firm may be postulated. The internal wage structure will be more predictable and stable, (1) the more the firm is a closed, isolated bureaucracy, (2) the more semiskilled jobs become bureaucratized, (3) the more professional jobs become bureaucratized, (4) the fewer the craft jobs, (5) the more social norms and tradition correlate with organizational values, (6) the weaker the pressures of groups within the organization. Conversely, the internal wage structure will be less predictable and stable, (1) the more conflict exists between bureaucratic values and social norms and customs in the community, (2) the less semiskilled jobs are bureaucratized, (3) the larger the proportion of professional employees and the more craftlike the professional groups, (4) the more craft jobs, (5) the greater the conflict between organizational values and social norms and tradition in the community, (6) the stronger the group pressures within the organization.

Finally, the effectiveness of money as motivation may be hypothesized in behavioral science terms. Money will become more effective as motivation as (1) physiological and safety needs are unsatisfied and esteem needs are satisfied off the job, (2) relevant reference

---

[58]This element is not absent in modern economic wage theory.

groups rate individuals on a monetary scale, (3) society values individuals in monetary terms and equates status with earnings, (4) higher pay provides ego-enhancement for the individual, (5) organizations are designed to assign higher pay as a reinforcement of achievement of organizational goals, (6) pay is perceived as a reward for productivity and productivity is perceived as a path to employee goals. Money will become less effective as motivation as, (1) social and self-actualization needs become important to the individual and attempts are made to satisfy higher order needs on the job, (2) relevant reference groups rate individuals on non-monetary scales, (3) society values individuals in other than monetary terms, (4) men work for reasons other than money, (5) organizations are designed on the assumption that money is the single motivator, positive and continuous in effect, (6) pay is not perceived as a result of productivity.

WAGE INEQUITIES, PRODUCTIVITY AND WORK QUALITY

J. Stacy Adams

Wage inequities are a perennial concern of management and labor. They are frequent causes of grievances, indeed, of strikes, and may lead to lower productivity.[1] They result in anguish, frustration, and, one might predict, a host of psychogenic complaints, absenteeism, and so on. It is the purpose of this paper to provide a theoretical framework within which inequity may be understood and to present experimental data that provide a test of the theory and demonstrate the effects of wage inequities upon productivity and quality of work.

THE THEORETICAL FRAMEWORK

The theoretical underpinnings of this article rest on a concept which psychologists call cognitive dissonance. Briefly stated, a man could be said to suffer from cognitive dissonance when things do not go as expected.[2]

The concept can be applied to wage administration as follows: every man expects

From J. Stacy Adams, "Wage Inequities, Productivity and Work Quality," Industrial Relations 3 (1), 9–16 (1963). Reprinted by permission.

[1] The author expresses his thanks to William B. Rosenbaum, New York University, and Francis Tweed, Columbia University, for assistance in collecting experimental data. Some of the data reported here were previously reported in J. S. Adams and W. B. Rosenbaum, "The Relationship of Worker Productivity to Cognitive Dissonance About Wage Inequities," *Journal of Applied Psychology* XLI, 161-164 (1962).

[2] For a more complete discussion, see J. S. Adams, "Toward an Understanding of Inequity," *Journal of Abnormal and Social Psychology* (in press); and Leon Festinger, *A Theory of Cognitive Dissonance* (Evanston, Ill.: Row, Peterson, 1957).

a certain relationship between his *input*, what he puts into his work in terms of effort, skill, etc., and his *outcome*, what he gets in terms of pay and other forms of satisfaction. When an individual compares himself with another person, he looks at his own inputs and outcomes in relation to those of the other person; for example, if two individuals receive the same pay, but are unequally qualified, then both parties may suffer from cognitive dissonance, even the man who is relatively overpaid. The cognitive dissonance hypothesis includes a prediction that when people suffer from such dissonance, they take steps to reduce it.

The three experiments reported here were designed to test how people behave when they are working on a relatively highly paid job for which they feel underqualified (that is, when they feel their pay, or outcome, exceeds their qualifications, or input). The first experiment suggests that if, under these conditions, people are paid by the hour, they may try to reduce their dissonance (that is, make up for their lower qualifications) by working harder and thus increasing their input. The second experiment suggests that if people under the same circumstances are paid for piecework, they may reduce dissonance by working less hard, thus reducing their earnings (outcome) and bringing them more in line with their input (qualifications). The third experiment was conducted under slightly different circumstances, but is consistent with the first two. It suggests that where it is possible for a person on piecework to increase the quality of his work, he will attempt to do so. Let us now look at these three experiments.

EXPERIMENT I

Twenty-two male students at New York University were hired through the Placement Service for part-time temporary work as interviewers. The rate of pay announced was $3.50 an hour and subjects were given the impression that interviewing would take place for a period of "several months." When they reported to their prospective "employer," they were assigned randomly in equal numbers to the *experimental dissonance* condition and to the *control* condition, as described below.

1. All the subjects filled out a Personal Information Questionnaire requesting demographic, educational, and previous employment data.

2. The experimenter studied each subject's questionnaire in his presence and then "discussed" his qualifications. But the "discussions" with those in the experimental group were very different from those with persons in the control group.

The *experimental* subjects were treated quite harshly. The experimenter proceeded as follows:

"You don't have any (nearly enough) experience in interviewing or survey work of the kind we're engaged in here. I specifically asked the Placement Service to refer only people with that kind of experience. This was *the* major qualification we set. I can't understand how such a slip-up could have occurred. It's really very important for research of this kind to have people experienced in interviewing and survey techniques. [Agonizing pause.]

"We're dealing with a limited alternative, open-end kind of questionnaire. There's no 'correct' answer to an item. Research in this area has shown that the nature of the response elicited by a skilled and experienced interviewer is more accurate and representative of the respondent's sentiments and differs substantially from the responses elicited by inexperienced people.

"Who interviewed you at Placement? [The experimenter scans the New York University phone directory, picks up telephone receiver, and dials a number; he gets a busy signal and slams the receiver down. Pause, while experimenter thumbs papers and meditates.]

"I guess I'll have to hire you anyway, but *please* pay close attention to the instructions I will give you. If anything I say seems complicated, don't hesitate to ask for clarification. If it seems simple, pay closer attention. Some of this stuff, on the surface, may appear to be deceptively easy.

"Since I'm going to hire you, I'll just have to pay you at the rate we advertised, that is, $3.50 an hour."

The *control* subjects were treated very differently!

"Well, this is very good. We can use you for this work. You meet all the qualifications required for the job. We often have to turn people down because they're poorly qualified. Poorly qualified people can really make a mess of a study of this kind. Why even the Census, where they were dealing with simple demographic material, got fouled up. They hired inadequately qualified people, some of their housewives for example, and the result was the gross deficiencies in their data that were so widely criticized in the press, if you recall.

"Well, anyway, I'm pleased you have the background we're looking for.

"So far as pay is concerned, the people at the Placement Service have probably advised you that we pay $3.50 an hour. This rate of pay is standard for work of this kind performed by people with your qualifications."

Referring to the theoretical statements made earlier, it should be noted that the subject's alleged qualifications are his inputs and the pay of $3.50 an hour is his outcome. In the experimental situation the subject is led to perceive that his inputs are out of line with his outcomes and the inputs and outcomes of other interviewers. In the control group, he is made to perceive that his inputs are in line with his outcomes and the inputs and outcomes of other interviewers.

3. The experimenter gave the subject instructions on the interviewing task. The subject was to interview adult members of the general public for approximately 2.5 hours and was to obtain approximately equal numbers of interviews with males and females. No restrictions were placed on where the subject was to obtain interviews. The interview was a simple one, requiring respondents to associate one of five automobile names (e.g., Ford) with six brief personal descriptions, such as "A professional athlete" and "A rising junior executive."

The task met the requirements of the experiment nicely. It was brief enough so that many interviews could be obtained during the subject's work period. More importantly, it could be perceived either as requiring more skills than the subject possessed or as requiring skills commensurate with his qualifications.

All subjects were given interviewing materials and a supply of 50 blank questionnaires (a number predetermined to be slightly greater than the most efficient interviewer could use in 2.5 hours). As the subject departed to begin work he was briefly reminded of the relation of his qualifications to his pay of $3.50 an hour.

4. When the subject returned at the time set by the experimenter, he was asked to fill out a brief questionnaire on his interviewing experience and his reactions to it. The experiment and its purpose were then explained to him and he was requested not to divulge information about it. In only one instance was this request not observed and the subject affected was eliminated from the experiment.

Results. Since there was some variation in the amount of time the subjects worked—a range of 143 to 165 minutes—and the dependent variable of interest was productivity, the number of interviews obtained per minute was the datum used in analysis. The results are given in Table 1. As predicted, the experimental subjects produced significantly more than did the controls. By median test a significant level better than .05 is achieved ($X^2 = 4.55$, df = 1).

TABLE 1   MEDIAN AND MEAN PRODUCTIVITY DISTRIBUTION OF EXPERIMENTAL AND CONTROL SUBJECTS

	EXPERIMENTAL	CONTROL
Cases above median	8	3
Cases below median	3	8
Mean productivity	.2694	.1899

EXPERIMENT II

In this experiment the hypothesis tested was

that whereas subjects who felt they were overpaid by the hour would show greater productivity than controls, subjects who felt overpaid on a piece rate would show less productivity than controls. Thus, what we will be looking at in this experiment is the relationship between method of pay and dissonance.

Method. Thirty-six male New York University students were hired through the Placement Service, as in the previous experiment, for the same interviewing job. When they reported to the "employer," they were randomly assigned in equal numbers to the following four conditions:

1. H_e: experimental dissonance condition; subjects paid $3.50 an hour (N = 9)
2. H_c: control condition; subjects paid $3.50 an hour (N = 9)
3. P_e: experimental dissonance condition; subjects paid 30 cents an interview obtained (N = 9)
4. P_c: control condition; subjects paid 30 cents an interview obtained (N = 9)

TABLE 2.   MEDIAN AND MEAN PRODUCTIVITY DISTRIBUTION OF HOURLY AND PIECEWORK EXPERIMENTAL AND CONTROL SUBJECTS

	H_e	H_c	P_e	P_c
Cases above median	8	4	1	5
Cases below median	1	5	8	4
Mean productivity	.2723	.2275	.1493	.1961

The procedure was identical to that in Experiment I, with an exception that the subjects in the P_e and P_c conditions were paid 30 cents an interview. The piece rate of 30 cents was determined from the performance of control subjects in Experiment I, who would have earned slightly less than 31 cents an interview, on the average, had they been paid on a piece rate. A minor, additional modification in procedure was that subjects were instructed to work 2, instead of 2.5, hours.

Results. The data are presented in Table 2 and support the hypothesis. As may be seen, hourly workers in the dissonance condition had a higher mean productivity than their controls, whereas pieceworkers in the dissonance condition had a lower mean productivity than their controls.[3]

CHI SQUARE ANALYSIS OF VARIANCE

SOURCE	df	X^2
Method of pay	1	4.00[a]
Dissonance	1	0.00
A × B interaction	1	7.11[b]

[a]$p < .05$; [b]$p < .01$
[a]$p < .05$; [b]$p < .01$.

EXPERIMENT III

The prediction that piecework subjects perceiving wage inequality (overpayment) would have a lower productivity than subjects perceiving their wages as fair was supported by the previous experiment. The rationale for the prediction was that because dissonance is linked with units of production, dissonance would increase as more units were produced, and, consequently, subjects would attempt to avoid increasing dissonance by restricting production. There is, however, an alternative explanation that would account for the same manifest behavior. It is entirely possible for subjects to *reduce* dissonance by increasing their effort on the production of each unit, for example, by increasing the quality of their work; this would have the effect of increasing the production time per unit and, therefore, have the consequence of reducing productivity. In terms of the theoretical framework presented earlier, this explanation assumes that pieceworkers would reduce their disso-

[3]Median tests of the difference between the two hourly conditions and between the two piecework conditions do not reach a satisfactory level of significance, although the directions of the differences are as predicted. A more powerful and appropriate test is that of the interaction between conditions of pay and dissonance. The interaction, tested by chi square analysis of variance, is significant at better than the .01 level as shown in the table below. The significantly lower productivity of pieceworkers is, of course, a necessary outcome.

nance by increasing their inputs, very much as hourly workers. Only the mode of increasing inputs varies: whereas hourly workers increase inputs on a *quantitative* dimension, pieceworkers increase them on a *qualitative* dimension.

Unfortunately, the task used in Experiment II did not lend itself to measuring quality of work. In Experiment III the work performed was designed so as to permit measurement of both amount of work and quality of work. The specific hypothesis tested is: pieceworkers who perceive that they are inequitably overpaid will perform better quality work and have lower productivity than pieceworkers who are paid the same rate and perceive they are equitably paid.

The interviewing task was modified so as to permit the measurement of quality. The modification consisted of making the three principal questions open-end. As an example, one question was, "Does a man who owns a shelter have the moral right to exclude others from it, if they have no shelter?" (Yes or No), which was followed by, "What are your reasons for feeling that way?" The subject's task was to obtain as much information as possible from a respondent on the latter part of the question. The measure of work quality thus was the amount of recorded information elicited from respondents. More specifically, the dependent measure of quality was the number of words recorded in the blank spaces following the three open-end questions. As before, the measure of productivity was the number of interviews obtained a minute during a total period of approximately two hours.

Quality of Work. The data indicated that the mean number of words per interview was significantly greater among the overpaid experimental subjects than among the control subjects ($t = 2.48$, $P < .02$, two-tailed test): experimental, 69.7; control, 45.3.

Productivity. The mean productivity of subjects in whom feelings of inequitable overpayment were induced was significantly lower (t = 1.82, P < .05, one-tailed test) than that of control subjects: experimental, .0976; control, .1506.

The quality and productivity data support the hypothesis that under piecework conditions subjects who perceive that they are overpaid will tend to reduce dissonance by increasing their inputs on each *unit* so as to improve quality and, as a result, will decrease their productivity. Thus, the alternative explanation for the results obtained with piece-workers in Experiment II has some validity. This is not to say that the dissonance-avoiding hypothesis originally offered is invalid; if a job does not permit an increase of work input *per unit produced,* dissonance avoidance may well occur. This, however, remains to be demonstrated; the fact that we were unable to measure quality of work in Experiment II does not mean that subjects did not reduce dissonance by some means, including the improvement of quality, on each unit produced.

DISCUSSION

In the experiments reported here, we attempted to extend the implications of the cognitive dissonance theory to a practical problem, and we tried to test relevant derivations of the theory in such a manner that they bear directly on the problem. The problem selected was that of wage inequities and their effects on workers' productivity. The experimental situation chosen was a "real" employment situation in which workers performed a real task for real wages. It may be noted that our subjects uniformly believed they had been hired for and had worked on a real job. In pretest experiments it was found that unless this condition obtained predictable effects were not observable.

In the first experiment reported, it was shown that hourly workers who were made to feel overpaid displayed greater produc-

tivity than control subjects who earned the same pay but were made to feel fairly paid. Although the prediction was derived from cognitive dissonance theory, an alternative explanation is that the experimental subjects worked harder and produced more simply in order to obtain greater job security. Having been hired reluctantly, they may have feared that they would lose their jobs unless they could demonstrate competence. This explanation is not entirely satisfactory, however. In the first place, if it were valid, the same effects would be predicted for pieceworkers, for there is no reason to assume that a threat to job security would result in different behavior among hourly paid and piecework subjects. But, as we have seen, pieceworkers reduce rather than increase their productivity and, under some circumstances, increase the quality of their work when overpaid.

Secondly, in a related study, Arrowood has argued that if the alternative explanation were valid, the results would obtain only when the experimenter was aware of the subjects' productivity.[4] He conducted an experiment in which hourly paid subjects worked under overpaid and equitably paid conditions, as in our first study, and under public and private conditions. In the public condition, subjects turned in their completed work to the experimenter; in the private condition they mailed their work to New York under the impression that the experimenter would not see it. Arrowood found that overpaid workers produced significantly more in both the public and the private conditions. His study, therefore, supports the dissonance-derived prediction and tends to invalidate the alternative explanation of our results.

In the second of our experiments, a further hypothesis was given support. If workers perceive that they are overpaid—which psy-

[4]A. J. Arrowood, *Some Effects on Productivity of Justified and Unjustified Levels of Reward under Public and Private Conditions* (Unpublished doctoral dissertation, University of Minnesota, 1961).

chologically is an inequity, as is being under-paid—and other means of reducing the resulting dissonance are not readily available to them, they will produce more or less than control subjects paid the same wages, depending on whether their wages are hourly or on a piecework basis.

In the third experiment described, it was demonstrated that, under conditions which permit subjects to vary the quality of their work and permit the experimenter to measure quality, subjects appear to reduce dissonance by increasing the quality of their work. This finding, we believe, is of particular interest, for it points up the fact that under some circumstances individuals behave so as to *earn less at the cost of greater effort.* This is clearly contrary to the usual assumption that workers behave so as to maximize their gains and minimize their effort.

PERCEPTIONS REGARDING MANAGEMENT COMPENSATION

Edward E. Lawler III
Lyman W. Porter

Despite widespread interest in the problems of compensation, experimental investigation in the field has only recently begun.[1] The present study differs from most of the work in this area for two reasons: first, it is concerned with members of *management* and, second, it deals with the *psychological* aspects of compensation. Previous studies have dealt with such topics as the effectiveness of different methods of payment[2] and the incomes of different demographic groups. Research has been neglected on such aspects of pay as: (1) the importance attached to pay, (2) perceptions regarding the amount of pay received, (3) satisfaction with regard to pay, and (4) the needs which pay satisfies. The purpose of the following study is to investigate, at all levels of management and at all income levels, each of these four aspects of managers' perceptions regarding their pay.

QUESTIONNAIRE

The data for this study were obtained by means of a questionnaire. The relevant part

From Edward E. Lawler and Lyman W. Porter, "Perceptions Regarding Management Compensation," Industrial Relations 3 (1), 41–49 (1963). Reprinted by permission.

[1]For suggestive examples of the kind of work which can be done in this area, see Robert L. Kahn, "Human Relations on the Shop Floor," in E. M. Hugh-Jones, ed., *Human Relations and Modern Management* (Amsterdam: North-Holland, 1958), and Elliott Jaques, *Equitable Compensation* (New York: Wiley, 1961).

[2]W. F. Whyte, *Money and Motivation* (New York: Harper, 1955).

of the questionnaire contained 13 items classifiable into a Maslow-type need hierarchy system,[3] plus one item concerned with pay. The instructions for this part of the questionnaire stated:

> On the following pages will be listed several characteristics or qualities connected with your management position. For each such characteristic, you will be asked to give three ratings:
> a. *How much* of the characteristic *is there now* connected with your management position?
> b. *How much* of the characteristic do you think *should be* connected with your management position?
> c. *How important* is this position characteristic to you?

For each of the 14 items, the respondents were instructed to answer the above three questions by circling a number on a rating scale extending from 1-7, where "low numbers represent low or minimum amounts, and high numbers represent high or maximum amounts." Each item, such as the one on pay, appeared as follows on the questionnaire:

> The pay for my management position:
> (a) How much is there now?
>   (min) 1 2 3 4 5 6 7 (max)
> (b) How much should there be?
>   (min) 1 2 3 4 5 6 7 (max)
> (c) How important is this to me?
>   (min) 1 2 3 4 5 6 7 (max)

The items were randomly presented in the questionnaire. However, each of the 13 items pertaining to the Maslow-type need hierarchy theory had been preclassified into one of the following five types of needs: security needs, social needs, esteem needs, needs for autonomy, and needs for self-actualization.[4]

[3]A. H. Maslow, *Motivation and Personality* (New York: Harper, 1954).

[4]A detailed description of these 13 items and the rationale underlying their classification can be found in a previous paper, L. W. Porter, "A Study of Perceived Need Satisfactions in Bottom and Middle Management Jobs," *Journal of Applied Psychology*, XLV, 1-10 (January, 1961).

PROCEDURE AND SAMPLE

The questionnaire was mailed to a random sample of 3,000 members (approximately 10 per cent) of the American Management Association and to another random sample of some 3,000 managers whose names were on mailing lists available to the Association.[5] Responses were received from 1,958 managers, with the number of usable questionnaires for this study being 1,913. (It should be noted that for a psychological research study dealing with managers this is an exceptionally large sample.) The method of distribution of the questionnaire resulted in a nationwide sample, one in which any particular company would not be represented by more than a few individual respondents.

From personal data questions asked on the last page of the questionnaire, it was possible to classify respondents on a number of independent variables. The three relevant variables for this study were salary, level within

For this study the amount of annual pay was the major independent variable. However, since pay is correlated with management level, it was felt necessary to classify individuals both by management level and by pay. In this way, the effects of the two variables could be assessed independently. This was particularly important since previous studies have found that satisfaction of psychological needs varies with level of management.[7] In this study we held pay level constant in order to see the effects of management level on perception of pay.

RESULTS AND DISCUSSION

Importance Attached to Pay. The data concerned with the importance attached to pay were obtained from respondents' answers to part (c) ("How important is this to me?") of the item, "The pay for my management position." A study by Kahn showed that superiors

TABLE 1. DISTRIBUTION OF N FOR TOTAL SAMPLE BY FIVE MANAGEMENT LEVELS AND TEN PAY GROUPS

MANAGEMENT LEVEL	PAY GROUPS										TOTAL N FOR LEVEL
	1 BELOW $5,900	2 $6–8,900	3 $9–11,900	4 $12–14,900	5 $15–19,900	6 $20–24,900	7 $25–34,900	8 $35–49,900	9 $50–74,000	10 OVER $75,000	
President	1	1	2	4	13	15	28	16	23	11	114
Vice-president	2	9	27	80	111	108	154	78	30	11	610
Upper middle	2	34	127	159	177	92	51	14	3	—	659
Lower middle	3	63	129	130	77	21	4	1	1	—	429
Lower	4	30	34	17	14	2	—	—	—	—	101
Total N for pay group	12	137	319	390	392	238	237	109	57	22	1,912

management, and staff or line management.[6] Table 1 shows the distribution of the sample by management level and pay group.

[5]The assistance of the American Management Association, and particularly Robert F. Steadman, in obtaining the sample of respondents is gratefully acknowledged.

[6]The specific methods used to assign respondents to different levels of management can be found in L. W. Porter, "Job Attitudes in Management: I. Perceived Deficiencies in Need Fulfillment as a Function of Job Level," *Journal of Applied Psychology* XLVI, 375-384 (December, 1962).

consistently perceived their subordinates as attaching more importance to pay than they themselves did.[8] Kahn's finding suggests that lower-level managers attach greater importance to pay than do higher-level managers. Since the size of a man's salary is highly correlated with management level, and is also a major determinant of the importance he

[7]*Ibid.*

[8]Kahn, *op. cit.*

attaches to pay, we held amount of pay constant in our analysis of differences among management levels. When we did this, we found no difference among managers at various levels in the importance attached to pay.

Then, to assess the effect of the amount of pay on the importance attached to pay, management level was held constant. When this was done, we found that higher-paid managers attached *less* importance to pay than did lower-paid managers at the same level. If we assume that higher-paid managers are better satisfied than lower-paid managers, then these results support current motivational theories which state that as a need becomes better satisfied it tends to decrease in importance.[9]

Line and staff managers who received the same pay and were at the same level in the organization showed no significant difference in the importance they attached to pay. The frequently stated opinion that the staff manager is less concerned with pay than the line manager is not supported by the data and, in fact, the trend, though not statistically significant, was in the direction of staff managers attaching more significance to pay. A study by Haire, Ghiselli, and Porter pointed out that the importance attached to different psychological needs seems to be largely a function of the individual and does not vary significantly with organizational variables.[10] The importance attached to pay appears to operate in a similar manner, since no differences were found on the organization variables investigated (management level and line-staff type of position).

How Current Pay Level Is Perceived. The answers to part (a) ("How much is there now?") and part (b) ("How much should there be?") of the question concerned with

pay provide data on managers' attitudes towards how much pay they receive and how much pay they feel they should receive. The answers to the first question are particularly interesting because the ratings of "How much pay is there now for your management position?" on a seven-point attitude scale can be compared with an objective measure in dollars of the respondent's actual pay as revealed by him in the personal data items at the end of the questionnaire. It is valuable to make such a comparison, because in any attitude study the question always arises as to whether or not expressed attitudes have any relationship to reality.

Figures 5.1 through 5.5 represent the answers to "How much should there be?" and "How much is there now?" for each of the five management levels classified by actual pay groups. As each of the charts shows, the managers who in fact got the most pay, also *felt* that they got the most pay. This is shown by the fact that the dotted line for "How much is there now?" rises from lower- to

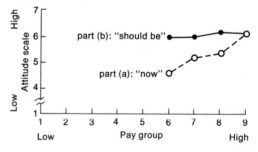

Figure 5.1 Responses of presidents to parts (a) and (b) of the pay item, as a function of actual pay.

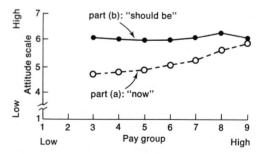

Figure 5.2 Responses of vice-presidents to parts (a) and (b) of the pay item, as a function of actual pay.

[9]Maslow, *op. cit.*

[10]Mason Haire, E. E. Ghiselli, and L. W. Porter, "Cultural Patterns in the Role of the Manager," *Industrial Relations* II, 95-117 (February, 1963).

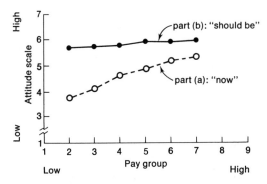

Figure 5.3 Responses of upper-middle managers to parts (a) and (b) of the pay item, as a function of actual pay.

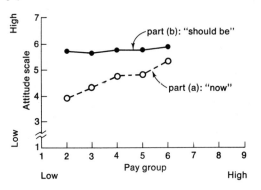

Figure 5.4 Responses of lower-middle managers to parts (a) and (b) of the pay item, as a function of actual pay.

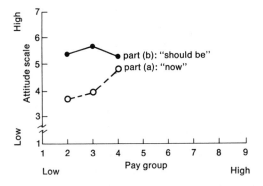

Figure 5.5 Responses of lower managers to parts (a) and (b) of the pay item, as a function of actual pay.

higher-paid groups within each graph. In contrast to this finding, when actual pay was held constant, managers at different levels showed no difference in their answers to this

question. Therefore, actual pay rather than management level is the most important determinant of a manager's perception of how much pay he receives.

When management level was held constant, higher-paid managers did not respond differently from those who were lower paid when asked, "How much pay should there be for your management position?" The agreement between managers at the same level on what pay they should receive is shown in Figures 5.1 through 5.5 by the solid line ("How much should there be?"), which runs parallel to the X axis in each figure and indicates similar expectations regardless of present pay. When actual pay was held constant, higher-level managers indicated there should be more pay for their management position than did lower-level managers. The influence of management level on what managers feel they should be paid is indicated in Figures 5.1 through 5.5 by the tendency for the position of the solid line (for "expectations") to drop as management level decreases between Figure 5.1 and Figure 5.5. Apparently the key determinant of managers' expectations as to what they should be paid is not present pay, but management level.

Satisfaction with Pay. The data relevant to the topic of *satisfaction* with pay were obtained from the difference in answers to part (a) ("How much is there now?") and part (b) ("How much should there be?") of the item, "The pay for my management position." The advantages and rationale for using these questions together as a measure of satisfaction were discussed in detail in a previous article.[11] An *a priori* assumption was made that the smaller the difference—part (a) subtracted from part (b)—the larger the degree of satisfaction or the smaller the degree of dissatisfaction. In other words, it is the relationship between expectations and perceived outcomes that determines satisfaction. Since it is established that actual pay

[11]Porter, "Job Attitudes in Management . . ." *(op. cit.).*

is an important determinant of an individual's perception of how much he receives, and that level is an important determinant of how much an individual feels he should be paid, these two variables must be considered in any analysis of satisfaction with pay.

Figures 5.1 through 5.5 illustrate the effect of actual pay on managers' satisfaction with their pay. Notice that at each management level, as pay increases, the difference between the solid line ("How much should there be?") and the broken line ("How much is there now?") decreases. Thus when management level was held constant, higher-paid managers were found to be better satisfied with their pay than were lower-paid managers. Holding management level constant has the effect of holding expectations constant, and the effect of increasing pay is to increase the individual's perception of how much he receives, resulting in a decrease in the difference between the individual's expectations and perceptions with regard to his pay.

When actual pay was held constant, higher-level managers were found to be *less* satisfied than lower-level managers. (Note in Figures 5.1 through 5.5 the differences between the lines for perceived pay and expected pay for a given amount of objective pay at different management levels.) Since lower-level managers have lower expectations with regard to pay than do higher-level managers and since both groups receive the same pay, it follows that there is a smaller difference between expectations and perception of reality for lower-level managers.

The question of which managers are the best satisfied with their pay can now be answered by looking again at Figures 5.1 through 5.5. At each management level, the smallest differences between expectations and perceptions of amount of pay received occur for the highest-paid managers at *that* level. For example, first-line supervisors making between $12,000 and $14,000 (Pay Group 4) are better satisfied with their pay than are company presidents who make less than

$49,000 (Pay Group 8 or below). It appears that a manager is very satisfied with his pay if he is paid well in relationship to others at his *same* level of management. As would be expected, since the lowest-paid managers at *each* level are the worst paid relative to others doing a similar job, they are the most dissatisfied. However, even the highest-paid groups at each management level are not completely satisfied.

There was no tendency for line and staff managers at the same level and receiving the same pay to report different satisfaction with pay. Apparently, not only do staff managers attach the same importance to pay as do line managers, but when pay and management level are held constant, they report the same degree of satisfaction as do line managers.

Relationship Between Pay Received and Satisfaction in Five Need Areas. Most discussions of pay emphasize that it does not satisfy a single need in the individual, but rather a variety of psychological needs (e.g., security and esteem needs).[12] In those need areas which are thought to be satisfied by pay, higher-paid managers should report greater satisfaction than lower-paid managers. Since management level has been shown in a previous study[13] to be correlated with satisfaction in the five need areas (social, esteem, security, autonomy, and self-actualization) considered in the present study, this variable was held constant in the analysis of the relationship of amount of pay to satisfaction in these need areas. When this was done, higher-paid managers reported no greater satisfaction in the social and self-actualization need areas than did lower-paid managers. However, higher-paid managers did show definitely greater satisfaction in the esteem and autonomy need areas and somewhat greater satisfaction in the esteem and autonomy need areas and somewhat greater

[12]Mason Haire, *Psychology in Management* (New York: McGraw-Hill, 1956).

[13]Porter, "Job Attitudes in Management . . ." *(op. cit.).*

satisfaction in the security need area than did lower-paid managers. It is interesting to note that the needs most frequently discussed as being satisfied by pay, namely, esteem and security needs, are according to the present study better satisfied for higher-paid individuals.

CONCLUSIONS

1. The importance attached to pay varied with objective pay received, but not with level of management. Higher-paid managers on each level attached *less* importance to pay.

2. There was no line vs. staff differences in either importance attached to pay or satisfaction with pay.

3. Managers' expectations about what pay they should receive were related to management level, but not to present actual pay.

4. Managers' perceptions about how much pay they received were realistic with regard to actual pay.

5. At a given management level, as pay increased, satisfaction with pay also increased.

6. For any given amount of pay, the amount of satisfaction with pay *decreased* the higher the level of management.

7. Higher-paid managers reported that they were better satisfied in the security, autonomy, and esteem need areas than did lower-paid managers at equivalent levels of management.

CAREER MOBILITY AND ORGANIZATIONAL COMMITMENT

Oscar Grusky

Organizational commitment refers to the nature of the relationship of the member to the system as a whole. Two general factors which influence the strength of a person's attachment to an organization are the rewards he has received from the organization and the experiences he has had to undergo to receive them. People become members of formal organizations because they can attain objectives that they desire through their membership. If the person discovers that he cannot obtain the rewards he originally desired, he either leaves the organization and joins another; or if this is not feasible, he accepts those rewards which he can obtain and, we suspect, at the same time feels less committed to that organization. On the other hand, obtaining the rewards sought, operates to further his felt obligation to the organization, and his commitment is strengthened. The expectation of reward operates in a like manner. Strength of commitment to an organization should be positively related to the strength of conviction that one will be rewarded by the organization. The nature of one's commitment to an organization may undergo radical change depending on the relationship between belief and reality.[1] Convergence of belief and reality would tend to strengthen commitment, while divergence should cause a decrease in commitment.

Whether one must overcome hurdles in order to obtain the rewards of the organization may be another important factor in determining one's commitment to the organization. If the rewards are readily obtained, one's obligation to the organization is likely to be weak; one becomes convinced that it was his attributes rather than those of the organization which provided the rewards. On the other hand, if one obtains great rewards despite apparent obstacles (such as starting out with a low status in the organization), commitment should be strong. This study examines evidence for the following two general hypotheses.

Hypothesis 1. All else equal, the greater the rewards an individual has received or expects to receive from an organization, the greater will be the degree of his commitment to the system.

Hypothesis 2. All else equal, the greater the obstacles the individual has overcome in order to obtain the organization's rewards, the greater will be the degree of his commitment to the system.

The theory suggests simply that if a person receives high rewards from the organization he will respond by demonstrating positive feelings toward the organization. The simplicity of the formulation may be deceptive, however; the concept of reward is useful to organization theory because of its generality, and yet, this same quality can impair its usefulness in empirical research. It is assumed that all human behavior patterns do not recur unless rewarded in some way. A fundamental problem lies in the relation between objective reward value and subjective reward value. Members evaluate the rewards they have received from an organization in terms of

From Oscar Grusky, "Career Mobility and Organizational Commitment," **Administrative Science Quarterly 10 (4), 488–503 (1966). Reprinted by permission.**

[1]Goffman has stated a related hypothesis: "Persons at the bottom of large organizations typically operate in drab backgrounds, against which higher-placed members realize their internal incentives, enjoying the satisfaction of receiving visible indulgences that others do not. *Low-placed members tend to have less commitment and emotional attachment to the organization than higher-placed members."* (Italics added.) *Asylums* (New York: Doubleday and Company, 1961), p. 201.

various standards or perspectives. The size of the reward received is frequently a function of the size of rewards received relative to those received by others who occupy a similar status. Numerous theorists in social psychology have recognized this problem, as indicated by Homans' use of the concept of distributive justice and Thibaut and Kelley's notion of comparison level and comparison level of alternatives.[2] Hypothesis 2 may be superior to Hypothesis 1 because it implicitly takes into consideration a comparative frame of reference. The person who overcomes obstacles compares himself with persons of equal status who did not do so.

Homans has described social approval as a general reinforcer.[3] Likewise upward career mobility in a corporation may be considered a general reinforcer in that it provides rewards of many kinds for the upward-mobile person; therefore the major measure of reward used in this study was the degree of upward career mobility experienced by the manager.

METHODS

This study is concerned with the relationship between managerial career mobility and organizational commitment in a large corporate enterprise.[4] A questionnaire was distributed to all 2,198 managers (as defined by the firm) of the United Utility Corporation (a fictitious name), the largest single enterprise of a major public utility holding company in the United States. Approximately 75 percent, or 1,649 usable, signed schedules were returned. A comparison by salary, sex, and position of the distributions of the sample with that of the total population of managers in the firm revealed a very close correspondence between the two groups.

On the basis of observation, a six-level corporate hierarchy was distinguished, as follows: (*1*) top management, (*2*) upper-middle management, (*3*) middle management, (*4*) lower-middle management, (*5*) first-level management, (*6*) clerical supervisors. The last group consisted almost entirely of females. Two managers in the firm (one at level *3*, and the other at level *4*) independently placed each of the 318 management positions in the corporation on one of the six levels, applying the criterion of amount of official authority associated with the position. Interrater reliability was 0.904 ($p < 0.0001$). When the raters were brought together to examine disagreement, none of which deviated by more than one level, complete agreement was reached when the criterion was restated, and the duties of the rated position discussed. Corporate level was related both to salary[5] (Cramer's $V = 0.58$, $p < 0.0001$) and perceived authority ($V = 0.21$, $p < 0.0001$).

Amount of career mobility for each manager was determined by comparing the level of his present position in the corporate hierarchy with the level of his first position in the firm; therefore, mobility referred to movement *across levels,* not merely movement from position to position. As in many public utilities, most of the managers (84.7 percent) started in nonmanagement positions

[2]This formulation follows that of Homans who notes: "The rule of distributive justice says that a man's rewards in exchange with others should be proportional to his investments." *Social Behavior: Its Elementary Forms* (New York: Harcourt, Brace & World, 1961), p. 235; J. Thibaut and H. H. Kelley, *The Social Psychology of Groups* (New York: Wiley, 1959), pp. 21-23.

[3]*Op. cit.,* pp. 34-35.

[4]I am grateful to John Vincent and Judith Ellis for research assistance; to the Graduate School of Business Administration, University of California, Los Angeles, for financial support for the larger study of which this is part; and to Charles Y. Glock, Director, and members of the staff of the Survey Research Center, University of California, Berkeley, for coding the data. Most of the data were gathered while the author held a Ford Foundation Faculty Research Fellowship in Social Science and Business. This is a revised version of a paper presented at the annual meeting of the American Sociological Association, August 1963, Los Angeles, California. I am indebted to Professor Peter Blau, session organizer for the field of formal organizations, for his many helpful comments on the manuscript.

[5]See H. M. Blalock, Jr., *Social Statistics* (New York: McGraw-Hill, 1960), p. 230.

(designated level 7); those starting in management positions were excluded from this study. Three mobility groups were isolated: (1) *minimum mobility,* those who had moved up only one or two levels; (2) *moderate mobility,* those who had moved up three levels, and (3) *maximum mobility,* those who had moved up four levels or more.

Levels in the corporate hierarchy and career mobility, though obviously highly correlated, were not identical. The mobility measure, because it necessarily excluded those who started in management positions, did not consider more than half (53 percent) of the top executives; that is, level 1. Similarly, almost one in five of the managers in levels 2, 3, and 4 were excluded.

One behavioral and three attitudinal indexes of commitment were used: (1) seniority, (2) identification with the company as a whole, (3) attitude toward the company's

administrators, and (4) general satisfaction with the company.[6]

RESULTS

Intercorrelations of the Indexes

Table 1 presents the intercorrelations of the four measures, revealing that five of the six possible correlations were statistically significant at or beyond the 0.001 level, and all were positive. Seniority was most highly related to identification with the company as a whole, but also significantly related to attitude toward company administrators. It was not associated significantly with general satisfaction. Identification with the company as a whole was positively correlated with general satisfaction as well as attitudes toward the company. Thus it would appear that the five indexes tapped related but differentiable components of what is here called "commitment."

---

[6]The measures of commitment were as follows:

(1) *Seniority.* Number of years employed by the company provided a simple index.

(2) *Identification with the company.* We attempted to tap the degree of commitment by this question: "Suppose you were offered a job exactly like your present position with another company located nearby, but with a 20 percent increase in salary. Would you accept it?" The alternatives offered were (1) Yes, definitely, (2) Yes, probably, (3) No, probably, and (4) No, definitely. Approximately half of the managers selected one of the two affirmative alternatives and half claimed they would not change jobs. Although one does not know whether the respondents would behave in a manner consistent with their signed questionnaire responses; nevertheless, the item did give a rough idea of the importance of economic incentives. It was assumed that those who claimed they would not take another position, despite the instrumental inducement of an increased salary, were guided in part by loyalty to the corporation. But this item attempted to measure loyalty by means of a technique which was essentially negative. A manager was defined as loyal if he said he would reject such an offer. In order to deal directly with the concept in a way seemingly consistent with its meaning, the managers were asked to report their degree of agreement or disagreement with this rather extreme statement: "The good of the company always comes before the good of the individual manager."

The alternatives permitted were: strongly agree, slightly agree, slightly disagree, strongly disagree.

(3) *Attitude toward the company administrators.* A Guttman scale of attitude toward the company administrators was devised consisting of the following three items:

1. Do you feel that the men who run the Company recognize your ability and what you are able to do?
2. How well do you feel that the men who run the Company understand your problems and needs?
3. In general, how well do you think the Company is run?

The coefficient of reproducibility of the scale was 0.96 and the coefficient of scalability was 0.80. Both figures were well above the suggested desirable levels. (See H. Menzel, A New Coefficient for Scalogram Analysis, *Public Opinion Quarterly,* 17 (1953), 268-280.)

(4) *General satisfaction with company.* Two open-ended questionnaire items asked respondents' opinions as to the major problems of the company and the department. Responses were evaluated for over-all satisfaction on a five-point scale ranging from very satisfied to very dissatisfied. Slightly more than one out of four managers (448) could be coded on the basis of their responses and the large majority of these (77 percent) were either dissatisfied or very dissatisfied. Since the question solicited problems rather than favorable comment, this was not surprising; however, the measure served the important function of an independent check on the validity of the Guttman scale measure.

TABLE 1. INTERCORRELATIONS OF INDEXES OF ORGANIZATIONAL COMMITMENT.†

	(1) SENIORITY	(2) IDENTIFICATION WITH THE COMPANY	(3) ATTITUDES TOWARD COMPANY ADMINISTRATORS	(4) GENERAL SATISFACTION WITH THE COMPANY
(1) Seniority		0.19*	0.09*	0.09**
(2) Identification with the company			0.15*	0.21*
(3) Attitudes toward company administrators				0.23*

†Correlations are zero-order values of V (Cramer's Coefficient). See H. M. Blalock, Jr., *Social Statistics* (New York: McGraw-Hill, 1960) p. 230, for a description of this measure.
*$p < 0.001$.
**$p < 0.10$.

Mobility and Commitment

This section considers the hypothesis that the greater the rewards received as a result of upward career mobility, the stronger the commitment to the organization. Following Homans, one can assume that the interaction of the manager and the organization continues only up to the point where the rewards the manager receives or expects to receive from the organization exceed the costs incurred. It is also assumed that it is rewarding to be more upwardly mobile than one's peers.

The formal structure of the corporation is

TABLE 2. CAREER MOBILITY AND FOUR MEASURES OF COMMITMENT.*

MEASURES OF COMMITMENT	CAREER MOBILITY		
	MINIMUM	MODERATE	MAXIMUM
Seniority†			
0–4 years	6%	9%	4%
5–9 years	22	18	8
10–14 years	57	57	54
15 + years	15	16	34
	(415)‡	(405)	(216)
Identification with company§			
Strong	30	25	40
Medium	43	45	46
Weak	27	30	14
	(411)	(394)	(211)
Attitude toward co. administrators			
Guttman Scale Types			
Favorable (I–II)	33	30	51
Less favorable (III–IV)	67	70	49
	(414)	(397)	(204)
*General satisfaction***			
Satisfied	10	25	37
Dissatisfied	90	75	63
	(112)	(126)	(48)

*Includes only male managers who started in management positions.
†$\chi^2 = 51.3$, df=6, p 0.001; Cramer's $V = 0.16$.
‡Numbers in parentheses indicate numbers of cases.
§$\chi^2 = 24.2$, df=4, p 0.001; Cramer's $V = 0.11$.
$\chi^2 = 27.8$, df=2, p 0.001; Cramer's $V = 0.16$.
**$\chi^2 = 17.8$, df=2, p 0.001; Cramer's $V = 0.25$.

such that upward career mobility automatically provides access to most of the major rewards the organization can provide. As noted, the data revealed that the higher one's position in the hierarchy, the greater one's salary and perceived authority.[7]

Table 2 presents the overall findings relating degree of career mobility to the commitment indexes.[8] The attitudinal data, without controls, did not support uniformly the hypothesized monotonic relationship between mobility and commitment. Among the three attitudinal indexes, only the general satisfaction measure clearly supported Hypothesis 1.

positively, although only slightly, correlated with seniority. Of the managers experiencing little mobility only 15 percent had been with the company at least fifteen years, but 16 percent of the managers experiencing moderate mobility and more than 33 percent of the highly mobile group had been with the company that length of time. These data contrast with Dalton's report of no significant relationship between seniority and career mobility at Milo.[9] Small but positive correlations were also found with the other three measures of commitment. The highest correlation, only 0.25, was found on the general satisfaction index.

TABLE 3.   IDENTIFICATION WITH THE COMPANY, AND CAREER MOBILITY, WITH SENIORITY CONTROLLED.*

| CAREER MOBILITY | IDENTIFICATION WITH COMPANY | | | N |
	STRONG	MODERATE	WEAK	
5 – 9 years with company				
Minimum	33%	40%	27%	90
Moderate	23	43	34	73
10 – 14 Years with company				
Minimum	22	46	32	229
Moderate	22	46	32	223
Maximum	29	52	19	129
15 or More years with company				
Minimum	50	34	16	62
Moderate	41	45	4	64
Maximum	64	32	4	72

*Includes only males who started in nonmanagement positions.

It was expected that seniority would be positively related to amount of upward mobility. This assumes that maintaining one's position with a company reflects commitment to it. As predicted, degree of mobility was

The relationship between career mobility and attitudinal commitment was examined separately for managers who had been with the firm five to nine years, ten to fourteen years, and fifteen years or more. Table 3 presents the findings with respect to iden-

[7]Also the greater one's political involvement and the greater one's chances of being a Republican. See Grusky, "Career Mobility and Managerial Political Behavior," *Pacific Sociological Review,* **8** (2), 82-89 (Fall, 1965).

[8]Since the study was based on a nonrandom sample, the application of statistical tests is questionable; therefore the interpretations of the findings are based primarily on patterns of differences rather than on statistical tests. In every case the interpretations should be viewed as tentative.

*Includes only male managers who started in management positions.
†$\chi^2 = 51.3$, df = 6, p 0.001; Cramer's $V = 0.16$.
‡Numbers in parentheses indicate numbers of cases.
§$\chi^2 = 24.2$, df = 4, p 0.001; Cramer's $V = 0.11$.
   $\chi^2 = 27.8$, df = 2, p 0.001; Cramer's $V = 0.16$.
**$\chi^2 = 17.8$, df = 2, p 0.001; Cramer's $V = 0.25$.
[9]M. Dalton, *Men Who Manage* (New York: Wiley, 1959), pp. 159-161.

tification with the company. Contrary to Hypothesis 1, the data suggest that managers with moderate mobility were *less* committed to the firm than were the managers who experienced minimum mobility. On the other hand, consistent with the hypothesis, the most committed managers were those who had been most mobile during their careers.

Some support for Hypothesis 1 was found with respect to the Guttman scale of attitude toward company administrators. Table 4 indicates that for two of three seniority categories, contrary to the hypothesis, commitment was weaker among the moderately mobile managers than among those who had experienced minimum mobility. However, among the group of managers who had fifteen years seniority or more, amount of career mobility was positively related to attitude toward company administrators.

greater the amount of upward career mobility experienced, the greater the proportion of "satisfied" responses (Table 5). Also, seniority and commitment were correlated in every instance except one. Strength of commitment was strongest in the highest seniority category and weakest in the lowest seniority category.

Considering the findings, one can draw the following conclusions: (*1*) In general, strength of organizational commitment was positively associated with seniority. (*2*) Managers who experienced maximum career mobility were generally more strongly committed to the organization than were less mobile managers. (*3*) Managers who were moderately mobile did not show any uniformity in their pattern of commitment that distinguished them from the less mobile managers. This latter finding may be due to differential mobility expectations. Managers receiving some promotion

TABLE 4. ATTITUDE TOWARD COMPANY ADMINISTRATORS AND CAREER MOBILITY, WITH SENIORITY CONTROLLED.*

CAREER MOBILITY	ATTITUDE TOWARD COMPANY ADMINISTRATORS		
	FAVORABLE (GUTTMAN SCALE TYPES 1–2)	UNFAVORABLE (GUTTMAN SCALE TYPES 3–4)	*N*
5–9 Years with company			
Minimum	27%	63%	87
Moderate	25	75	72
10–14 Years with company			
Minimum	32	68	234
Moderate	30	70	229
Maximum	47	53	127
15 or More years with company			
Minimum	38	61	62
Moderate	39	61	63
Maximum	60	40	69

*Includes only males who started in nonmanagement positions.

The hypothesis fared best on the index of general satisfaction with the company, which was based on responses to two open-ended questions. In all three of the seniority categories, there was a monotonic relationship between amount of upward career mobility and degree of commitment on this index. The

may have felt a weaker commitment when their rewards proved smaller than anticipated.

A note on causality is appropriate. The data do not permit one to ascertain whether career mobility produced strong organizational commitment or vice versa. Nor does

TABLE 5. **GENERAL SATISFACTION WITH THE COMPANY AND CAREER MOBILITY, WITH SENIORITY CONTROLLED.***

| | GENERAL SATISFACTION | | | |
CAREER MOBILITY	SATISFIED	NEUTRAL	DISSATISFIED	*N*
5 – 9 Years with company				
Minimum	4%	—%	96%	27
Moderate	10	14	76	11
10 – 14 Years with company				
Minimum	7	3	90	61
Moderate	10	9	81	70
Maximum	21	2	77	34
15 or More years with company				
Minimum	6	5	89	17
Moderate	23	13	64	22
Maximum	27	18	54	11

*Includes only males who started in nonmanagement positions.

TABLE 6. **FORMAL EDUCATION AND CAREER MOBILITY, WITH SENIORITY CONTROLLED.***

| | FORMAL EDUCATION | | |
CAREER MOBILITY	H.S. GRADUATE OR LESS	SOME COLLEGE	COLLEGE GRADUATE
5 – 9 Years with company			
Minimum	66.7%	52.2%	34.5%
Moderate	33.3	47.8	65.5
	(66)†	*(69)*	*(29)*
10 – 14 Years with company			
Minimum	51.2	32.3	15.2
Moderate	36.1	41.4	32.6
Maximum	12.7	26.3	52.2
	(252)	*(297)*	*(46)*
15 or More years with company			
Minimum	44.8	21.4	4
Moderate	27.6	41.5	28
Maximum	27.6	37.1	68
	(105)	*(70)*	*(25)*

*Males who started in nonmanagement positions only.
†Numbers in parentheses are number of cases.

common sense permit one to make a judgment on the causal relationship. Expressions interpreted as evidence of loyalty to the firm may very well be a condition favoring movement upward in the hierarchy. One could assume that these two variables exercise a reciprocal influence upon each other.[10]

Overcoming Obstacles to Career Mobility

The second hypothesis proposed that the greater the obstacles the individual had to overcome in order to obtain the rewards of upward career mobility, the stronger would be his commitment to the organization.

Two barriers to upward mobility in the company are considered: (*1*) formal educa-

[10]The sample survey design has the weakness of providing data only for a particular period of time. Resurveys or a panel design are required to assess clearly the effects of experience with the company on identification.

tion, which is an achieved characteristic; and (2) sex, which is ascriptive. Specifically, it is hypothesized that within each career mobility level, managers who had overcome a barrier would be more fully committed to the corporation than those who had not. Therefore, less educated managers should show greater commitment than managers possessing more formal education, and female managers should be more strongly committed to the organization than male members.

First, however, it is necessary to establish the two attributes as barriers to upward mobility in the firm. Dalton has shown that formal education was *not* a critical factor in promotion at Milo.[11] Table 6 demonstrates a consistent positive correlation between years of school completed and amount of upward mobility in United Utility when seniority is controlled. The greater the amount of formal education, the greater the degree of upward career mobility in the firm.

Of 352 female managers in United Utility from whom mobility data were gathered, only one (less than one percent) had attained maximum mobility. This contrasts with approximately 20 percent of the male managers who similarly had started in nonmanagement positions and had moved up at least four levels in the hierarchy. Where slightly over 10 percent of the female managers were moderately mobile, more than three times as many male managers (38.7 percent) experienced an equal amount of mobility. When controls for seniority, age, and formal education were applied, the differentials remained. These data suggest that lack of a formal education and being a female were barriers to advancement in the company studied.

Table 7 compares the degree of commitment on the three attitudinal indexes for managers with a high school education and those with college education for each of the three levels of upward mobility. The hypoth-

TABLE 7. ATTITUDINAL INDEXES OF COMMITMENT AND FORMAL EDUCATION, WITH CAREER MOBILITY CONTROLLED.*

FORMAL EDUCATION	IDENTIFICATION WITH COMPANY		ATTITUDE TOWARD COMPANY ADMINISTRATORS		GENERAL SATISFACTION WITH COMPANY	
	HIGH	*N*	FAVORABLE	*N*	SATISFIED	*N*
Minimum						
High school†	31%	*(172)*	35%	*(174)*	13%	*(41)*
College	23	*(115)*	28	*(118)*	5	*(38)*
Moderate						
High school	28	*(116)*	39	*(119)*	24	*(34)*
College	24	*(168)*	28	*(173)*	24	*(56)*
Maximum						
High school	47	*(59)*	56	*(54)*	34	*(15)*
College	41	*(125)*	52	*(125)*	31	*(26)*

*Includes only males who started in nonmanagement positions and have been with the firm ten years or more.

†Includes those completing high school or less.

It is well known that females tend to be discriminated against with respect to promotion, both in civil service and also in industry.

[11]*Op. cit.,* pp. 161-167.

esis was supported in eight of the nine comparisons; in each of these cases, managers with a high school education showed a stronger commitment to the organization than did managers with college experience.

In one instance, level of education did not differentiate: managers with a high school background and those who went to college who experienced moderate mobility demonstrated a similar strength of commitment on the index of general satisfaction with the company. Also, it should be noted that with but one exception, if each educational group is examined separately, there is a positive relationship between level of upward mobility and strength of commitment.

Although the sample of female managers was adequate for those experiencing minimum upward mobility, it was not adequate for those experiencing moderate or maximum

the seniority variable operated against the hypothesis. Although only 45 percent of the female managers had been with the company ten years or more, 72 percent of the male managers in this group had equivalent seniority. In the moderate mobility category, the distributions were similar, 74 percent of the males compared to 75 percent of the females had been with the firm at least ten years. Seniority it appears was a more critical factor in upward mobility for females than for males.

These findings can be interpreted in terms of reference group theory. Managers compare their progress up the ladder with others who

TABLE 8.   ATTITUDINAL INDEXES OF COMMITMENT AND SEX WITH CAREER MOBILITY CONTROLLED.*

SEX — FORMAL EDUCATION	IDENTIFICATION WITH COMPANY		ATTITUDE TOWARD COMPANY ADMINISTRATORS		GENERAL SATISFACTION WITH COMPANY	
	HIGH	*N*	FAVORABLE	*N*	SATISFIED	*N*
Minimum						
Males	30%	*(411)*	33%	*(414)*	10%	*(112)*
Females	38	*(295)*	42	*(306)*	31	*(78)*
Moderate						
Males	25	*(394)*	30	*(397)*	25	*(126)*
Females	53	*(34)*	47	*(34)*	33	*(9)*
Moderate and Maximum						
Males	25	*(603)*	34	*(601)*	26	*(173)*

*Managers who started in nonmanagement positions only.

mobility. The original 37 female managers who were moderately upwardly mobile were reduced to 34 on two of the commitment indexes and to nine cases on the third one, which was one based on open-ended questions.

As Table 8 demonstrates, female managers were more strongly committed than male managers on each of the three indexes, within the two mobile categories. In the minimum mobility category the average percentage difference was 13 percent, while in the moderate mobility group it was almost 18 percent. Moreover, in the minimum mobility category,

presently occupy and who have occupied similar positions in the corporate hierarchy. They are aware that being male and having a college background influences promotion opportunities in the firm. Hence, the female manager and the manager with only a high school education or less who find themselves promoted rapidly or on a level with managers of higher status (male, college-educated managers) feel strongly obligated to the firm, because the rewards they have received have been greater relative to the others. Strong commitment is also encouraged by job opportunities. The male manager and the college-educated manager have considerably more desirable job opportunities elsewhere than do female managers and those with only a high school education or less. The lack of available opportunities at a similar status level should function to promote strong commitment to the company.[12]

SUMMARY

To summarize briefly, this study has examined the relationship between career mobility and strength of commitment among managers of a large corporation. Two hypotheses were formulated. The first proposed a monotonic relationship between rewards received (as measured by degree of career mobility) and the degree of commitment on four indexes. The second hypothesis suggested that

the greater the obstacles the individual had to overcome in order to obtain the organization's rewards, the stronger would be his commitment. Although the first hypothesis received only slight and scattered support, the second was uniformly sustained.

[12]Festinger has suggested that likelihood of persistence in learned behavior is influenced by the amount of effort required when that behavior was acquired. The dissonance created by the amount of effort in learning is decreased by an extra preference for the learned response. [See "The Psychological Effects of Insufficient Rewards," *American Psychologist* **16**, 1-11 (1961).] A related type of phenomenon may be applicable to the present situation. The strength of the manager's attachment to the organization may be affected by the nature and extent of obstacles he found it necessary to overcome in order to attain success. If he succeeded in attaining success, that is, career mobility, despite these hurdles, an extra preference for the company may have developed.

PART SIX

FEEDBACK PROCESSES

In Part IV we talked about monitoring employee performance. Information concerning how well an employee is performing his assigned duties is a form of feedback. It is feedback to management and has implications for rewards, development, counseling and the like. It is also feedback to the individual employee. It provides him with needed information concerning his behavior. Feedback in general, then, is the process which provides individuals or organizations the information needed to determine the extent to which objectives are being met. Additionally, it provides a basis for taking appropriate corrective action, if there is a deviation from objectives.

There are virtually an infinite number of sources and situations which may either provide or require feedback to the personnel function. The articles in this section are representative of some of these sources and situations.

The first article, "Validity of Exit Interviews," focuses on an underutilized source of feedback—the terminal interview with a departing employee. To the extent that the real reasons for an employee's decision to leave the organization can be uncovered, the employee may be salvaged or at least poor personnel practices or other sources of job dissatisfaction may be identified. This "feedback" information may then form the basis of corrective action to minimize the probability of further turnover. In this article, the author attempts to demonstrate the validity of exit interviews and advances recommendations for improving their usefulness.

"Union-Management Relations: From Conflict to Collaboration" has as its focus an attempt to move the union-management process from one of conflict and limited warfare to one of mutual communication and collaborative problem solving.

In the final article, "Handling Grievances Where There is No Union," the author explores the implications of the fact that grievance handling may be more difficult in a non-union shop than in a union shop. Ways to make a grievance system contribute to effective feedback rather than detract from it are suggested.

VALIDITY OF EXIT INTERVIEWS

Joel Lefkowitz
Myron L. Katz

The high cost of employee turnover has led to increased concern, in recent years, with methods of systematically reducing organizational rates of attrition. Published research has focused primarily on attempts either to predict employee tenure or to explain the reasons for job separations after they occur.[1]

Part of industry's systematic approach to the problem has been the use of some form of exit interview—a formal or informal, structured or relatively unstructured information-gathering session with departing employees. Rarely is the interview seen as a means of attempting to salvage the departing employee. The present emphasis seems to be on its usefulness as a means of creating better public relations, checking on the soundness of initial selection procedures, or uncovering poor personnel practices, specific sources of job dissatisfaction, unsatisfactory supervisors, etc.[2]

The traditional criticisms of the technique involve the difficulty of obtaining enough trained interviewers, the (unknown) accuracy of the interviewee's comments, and the possibility of his distorting or being unwilling to discuss frankly the reasons for his departure.[3]

Most published studies ignore the criticisms regarding the reliability and validity of the procedure and focus on merely categorizing the verbalized reasons for leaving, as obtained during the interviews.[4]

Where recognition of these shortcomings is acknowledged, a post-separation follow-up is often advocated, either by means of a mailed questionnaire or telephone survey.[5] Few authors have agreed with the all-inclusive criticism of van Blokland[6] that the exit interview is relatively valueless on the grounds that a well-balanced personnel policy can give all the information obtainable in an interview program—and often in time to prevent the employee's desire to terminate.

Even those who have advocated the post-separation check on the accuracy of offered "reasons for termination" have presented no data to support the procedure. They have merely assumed that the technique should obviate the problems of "obtaining a rational assessment of the situation from an employee who is still emotionally involved," and the reluctance of employees "to discuss the real reasons for their leaving, for fear they would not get good letters of recommendation when seeking their next job."[7] The closest we have come to an empirical presentation is Yourman's allusion to the fact that

... when the mail questionnaire results were

From Joel Lefkowitz and Myron L. Katz, "Validity of Exit Interviews," Personnel Psychology 22 (4), 445–455 (1969). Reprinted by permission.

[1]J. Lefkowitz, *How to Diagnose and Control Personnel Turnover* (New York: BFS Executive Communications, 1967); A. J. Schuh, "The Predictability of Employee Tenure: A Review of the Literature," *Personnel Psychology* **XX**, 133-152 (1967).

[2]S. Habbe, "The Exit Interview: A New Interpretation," *Management Record* **XIV**, 337-338, 371-372 (1952); R. P. Kreuter, "Exit Questionnaires Help Our Employee Relations," *Factory Management and Maintenance* **CIX**, 90-91 (July, 1951); L. This, "Exit Interviews: Do They Pay?" *Personnel Journal* **XXXIV**, 58-60, 70 (1955).

[3]Kreuter, *op. cit.;* E. Schoenfeld, "The Non-Directive Exit Interview," *Personnel* **XXXIV**, 46-50 (1957); J. Yourman, "Following up on Terminations: An Alternative to the Exit Interview," *Personnel* **XLII**, 51-55 (1965).

[4]R. D. Melcher, "Getting the Facts on Employee Resignations," *Personnel* **XXXI**, 504-514 (1955); E. J. Moran, "The Exit Interview—An Experimental Study," *Personnel Practices Bulletin* (Melbourne) **XII**, 31-42 (1956); F. J. Smith and W. A. Kerr, "Turnover Factors as Assessed by the Exit Interview," *Journal of Applied Psychology* **XXXVII**, 352-355 (1953).

[5]Kreuter, *op. cit.;* Lefkowitz, *op. cit.;* Yourman, *op. cit.;* H. G. Heneman and Mary Sue Kern, "Exit Interviews," *Nursing Outlook* **IV**, 436-438 (1956).

[6]G. G. van Blokland, "Het Exit-Interview: Mosterd Nade Maaltijd," *Mens Onderneming* **XIII**, 237-245 (1959).

[7]Lefkowitz, *op. cit.*

compared with the findings of the (exit interviews) they showed a sufficiently high measure of agreement on both favorable and unfavorable aspects as to convince management, as well as the research team, that the mail interview was just as valid a tool as a highly competent personal interview . . . [8]

PURPOSE OF THE STUDY

In the endeavor to assess the validity of the exit interview, it is apparent that no "ultimate" criterion exists apart from employees' reports of the circumstances leading to separation. It is, perhaps, illogical to assume that one set of proffered reasons (say, several months after termination of a job) has any more value as a criterion assessment than some other set (say, immediately prior to termination, during an exit interview). This dilemma, of course, is the characteristic difficulty with most correlational type research. However, the previously noted advantages of post-termination data *do* make sense, and the utilization of such data as a criterion with which to validate exit interviews appears to be the most tenable procedure. As such, it is the procedure followed in this study.

An assessment of the validity of the exit interview, therefore, entails a comparison between the specific "reasons for termination" listed in one company's personnel records (as obtained via exit interviews) with those elicited from the employees involved several months following termination of their employment. To the extent, however, that some specific disagreements between these two sets of data may be insignificant, we may obtain a deflated measure of the value of exit interview information. This suggests, then, a "pre vs. post" comparison not only of the *specific reasons* given for termination, but also of the *general categories* within which those reasons are contained.

This procedure involves a more analytical breakdown of "job separations" than is

usually performed. It has been pointed out elsewhere[9] that managements as well as industrial psychologists occasionally overlook the distinction between "voluntary" (resignations) and "involuntary" (dismissals) job separations. Even more rarely is explicit recognition given to reasons that may be considered "avoidable" vs. those that may be considered "unavoidable."

An assessment of the meaningfulness of exit interview data will entail "pre vs. post" comparisons of these categories. Theoretically, it would seem that these two dichotomous variables should yield a 2×2 or four-fold table: voluntary avoidable, voluntary unavoidable, involuntary avoidable, and involuntary unavoidable reasons for termination. However, it is the writer's position that the last-mentioned category does not (should not?) exist. That is, there is no occasion when an employee is discharged for reasons which are not, at least potentially, avoidable. While that position is subject to refutation, it is felt that even if it were demonstrated to be incorrect, "involuntary unavoidable" separations represent an exceedingly small proportion of actual reasons for separation. Accordingly, the present study utilizes three general categories: voluntary avoidable, voluntary unavoidable, and involuntary.

METHOD

The Research Site and the Sample

The study was conducted at a medium-sized factory which employs approximately 750 people in the manufacture of women's lingerie. The factory is located in a suburb of a medium-sized town in the eastern United States. Approximately 650 of these employees are female sewing machine operators, and the present study refers to this group.

The population from which the sample was drawn consists of all those women who terminated their employment during the six-

---

[8]Yourman, *op. cit.*, p. 55.

[9]Lefkowitz, *op. cit.*

month period January–June, 1967 ($N = 164$). Questionnaires were mailed directly to the homes of these former employees on an average of approximately six months after job separation. Participation was completely voluntary, and the return envelopes were addressed to a consulting organization employed by the manufacturing company.

Eighty questionnaires were received, for a return of 48.8%. However, 16 envelopes were returned marked "addressee unknown," yielding an effective return of 54.1% (80 of 148).

Because participation in the study was voluntary, the possibility exists of self-selection bias having influenced the determination of the sample. As a partial check on such factors, comparisons were made between the sample and the parent population on the factors of Age and Job Tenure. With respect to age: $X = 26.30$ years, S.D. $\times 9.61$ years; $\mu = 26.58$ years, $\sigma = 8.77$ years ($Z = -.28$, n.s.). For job tenure: $X = 17.80$ months, S.D. $= 32.26$ months; $\mu = 19.15$ months, $\sigma = 29.66$ months ($Z = 1.40$, n.s.).

Data Analysis

This study involves a comparison of "reasons for termination" recorded in the company's personnel records as obtained during an unstructured exit interview, with reasons listed by these same employees on the mailed follow-up questionnaire.

All responses were coded as falling into one of the following 19 reasons for termination:

A. Involuntary
  A1. Low Production Efficiency
  A2. Inferior Quality of Production
  A3. Taken off Company Records: Not Reporting In (Absence)
  A4. Personal Relations—Supervisor
  A5. Laid Off—Not Enough Work Available
  A6. Not Enough Information Given—or No Reason Specified.

B. Voluntary Avoidable
  B1. Inability to cope with the felt pressure of production
  B2. Dissatisfaction with the nature of the work itself
  B3. Dissatisfaction with some aspect of physical working conditions
  B4. Personal relations—Peers or Supervisors
  B5. Dissatisfaction with piece rates
  B6. Dissatisfaction with absolute amount of money to be earned
  B7. Accepted another job
  B8. No specific reason given

C. Voluntary Unavoidable
  C1. Needed at home due to physical health problem, lack of baby sitter, or unspecified
  C2. Pregnancy
  C3. Leaving town: as a result of marriage, or husband's vocational relocation
  C4. Lack of transportation
  C5. Enrolled in school full time

Some of the reasons in category (C) might actually be better represented as falling in category (B). However, without additional information beyond that available, we have to assume that "needed at home" and "lack of transportation" actually represent "unavoidable" rather than "avoidable" conditions.

RESULTS

Specific Reasons for Termination

Table 1 presents the frequency count of specific reasons for termination as obtained during the exit interviews and the follow-up questionnaires. In addition, the reasons are rank-ordered for both sets of data.

The rank order correlation coefficient

Exit Interview "Reason"

Follow-up "Reason"	A1	A2	A3	A4	A5	A6	B1	B2	B3	B4	B5	B6	B7	B8	C1	C2	C3	C4	C5	Σ	Rank
A1	3	1																		4	7
A2																				0	18.5
A3	1							1					1							3	9
A4	1	1																		2	12.5
A5	1	1																		2	12.5
A6	2																			2	12.5
B1	2		1					2	1	1			2		4		2			15	1
B2									1					1						2	12.5
B3								1												1	16
B4			1				1	1					1	4	1					9	4
B5							1													1	16
B6													1		1			1		3	9
B7													1	1	1					3	9
B8																				0	18.5
C1			4												9					13	2
C2	1														1	6				8	5
C3	1		2										1	1	1		5			11	3
C4													1	1				3		5	6
C5							1													1	16
Σ	12	3	8	0	0	0	3	5	2	1	0	0	8	8	18	6	7	4	0	85[a]	
Rank	2	10.5	4	16.5	16.5	16.5	10.5	8	12	13	16.5	16.5	4	4	1	7	6	9	16.5		

* See text for definitions of coded "reasons for termination."

[a] No. of Subjects — 80, less 4 (missing data) plus 0 (multiple responses) — 85 responses.

R_s = .42 (corrected for ties) is statistically significant ($p <$ .05, one-tailed test), but we would evaluate it as low for these data.

The most frequently-given reason for termination at the time of the exit interview is the general "needed at home" explanation. At the time of the follow-up, the most frequent reason involves the inability to cope with production pressures.

The reasons which show the greatest discrepancy between the two rankings are (in decreasing order of degree of discrepancy) B8, B1, B4, A2, and B6. The 14 percent of the voluntary terminators who, during the exit interview, said they were resigning "for no specific reason" *all* listed specific reasons at the time of the follow-up. Half of these reasons were related to problems in personal relations—with peers or supervisors, and about which the employees apparently would not discuss at the time.

Production pressures would seem to account for few terminations—if measured at the time of termination. The questionnaire data, however, indicate it to be the single most frequent "cause" of termination (among both voluntary and involuntary reasons).

Most published research deals only with voluntary terminations of employment. For this reason and because a portion of the involuntary terminators in our sample were "taken off company records," thus presumably receiving no interview, Table 2 presents the rank order of reasons for termination for a sample restricted only to those who voluntarily resigned.

The rank order correlation coefficient r_s = .31 (n.s., corrected for ties) lends little

TABLE 2. FREQUENCY AND RANK ORDER OF "REASONS FOR TERMINATION" AS
OBTAINED FROM EXIT INTERVIEWS AND FOLLOW-UP QUESTIONNAIRES, FOR
A SAMPLE OF VOLUNTARY RESIGNATIONS ONLY

	FREQUENCY		RANK ORDER	
REASON[a]	EXIT INTERVIEW	FOLLOW-UP QUESTIONNAIRE	EXIT INTERVIEW	FOLLOW-UP QUESTIONNAIRE
A3[b]	0	2	12.5	9.5
B1	3	12	8	1
B2	5	2	6	9.5
B3	2	1	9	12
B4	1	8	10	3.5
B5	0	1	12.5	12
B6	0	3	12.5	7.5
B7	8	3	2.5	7.5
B8	8	0	2.5	14
C1	18	9	1	2
C2	6	7	5	5
C3	7	8	4	3.5
C4	4	5	7	6
C5	0	1	12.5	12
Total	62	62		

[a] See text for definitions of coded "reasons for termination."
[b] Two individuals who apparently resigned voluntarily but who, not reporting in, admit to actually having been "taken off Company records."

support to one's faith in the validity of the exit interview.

General Categories of Reasons for Termination

The validity coefficients noted above indicate widespread discrepancies between initial and follow-up "reasons for termination" as ob-tained from employees. It is likely that the extent of such specific discrepancies is related to the general kind (category) of termination. Table 3 presents this data.

The total proportion of discrepancies, as well as the proportion within each category, is significantly greater than zero. In point of fact it represents a majority (59% of all those for whom we have complete data, $N = 76$).

TABLE 3. AGREEMENTS AND DISCREPANCIES BETWEEN EXIT INTERVIEW AND FOLLOW-
UP QUESTIONNAIRE "REASONS FOR TERMINATION," AS A FUNCTION OF
GENERAL CATEGORY OF INITIAL "REASON"

INITIAL CATEGORY	AGREEMENT	DISCREPANCY	NO RESPONSE
A. Involuntary	3 (14%)	18 (82%)*	1 (5%)
B. Voluntary Avoidable	5 (21%)	18 (75%)*	1 (4%)
C. Voluntary Unavoidable	23 (68%)	9 (26%)*	2 (6%)
Total	31 (38%)	45 (56%)*	4 (5%)

Note. Any multiple questionnaire response was scored as an "agreement" if any one of the several reasons agreed with the initial (exit interview) reason.
*Significantly greater than zero ($p < .05$).

Responses in category C, consisting of "voluntary unavoidable" reasons for termination, are significantly less discrepant (26%) than those in either category A (82%) or category B (75%) [$Z = 4.05$, $p < .0001$; $Z = 3.65$, $p < .0002$, respectively]. Obviously, pregnancy, leaving town, being needed as a "baby sitter," or not having transportation to get to work are reasons for termination which are less subject to distortion than others.

The meaningfulness of the data presented in Table 3 is limited since many of the discrepancies represent different *specific* reasons within the *same general category*. It would be of particular interest to note, for example, the number of "unavoidable" terminations which, upon later questioning, were actually "avoidable." Table 4 presents these data.

Summarizing the results presented in Table 4, we see that 36 percent of the sample (28 of 78) indicate reasons for termination on the follow-up questionnaire which fall into different general categories from that recorded at the time of termination. In addition, category A (involuntary) is significantly less stable than either category B ($Z = -1.64$, $p = .05$) or category C ($Z = -2.04$, $p = .02$).

Comparing the data in Tables 3 and 4 reveals that the three categories maintain the same rank order of stability (C,B,A) whether specific reasons are noted (Table 3) or general category of reason is the focus (Table 4).

Although this general trend is consistent, there are specific differences worth noting. The percentage figures for category C (voluntary unavoidable) in Tables 3 and 4 are highly similar, indicating that, whatever discrepancies in particular reasons for termination occur among individuals in this category, they are nevertheless restricted to discrepancies within the same category. The data for categories A and B, however, reveal that a majority of the discrepancies between exit interview and follow-up questionnaire "reasons" consist of shifts to one of the other general categories.

Worthy of special note are the following particular "shifts":

Fifty-four percent of those who were dismissed later report having voluntarily

TABLE **4.** **AGREEMENTS AND DISCREPANCIES BETWEEN EXIT INTERVIEW AND FOLLOW-UP QUESTIONNAIRE GENERAL CATEGORIES OF "REASONS FOR TERMINATION"**

GENERAL CATEGORY OF REASON

EXIT INTERVIEW	FOLLOW-UP QUESTIONNAIRE	*N*	PERCENT	
	A (same)	10		45
A. Involuntary	B	4	18	
				54
	C	8	36	
	B (same)	16		70
B. Voluntary Avoidable	A	2	9	
				31
	C	5	22	
	C (same)	24		73
C. Voluntary Unavoidable	A	0	0	
				27
	B	9	27	

resigned (A → B or C). (This is a somewhat overly-impressive figure due to the inclusion of those who "resigned" by not showing up for work and were subsequently, therefore, "dismissed" by management.)

Nine percent of those who (from management's exit interview data) voluntarily resigned for "avoidable" reasons report having been dismissed (B → A).

Twenty-seven percent of those whose exit interviews indicate their resignations to have been "unavoidable," report later having resigned for reasons classified as "avoidable."

DISCUSSION

Several types of data analyses were employed in the study based on a predictive validity model, using the exit interview as predictor and post-termination questionnaire data as criteria.

The several analyses focused on:

Validity coefficients representing the correlation between rank order of frequencies of "reasons for termination."

The proportion of the sample revealing discrepancies between their reported "reasons for termination" on the two sets of data.

The stability (proportion of discrepancies) of the three general categories of "reasons for termination."

All three analyses substantiate the traditional but heretofore undocumented criticisms of the exit interview regarding its questionable accuracy and tendency to obtain, from departing employees, noncommital and/or distorted verbal reports.

The distortions are revealed by the fact that 59 percent of the sample report different "reasons" on the two sets of data. The tendency to "clam up" is illustrated best by the fact that *all* of those, who at the time of the exit interview, said they were resigning "for no specific reason," later report specific reasons for their resignations. The general lack of accuracy is demonstrated by the reported rank order correlation coefficients of .42 and .31.

Since most published research deals with voluntary resignations it is important to note the distinction between "avoidable" and "unavoidable" voluntary resignations.

Unavoidable terminations appear to be the only kind about which exit interviews elicit accurate information. This is apparently due to the unambiguous nature of "leaving town," or being pregnant. However, another interpretation is possible. This category of terminations is composed uniformly of specific reasons which are extra-organizational in origin. As such, they pose little or no threat when revealed to a management representative during an exit interview.

The results of this study substantiate the oft-voiced necessity for extensive training in interviewing techniques for those whose responsibility it is to conduct exit interviews. The data suggest, moreover, the advisability of supplementing (and possibility of completely replacing) exit interviews with a post-termination questionnaire approach.

UNION–MANAGEMENT RELATIONS: FROM CONFLICT TO COLLABORATION

Robert R. Blake
Jane S. Mouton

Not long ago, the senior author of this article was talking with the president of a chemical company that had just reached a strike settlement.

Armed only with some raw newspaper facts, he asked, "How did it turn out?"

"We won! We made them crawl back through the gate on their bellies," the president answered exultantly. Then, with somewhat muted enthusiasm, he went on, "The company is in bad economic shape. We lost several contracts we would have had if we had been able to make delivery. But we taught the union a lesson—we won!"

"What," asked the author, "really started the conflict?"

The president answered, *"I don't know. There were some disagreements, but they were not the real reasons for the antagonism."*

Later on, the author talked with the president of the union in question. When he asked him how the strike had turned out, the union man said grimly, "We lost. They forced us to submit, but we were right. We'll build strength. We won't make the mistake tomorrow that we made yesterday."

"What was the real problem?" the author asked.

The union president said, *"I don't know. There were some differences, sure, but*

From Robert R. Blake and Jane S. Mouton, "Union–Management Relations: From Conflict to Collaboration," Personnel 38 (6), 38–51 (1961). Reprinted by permission of the American Management Association.

management took arbitrary positions—tough positions and attitudes that we can't understand."

Thus what seemed from management's viewpoint to have been a successful resolution of a union-management conflict had, in fact, solved nothing. Nor was this by any means an isolated case: such episodes take place so often that we more or less take them for granted.

Indeed, the almost universal tendency is to look upon clashes of this kind as one of the inescapable facts of life that we all have to learn to live with. To the behavioral scientist, however, such intergroup conflicts are merely the outward and visible signs of something radically wrong with the relations between the warring parties—the symptoms, in other words, of an underlying intergroup pathology. And just as modern medicine focuses on treating the causes of disease, not its symptoms, so behavioral science aims at identifying the socio-psychological causes of intergroup conflict and treating them, not the conflict itself.

At the University of Texas, we have been working for the past decade on a two-pronged approach to this problem. One prong has been concerned with the development and continuous expansion of a comprehensive theory of intergroup warfare and collaboration, which we have validated through experimental work. The other prong has taken the form of applying this comprehensive theory of actual union-management situations with the aim of shifting them from a condition of mutual suspicion to one of mutual respect and joint problem solving. In this article we shall survey both theory and application and evaluate their more sweeping implications for the future of union-management relations as we now see them.

THE WIN-LOSE APPROACH

First, we must consider three questions: What are the causes of unhealthy intergroup relations, as manifested in such symptoms as discord and conflict? What are the causes of intergroup health, as manifested in the cooperative problem solving that leads to concord? Once the malady has appeared, how can it be treated so that the intergroup system can be restored to better health?

We begin with the hypothesis that warfare follows when the response of two contending groups to the differences separating them is based on a two-valued orientation to the situation—good-bad, right-wrong. A major two-valued orientation, often characteristic of industrial strife, is win-lose. There is nothing in between; the cleavage is absolute. Each side is bent on winning, on defeating the other, by ramming fixed, inflexible "positions" down the other's throat.

By comparison, cooperation is based on a multivalued orientation that provides the mental flexibility and intellectual freedom to explore a whole spectrum of alternative approaches to the problem. Under these circumstances the win-lose orientation tends to disappear and to be replaced by efforts to find acceptable solutions rather than to "win."

It is not too difficult to see that the multivalued, problem-solving approach is likely to be a far more constructive way of resolving intergroup differences than the search by each side for the conditions under which the other will be compelled to yield. The question is, then, "How can the simple win-lose orientation be replaced by the problem-solving approach?" Some guidance for making this shift in union-management relations can be drawn from a series of experiments we have carried out over the past few years.

Our work has been based on a prototype experiment designed and carried out by Sherif, who placed two groups of children in a competitive situation from which there was no realistic possibility of escape.[1] First,

Sherif studied the ingroup and intergroup phenomena generated by the competitive circumstances. Then he went on to identify the conditions that were effective and those that were ineffective in reducing competitive tensions and conflict between the groups.

Our experiments have been concerned with the same basic problem but have been conducted with adults drawn from industrial organizations. In all, they have involved approximately 1,000 subjects divided into more than 150 groups matched, on a paired basis, in size, personal characteristics, and other relevant dimensions. Each of the 30 experiments we have conducted has dealt with a different systematic problem and has proceeded through a series of phases extending over a two-week period.[2]

The first phase in each experiment has consisted of 10 to 18 hours of interaction during which the groups develop goals, norms of conduct and performance, and power relations among their members. In the second phase, conditions are created to throw the groups into competition; each group develops its own solution to some basic issue with which all members are familiar. The third phase begins when one group has "won" by producing a better solution and the other group has "lost" by producing a poorer one. The fourth and fifth phases deal with the reduction of conflict and the restoration of intergroup problem solving.

APPLYING THE EXPERIMENTS TO UNION-MANAGEMENT RELATIONS

Before we go on to generalize from these experiments, it may perhaps be advisable to explain why we elected to use the win-lose design. Is the win-lose orientation typical of union-management relations in general? There is no doubt that it characterizes such

[1]M. Sherif and C. W. Sherif, *An Outline of Social Psychology* (New York: Harper & Brothers, 1956), revised ed.

[2]These studies were partially supported by grants from the National Institute of Health and Esso Division, Humble Oil and Refining Company.

forms of open conflict as strikes, lockouts, and demands for coercive legislation. But what of the numerous situations where no open conflict manifests itself?

Our feeling on this question was that the absence of open conflict could not be construed as equivalent to constructive intergroup problem solving. Indeed, many union-management situations that look "healthy" are, under closer examination, better characterized as win-lose situations held in equilibrium by an uneasy truce. The conditions for conflict are there, but neither side feels strong enough to fire the opening volley. Hence, we concluded that the win-lose design was critical for developing a theory of intergroup relations that would be useful for unraveling the causes of industrial strife.

In any case, there is widespread evidence that labor and management do approach many outstanding issues from a win-lose point of view. The shift away from the idea of complete and total victory is made only when the chips are down and economic and social realities intrude to blur the situation. Moreover, even when new issues and realities invade the scene, and the urge to compromise takes over, the desire to win is not always obliterated. Often, it is merely driven underground, with each group pledging itself to a stronger position that will lead to total victory in the next round.

One direct result of the prevalence of the win-lose orientation and fixed-position taking, which generates acrimony and makes the redefinition of problems and the give-and-take of compromise more difficult, has been the development of federal, state, and private mediation services. Another, the building into union contracts of arbitration clauses as a mechanism for invoking outside aid when a total impasse has been reached.

Our experiments with intergroup win-lose dynamics have their parallels, in fact, whenever a union and a management approach bargaining, grievances, work assignments, and similar issues from fixed positions and with the intention not to compromise but to prevail over the other side.

WHEN THE GOAL IS TO WIN

The details of our individual experiments have been reported elsewhere. Here we shall summarize the insights they have yielded that we have found most central for understanding unhealthy union-management situations and for pointing out what might be done to help the parties develop more healthy interdependence in their problem-solving relations.

It is at the point where competition emerges that the fundamental significance of the win-lose dynamic appears. As soon as a group is possessed of the urge to win over the other side, marked changes appear both in the group itself and in its attitude toward its opponents:

1. *Greater Group Cohesion.* Prominent among these changes is an increase in the cohesiveness of the group. When an adversary approaches, the members close ranks to stave off defeat. Spirits go up, former internal disagreements are put aside, members "pitch in." All pull together toward the common goal of victory. (The heavier turnout of members at union meetings during periods of tension is typical of this phenomenon.)

But exciting though it is to march together toward victory, the urge to win is a primitive one. Here is a first sign of group pathology. Disagreement—the raw material of the creative thinking that alone can lead to the re-examination and enrichment of the group's position—tends to be snuffed out. Failure to go along after a certain point can arouse insidious group pressures toward conformity and, in the extreme, may even lead to the expulsion of members who resist the tide.

2. *Shifts in the Pecking Order.* At the start, power relations in our groups tend to be loose and rather poorly worked out. With neither

time nor performance pressures bearing down upon it, the pecking order is fuzzy and unclear.

But when clear, sharp competition arises, stakes are involved; personal reputations merge with the reputation of the group. Some members, who are better able to talk than others, or for whom the thought of victory has particular relish, begin to carry more weight than before. Sometimes there is, in effect, a complete takeover by one or two persons. Those who are less aggressive and more dependent fall in line.

What happens? There is definitely group accomplishment. A more differentiated pecking order is established. But if those who control the group fail to exercise their influence in ways that recognize the "legitimate" rights of others, the seeds of civil war have been sown. Later on, defeat will be the fertile soil that nourishes their growth and the development of dissension and discord within the group itself. The surge toward victory may, in fact, raise strong barriers to future ingroup cooperation.

3. *Distorted Judgments of Competing Positions.* After group positions have taken shape and have been exchanged between the contending groups, the members quickly develop attitudes toward both solutions. But judgments of the position adopted by the opposing group are invariably distorted by membership considerations. This distortion takes the form of judging one's own position to be superior to the other, with little or no regard for any qualitative differences that may actually exist between them. The group members strongly identify with their own position; they rationalize, or justify the comparison, and downgrade the competitor's proposals.

Thus the win-lose conflict disrupts realistic judgment. It tends to obliterate objectivity—a primary condition of intergroup problem solving. When win-lose attitudes increase subjectivity to the point where appraisal is no longer realistic, then the conditions of future cooperation are effectively eliminated.

4. *Belittlement of the Opposite Side.* In our experiments, the groups study the two solutions and then interact through their representatives to determine victor and vanquished. But before coming to the final decision, they are given an opportunity to clarify their similarities and differences. During this clarification stage, questions are formulated by each group to be answered by the other.

Study of these questions shows that, far from being intended to clarify the issue, they are for the most part couched in such a way as to belittle the competitor's proposal, cast doubt on its validity, and in fact demonstrate its inferiority. We see precisely the same process at work in the handouts, full-page newspaper advertisements, and other media used to state either management's or the union's case and belittle that of the other side: all are examples of hostile messages that purport to "clarify" the issues at stake but, all too often, produce no more than an incendiary effect.

Thus instead of reducing conflict and increasing objectivity, intergroup contacts for the purpose of clarification have precisely the opposite effect. Each side's suspicion of the other's motives is intensified.

5. *Development of Negative Stereotypes.* As groups interact over a period of time, under conditions where the activities are competitive and mutually frustrating, the members of each group develop hostile attitudes toward the members of the other group and express them in the form of negative stereotypes whose provocative effect simply leads to counterprovocation. Thus the conflict is intensified, and there is a further erosion of mutual respect and confidence.

This process was well exemplified in a recent strike when negative thrusts by each group against the other filled the airwaves as the conflict reached its peak. The union called management's approach "bargaining by ultimatum." Management accused the union of wanting "auction type" bargaining. By blurring the real issues and focusing attention on "labels" instead of on the existing problems, this stereotyping made the problem-solving process itself more difficult, quite apart from the difficulty of resolving the issues involved.

6. *Distortions in Comprehension.* Another feature of our experiments is that when all group members on both sides aver that they fully understand the adversary's position they are given an objective test of their knowledge of the stands taken by both groups. Our analysis of their test papers not only shows how win-lose attitudes contaminate objective thinking but also throws some light on the character of the resulting distortions.

Not too much attention is paid to points of agreement on both sides, the test results show, but areas of actual differences are highlighted. The items most often missed are the ones identical in both proposals. While the testees correctly recognize that such items are part and parcel of their own group's position, they frequently fail to see that the opposing group has adopted them as well. In other words, similarities tend to be overlooked when groups are in competition with one another. Thus further barriers to agreement are created, since people can't very well agree to what they don't understand.[3]

By contrast, items that form part of the position of one side alone are correctly recognized much more often. But even here group members identify the distinctive elements in their own position better than they identify those of their adversary's.

These findings show how one's mental outlook is affected by the desire to win. Obviously, this underattention to areas of

[3]The authors recently had occasion to scrutinize a summary prepared by one company's management, entitled "Differences Between Union and Management Bargaining Positions." The summary listed 62 items. Management had never bothered to list the 182 points of agreement in the two positions.

agreement and overattention to areas of disagreement must increase the difficulty of reaching common understanding.

7. *Loyalty Before Logic.* When the representatives of the competing groups meet to decide the winner and the loser, deadlock is the most likely result. If, by being impartial and taking an objective point of view, a representative is in danger of losing, the pressures of loyalty to the group are often sufficient to overwhelm logic. Even though the representative is theoretically under the intellectual compulsion to exercise objectivity in judgment, he rarely does so.

Underlying the pressures on the representative to stand by his group through "thick and thin," and "for better or worse," is the threat of being labeled a traitor. A traitor is one who capitulates to the enemy and thus loses for his group, while the member who wins for his group by devastating his adversary is, of course, a hero. Deadlock, though it does not carry with it the elevation in status accorded a hero, at least is one way to avoid the stigma of "traitor."

In the background of intergroup contact under win-lose conditions there often lurk the shadows of hero-traitor dynamics. To be a hero is its own reward. Yet the behavior required for this reward can be at variance with the actions called for by objectivity and problem solving. On the other hand, and equally unfortunately, objective, problem-solving behavior may be abandoned to escape the "traitor" threat.

8. *Resistance to Any Unfavorable Neutral Judgment.* Since, for these reasons, it is difficult to determine the winner in our experimental situations, an impartial judge is called on to make the decision, in circumstances paralleling arbitration. Not being vested with membership interests, he is usually able to render his verdict without too much hedging. One group wins; the other loses.

How is the impartial judge perceived? Before he hands down his verdict, both groups agree that he is intelligent, fair, honest, thoughtful, unprejudiced, tactful, and capable. After the verdict, the picture shifts dramatically. The group members who have won are reinforced in their positive perceptions of him. His verdict "proves" he was a "good" judge. But the defeated group immediately questions the judge's ability to render a competent verdict. While the members still think he is intelligent and basically honest, they now look upon him as unfair, thoughtless, biased, and tactless. Their response is "We weren't wrong. It was the judge who failed to comprehend."

Thus there is an inability to accept the unfavorable judgment of a neutral party as valid. Rationalizations are immediately erected to protect the losing position despite its defeat.

9. *Complacency vs. Ingroup Fighting.* There are still other differences between the groups after the verdict is rendered. Victory or defeat has predictable outcomes that influence the conditions of subsequent contacts between the groups.

In the winning groups, those who led the march to victory are congratulated. Their positions are strengthened, and those who followed them become even more dependent on them for future direction and guidance. In the defeated groups, however, there is ingroup fighting and splintering into factions. The leaders who failed the group fight back. If they don't succeed in reinstating themselves, they pout and sulk and eventually cease to take any interest in the group.

The "group mentality," bad though this concept is said to be, is dramatically different too in the winning and losing groups. This is apparent not only in their reactions to the judge and to their representatives but also in the group "atmosphere." Members of victorious groups bask in the glow of victory. Success makes them complacent. They are content to coast and rest on their laurels. But in the defeated groups there is a "lean and

hungry" atmosphere filled with tension that must be discharged. Members immediately start ferreting out the causes of failure. This process was clearly at work after the 1960 election: less than one week later *The Wall Street Journal* reported, "The Republican Party, scarcely stopping to lick its wounds after a narrow national defeat, today enters a period of protracted, intense—and possibly destructive—civil war."

Without going into further details, it can be said that by failing to come to grips with the problems of the future, the complacency that follows victory is no less unhealthy than the destructive ingroup fighting that is too often associated with defeat.

These observations of the behavior of groups deliberately placed in competitive situations clearly indicate the futility of the win-lose concept as a basis for healthy, constructive intergroup relations. The question still remains, however: "How can this competitive relationship be changed into a collaborative one based on mutual respect and trust and joint problem solving?"

FIRST STEPS ALONG THE PATH TO COLLABORATION

Experimental attempts to solve this problem have taken two main forms. One has sought to reduce conflict by trying to eliminate the boundaries that separate people into groups. The other, more realistic, recognizes that people are inevitably segregated into groups of one kind or another, and hence has focused on devising ways to protect group identification and membership while promoting intergroup cooperation.

The former approach clearly has little applicability to industrial strife, since it is essentially contradictory to the legal definition of the appropriate relations between union and management. It is true that there have been many times when management and union have joined forces, as it were, against the threat of external competition to insure the company's survival. But in a thriving, growing economy, survival is seldom in question. Since it is a need that is more or less satisfied, it does not furnish a compelling motivation as the basis for cooperation. Furthermore, many goals of the two groups are essentially distinctive, i.e., not shared by both, once the question of survival is no longer of functional signficance. Labor-management cooperation, therefore, would seem to be a practical alternative to labor-management competition only when both sides share the motivation to solve their common and distinctive problems while maintaining their legitimate group boundaries.

At the University of Texas we have followed this approach in the various training procedures briefly described below. These procedures have been employed in four union-management warfare situations and in each case have demonstrated that groups locked in conflict with one another *can* re-establish a collaborative relationship.

1. *Training in the Theory of the Win-Lose Conflict and in Recognizing the Phenomena Associated with It.* Deep-rooted human attitudes are not changed by an expert's saying, "This is how it should be," or even pointing the way. Yet attitudes can be changed once one has become aware of one's own reactions to warfare, first through experiencing them in the direct heat of conflict and then through talking about them systematically.

A laboratory training program in which participants directly experience the conditions that arouse intergroup hostility and conflict and then compare their experiences with the conditions necessary to bring about collaboration provides this first step. The program includes miniature situations illustrating the generalizations outlined above.

2. *Laboratory Skill Training in the Procedural Steps Leading Toward Intergroup Cooperation.* Recognition of the dynamics of intergroup conflict, though indispensable, is insufficient. If collaboration is to be achieved,

practical ways of facilitating it must be demonstrated. Hence the next phase of the laboratory training covers the following five procedures for facilitating intergroup cooperation:

(a) Defining the problem on the basis of facts that are interdependently agreed upon.

(b) Presenting a range of alternatives instead of taking up a fixed position.

(c) Seeking points of similarity in the two sets of proposals, as well as tackling their differences.

(d) Avoiding the "traitor" threat by involving as many members as possible in the problem-solving process.

(e) Having representatives cross-check with their groups before diverging from the group position.

To date, we have conducted some 50 laboratory training programs of the type outlined above for management groups within various companies. Here it might be added that this kind of training does not necessitate the participation of two actually conflicting groups. A management team, or a union, can derive positive benefits by following this path on its own, provided of course, it has the genuine desire to substitute collaboration for the win-lose approach.

Two additional steps that can be used to train either one side or the other are:

3. *The Norm-Setting Conference.* Here the aim is to achieve uniformity in opinions and attitudes toward collaboration as a basis for intergroup relations. A real shift cannot be made simply by changing individuals in isolation from the social framework in which they normally operate; to do so would be to increase the "traitor" threat. In any case, no one member of the group can compel it to "cooperate" from now on. Hence, in order to consolidate attitudes as the basis for future action, we conduct norm-setting conferences in which the group members talk through their own attitudes, reservations, doubts, and

hopes about cooperating with a former adversary. Once the group as a whole has a shared perception of this goal and is committed to it, the energies of the individual members can focus in the same direction. Each member moves with the assurance that he has the support of the group.

4. *Intervention of a Behavioral Scientist in Actual Intergroup Conflicts.* The fourth step lies in using a behavioral scientist to intervene in actual intergroup activities that are going badly. In the heat of battle, even laboratory-type "learning through experience" can be forgotten and lose its potency. It is at these points that the outsider can step in and "freeze" a problem situation long enough to recast it into theoretical terms so that alternative ways of behaving can be examined before an incendiary, win-lose event occurs. If there is heavy tension, then it is all the more important that alternatives be explored *before* any action is taken.

Finally, for groups locked in actual conflict, there are two further procedures that have proved useful. Both require the contending groups themselves to tackle the differences between them:

5. *The Intergroup Leveling Conference.* This can be introduced at any point in the developing relationship where tension has arisen to the extent that efforts at collaboration are being stifled.

Instead of convening for a session of charges and countercharges, the warring factions explore with one another the attitudes, feelings, and emotions that underlie distrust and the motivation to frustrate and destroy. Amazing though it may sound, once leveling starts, the tension in the situation is reduced. People disclose to one another the very attitudes they ordinarily withhold—the underlying ones that are at the root of mutually destructive overt action.

With the leveling started, usually through the intervention of a behavioral scientist, the way is opened for much more extensive joint exploration of the history that has led to the present situation. A historical review of the previous decade helps to place the current conflict in its proper perspective, provides diagnostic cues to account for the dilemma, and suggests what kinds of altered thinking are necessary to achieve a constructive relationship.

6. *Intergroup Therapy.* Intergroup therapy is a more extensive approach that is useful for digging directly into the sources of unhealthy intergroup relations instead of skirting around their surface symptoms. The rationale underlying intergroup therapy is that groups may hold perceptions and stereotypes of one another that are distorted, negative, or so hidden that they prevent effective interaction. Such interaction is possible only *after* the basic problems in the relationship have been eliminated.

Intergroup therapy is an extension of the leveling conference described above. The contending groups are brought together as groups. In private, each group discusses, and seeks to agree on, its perceptions of the other group and attitudes toward it and its perceptions of itself as well. Then representatives of both groups talk together in the presence of other group members, all of whom are obliged to remain silent.

During this phase, the group representatives are responsible for accurately communicating the picture that each group has constructed of the other and of itself. They are free to ask questions aimed at clarifying the other group's point of view, but the ground rules forbid them to rationalize or justify their attitudes. The use of representatives allows for more orderly communication than would be possible if the groups participated as a whole and also increases the communicants' sense of responsibility for providing an accurate version of the situation.

Members of both groups then discuss *in private* the way they are perceived by the other side. This is done in order to develop an understanding of the discrepancies between their adversary's viewpoint and their own view of themselves. Finally, again working through representatives, each group helps the other to appreciate the points of difference, to correct invalid perceptions, and to consider alternative explanations of past behavior. Fundamental conflicts in values can also be identified and examined. Then, suggestions can be developed for ways of tackling the problems at issue.

AN ACTUAL EXAMPLE

What happens when the behavioral science approach is actually applied in industry may be illustrated by the experience of a company that had just "won" a two-year contract that was very close to its initial position in bargaining. At that time, however, management sensed that in the next round of bargaining victory would be less sure. Accordingly, it decided to enlist the aid of behavioral science in making the switch from conflict to collaboration.

As the first step, all members of management were brought together for a laboratory training program, which gave the participants direct experience in the intergroup experiments and theory described above. In addition, the organization had the assistance of a behavioral scientist who worked closely with management, especially at times when emotions came to the fore.

The turning point came in the next round of negotiations, when an impasse was reached. For two weeks, the sides remained very sharply divided on a number of issues that could not be resolved. Each side tried to force the other to capitulate, but deadlock was the only result.

With the assistance of the behavioral scientist, management then formulated a plan for moving ahead that the union accepted. First, the bargaining committee dropped all discussion of the issues in dispute and set about identifying the problem areas underlying them. Subcommittees were then set up to study each problem area and to develop solutions consistent with the newly obtained facts for presentation to the main bargaining committee. (As evidence of management's willingness to collaborate, union representatives were in the majority on each subcommittee.)

In each of the subcommittees, unanimity was achieved through essentially the same sequence of interactions. As significant issues arose, win-lose conflict manifested itself, positions became rigid, and problem-solving procedures were shelved. But at this point, instead of admitting defeat, the committee members took a fresh look at the situation. As they worked through each subject of dispute to the point where mutual satisfaction was achieved, their former group alignments and loyalties tended to disappear. After three weeks, the committee members spoke with a single voice. They drew together with unanimity, focusing on problems and their solutions rather than on traditional positions.

In the end, the ten subgroup recommendations were accepted by the bargaining group as the bases for further negotiations. Thus creative subgroup thinking unfroze the actual negotiating body, and more constructive, cooperative action between the two groups followed. Once the critical hurdles of establishing a posture of cooperation and of achieving some degree of successful problem solving on a joint basis had been surmounted, a more healthy union-management relationship evolved.

In conclusion, perhaps we may reiterate that the theory of intergroup conflict presented here is one that we feel to be basic in understanding the nature of union-management relations that are characterized by tension, strife, and inability to work together harmoniously without the intervention of such outside parties as mediators and arbitrators. The basic proposition we have tried to demonstrate is that problem solving and the resolution of intergroup differences are possible once the pathology of win-lose conflict is understood.

At all events, our experience has been that when management is exposed to laboratory training programs that provide direct experience in intergroup conflict and collaboration, a shift both in orientation and in action takes place. What was formerly a state of chronic conflict and tension subsisting between union and management gives way to constructive problem solving. We have seen this happen in a number of industrial situations, confirming our belief that with the aid of behavioral science union-management conflict can be replaced by the kind of collaboration that serves both the common interests of the parties and the distinctive goals of each.

HANDLING GRIEVANCES WHERE THERE IS NO UNION

Robert E. Sibson

Regardless of how effectively management operates a company, employees are bound to have questions and complaints from time to time. Unless these grievances are settled satisfactorily, efficiency of operations will probably suffer.

The thinking and experience of persons who have worked out successful procedures in non-union shops indicate that there are a number of exacting requirements for success in handling grievances. An employer who is thinking of setting up a grievance system, or reviewing an existing system, should check it against these requirements.

1. The company must have definite and fair personnel policies and these must be effectively communicated to all employees and all members of management.

2. Management at all levels must sincerely believe in the importance of solving grievances and they must vigorously support the grievance system.

3. The system must expressly and formally handle all questions and complaints which may arise.

4. Employees must have complete confidence in the sincerity of management and the effectiveness of the grievance procedure.

5. The grievance procedure should not undermine the effectiveness of line management, interfere with line management responsibilities in personnel matters, or align managers against each other.

6. The system must recognize in a

From Robert E. Sibson, "Handling Grievances Where There Is No Union," Personnel Journal 35 (2), 56–58 (1956). Reprinted by permission.

straightforward manner that management is always the final arbiter of grievances in a non-union shop.

7. The grievance procedure should be a positive tool in human relations.

Written personnel policies are absolutely necessary to the success of any grievance procedure in a non-union shop. For the employees, they set forth top management's position on important personnel matters. For members of management they provide a yardstick for deciding specific questions and grievances which occur during day-to-day operations, rather than each following his own ideas.

Both supervisors and employees need a common guide of company policy. Employees are given some way to judge when they have a reasonable grievance. Supervisors are enabled to resolve grievances consistently throughout the company and in conformance with top management thinking. Therefore, the first step in working out an effective grievance procedure in a non-union shop is for top management to formulate sound personnel policies and reduce them to writing.

The second essential for a sound grievance procedure is management support at every level. Management support requires a sincere recognition of the need for handling grievances effectively. It also requires that all members of management be willing and able to take necessary actions, and exercise restraint in dealing with day-to-day questions and complaints.

MUST SEE WORKERS' SIDE

Unless managers at all levels are able to see two sides of a question, there is no chance for an effective grievance-handling system. Unfortunately, too many company executives and supervisors bask in their own benevolence and righteousness when it comes to the problem of employee complaints. They are convinced that they are doing what is best for employees. Some managers even believe that employee problems or grievances which arise merely reflect a break-down in employee communications; that if employees are only told the company's views and if the situation is "explained," all right-thinking employees will accept the company view. Any grievance system designed to "educate" employees in this way, regardless of how gently that educational job is performed, is doomed to failure. Only a system which realistically recognizes that mistakes will be made has a chance of success.

The fact of the matter is that management at all levels does make mistakes in handling employees. Furthermore, fine-sounding and well-conceived policies may be grossly unfair in individual applications, at different times or under different circumstances. Finally, there are many times when employee views or interests are in direct conflict with the company interests or management's views.

Because of all of these considerations, management support of the grievance system requires that management, and particularly top management, must be willing to:

1. Seek out employee grievances;
2. accept reversal of decisions as a result of grievance handling;
3. stand ready to adjust and modify policies.

In the non-union company it is also very important that all questions or complaints be handled in the grievance procedure. There is no fixed period in the non-union company when all working conditions, shop rules, etc. are subject to review. Therefore, there is no reason why the definition of a grievance should be restricted in any artificial manner. In fact, new problems brought up through the grievance procedure should be a major source of suggested improvements to written company policy. Furthermore, if complaints and questions are handled as they arise there will be no problem of small grievances grow-

ing into major complaints because of neglect or unnecessary delay.

CONFIDENCE IN SYSTEM ESSENTIAL

Another requirement for success in grievance handling in the non-union shop is that employees have complete confidence in the effectiveness of the procedure. In general, this requires an aggressive but low-pressure selling program on the part of all members of management. Managers must emphasize that it is important to the company as well as to the employees to have questions and complaints solved satisfactorily. They must convince employees of the soundness of the system. And they must impress employees with their sincere desire to solve problems quickly and fairly.

Employees will gain confidence in the grievance system only through experience. If management is going to demonstrate to employees, through their experiences, that the system will satisfactorily resolve their problems, they must make sure that the following four requirements are met:

1. *No Fear of Reprisal.* There can be no fear of reprisals on the part of employees. If employees believe that by submitting a grievance they might expose themselves to any type of reprisal on the part of their immediate supervisor they will not use the system. To avoid fear of reprisal, the operation of the procedure must be audited carefully by the person responsible for its operation. And all members of management must exercise self-restraint and good judgment in dealing with employee grievances.

2. *Employees Understand System.* The grievance system must be formalized and reduced to writing. Employees must know how to present a grievance, where they should do it, when they should do it and exactly what will happen, step by step, when they do it. Uncertainty in their minds will

surely tend to discourage the use of a grievance system.

3. *A Problem Solving Atmosphere.* Grievances must be handled quickly. The grievance system which eliminates all unnecessary legalism and which is geared to solve problems in the shortest practical time, encourages a problem-solving atmosphere. Such an atmosphere is bound to win employee confidence and demonstrate the company's sincere desire to settle all grievances fairly.

4. *No Skill Disadvantage.* The employee should not be at any disadvantage in handling grievances because of lack of skill in presenting his case. Generally speaking, grievances involve questions of interpretation, motive, intent or opinion. Under these conditions, the manner in which facts are presented, and the skill with which views are expressed, may influence the results. The average plant employee is generally at a disadvantage in obtaining facts, expressing views, etc. Unless this skill disadvantage is discounted in the grievance system, employees will recognize their disability and lose confidence in the system—or develop contempt for it.

In its enthusiasm to inject the necessary safeguards and restraints into the grievance system, management must be careful not to weaken the effectiveness of management or pit various members of the management group against each other. The primary responsibility for handling employee grievances must always rest with line supervision. A system which sets up two "foremen" in every operating department—the line foreman and the grievance representative—is bound to affect employee relations adversely.

Generally speaking, the grievance procedure should be designed so that line supervisors handle first-step grievances. The personnel department should, at best, only handle appeals from the decision of line management. The primary function of the personnel department should be to assist and advise line management.

MANAGERS REMAIN FINAL ARBITERS

Unless managers are willing to give away some of their rights to manage, they will always stand as final arbiters of grievances in a non-union company. But this does not mean that the system cannot be successful. Rather, it merely points up to the need for management in the day-to-day administration of grievances to demonstrate to all employees that management is willing and able to work out satisfactory answers. There is no reason why management should hedge on this essential characteristic of a grievance system in a non-union company. Rather, it should be emphasized so that management may take credit for the grievance settlements.

The grievance procedure cannot be an isolated segment of the company's policies and practices. Rather, it must be an integral part of the company's overall personnel program. Essentially, the grievance system is a "fire fighting" apparatus. It is designed to answer problems which have already occurred.

Grievances can, however, provide management with the opportunity of determining the causes of employee unrest. Armed with such information, management can initiate such policies and procedures as are necessary to eliminate or at least reduce employee dissatisfaction before it occurs. In this way the grievance procedure in the non-union shop can serve as a means of "fire prevention"—a positive tool in a sound human relations program.

PART SEVEN

SPECIAL TOPICS

The sections in the Special Topics part of this book deal with a variety of considerations and issues which impact the personnel management function. There are four sections and twelve articles in this part. Both the sections and the articles were chosen for inclusion on the basis of one of two criteria: a relationship to an emerging problem or process which heretofore has had little or no impact on personnel, or a relationship to a problem or process which has virtually always been important, but which has not generally been treated in personnel texts.

EDP APPLICATIONS

The first section on EDP applications highlights an important technological advance, the impact of which is posing problems, as well as opening new horizons, for personnel management. One of the articles focuses on particular applications—long-range planning and recruiting—while the second explores the positive contributions EDP is making to the personnel process.

CIVIL RIGHTS AND EMPLOYMENT

The second section deals with problems, programs, and issues in the area of civil rights and employment. While EDP has its origin in technology, the origin of civil rights considerations is social. Civil rights demonstrates that personnel management functions must relate not only to the immediate organization, but to the organization's operating environment as well. The articles in this section are addressed to the implications for personnel management of various government programs and legislation, and to problems involved in recruiting, hiring, training and retraining hard-core unemployed and minority group members.

ENVIRONMENTAL QUALITY

The section on environmental quality focuses on various factors which affect the quality of the work environment. Many other articles could have been included, but the two presented provide a sample of some of the concerns in this area. The physical environment of offices and the organization's role in mental health are the topics.

COUNTER-PRODUCTIVE BEHAVIORS

Counter-productive behaviors is the theme of the fourth section which deals with special "people problems" of concern to personnel management. The problem of how to deal with the employee who is an unsatisfactory performer is the topic of the first article. The remaining three articles deal with the subjects of problem drinkers and drug abuse. One of these articles, "Young Drug Users and the Value Gap," is an unsusal selection for a personnel book. It was included not only to provide background to aid in understanding how to cope with the drug user, but also to reveal some of the value differences which exist today and which may ultimately have a more profound effect upon personnel management.

EDP APPLICATIONS ══════════

HOW EDP IS IMPROVING THE PERSONNEL FUNCTION

Richard T. Bueschel

Efficiently used, electronic data processing can lead to significant improvement in the company's personnel activities. In fact, progressive personnel departments are already realizing considerable operating benefits from the better and more timely information that the computer can provide. The personnel manager who has hitherto bypassed these developments owes it to himself—and his company—to take a closer look at what EDP can do to assist in his function.

In most companies, the first application of EDP to personnel work is usually merely an extension of some record-keeping system that has formerly been handled manually. But with growing experience in the use of the computer wholly new approaches are developed, broadly expanding the scope of data available for better personnel decisions.

This article will briefly discuss some current applications of EDP in four broad personnel areas: Records and Administration; Wages and Salaries; Skills Inventories; and Employment. It will also touch upon the planning and design called for in applying EDP to the personnel function.

From Richard T. Bueschel, "How EDP Is Improving the Personnel Function," Personnel 41 (5), 59–64 (1964). Reprinted by permission of the American Management Association.

Personnel records and administration is the area where computer equipment has found its most frequent application thus far. This is not surprising, because here usually is the biggest time consumer of clerical labor in the personnel office, so that results can be measured in clerical savings alone. More important, though, is the more timely and more significant information that the computer can provide.

Information maintained on employees generally enters the "system" through some form of change notice that is keypunched onto a card and "read" into the computer. The personnel department must, of course, control this input of information to insure its accuracy and completeness. The amount and type of information recorded and the kinds of reports produced therefrom will naturally vary with the company's particular needs. Most reports are, however, provided monthly or quarterly.

Many companies have used the computer to develop extensive personnel records for specific purposes. One large manufacturing company, for example, maintains a considerable amount of data on its employees with particular reference to labor relations. A major automobile company maintains on the computer centralized information on the status of over 50,000 salaried employees. This file includes the salary, position, age, date of hire, plant location, and insurance data on each employee. A prominent bank has an elaborate system for keeping management abreast of attendance figures, as well as manpower strength.

At Honeywell, our Employee History system provides over 30 reports on a monthly or quarterly basis, with some available on demand when required. The file is updated once a week by the use of four documents—the Salaried Employee Change Notice, Hourly Employee Change Notice, Tuition and Professional Society Refund Request, and the Personal Background Sheet.

MAIN ADVANTAGES OF EDP

Despite the varied nature of the reports provided, all are produced from the same file of information so that the data are recorded only once. This is one of the main advantages of EDP—multiple uses can be made of a single file. Among its other significant advantages are the reduction of clerical workloads; the provision of more timely data for decision making; the supply of broader information for salary comparison, forecast, and simulation purposes; and increased accuracy of personnel reports.

One of the most interesting automated systems in this area is SPARTAN (System for Personnel Automated Reports, Transactions, and Notices), which has been developed by the Bureau of the Census. Here, information on employee changes is taken from a Request for Personnel Action form and inserted into the computer. Though some of the information is keypunched onto cards before entry into the system, most data is "read" into the computer by a machine known as FOSDIC (Film Optical Sensing Device for Input to Computers). The system provides a number of reports on employees. Additionally, and more unusual, the computer prepares and addresses memos to managers alerting them to the imminence of certain events, or to activities that have been accomplished by the computer. Scheduled step increases, time and salary limits on appointments, eligibility for retirement, sick leave limits, eligibility for service awards, performance rating periods, placement and training follow-ups, probation periods, and so forth, are among the events that are thus

examined by the computer and reported upon as required.

WAGE AND SALARY APPLICATIONS

Compensation information, such as salaries and benefits, has long been available from the company's payroll tabulating equipment. However, more extensive use of the computer is now beginning to yield significant improvement in the wage and salary program. As a rule, the basic personnel records include data that are relevant to the needs of the wage and salary administrator.

Among the more frequent applications in the wage and salary area is that exemplified by the system of a well-known research laboratory, employing many scientists, which examines its competitive position on a quarterly basis. The results of salary surveys that the laboratory participates in are "read" into the computer. By extrapolation, the surveys are brought up to date and matched against the salaries of the laboratory's scientific employees. Some of the surveys rely on maturity curves, and others compare job content. By means of these comparisons, the laboratory is able to assess the strengths and weaknesses of its salary program—information that is carefully considered at the time salary increases are being budgeted.

Incidentally, this kind of comparison is by no means the exclusive province of the large, research-oriented organization. I know one machine shop, employing under 800 employees, that rents time on a computer to compare its wage rates with those prevailing in the local labor market. The company feels that the savings achieved on the one hand by reducing turnover, and on the other by not paying higher rates than is necessary, far exceed the modest cost of computer rental time.

Another advantage of computerized wage and salary data is the speedy control these afford the salary administrator. Mid-points, red-circle rates, and misclassified rates can be automatically flagged. Salary increase budgets can be compared with projections or with the budgets of comparable departments elsewhere in the company.

An especially valuable application of EDP is the use of the computer to simulate wages and salaries. By simulating various wage and salary trends the company can obtain a projection of its position at a future point in time. Thus, the impact and potential costs of a general salary increase can be simulated to enable management to decide whether this course is justified or not. When wages and benefits are determined through collective bargaining, the ability to simulate and quickly assess the costs and implications of alternative proposals is an essential managerial tool. Simulation, in short, offers a ready means of testing alternative solutions to facilitate choosing the best course of action.

Finally, the computer is widely used in processing data for salary surveys. In fact, participants in many surveys are now asked to supply their data in punched card form so that the information can be quickly fed into the computer.

SKILLS INVENTORIES

Most recently, a good deal of attention has been focused on the use of the computer to implement a skills inventory program. These systems go by various names—Skill Banks, Manpower Assessment Programs, and so on; but whatever they are called, their goals are the same—to speedily locate the company's resources of talent and maximize its use.

Skills inventories have largely been developed by engineering and research organizations where the high costs of recruiting and the shortage of skilled professionals make it essential to use the talent already available in the company to the full. By thus offering greater internal growth to its employees, the company with a skills inventory program also tries to reduce turnover among its hard-to-

find professionals. The technically oriented concerns are not the only users, however of such systems. Many companies operating in less critical labor markets have also turned to the computer to assist in implementing their personnel inventory programs.

There are two main ways to design such systems; the difference between them lies in their methods of collecting the data. Some companies develop their inventory information from data that have been specifically gathered for the skills program, while others use data that have been collected for personnel administration generally. Both systems, in fact most successful systems, prepare listings of skills and traits on a regularly scheduled basis instead of searching through the computer each time a need arises.

One example of a system that uses specifically collected information is that of a well-known mining company that has developed a skills questionnaire and program to inventory its many different types of mining engineers. The system provides data on some 1,400 professionals at over 100 different locations. The questionnaire is a self-contained writing pad, designed for use in the field, which asks the employee to either check off or fill out pertinent information on his background, education, previous job history, and skills. Reports depicting individual skills and proficiencies are then prepared by the computer from the information on the questionnaires. A new questionnaire is sent out each year to update the employee's file.

An example of the alternative system, using data collected for general personnel administration, is in use at Honeywell EDP. Here skills information on each employee is prepared from the same file that is used to prepare personnel and salary reports. The reports on skills inventories list job history within the company, prior three jobs before employment with Honeywell, educational background, special achievements, and proficiency in foreign languages.

AUTOMATING THE COMPANY'S EMPLOYMENT RECORDS

With the increasingly high cost of recruiting technical personnel, the application of EDP to the employment function is a logical development. Here, the aim of the system is to enable the employment office to:

1. Move quickly in making hiring decisions, and provide follow-up on job offers.
2. Keep track of internal routing of information and files.
3. Promptly advise applicants of the disposition of their applications.
4. Evaluate the effectiveness of the company's recruiting programs, to better determine where recruiting funds should be spent.
5. Cut clerical costs.

In the usual manual system, a 3 × 5 card index is set up for applicants, for all résumés routed to a department, visitors, and so on. Each time a file is returned or acted upon, the index card has to be pulled out, updated, and refiled. Furthermore, additional entries are often called for, such as a record of the advertisement to which an applicant has responded.

At Honeywell, employment records have been automated by means of a program that prints out, twice a week, the status of all applicants and visitors. The system is also designed to identify, once a week, all files that have exceeded certain time limits. Some of the tasks this program performs are:

1. Provision of a complete report on the status of all résumés and applications, so that delays can be spotted and decisions made quickly.
2. Elimination of over 22 separate posting and routing activities previously performed by clerical help, thereby freeing their time for more productive work.
3. Printing and updating of a complete set of indexing cards that provide cross-reference to all files placed in storage, thus eliminating

a posting job that formerly required over 20 clerk-hours a week.
4. Provision of a highly selective system of retrieval on all applicants who visit the plant.
5. Speed-up of the preparation of reports on employment activities.
6. Measurement of the effectiveness of different recruiting sources, such as advertising and employment agencies, based on source-of-hire data.
7. Provision of up-to-the-minute budget information, cost-of-hire figures, and other pertinent cost data.

There are, of course, other purposes the system could be designed to serve, depending on a company's particular needs.

If you are not yet using EDP in the personnel department, you may be wondering how to get started, what alternatives to follow, and how ambitious a program to undertake. A critical look at how your company now operates and the policies it has developed should help to point the way.

SOME POINTERS ON HOW TO GET STARTED

First, examine your present system. Look closely at the forms you now use and the records you keep. Determine how valuable they really are, what purposes these statistics and reports really serve, who gets them, and how much work is entailed in gathering the information needed to service your report. It is not unusual to find that if reports have been developed sporadically, as the need arises, there is a great deal of duplication of content in the various reports going the rounds. Moreover, the forms developed for particular reports are often similar and can readily be consolidated. Recently, one company found that it was using 110 different forms to collect personnel data. It promptly reduced these to fewer than 20.

Remember that though the computer can make available information that could not previously be obtained and produce it faster, it can only handle information in a prearranged fashion. Flexibility, therefore, is reduced to the extent that each action of the computer must be planned. In a manual system you can tell your secretary to look through each file and find all the left-handed plumbers. With the computer you must anticipate that somebody, sometime is going to ask for a left-handed plumber, and write the relevant information into the program beforehand. In other words, information on left-handed plumbers must be collected and inserted into the computer long before anyone ever requests it.

The essence of a well-designed system, therefore, is good planning. Here, your best approach is to analyze all information Personnel is called upon to provide to the government, to management at all levels throughout the company, and to your own department.

In general, planning is likely to represent somewhere between 60 to 80 percent of the total effort and cost of the completed system. The rest of the job (the actual writing of the program, and its checkout and setup on the computer) is up to the programmer.

Many problems will be encountered before the system works smoothly, but on balance the gains should far outweigh any possible pitfalls or difficulties along the way. Increasingly, the personnel function is being called upon to contribute directly to the company's profitability, and more and more its activities are being judged by objective comparisons between predetermined, specifically stated objectives and actual measured results. In this new environment, there is little doubt that the computer can be an indispensable aid.

EDP: A MANAGEMENT RECRUITING TOOL

R. H. Hawk
G. A. Bassett

Meeting the heavy demand for specialists in recent years has led to an increase of large, professional and technical recruiting operations in many organizations. Where the development of sources for technical personnel was formerly a one man show in most organizations, it is very often now a complex, integrated operation.

In a diversified, decentralized company such as General Electric with many geographically distant and semi-autonomous components, striking the right balance between coordinated and independent recruiting is a necessity, and especially so if internal company resources of manpower are to be best applied to meet overall requirements. Maintaining coordination between components is largely a matter of establishing the "big team" climate. Assuring coordination within a component, however, is a managerial issue.

Where recruiting has been uncoordinated, it has not been uncommon to find two adjacent and related components simultaneously recruiting the same man. He may have come in for interviews two different times, and received competing offers of employment at different salary levels on virtually the same letterhead. If he did not fit in one component, he was very likely to be shelved, despite the fact that he has a strong potential fit in another. Uncoordinated recruiting efforts have put many companies in

From R. H. Hawk and G. A. Bassett, "EDP: A Management Recruiting Tool," Administrative Management 26 (8), 22–24 (1965). Reprinted from Administrative Management © Geyer- McAllister Publications, Inc.

the curious position of unwittingly being in competition with themselves, and of using expensive applicant contacts at only fractional efficiency.

Informal lines of communication have sometimes been established between independent technical recruiters to control some of these problems. In such an arrangement there is never any assurance that a breakdown in communications will be repaired, however, or that competition for particularly scarce candidates will be controlled. The only certain answer to these problems of cost control, coordination, and applicant source utilization is the organization of these efforts under a single manager. This kind of organization brings with it new problems, however, which are almost as big as the old ones. In servicing a large number and variety of requests for personnel, the recruiting team will, of necessity, organize these requirements into a set of more or less generic job families, and must then stimulate the volume of employment inquiries necessary to meet these requirements.

In the process there may be a tendency to lose some very valuable day-to-day contacts with individual hiring managers. The recruiting effort may easily become depersonalized, and in the bargain a close intimate knowledge of each individual job may be sacrificed. Another of the mandates placed upon the management of a centralized recruiting effort is that it constantly measure and maintain a balance in referrals which will assure fair service to all managers. Strict impartiality in the servicing of requests for personnel must be assured. If it is not demonstrable that this service is fair and impartial, hiring managers will insist upon a rigid system of priorities form higher management. Attaining a reasonable ranking of priority is difficult, if not impossible, and is seldom likely to be in accord with the realities or organizational manpower needs. Proving that a recruiting system is equitable is a large bookkeeping and fact-gathering task. This fact must be established, however, if an integrated recruiting effort is to succeed.

The heavy volume of employment inquiries required by a large recruiting effort means that there will be oversized paper handling problems. Resumes must and will arrive in massive quantities. Prompt response to all inquiries is essential from both a recruiting and a public relations point of view. It is not uncommon for an applicant to telephone the office several days after he has submitted his resume. His file must be quickly identified and located among hundreds or even thousands of similar resumes. Comprehensive up-to-date activity records which can be referred to quickly are necessary to the efficient handling of such an inquiry.

In addition, the volume of resume activity makes it impossible for anyone to keep up with every file. The opportunity for loss or sidetracking of a resume is increased. Some applications are bound to be lost in the shuffle if there are no means for keeping track of all activity. Finally, recruiting is a dynamic function, and it is often necessary to obtain a summary analysis of all current recruiting activity at a given point in time in order to plan further activity. Detailed, current, accurate, comprehensive records are a "must."

A centrally coordinated recruiting effort must include the development and maintenance of a rather complex record-keeping system in order to solve old problems and to avoid new ones. Comprehensive records on recruiting activities, though, have some innate advantages of their own. From such records it is possible to analyze in detail different recruiting approaches. It is also possible to determine the quality of differential advertising sources. Measures and analyses of the recruitment strategies which were formerly impossible become feasible. Such a record system must meet most of the following criteria:

1) It must provide an easy, natural method for input of information into the system. If possible, the document from which records are updated should be a fully integrated part of the recruiting operation, and should serve more than just a record-keeping function.

2) The time lapse between action and updating of records should be as short as possible, and it should be at least theoretically possible to update all data to within the previous two hours.

3) Routine activities such as posting of action, preparation of reports and development of listings should be systematized and, where possible, automated to gain the greatest possible efficiency from the system.

4) The loop must be closed. All information fed into the system must be fed back to the recruiter or manager. In this respect, the system should be a positive support to the recruiter in his day-to-day recruiting activity so that he will keep information in the system accurate, reliable and complete. The feedback mechanism should provide incentive to make the record-keeping system work.

Other secondary criteria might include provision of some means for retrieving resumes on people with specific qualifications, provision of comprehensive records for analysis of recruiting programs and activities, or provision of specific managerial controls in the system.

Key-punching of cards, especially when the cards are laid out properly, is a very rapid process. The capability of the computer can be used to replace the record search function, checking and posting of records can be accomplished automatically, and the entire file can be updated and printed out, all in a matter of minutes. In fact, unless the volume of activity is high, it hardly seems justifiable to spend the time necessary to set the computer up for the program. Features of record keeping which consume so much time and manpower can be reduced to just minutes of computer time by use of an EDP approach. This can result in substantial manpower cost savings, and make it possible to obtain quickly more current and comprehensive information.

Because of the high investment that must be put into EDP equipment, it is often operated on the basis of two or even three shifts a day. This means that it may often be possible to arrange for necessary production runs to be accomplished between the close of work one day and beginning of work the next. Activity which is current as of 4:30 p.m. one day can be processed and returned for use by 8:30 the next day, with no strain whatsoever.

Finally, because of its ultra-high speed in handling data, the computer can take on data for a day, a week or a month with no stress. This means that EDP can be used as often or as infrequently as necessary to keep records useful. The amount of computer time paid for can be adjusted to the level of recruiting activity.

As with any record-keeping system, it is essential that all incoming resumes be put into it. This can be made part of the mail handling operation. Resumes are sorted from the rest of the mail, date stamped, checked for duplication in the record system, serially numbered, coded by source from which they were received, and assigned to a specific recruiter. With this information entered on the resume, full background data on each applicant can be either key-punched directly from the resume or entered on a key-punch instruction sheet for processing.

PROCEDURE

This assures that previous or concurrent activity is detected and noted on every resume. It is then put into the active EDP system. All further action will be entered on action cards and processed expeditiously and routinely.

The background data entered on each applicant in the EDP system must be chosen on two criteria: First, there must be adequate information to allow detection of duplicate activity when the resume is compared with the EDP listing. Secondly, basic statistical information must be included upon which to base later analysis of recruiting activity.

Our department, through experience, has found that the following basic information satisfied both these criteria reasonably well:

1) Full last name and two initials.
2) Source of contact (i.e. advertising, employment agency, etc.).
3) Geographical location of contact.
4) Degree, category (field) of degree, and year of degree.

The assigned serial number (essential to EDP processing), recruiter code and date of receipt of resume are entered with these four items of information when the resume first comes into the office.

CIVIL RIGHTS AND EMPLOYMENT ━━━

THE IMPACT OF THE CIVIL RIGHTS ACT ON EMPLOYMENT POLICIES AND PROGRAMS

Fred Luthans

What effect has Title VII of the Civil Rights Act, 1964, had on employment policies and programs? An answer to this question is of timely interest. On July 2, 1968, the last phase of the Act goes into effect. After this date it becomes unlawful for companies with 25 or more employees, engaged in interstate commerce to discriminate in any aspect of employment because of race, color, religion, sex or national origin.

The practicing manager can easily determine the impact of the Act in terms of his increased work load and additional restrictions.[1] As a result of Title VII, managers must now answer to more people (both governmental and interest groups); face the threat of court action for noncompliance; keep more detailed records and submit more reports; and even answer more questionnaires for studies such as this. Yet, despite these additional burdens, business executives seem to have generally accepted the Act and see pos-

itive value in it. This conclusion is substantiated by a National Industrial Conference Board study conducted shortly after the Act was passed in July 1964. The study found the following values mentioned most frequently by the chief executives who were interviewed:[2]

"The Act focuses attention on an important national problem."

"It puts the law on the side of what's right."

"Companies that want to move ahead will be encouraged; laggards will be prodded."

Athough virtually all the executives in the NICB study felt there were these positive values attached to the Act, only about one out of five thought it would affect their particular company.[3] It would be interesting to determine whether this expressed feeling is, in fact, the case.

SOME MAJOR TRENDS IN ANTIDISCRIMINATION POLICY

The author has been involved in a continuing research program to systematically analyze the impact Title VII has had on companies in selected Midwest locations. These studies were timed to fall prior to the Act, about the time the Act was passed, and finally, to coincide with the last phase of the Act's going into effect.

The first study in June 1961 analyzed Minneapolis-St. Paul firms' union contracts for their inclusion of antidiscrimination clauses.[4]

From Fred Luthans, "The Impact of the Civil Rights Act on Employment Policies and Programs," Labour Law Journal 19 (6), 323–328 (1968). Reprinted by permission.

[1] For instance see, Keith Davis, *Human Relations at Work* (New York: McGraw-Hill, 1967), 3rd ed., p. 272.

[2] National Industrial Conference Board, "Company Experience with Negro Employment," *Studies in Personnel Policy, No. 201,* p. 159 (1966).

[3] *Ibid.,* p. 130.

[4] Max S. Wortman, Jr. and Fred Luthans, "How Many Contracts Ban Discrimination in Employment?" *Personnel* **41** (1), 75-79 (January-February, 1964).

A follow-up study in February 1964 was then made on a large sample of both union and nonunion firms in the State of Iowa.[5] The most recent study, conducted during November 1967, asked all firms in Lincoln and Omaha with 50 or more employees in manufacturing firms and 100 or more employees in nonmanufacturing firms to participate. One hundred and eighty-four usable responses (63 per cent) were obtained for a comprehensive analysis of all aspects of antibias in employment. These three studies, plus a review of the growing literature, form the basis for the following analysis.

Unionized Firms

No clear trend evolved from the analysis of nondiscriminatory union contract clauses. Table 1 shows that prior to the passage of the Act in 1961, only 12 per cent of Minneapolis-St. Paul firms' contracts contained the clause. This percentage climbed considerably (up to 34 per cent in the Iowa study) by the time the Act was passed in 1964. The most recent study in Lincoln and Omaha shows the percentage of contracts having a nonbias clause to drop back down to 22 per cent.

TABLE 1. **PREVALENCE OF ANTIDISCRIMINATION CONTRACT CLAUSES FOUND IN THREE REGIONAL STUDIES**

UNION CONTRACTS		ANTIDISCRIMINATION CLAUSE	
LOCATION	DATE	PER CENT YES	PER CENT NO
Minneapolis-St. Paul	June 1961	12	88
State of Iowa	Feb. 1964	34	66
Lincoln-Omaha	Nov. 1967	22	78

Union representation may explain this pattern. In Minneapolis-St. Paul and in Lincoln-Omaha, most of the food industry is organized by the Grain Millers, and the greatest share of the machinery industry is organized by the Machinists' Union. Only

[5]Max S. Wortman, Jr. and Fred Luthans, "The Incidence of Antidiscrimination Clauses in Union Contracts," 16 *Labor Law Journal*, p. 523-532 (September, 1965).

a sprinkling of Auto and Packinghouse locals are found in the two industries at either location. Contracts negotiated with the Grain Millers and Machinists notably lacked nonbias clauses in the Minnesota study, and the same absence was found in the Nebraska study over six years later.

Iowa, on the other hand, has most of its food industry organized by the Packinghouse Workers and most of its machinery industry organized by the Auto Workers. The Packinghouse and Auto Workers have practically all their contracts containing a nonprejudice clause in all three studies. Therefore, the large number of Auto and Packinghouse locals may account for the greater number of antidiscrimination clauses found in Iowa labor agreements.

The above analysis refers only to contract clauses and not to policies per se. In fact, in the most recent study, three out of four unionized firms stated they had specific policies, but only 22 per cent said there was a clause in their contracts.

Nonunion Firms

There seems to be a clearer trend in unorganized firms' policies. Although nonunion firms were not examined in the Twin Cities study. Table 2 shows only 19 per cent of the Iowa nonunion firms had antibias policies in 1964, compared to 57 per cent in the Nebraska unorganized firms approximately four years later. When asked if the policies were written, only 7 per cent of the nonunion companies in Iowa responded positively, but almost four years later this figure is 43 per cent in Lincoln and Omaha (see Table 2). When these Nebraska nonunion firms were asked to supply tangible evidence of their written policies, 55 per cent sent along a copy of the policy, another 27 per cent quoted the policy verbatim and 18 per cent ignored the request. Overall, there seems to be a definite trend in the direction of more specific antidiscrimination policies stated in unorganized firms.

TABLE 2. NONDISCRIMINATION POLICIES FOUND IN IOWA AND LINCOLN-OMAHA NON-UNION FIRMS

NONUNION ANTIBIAS POLICIES

		SPECIFIC POLICY		WRITTEN POLICY	
LOCATION	DATE	PER CENT YES	PER CENT NO	PER CENT YES	PER CENT NO
State of Iowa	Feb. 1964	19	81	7	93
Lincoln-Omaha	Nov. 1967	57	43	43	57

Size of the Firm

All three studies found that the larger the firm, the more the tendency was to have a specific policy. In Minnesota, 9 per cent of the small companies (less than 200) compared to 38 per cent of the large companies (1,000 or more) had antibias clauses. In the Iowa study, 45 per cent of the organized firms with 250 or more had contracts with such a clause, whereas smaller firms (less than 100) provided these clauses in only 18 per cent of their agreements. Similar results were found in the nonunion firms of Iowa. In the recent study in Nebraska this trend held steady. Practically all firms with over 500 employees had a policy compared to slightly over 40 per cent of those with 50 to 100 workers.

STATUS OF NONDISCRIMINATION PROGRAMS

The discussion so far has been concerned only with antibias policies in employment. The next logical area of analysis would seem to be the plans or programs designed to carry out these policies in actual practice. The analysis of these programs played a minor role in the two earlier studies. The 1964 Iowa study did ask nonunion firms how they carried out their policies. Many of the responding companies ignored the question and those who did answer were very vague. Representative of the antibias programs described in the Iowa study were the following:

"Simply by judging each applicant on his qualifications."
"We hire anyone who can do the job."

"Every applicant is treated on the basis of ability, regardless or race, color, sex or anything else."

The status of nondiscrimination programs played a larger part in the most recent study in Lincoln and Omaha. To obtain data, all companies were asked what they did to insure nondiscrimination in employment. Of those who responded, 40 per cent said that at present there were no specific programs. Most of the 60 per cent who said they had specific programs described very vague and inconclusive programs which were similar to those described by the Iowa firms about four years earlier.

A minority of the firms described fairly detailed, active programs such as the following:

"In the *recruitment program* by 'continual contacts with the Urban League and other similar agencies that are sources of non-white referrals. We appear before minority audiences whenever possible to encourage the students to stay in school and to express our desire to employ people without regard to race, religion, or sex.'

"In the *hiring procedure* by 'evaluation of potential—not complete reliance on testing.'

"In the *promotion process* by 'reviewing those employees whose attitude and job performance show greater potential, e.g., janitor promoted into an apprentice program.' "

In total, the current status of antibias programs indicate that 40 per cent had no programs whatsoever. About 35 per cent had, at best, made very slight attempts to develop a program of action; and only about 25 per cent seemed to have a fairly well-conceived program to eliminate discrimination in practice.

CONCLUSIONS AND IMPLICATIONS

The preceding sections form the basis for the conclusions on the impact that Title VII of the Civil Rights Act has had on employment policies and programs. The NICB study, discussed in the introductory comments, reported that business executives did not feel the Act was going to affect their particular companies. Is this expressed feeling substantiated by the three strategically timed regional studies? The analysis suggests there are some clear trends in certain aspects of employment policies on nondiscrimination. Although no clear trend emerged in the area of antidiscrimination clauses in labor agreements, there was a clear tendency for an increasing percentage of nonunion firms to have a policy and to put it into written form. The larger firms continued to have more stated policies than did the smaller companies.

The question now becomes—what caused these trends or nontrends to develop? Was it the Civil Rights Act or are there other precipitating causes?

Possible Causes of the Trends

In organized firms, the union representation, and not the Civil Rights Act, seemed to be the determining factor whether the contract contained or did not contain an antidiscrimination clause. In all three studies there appeared to be a consistent pattern of certain unions entering contracts that had the clause and certain other unions involved in contracts without the clause. This finding could lead one to conclude that the Act was not as important as union influence in negotiating antibias clauses in union contracts.

If the Civil Rights Act has no apparent impact on contract clauses, is this also true for the policies of unorganized firms or even the policies, other than the union contract, for unionized firms? The answer seems to be that the Act is at least one of the major causes for the other trends. This conclusion is very difficult to substantiate objectively. However, the starting point would seem to be the analysis of other possible causes for the trends found.

Outright minority group pressures may cause a company to declare a nonbias policy. This pressure may be direct in the form of consumer boycotting, picketing, organized calling committees or indirect pressure from churches, communication mediums or government agencies. The November 1967 study in Lincoln and Omaha found that this outright pressure is not widespread. Only nine respondents (5 per cent) reported any outright pressures put on their companies. Eight of these nine companies reported specific nondiscrimination policies and five of the policies were in written form. Although this finding would indicate that companies are not generally experiencing outright pressures, the threat of such pressure may be ever-present. Therefore, the data would lead one to conclude that outright pressures are not a direct cause for declaring nonbias policy, but the threat cannot be ignored as a possibility.

Another possible cause may be that firms institute a policy to eliminate a problem area. In other words, the reason a company declares an antibias policy is to alleviate a perceived problem of discrimination in employment. Analysis of the data from the recent study does not substantiate this reason. In the first place, a large majority (77 per cent) of the respondents did not perceive discrimination as a problem. Secondly, there was no appreciable difference between those companies that felt there was a discrimination problem and had a specific policy and those companies that felt there was not a problem but had a specific nondiscrimination policy anyway. This could lead one to conclude that there is no correlation between stating a nondiscrimination policy and perceiving a problem of discrimination.

This leaves the Civil Rights Act as a major explanation for the trends which have developed—a conclusion based on the overall analysis of the three strategically timed regional studies. The latest study showed a marked increase over the 1964 study on specific nonbias policies in unorganized firms. The current data on nondiscrimination policies showed that two out of every three companies declared they had taken a firm policy stand on nondiscrimination in employment. One-half of the total firms responding sent tangible evidence of their nonbias policies.

Antibias programs, like the contract clauses, have not been affected by the Act. The current study uncovered only a small minority of companies that have developed or borrowed comphrehensive, active programs to wipe out discrimination in employment practices.

In summary, the Civil Rights Act had no apparent impact on nondiscrimination contract clauses or programs, but the overall analysis suggests the Act has caused many companies to include nonbias policies. The impact of the Act has certainly not been very great, and there are many areas of concern for the future.

Implications for the Future

The three reported studies reflect only stated antidiscrimination policies and programs. The results do not indicate actual day-to-day practices in the companies surveyed. Although the firm may have a specific statement outlawing discrimination and a detailed program designed to implement this policy, it is by no means assured that discrimination does not exist in actual practice. Moreover, just because a company does not have a specific policy and/or program does not mean that the company practices discrimination. Nevertheless, on a policy and program level, the regional surveys do indicate how the business community is generally reacting to legislative and social pressures. The reaction so far has not been very dramatic.

The studies show a gradual trend toward more policies and programs designed to eliminate discrimination in employment. The fact remains, however, that the policies generally take a moral, unwritten approach and seldom have a program of action to implement the policies in actual practice. Managers who are attuned to the social mood of the country and are well informed in state and federal legislation should realize that this approach is not sufficient.

To meet the future challenge of equal opportunity employment, management should logically start with a carefully thought-out policy reflecting the philosophy and goals of their companies on nondiscrimination. This policy should be in written form and fully communicated to everyone in the firm and relevant persons or groups outside the firm. Stating the policy is only the start; a program must also be designed to put the policy into action. Some areas the program should cover are methods of communicating the policy; specific areas of aggressive application, such as in recruitment, hiring, training, promotion, and employee facilities; and specific rules for practice within each of these areas. Finally, periodic audits and reviews should be utilized to determine if policies and programs are actually being carried out in practice.

In the final analysis, it will not be actual legislation, such as the Civil Rights Act, which will end discrimination in employment. Rather, it will be enlightened managers living up to the spirit, as well as the letter, of the law.

BUILDING GROUNDWORK FOR AFFIRMATIVE ACTION EEO PROGRAM

Dean B. Peskin

A decade ago many managers would have considered the subject of race relations as something sociologists worried about, not as an integral part of their responsibilities. The subject of race relations was an ill defined category of human interaction that historians found difficult to reduce to classic historiography. Things have changed. Race relations has become an extremely important, in fact, critical area of understanding for today's managers. Where once it was an intangible, vague kind of human responsibility that nagged the conscience of a few, today it becomes, for many, a living, breathing, pulsating, sometimes agonizing and challenging fact of life. How are managers and personnel administrators, in particular, going to meet this challenge? What will they contribute to the archives of personnel administration, human relations and business management as a result of this involvement?

Each citizen is confronted with the challenges, obligations, doubts, fears and frustrations of race relations. But probably few occupations are confronted with the real meaning of race relations as are personnel executives. In the final analysis, when the demonstrations, the placards and signs, and the barrage of congressional oratory have become a matter of record, the buck will finally stop at the desk of the personnel administrator. When he comes face to face with members of minority groups, in that moment, all of the cataclysmic forces, historic, eco-

From Dean B. Peskin, "Building Groundwork for Affirmative Action EEO Program," Personnel Journal 48 (2), 130–138, 143 (1969). Reprinted by permission.

nomic, social, political and racial come to bear in microcosm. But even before that confrontation, the personnel administrator should, and in fact, must, advise his organization in the ways and means, the arts and sciences, the how-to-do of building the groundwork for an effective Equal Employment Opportunity program. If personnel, as a profession and occupation, cannot meet this challenge, it cannot remain a viable force in our changing economic and social patterns of life. The purpose of this discussion is to offer some suggestions on how to initially establish an effective, affirmative action program (with emphasis upon equal opportunity in employment).

It will become increasingly necessary for the personnel administrator or the individual whose responsibilities include the functions of personnel, to develop a program to meet this challenge—a blueprint, a standard operating procedure whereby the many problems his organization may face in attempting to understand and meet the responsibilities of equal employment opportunity can be resolved. The most logical approach to the questions of race relations for businesses today is to adopt the basic concept of management by objective to accomplish affirmative action. This article is not a plea for social action or for political moderation or rationality. Rather, this is simply a discussion of the ways and means by which personnel people can face these new challenges and begin to build workable programs.

UNDERSTAND THE PROBLEM

The first step is understanding what is required. It is incumbent upon each personnel administrator to have more than a general understanding of local, state and federal laws regarding Equal Employment Opportunity (Title VII, The Civil Rights Act of 1964). Of course, a deep working knowledge would be more desirable. The personnel administrator should, in fact, be the expert in those phases of current, applicable laws which most specifically affect his organization whether it be Title VII, Wage and Hour Provisions or conditions regarding government contracts; provisions of the public accommodations law and certainly age and sex discrimination provisions; in short, any and all applicable provisions and statutes. The interpretation of laws changes as court decisions hammer new concepts into shape; humanize the word of the law and exemplify its spirit.

DEVELOP CLEARLY UNDERSTOOD GOALS

Once the word, the spirit, and the correct practice of the applicable statute are understood it becomes necessary for personnel people to attempt to effectively mesh these requirements and obligations with the goals of the organization for which they work. This, of course, assumes that they know where the organizations are going, what they intend to accomplish and how they can best be helped to meet these goals. This is not a matter of hearsay at the coffee break or luncheon table but rather, a matter of clearly understanding the specific objectives of management to which, hopefully, the personnel administrator has contributed.

Accordingly, this assumes that management has taken a clear position regarding the subject of race relations (EEO) and that the personnel administrator understands the attitudes of management. These attitudes may be in conflict or in concert with the statutes, laws and orders under which that business operates. It is then the responsibility of the personnel administrator to discuss these differences with top management so that a course can be charted by which business can accomplish its goals and satisfy its obligations and do both without unnecessary difficulties and costs.

There will come a time when a nondiscrimination policy becomes an affirmative action program. In the broad sense, business continues to be concerned with its image and, needless to say, business has different images on any given strata of our society. Business may elect to ignore the social change which seems to be current in the land and, it may choose to ignore the legislation under which it is expected to operate. But it is also a responsibility of business to evaluate whether such actions are to be considered as ongoing organizational policy or whether they are, in fact, a temporary blush of rebellion and reaction rather than a prudent business course. This type of analysis should be made by management.

The question of affirmative action versus nondiscrimination is a vital base of understanding. One might categorize the former as, "positively getting something done with tangible proof of results," while the latter might be described as "waiting for something wonderful to happen." Assuming that positive, affirmative action is going to be taken, certain positive, clearly defined steps can be taken to help implement the goals of management. The following discussion is directed toward that need.

POLICY DEVELOPMENT: THE KEYSTONE TO AFFIRMATIVE ACTION

Once the intentions of management have been determined, it is necessary to develop a stated policy. The best approach is an affirmative action policy which attributes to the Board of Directors or the Chief Executive Officer the impetus for this statement of goals and general policy. The statement itself, in order to be effective and to serve the best interests of the organization, should be clear and concise. It should not hedge the issue or pay lip service to a "something wonderful will happen" philosophy. Obviously, a policy of this kind will be meaningless if it is only known to the personnel administrator and the executive staff of the organization. The statement should be widely circulated. This can best be done by distributing copies of the printed policy to all employees of the organization, making it a part of the Personnel Policy Manual and making it known to recruitment sources in the community.

Obviously, once the policy has been established it must be humanized. Humanizing breathes life into the statement of intentions which have been developed. Then the policy must be made to work. The personnel administrator is in an enviable position because, hopefully, he has helped contribute to its development and understands the spirit under which it was created. Humanizing this type of policy is not a simple task. An affirmative action inventory needs to be developed by the personnel department as the next step.

AFFIRMATIVE ACTION INVENTORY

Fundamentally, the personnel administrator must look at every facet of employment to see where and how the policy of affirmative action can be implemented. Review the Personnel Policy Manual, the benefits program; lunchroom and restroom facilities; parking facilities; the testing program; the Wage and Salary Program; the promotion system; job titles; performance appraisal methods; job grades; working conditions in general; absence rules; rules regarding tardiness; job descriptions; training programs; apprenticeship trainee programs; on-the-job training facilities—in short, all aspects of work. This also includes a review of forms to make certain that discriminatory statements or comments or questions that could be interpreted to be discriminatory are eliminated and that, particularly, where the application is concerned, an affirmative action statement is included. All these must be viewed in light of the policy statement which management has issued.

A *simple* inventory follows. The basic way of starting such an inventory, admittedly unsophisticated, would be to draw a line down the center of a sheet of paper and caption the column on the right *"Present Circumstances or Conditions";* caption the left column *"Circumstances and Conditions in View of Affirmative Action Policy."* Now, list conditions and circumstances relative to all phases of employment and on the left indicate in what ways these circumstances or conditions need to be modified, changed or clarified in view of the policy. When this has been done, a pattern begins to develop. You will soon find that both quantitative and qualitative changes may be in order. You are now in a position to draft recommendations after having carefully reviewed existing conditions in the organization, so that management is in a position to accept or reject, humanize and implement, *put up or shut up* with regard to affirmative action programming. Simply stated, the inventory indicates where you are and where you should be in terms of the goals you have established. It may be that, in more sophisticated programs, target dates can be established in a third column. Fixed assignments should be given to specific individuals regarding the implementation and followthrough of such a program. Listing their names following the specific project in a fourth column is yet another level of sophistication.

FOLLOW-THROUGH

We have thus established where we want to go and how we are going to get there. A good idea is to schedule the program in terms of Phases: Phase 1; Phase 2; Phase 3; and so forth, with target dates. It will also be helpful to develop report forms for each Phase. For example, Phase 1 may be the dissemination of the policy statement. On a Project Follow-Through Report, you might list the project, the purpose, the date of inauguration, the steps to be taken, the person responsible and the target date. There could also be space on this form for notations of difficulties that might delay the project. This will provide a rapid and accurate reflection of your progress.

Once you have established the program which personnel will implement, it will be necessary to advise the supervisory staff of these definitions and clarifications. This may be the responsibility of a training department or, depending upon the size and complexity of the organization, the personnel or employee relations function. In any case, a face to face meeting with the supervisory staff is essential if the supervisors and managers of the organization are to realize their responsibilities in regard to achieving these goals.

A word about the presentation. In one way or another, we are all salesmen. When we recommend a program to management we are, in effect, trying to sell something. Perhaps we are trying to sell our knowledge and expertise; perhaps we are trying to sell an idea. In any case, the best methods of salesmanship must be used. What is that old saw about selling the sizzle and not the steak? The way you present this program to your supervisory staff may make all the difference in the world in its success or failure. It would be impossible to anticipate all the circumstances that could affect your presentation. Probably the attitudes of your supervisors regarding an affirmative action program of Equal Employment Opportunity and the entire subject of race relations will, in part, be determined by the background of each of the individuals to whom you are speaking, the history and precedent of the area in which your organization is located, or the historic experience of your organization in this phase of operation. Personnel would be well advised to understand these sentiments and attitudes.

One of the best methods of presenting this program is on the basis of simple, objective operational results. Every operations man who is haunted by production quotas, cost reduction drives and the constant pressures that business experiences is interested in knowing one thing: "What's in it for me as an operational supervisor?" That question,

indirectly or directly, needs to be answered and will be answered effectively once the goals, objectives and methods of the affirmative action program have been firmly established and clearly understood. This is the time during which old wives' tales, rumors and misunderstandings can be clarified. This is not the time to editorialize or air personal attitudes. The best approach is an objective one which simply states the goals of the organization and the methods of implementation. Few if any tangible and meaningful results will ensue with a presentation that begins with, "Well, boys, here it is. Like it or lump it!" Putting "the blame" on the *Feds* won't help your course, either. Likewise, a winsome, naively optimistic presentation may have just as harmful results. Face the problem openly and honestly, while attempting to indicate that you are available to advise and counsel as needed.

Hopefully, this type of training program for supervisors will be conducted *before* the policy statement of the organization is distributed to all employees. This will give you and/or the training department (or even public relations) an opportunity to inform the supervisory staff of the goals and intentions of the organization so that each is in a better position to answer whatever questions or consider whatever reactions are submitted to them by the employees. Again, it is extremely important to indicate to all supervisory personnel that the personnel department or the individual charged with the responsibility for affirmative action in Equal Employment Opportunity stands ready to answer questions at any time, and is anxious to know the reactions and feelings of the staff as they are communicated to the supervisors and line (operations) people.

An important part of building long-serving foundations for your affirmative action program has to do with building effective communications with leaders in the community who are in a position to help you reach the goals stated in your policy. I have heard many personnel directors ask, "How do you reach the Negro community?" (or any minority "community" for that matter). It is not always easy. Building effective relationships with anyone is not simple. It requires mutual understanding, trust and respect—the basic elements of human relations.

First, you have to be aware of what sources are available to you with respect to minority recruitment. The first two that come to mind are usually the Urban League and the NAACP. Obviously, the best approach is a face-to-face contact. You may want to invite the Executive Director of your local Urban League or NAACP to your office or you may wish to call him for an appointment to see him in his. In either case, it is better to have a face-to-face meeting than to write a stiff, carefully worded letter inviting applicants or to rely on a routine telephone call from your assistant indicating that there are "some vacancies" in your organization.

EFFECTIVE COMMUNITY RELATIONS— SOLVING THE CREDIBILITY GAP

One of the biggest problems you may face is one of credibility. You must demonstrate clearly that your affirmative action policy and programs are not just lip service, not intended to cloud the issue, or act as a smokescreen in the defense of a government contract, or to keep the investigative wolves from the door. Obviously, the best proof is through your actions. It is advisable to bring with you at the time of your meeting, or to have available for reference, a copy of your policy statement, a sample application, a written procedure indicating how promotions are facilitated and how work performance is evaluated, and in general, give the individual to whom you are speaking a clear understanding of the ways in which your personnel operation functions.

This is *not* an effort to patronize or placate anyone. It is not an effort to showcase what your organization "plans" to do. Instead, it

is an effort to communicate the factors which are important to you and those involved in this program so that little misunderstandings and minor breakdowns in communications do not become monumental difficulties. And it is important for you to understand (not just listen to) the problems being faced by these leaders, too. It is also helpful to explain the routine procedure that takes place in the personnel office. Keep in mind that there may be some percentage of minority group members applying for work who have never set foot in a sophisticated employment or personnel office. They may not understand many of the things involved in personnel recruitment, screening, interviewing, testing, etc. If the standard procedure is explained to the leadership in the community, it will be in a better position to help you if there should be any frictions. Too many times, formal discrimination charges are lodged as a result of a mutual misunderstanding or breakdown in communications. This is the first step in attempting to alleviate this problem.

RECRUITMENT—SEARCH AND FIND OPERATIONS

The question of where to get "qualified" minority group applicants continues to arise. Obviously, social action organizations representing various minority groups, whether they be Negro, American Indian, Spanish-American or any other minority group, are probably the first recruitment sources that should be contacted and are usually the first ones to come to mind. In addition, however State employment offices (part of USES) and numerous Federal and State bureaus are usually in a position to help. A growing number of private employment agencies are beginning to cooperate with such programs. You will find that religious leaders are particularly attuned to this problem and will be quick to make your job vacancies known. Contacting Negro real estate agents can also be a particularly fruitful approach. (You would be surprised how much these agents know about their clients!' They are interested in finding their clients jobs or referring them to better paying possibilities. High schools in the inner-city districts are particularly good sources. In this connection, if personnel administrators or selected members of their staffs would make themselves available for lecturing, counseling and advising students, and supporting and/or assisting the counselors of these high schools, they will have a rich source of applicants.

In the final analysis, the results you gain in recruitment will be limited only by your imagination in seeking out sources. Advertising in minority group newspapers and even making sure that bulletins regarding job vacancies appear on bulletin boards in businesses in ghetto areas are other possibilities. Asking the assistance of minority group members currently working for you usually proves highly productive. When it comes to college recruitment, one of the best sources would be College Placement Services, Inc., of Bethlehem, Pennsylvania, which is a non-profit organization assisting Negro Colleges in developing career counseling and placement services.

THE SELECTION PROCESS

Sooner or later the question of "qualified" versus "qualifiable" applicants must be answered. Fundamentally, when we use the term "qualified" we are referring to an individual who completely meets all or the most critical or pertinent specifications and standards of a particular job. This means the individual has *all* of the necessary experience, education, job skills and potential required, with particularly heavy emphasis upon current job skills. When we speak of "qualifiable" we are speaking about an applicant who may not meet *all* or even any of the minimum standards. They are qualifiable to the extent that with proper training and exposure they

can accomplish specific job functions within the organization. This places particularly heavy emphasis upon potential but, for many personnel people this is an uncomfortable category. It is often unwieldy, ill defined and fails to fit into neat, easily recognized categories. The factor that personnel people must determine is the degree, the amount or the nature of—qualitatively and quantitatively—the disqualifying factors they will allow and the extent to which they are prepared to provide job related and non-job related training. It could be argued that until an affirmative action program incorporates the qualifiable along with the qualified, it remains more "nondiscriminatory" as a matter of comparison rather than "affirmatively action oriented" (and the same would be true, in a sophisticated sense, in terms of several forms of discrimination such as the employment of only light-skinned Negroes or minority group members with post-graduate degrees).

THE NEED FOR INTERVIEWING TECHNIQUES TO MEET THESE CHALLENGES

There has been much discussion about the need to develop interviewing techniques designed to help personnel people obtain better interview results when dealing with minority group applicants who lack experience in participating in interviews. There are those who argue that to do so would be to effect a reverse type of discrimination and would result in altering or modifying standard employment procedures to the benefit of one group of applicants while failing to do so for another. Most personnel people are aware of these different positions, but regardless of the position you may take, it is obvious that there will always be special techniques in the interview phase of employment. The final answer may lie in our ability to select only the best interviewers, i.e., those who can do the most effective job of objective applicant

Figure 7.1
Interview Report

NAME OF APPLICANT _____

DATE OF INTERVIEW _____

APPLYING FOR _____

INTERVIEWER _____

Please Report Your Interview Impressions By Checking the One Most Appropriate Box in Each Area

1. APPEARANCE: very untidy; poor taste in clothes	Somewhat careless about personal appearance	Satisfactory personal appearance	Good taste in clothes; better than average appearance	Unusually well groomed; very neat; excellent taste
2. FRIENDLINESS: appears very distant and aloof; cool	Approachable; fairly friendly	Warm; friendly; sociable	Very sociable and outgoing	Extremely friendly and sociable
3. POISE, STABILITY: ill at ease; "jumpy"; appears nervous	Tense; easily irritated	About as poised as the average applicant	Sure of himself	Extremely well composed; probably calm under pressure
4. PERSONALITY: unsatisfactory for the job	Questionable for this job	Satisfactory for this job	Very desirable for this job	Outstanding for this job
5. CONVERSATIONAL ABILITY: talks very little; expression poor	Makes attempts at expression; fair job at best	Average fluency and expression	Talks well and to the point	Excellent expression; extremely fluent; forceful
6. ALERTNESS: slow to catch on	Rather slow; requires more than average explanation	Grasps ideas with average ability	Quick to understand; perceives very well	Exceptionally keen and alert
7. INFORMATION: poor knowledge of field of interest	Fair knowledge of field of interest	Is as informed as the average applicant	Fairly well informed; knows more than average applicant	Has excellent knowledge of the field
8. EXPERIENCE: no relationship between applicant's background and job requirements	Fair relationship between applicant's background and job requirements	Average amount of meaningful background and experience	Background very good; considerable experience	Excellent background and experience
9. DRIVE: has poorly defined goals and appears to act without purpose	Appears to set goals too low and to put forth little effort to achieve these	Appears to have average goals; puts forth average effort to reach these	Appears to strive hard; has high desire to achieve	Appears to set high goals and to strive incessantly to achieve these
10. TEST RESULTS: too low to be considered	Substandard but possibly acceptable	Average	Above average and shows potential	Outstanding

ELIGIBLE FOR EMPLOYMENT: YES_____ NO_____ _____

SIGNATURE OF SUPERVISOR

Figure 7.2
Personnel Department
Kansas City Blue Cross-Blue Shield
Interview Check List

This form is to be completed *ONLY* if the applicant is not eligible for hire. Check the item or items that contributed to the applicant's ineligibility for employment. Under "Comments," indicate factors that might alter this ineligibility and action taken.

APPLICANT'S NAME: _____

Date of Application: _____ Job Sought: _____

1. Appearance not in keeping with the job. _____

2. Little interest in the job for which applicant applied. _____

3. Apparent disinterest in working. _____

4. Applicable test scores. _____

5. Physical condition applicable to work responsibilities. _____

6. Insufficient training for job sought. _____

7. Insufficient experience when applicable. _____

8. Insufficient job "Know-How" (aptitude). _____

9. Not bondable. _____

10. Salary requirement above authorized level. _____

11. References. _____

12. Transportation problem. _____

13. Hours not suitable to applicant. _____

14. Want part-time or temporary work. _____

15. Former employee not eligible for rehire. _____

16. Other: _____

COMMENTS:

and company oriented interviews. Probably those who are the best interviewers will do equally well with minority and majority applicants. It is unrealistic to presuppose the existence of total objectivity and complete lack of discrimination on the part of interviewers, but it seems reasonable to expect that those emotions which could hamper effective screening will be controlled in a professional way. This is best accomplished by training and dedication to the principles of professional and ethical personnel administration. Obviously, it places a burden upon personnel administrators to screen staff members and to evaluate the staff within this additional dimension. Even those with a minimum amount of interviewing experience will know that it takes very little effort to turn a "routine" interview into an accusatory and inflammatory session of strained human relations which can only result in damaging company image and emasculating the community relations program. The personnel administrator who evaluates his interviewers with these concepts in mind must take into account the possibility that there will be experiences which the white Anglo-Saxon, Protestant, middle class interviewer may find objectionable. This may also be true of line supervisors who will participate in subsequent interviewing and evaluation. Specific examples might be unmarried mothers, certain misdemeanors, numerous changes of address, long periods of unemployment without dramatic justification except for the simple reason, "I could not find a job," salary histories revealing extremely low earnings, etc. How personnel people are influenced by such factors and the extent of this influence is a matter of our orientation as professionals and as citizens.

You may find it helpful to develop an interview report form for use in analyzing applicants. This is good personnel practice, but it is particularly helpful in the establishment of the affirmative action program. It will provide a permanent record of what has transpired and give you an opportunity to evaluate the performance of interviewers in terms of EEO. Sample forms (Figs. 7.1 and 7.2) or a modification of them could be considered.

TESTING

One area of particular concern is that of testing. What constitutes a *good* test too often depends upon the person analyzing the test. Tests can be used to *screen in* or *screen out* and so it becomes incumbent upon the personnel department to validate tests so that the foundation of a strong affirmative action program is not weakened by a faulty test program that cannot accommodate the "qualifiable" applicant. You can analyze your tests further by examining carefully the type of tests you are using. There are aptitude tests which attempt to measure the mechanical skills and adaptability for specific jobs; there are tests which attempt to indicate the amount of knowledge an individual has, or simply put, what he is capable of doing in the form of achievement tests. There are typical I.Q. tests which are presumed to measure mental ability, and there are personality tests which run the gamut from Occupational Interest to Promotional Quality. Regardless of the tests you are using, you want the test to help you predict the type of job performance an applicant may be expected to produce once he is on the job. If a test cannot do that it is not a good test, or, put another way, it is invalid. An invalid test results in work for the personnel executive.

It is not always necessary to hire a professional consultant to validate tests. However, depending upon the size of the organization, the complexity of job responsibilities and the scope of the testing function, in the long run, it may be the wisest approach. Test validation is not that difficult although it takes time and willingness.

Conducting a job analysis is basic. This is based on nothing more than a job description which indicates the critical factors of the job. You then decide, as you normally would, what is required of the individual. The tests which you are using are simply analyzed and listed in terms of scores. The results of job performance appraisals are then analyzed and a statistical summary of the relationship between test scores and performance is made. Test validation is an almost natural adjunct of the personnel function and should be attempted even in the rudimentary stages. Most important, of course, is to develop tests that are appropriate and meaningful. Ask yourself *why* you are using a certain test and *what* you hope to gain by its specific use. Testing for the sake of testing is an approach that can never be justified. You might consult with federal representatives, specifically connected with the bureau of the government having jurisdiction over your specific government contracts (if you have such), or obtain consultation from governmental sources, either state or federal. You could also contact private sources such as consulting firms or a faculty member of a local college whose interests are in statistics or testing.

CONCLUSION

Needless to say, the subject of Equal Employment Opportunity is too vast to cover in a brief article. The purpose of this article has been simply to indicate guidelines by which to begin building the foundation of an effective, affirmative action program. The implementation and follow-through in all facets of employment and personnel cannot be dealt a broad brush stroke and certainly should be future topics for personnel administrators to explore.

A HIDDEN ISSUE IN MINORITY EMPLOYMENT

Richard Alan Goodman

There has been considerable foot-dragging on the part of corporations with relation to the employment of minority members. Part of this foot-dragging is "economic"; minority members are unskilled and educationally disadvantaged, and therefore a training program is required to make productive employees. Such a training program is often considered economically unfeasible vis-à-vis an adequate return on investment. Part of this foot-dragging is prejudice, to varying degrees and at many levels in the organizational hierarchy, against the minority groups. Part of this foot-dragging is the unconscious recognition that even the white members of the organization cannot effectively influence the operational value system of the organization. That is, organizations do not effectively deal with value conflict among their white members, and the appreciation of this unarticulated phenomenon tends to engender a go-slow attitude when considering the employment of personnel who might not "fit."

While not intending to negate the issues of "economics" or prejudice, I will explore the hidden issue of low tolerance for value conflict. This issue is raised clearly by the recent work of William McKelvey who states:

In recent years the conflict between [personal] . . . objectives . . . and the goals of large . . . organizations has been the subject of an increasing number of books and articles. This conflict, which may conceivably arise in any kind of an organi-

zation, is one where expectations, aspirations, and values of an employee are different from those of the organization.[1]

There is a growing appreciation, illustrated by various organizational theorists, that the value systems inherent in organizations and in individuals are not sufficiently similar to allow the assumption of commonality.

Chris Argyris articulated this when he described the tendency of organizations to inhibit the maturing process of their members.[2] That is, organizations tended to restrict independence, to limit alternate behavior patterns, to demand a relatively short time perspective, and to discourage the development of a deep interest pattern.

Similarly, Robert Dubin, in an early study of the "central life interests" of workers tended to find that they did not view the work situation as a place to get their satisfactions.[3] He continues by noting that organizational devices to encourage commitment to organizational objectives normally have been based on the assumption that the working time of an employee is one of his central life interests. Within the limit of Dubin's study, however, this is not true. Small wonder that progress toward stronger organizational commitment has been slow.

NONCONFORMIST EMPLOYEES

The preceding discussion suggests that the incidence of value conflict between employee and organization is likely to be significant. It then becomes interesting to speculate on what behavior ensues from a value conflict

[1]William McKelvey, "Expectational Noncomplementarity and Style of Interaction Between Professional and Organization," Research Paper No. 15, Graduate School of Business Administration, UCLA, Division of Research (Los Angeles, Nov. 1967), p. 1.

[2]Chris Argyris, "Understanding Human Behavior in Organizations: One Viewpoint," in Mason Haire, ed., *Modern Organization Theory* (New York: Wiley, 1959).

[3]Robert Dubin, "Industrial Workers' Worlds: A Study of the 'Central Life Interests' of Industrial Workers," *Social Problems* **III**, 131-142 (1956).

situation. This raises the issue which served as a focus in the McKelvey study: "What happens when [employees] begin to see that the organization they are working for is not fulfilling their . . . expectations?"[4]

Athough McKelvey used a framework which allowed several typical behaviors, his study identified a predominant form. This form he called "active, cynic" or "insurgent." His findings are thus stated:

These results suggest that scientists and engineers who perceive that their professional expectations are not being fulfilled by the organization are most likely to feel that they have little control over their career advancement (cynicism). They are quite likely to choose not to change their own values and expectations to fit well with those of the organization (non-passivity).[5]

The employee who is behaving in the active, cynic style can be characterized as one who is working for a change in the organizational system. He continues to believe that his criticisms will actually affect the alteration of that system. This continual belief in the eventual ability to accomplish change and the behavior which often follows from such a belief leads to a further major finding of McKelvey. This style (active, cynic) is "the style least likely to be coupled with high eligibility for promotion."[6] The low eligibility for promotion tends to ensure that people in the upper echelons of an organization have relatively similar value systems.

This work of McKelvey and that of authors such as William H. Whyte, Jr. and Melville Dalton seem to support the conclusion that sameness in values is an attribute treasured by organizations.[7] Further, their work suggests that value sameness is more prevalent the higher one looks in the organizational hierarchy. The end result of this sort of behavior is to disenfranchise people who have different value systems and who do not conform. American industry does not seem to have the organizational abilities to tolerate value conflicts, and it is this hidden issue which seems most likely to contribute to turbulent progress in the minority employment programs of various organizations.

One of the clear trends in the question of minority problems is the fact that the Negro and, to some lesser extent, the Mexican-American are becoming more and more insistent upon a satisfactory role in United States society. A satisfactory role means being actually represented in the society and thereby contributing to the fashioning of the future of this society. It explicitly requires the ability of the minority group to influence the operational value system of the society. The ability to influence is a complex and troublesome concept when considered on a societal level, but when transformed to an organizational level this ability and its corollary, the achievement of a satisfactory role, appear possible.

At the organizational level the complexity associated with assuring a satisfactory role for minority members is greatly reduced. Here the question of a satisfactory role continues to require that the minority groups have the ability to influence, but in this case it is the operational value system of the organization that is influenced.

Turning to the specific problem of minority employment, an initial axiomatic statement would be as follows: as the influx of minority group employees grows in number, more and more members of the organization will have value systems which are at variance with that of the organization. It then follows that unless an organization can devise some process of adapting to this value conflict and making it "constructive value conflict," the influx of minority members will simply lead to frustration and turmoil.

The issue raised is not one that has an easy solution. Only limited guidance is avail-

[4]McKelvey, *op. cit.*, p. 1.
[5]*Ibid.*, p. 25.
[6]*Ibid.*, p. 24.
[7]William H. Whyte, Jr., *The Organization Man* (New York: Simon and Schuster, 1956); and Melville Dalton, *Men Who Manage* (New York: Wiley, 1959).

able from the literature on organizational behavior.

The most prominent recommendation for an adaptive device which potentially allows for constructive value conflict comes from Rensis Likert. His recommendation of a "linking pin" organizational form is well known.[8] (See Fig. 7.3.)

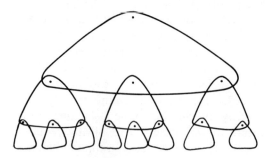

Figure 7.3 The linking pin organization.

The essence of his recommendation is that decision making should be done by the entire group of men, with the man who "supervises" serving as a linking pin to the next level of the organization. The essential assumption of Likert's proposal is that each man in any specific triangle is equally influential. An organization which operates under this recommendation has great potential for handling value conflict. But it does not necessarily avoid the issue of promotions being given to the men whose values match those of the organization. It seems, therefore, that while Likert's proposal has the potential for handling value conflict it does not protect an organization from value-oriented promotion practices. Parenthetically, it does seem that task conflict can be handled well by this device, regardless of the value conflict problem.

Another model or organizational behavior which has potentiality for handling value conflict is that of Richard Cyert and James

March.[9] They describe organizations as a set of "viable coalitions." The coalitions are formed by various forms of negotiating and are relatively stable over time. A coalition mapping of an organization can be seen in Figure 7.4. The coalitions tend to determine organizational objectives which are forged from the value systems of the coalition participants by the negotiation process. The basic ingredient necessary for this conceptualization to be operational in the minority area is the provision of a source of bargaining power for the minority groups. To more fully allow for effective value conflict the minority participants must have some measure of power. To date, most of this power has resided external to the firm in the hands of various civil rights groups.

For a considerable period of time, the major influx of minority group employees will be seen in the lower echelons of the organization. David Mechanic has described how occupants of an organization's lower echelons can exert power and influence.[10] His definition of sources of power include access to people, information, and instrumentalities.

The power of participants who control access to people can be exemplified by the secretary who screens calls and callers for her boss or the machine shop supervisor who does or does not allow you to speak directly with the men working on your project. Control of access to information concerns a wide variety of actions, including whether or not to report an impending schedule variance and who to inform in advance about organization switches. Examples of control over access to instrumentalities are the "actual" assignment of priorities on computer runs, illustration work, or the use of company special facilities. To a large extent, the initial

[8]Rensis Likert, *New Patterns in Management* (New York: McGraw-Hill, 1966).

[9]Richard M. Cyert and James G. March, *A Behavioral Theory of the Firm* (Englewood Cliffs, N.J.: Prentice-Hall, 1963).

[10]David Mechanic, "Sources of Power for Lower Participants," in William W. Cooper *et al.,* eds., *New Perspectives in Organization Research* (New York: Wiley, 1964).

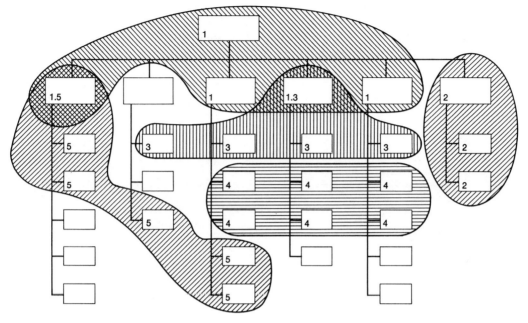

Figure 7.4 Coalition mapping of an organization.

positioning of newly hired minority members will not even give them access to these sources of power. As such, even this coalition concept will not encourage the desired effective value conflict since there is little power available to the lower participants.

A POWER ROLE

The logical conclusion to this discussion is simply to provide some source of power to new entrants to the organization. This would then set the stage for a mode of value conflict which would provide most organizational participants with a role in defining the operational value system. But it does not provide for a constructive value conflict situation. It only provides for value conflict per se. I can go either way.

The situation must be leavened with a dose of "winning while losing."[11] Dubin has de-

[11]Robert Dubin, "Winning While Losing," a speech delivered to the Academy of Management, Western Division, at Boulder, Colo., March 17, 1967.

scribed a situation which encourages conflict without destroying conflict resolution capabilities. The essence of his discussion is that an organization must create conditions that encourage participants to:

1. Strongly present their views on a given situation.
2. Not affect the decision.
3. Come back the next time equally willing to present their views.

This continues to allow a decision-making body to understand the full implications of a decision, both functional and dysfunctional.

With this in mind, my concluding recommendation is as follows: Consider carefully the areas of an organization within which lower participants have relevant contributions to make. Within those areas, encourage participative decision making under conditions which provide a winning-while-losing atmosphere. In such a situation a constructive conflict of values might be worked out and, at the same time, provide an ever-increasing satisfactory role. for minority participants. It is important to note that such a recommendation is only an enabling condition for the development of constructive value conflict. It is not a final answer. The final solution to these problems will continue to be elusive for many years to come.

PAYCHECK AND APRON— REVOLUTION IN WOMANPOWER

Eli Ginzberg

Before World War II, in many states women teachers and others holding civil service positions had to resign their positions if they married. The same practice was widespread throughout private industry. Shortly thereafter, as the economy of the United States was transformed under the impetus of the war, it became necessary for senior military officers to ring doorbells to persuade housewives that they were needed in office or factory.

The tradition that the place of a married woman, particularly if she had children, was in the home was shattered under the hammer blows of war when women were exhorted that it was their patriotic duty to take a job. As frequently happens in major social changes, neither men nor women, according to the various wartime polls, understood that this move of married women into paid employment would be not solely for the duration, but would represent a revolution in the American way of life. While many women, of course, gave up their jobs when the war ended, they had eaten of the apple: they liked the independence and esteem that they found associated with holding a job; they even liked the idea that their husbands and children had to pitch in with the housework; they liked, above all, the wider horizons that work created.

To put the record straight, it is necessary to point out that some married women had long worked out of the home. For the most part, these were women whose husbands were unable to support their families and a minority of middle class women, usually with very small families, who were professionals.[1] The dominant pattern, however, was that a woman who was working gave up her job *permanently* when she married or during her first pregnancy. It was almost unheard of for a married woman, in the absence of family misfortune, to seek paid employment for the first time in her mature years.

THE SITUATION TODAY

In 1965, 33.8 million women worked at some time during the course of the year. An additional number of about 900,000 did not work, but looked for work. Approximately 2 out of every 3 women between the ages of 18 and 25 worked, as did more than 1 out of 2 of those between 25 and 60. In the 45 to 54 year old group, the percentage who worked was just under 58—the highest proportion of any group of women over 25 years.[2] Since approximately 95 out of every 100 women marry, these proportions refer overwhelmingly to women who are or have been married. In fact, if we disregard those who are 65 or older, we find that approximately half of all women who were married and living with their spouses in 1965 had worked during the year; if they had been married, but were then widowed, divorced, or separated, the chances were 2 out of 3 that they worked; if they were single, the probability of their working was 4 out of 5.[3]

It is not generally understood either by the American public or by most labor economists, for that matter, that the prototype of the full-time, full-year worker barely comprises a majority. Of the 87.6 million people who worked or looked for work in 1965, only 48.4

From Eli Ginzberg, "Paycheck and Apron—Revolution and Womanpower," Industrial Relations 7 (3), 193-203 (1968). Reprinted by permission.

[1] Robert W. Smuts, *Women and Work in America* (New York: Columbia University, 1959), Chaps. 1 and 2.

[2] "Work Experience of the Population in 1965," *Monthly Labor Review* **LXXXIX**, 1371 and A-5 (December, 1966).

[3] *Ibid.,* Table A-13.

million or 55 per cent fell into this category. The other 45 per cent represented two major subgroups: those who desired, but were unable to find, full-time employment; and those, including a high proportion of all women workers, who preferred to work less than full time.[4] Of the 33.8 million women who worked, 13.1 million, or about 39 per cent, worked full time, full year. About 10 million worked full time for less than a full year, and the other 10.6 million worked part time throughout or for part of the year.[5]

A critical question about individuals who work less than full time throughout the year is whether they work less out of preference or necessity. Of the 17.6 million women who fell into this category, just over half (52 per cent) indicated that they were out of the labor force for part of the year in order to take care of their homes. The second largest group, about 22 per cent were going to school. The remaining 26 per cent were about evenly divided between those who could not find jobs and those who were kept from working because of illness, disability, or other reasons.[6]

It would be easy to conclude that a weakness in the demand for labor is a factor of relatively minor importance in explaining why women work part rather than full time. But before making this deduction, we must note that for 2.2 million women, unemployment was identified as the key variable and that another 900,000 women wanted to work, but could not find jobs. Some part of the 2.5 million who worked less than full time because of disability or other reasons might have worked full time had the demand for labor been stronger. The proof of the sensitive relations between the strength of demand for labor and the full-time employment of women is found in the following four-year

trend. From 1962 through 1965 the total number of women who worked increased by 2.4 million. The corresponding increase in those working full time, full year was 1.5 million. The proportion of women who worked full time increased from 36.8 per cent to 38.8 per cent, which suggests that many women will respond to the opportunity to shift from part- to full-time employment.[7]

While most women who hold jobs work less than full time, it is worth noting that in any week about 1 out of 8 women who are employed work not only full time, but overtime. In May 1966, there were 3.4 million who worked overtime and slightly over 1 million received premium pay. Just about half of all those who worked overtime were women who were living with their husbands.[8]

Another important dimension of the role of women in the world of work relates to the jobs which they hold and the income which they earn. Of the women who were employed in 1966, those in white-collar occupations accounted for just about half. Approximately 1 out of every 3 women who was employed was a clerical worker. Another 1 out of 3 was a blue-collar worker, usually a factory operator or a service worker in other than private household work. The remaining third were about equally divided between two major groups, "professional workers, managers, or officials" and "private household workers, sales workers, farmers, or farm laborers."[9]

Women workers are concentrated in a relatively few occupational fields, and they often account for a high proportion of all workers within that occupation. Over 97 per cent of all stenographers, typists, and private household workers are women. Women ac-

[4]*Ibid.,* pp. 1370-71.
[5]*Ibid.,* p. 1370.
[6]*Ibid.,* p. 1373.

[7]*Ibid.,* p. 1370.
[8]"Overtime Hours and Premium Pay," *Monthly Labor Review* **LXXXIX,** A-8 (September, 1966).
[9]Women's Bureau, U.S. Department of Labor, *Background Facts of Women Workers in the U.S.* (Washington, D.C.: May, 1967), p. 11.

count for 6 or 7 out of every 10 workers in the following fields: health service workers; teachers, except college; waitresses and cooks; clerical workers, other than secretaries and typists. In contrast, women represent a relatively small minority of such occupational fields as craftsmen, farmers, managers and officials, and professional and technical workers, other than health service workers and teachers.[10] The concentration of women workers is further pointed up by the fact that they account for approximately half or more of all employees in the following major industries: banking, insurance, local government, apparel manufacturing, general merchandise stores, eating and drinking places, apparel and accessory stores, medical and health services, personnel services, and communications.[11]

In 1965, when about 29.5 million women received wage or salary income for at least part of the year, the median annual earnings amounted to $2,098, or 40 per cent of the male median ($5,194). Over 6 out of 10 women earned less than $3,000; about 1 in 4 earned between $3,000 and $5,000, and under 15 per cent earned over $5,000. One ready explanation for low average earnings is to be found of course in the fact that under 40 per cent of all women workers were regularly employed throughout the year. But that this is not the whole of the explanation can be seen if comparisons restricted to year-round full-time workers; then a marked discrepancy is found in each major occupational field. The greatest absolute and relative discrepancies are found among sales workers: the median annual earnings of women totaled about $3,000 and those of men totaled in excess of $7,000; among managers and officials, women averaged about $4,500 and men earned over $8,600. Differentials in favor of men are also found among: profes-

sionals, $5,500 to $8,200; clericals, $4,200 to $6,200; craftsmen, $3,900 to $6,700; operatives, $3,200 to $5,700; and service workers, $2,800 to $4,900.[12]

There are several factors which help to explain the marked differences in earnings between men and women in the same occupational category. Within each category women are likely to be employed in the less remunerative branches—e.g., nursing instead of medicine, operatives in apparel manufacturing instead of the chemical industry; tearoom waitresses instead of hotel waiters. Since women are more likely than men to have a discontinuous work experience, they are normally concentrated at the lower end of the job ladder; moreover, they are less likely than men to work overtime. But part of the explanation—how much remains uncertain until experience accumulates under the Civil Rights Act of 1964—lies in the reluctance of many employers to promote women to the more prestigious and higher paying positions in their organizations. While the last several decades have seen a weakening of the dual job market based on sex, the evidence of concentration by sex among occupations, reinforced by data on income, indicates its persistence.

Other important determinants of the substantial wage and salary differential in favor of men has been (1) the lag in the number and proportion of women who have been willing to pursue their studies to the doctoral level, which has precluded their sharing fully in the employment and income opportunities that have opened up for professional workers since the end of World War II, (2) the inability of many women to respond to job opportunities that require more time than the regular work week, and (3) the inability of many women to accept jobs which are not near their homes.

---

[10]*Ibid.*

[11]*Ibid.*, p. 13.

[12]*Ibid.*, pp. 16 and 17. The median wage and salary income of full-time workers in 1965 came to $3,823 for women, compared to $6,375 for males.

A BACKWARD AND FORWARD LOOK

Between 1947 and 1966, the civilian labor force increased by 17 million from slightly over 59 million to about 76 million, or almost 30 per cent. Of this increase, the expansion of the male labor force accounted for approximately 6 million; the female labor force almost doubled—it increased by about 11 million.[13]

These figures make it clear that had it not been for the much heavier involvement of women in the world of work, the rapid and sustained economic growth that characterized the American economy during these two decades would have been impossible. The slow additions to the civilian male labor force in the fifties reflect the depressed birth rates of the thirties and the buildup of the armed forces during the Korean War and its aftermath. The elongation of the educational cycle was a third factor which reduced the numbers of young male entrants into the labor force. During the 20-year period, the civilian male labor force grew by only 14 per cent. In sharp contrast the female labor force increased by 66 per cent.[14]

In each of the strategic age groups the labor force participation rates for women increased substantially. But the biggest gains were scored in the older age groups. By the middle sixties, 1 out of every 2 women between 45 and 54 was working or looking for work.[15]

The post-World War II decades provided a conducive environment for women to find employment out of the home, not only because of reduced competition from males but also because the service sector of the economy was expanding rapidly, a sector that traditionally makes heavy use of part-time workers and of women. For instance, in the period 1950 to 1965, the average annual increase of part-time women workers totaled about 300,000, a figure just below the average increase of full-time male workers. In the four-year business cycle following the end of the Korean hostilities (1953 to 1957), the contrast between the average annual increase of part-time jobs and the average increase of full-time jobs was most pronounced—in the ratio of 11 to 1. In the last decades the increase in favor of part-time jobs was much smaller. Taking the entire 15-year period (1950-1965) as a whole, the proportion of all workers who were employed at part-time jobs increased from 16 to 20 per cent.[16]

The above data emphasize that the key to the new role of women in the labor force since the end of World War II has been, in the first instance, the entry or re-entry into work of mature women, those over 35 years of age. But a closer look at the data reveals the interesting finding that, in the last decade, from 1956 to 1966 the proportion of younger women (below 35) in the labor force increased even more rapidly than the proportion for those over 35, with the result that in 1966 the proportions of the two groups in the labor force were almost the same (below 35, 34.3 per cent; 35 plus, 36.0 per cent).[17]

What has been happening among younger married women who are living with their husbands and usually have young children? In 1947, about a quarter of those in the 20 to 24 year old bracket were in the labor force; two decades later the proportion was approaching 2 in 5. In the next age group, 25 to 34, a parallel increase occurred—from about one-fifth in 1947 to one-third in 1966.[18] One of the major determinants of whether or not a woman seeks employment is whether she has children, particularly children of pre-school age. For instance, among women in

[13]U.S. Department of Labor, *Manpower Report of the President* (Washington, D.C.: 1967), p. 201.
[14]*Ibid.*
[15]*Ibid.*, p. 202. See also the McNally article in this symposium.

[16]"Work Experience, 1965 . . . ," p. 1375.
[17]U.S. Bureau of Labor Statistics, *Marital and Family Characteristics of Workers,* Special Labor Force Report No. 80 (Washington, D.C.: March, 1966), p. 32.
[18]*Manpower Report of the President . . . ,* p. 229.

their early thirties (30-34) who live with their husbands and have a child under the age of 3, 21 per cent work; 32 per cent work if they have a child between 3 and 5; 44 per cent if they have a child between 6 and 11; and 53 per cent if they have a child between 12 and 17. The total number of children that a woman has, as well as the age of the youngest, influences working patterns. The more children a woman has, the less likely she is to work.[19]

Since 1957, important changes have been occurring in the birth rate or, to use a preferred measure, the general fertility rate, which indicates the number of births per 1,000 women between the ages of 15 and 44. In 1957, this rate reached a high of 123.0. By 1966 it had declined to 92.6. The 1966 rate was considerably below that of any of the post-World War II years, but it was still considerably in excess of the low rates of the thirties when the rate fluctuated in the high 70's.[20]

A recent bulletin of the Metropolitan Life Insurance Company (October 1966) on "Baby Boom Ending" adds some important facts. It explains that the drop in the birth rate reflects "reductions in the rates for second and subsequent children." Between 1947 and 1957 the rate for second children was 45 per 1,000; since 1957 it has declined to under 35 per 1,000. Similarly, the annual rate for third births had declined from a peak of 33 per 1,000 in 1957 to slightly over 24 per 1,000 in 1965.

Such radical reductions in the birth rate during a period of continuing high level employment and income are not easy to comprehend. They unquestionably reflect a multitude of influences, including the growing perception among the middle class that

while the marginal cost of a third or fourth child might be small in the early years, contingent expenses loom large, since tuition in good private colleges is now in excess of $2,000 annually. The dissemination and use of improved birth control methods must be considered. The declining attractiveness of the suburbs, as a consequence of rapidly increasing population pressures, may be a factor. But it is a reasonable assumption that part of the decline must be the result of the growing recognition by many women that their ability to combine home and work will be significantly affected by the number of children they have. If a woman limits her children to one or two and spaces them closely together, she has much less difficulty returning to work than if she waits to return until the youngest of four children is in school.

While it is never safe to project recent population data—witness the radical change in our fertility rate after 1957—the U.S. Department of Labor is probably correct in its assumption that the labor force participation rates of women will continue to increase during the period 1965-1980. The Labor Department's estimates allow for an overall rise of 3 percentage points from 37.5 to 40.6 between 1965 and 1980. In the age group under 35 years the anticipated increase is considerably smaller than in the upper age groups. Without contesting the relatively substantial increase anticipated among older women, which would bring the rate for the 45 to 54 year old group to 60 per cent in 1980, some question may be raised about the postulated small increases among the 20 to 34 year old groups.[21] Developments during the past decade, we have found, point to the much heavier involvement of young married women in paid employment. Of course, the participation rates of women will be greatly influenced by the availability of jobs and by

[19]U.S. Department of Labor, Manpower Administration, *Manpower Report,* No. 12 (Washington, D.C.: May, 1967), p. 3.

[20]U.S. Bureau of the Census, *Current Population Reports,* Series 25, No. 368 (Washington, D.C.: June 27, 1967), p. 3.

[21]"Labor Force Projections by Color, 1970-1980," *Monthly Labor Review* **LXXXIX,** 966 (September, 1966).

competition from men. And in the 15 years ahead there will be many more young men entering the labor force for the first time than in the period we have just passed through.

EDUCATION AND INCOME

Whether a woman works regularly, periodically, or not at all is greatly affected by the education level which she has achieved. In turn, the income which her husband earns will influence her decision to seek a job, just as her earnings will have a significant effect on the standard of living that the family is able to maintain. These three variables, a woman's education, husband's income, and her earnings, warrant more careful consideration.

The most important single finding about women's education and their labor force participation is that the more education a woman has had, the more likely she is to work. In 1966, about 70 per cent of those with one or more years of post-graduate study were in the labor force, compared with about 50 per cent of college graduates, 40 per cent of high school dropouts, and 30 per cent of those who graduated from elementary school, but went no further.[22] Among women who have had at least one year of postgraduate study, the proportion who are in the labor force never drops significantly below two-thirds and in the age group, 45 to 54, reaches the astonishing high of 85 per cent. In the case of college graduates, more than half work at all times except in the 35 to 44 year old group, where the percentage drops to 44.[23]

Since there have been rapid changes under way which affect all women in the labor force, the cross-sectional data presented above do not disclose the full force of education in pulling women into work. This force is clearer

if we compare the labor force participation rates in 1952 and in 1966 of women in the strategic age group of 25 to 34 according to their education. There was an overall rise of less than 3 percentage points—36.3 to 39.0; high school graduates showed an increase close to the average, college dropouts a slightly smaller increase, while the group composed of those with 4 years or more of college showed a rise of more than 9 percentage points—three times the average.[24]

A significant relationship between level of education and participation in work is not surprising. Many women, like men, undertake additional education for occupational reasons. Hence the achievement of an occupational goal is a strong force in their planning and action. Moreover, once they have made the investment of time, money, and energy in attaining a college or higher degree, their interests in a particular field are likely to be awakened or strengthened to a point where they will seek to gratify them through work.[25]

The relationship between working and family income runs in two directions. On the one hand, the level of family income influences whether women seek jobs. And the income that women earn from work influences the level at which the family is able to live. We noted earlier that single women and women whose marriages have been broken by death or divorce are likely to be employed unless they have young children at home. We will therefore focus on wives living with their husbands who are or are not in the labor force.

In 1965, the median income of white men whose wives did not work was $6,300; men whose wives worked had a slightly lower median income—$6,000. Of the white women who worked, 28 per cent were married to men whose earnings were between $5,000 and $6,999, and 36 per cent were married

[22]Women's Bureau, U.S. Department of Labor, *Trends in Educational Attainment of Women* (Washington, D.C.: June, 1967), p. 9.

[23]*Ibid.*, p. 17.

[24]*Ibid.*, p. 18.

[25]Eli Ginzberg and Associates, *Life Styles of Educated Women* (New York: Columbia University, 1965), *passim.*

to men who made over $7,000. Of the white women who were *not* in the labor force, 23 per cent were married to men earning between $5–6,999 and 42 per cent to men earning over $7,000. Thus we see that as far as these gross categories are concerned, it is only when men earn $7,000 or more that their wives are somewhat less likely to seek outside employment.[26]

An interesting facet of the problem is the effect of women's working on family income. In families with a total annual income of under $3,000, only about 1 out of 4 wives work and those who do are employed for a relatively small part of the year. In families with $10,000 or over, more than half of all the wives work (55 per cent in 1965). Another finding is that significant differences in family income depend on whether wives work little (1-26 weeks or 1-52 weeks part time), moderately (27–49 weeks full time), or regularly; median family income reflects this variable as follows: $7,200, $8,700, $9,600.[27]

In 1965 the median annual wage or salary of all women who worked was $2,100. However those who were regularly employed year-round earned $3,800.[28] The median income of families with both husband and wife in the labor force in 1965 was $8,600 (for white families only; if nonwhites are included the median falls to $8,400), indicating that middle-class status, at least as defined in terms of income, can be achieved by most families if both husband and wife work.[29]

WHAT THESE DATA REVEAL

These are the contours of the revolution revealed by the data:

1. Except for those with young children, women are likely to be employed outside the home.

[26]*Marital and Family Characteristics . . . ,* Table A-6.
[27]*Ibid.,* Table A-17.
[28]*Background Facts . . . ,* p. 16.
[29]*Marital and Family Characteristics . . . ,* Table A-17.

2. However, most women who work do not hold full-time year-round jobs; they work part-time or part-year.

3. The more education a woman has, the more likely she is to be employed.

4. Although women with husbands at the upper end of the income distribution are less likely to work, a significant proportion do.

5. A large number of families move into the middle-income bracket on the basis of supplementary earnings of wives.

6. Mature women in the age group of 45 to 55 are more likely to be employed than any other age group.

7. An increasing proportion of women in the childbearing years (25–35) are finding it possible to hold a job.

8. The employment of women has been facilitated since the end of World War II by the reduction in the percentage of young men entering the labor market and by the growth of the service sector.

9. Government forecasts anticipate a continuing rise in the labor force participation rates of women in all age classes (20 to 64).

10. Women continue to be highly concentrated in certain occupational and industrial fields, particularly in clerical work and service occupations.

THE CHALLENGES THAT REMAIN

In the early days of the revolution in womanpower many leaders were disturbed by the development. They were afraid that the increasing participation of women in the labor force would greatly increase the difficulties of many men in their effort to get and hold jobs. More generally, there was widespread uneasiness that with mothers away from home many children would be neglected and become delinquent. Some critics worried about the psychological upsets that might follow upon a woman having a better job and earning more than her husband. Many other fears and apprehensions were bruited about. Most of these have now been stilled, although some people believe that working mothers must be a major contributory factor to delinquency. If the children of working mothers are neglected, the critics are probably right, but they ignore the fact that many women who do not hold a job neglect their children and most of those who work do not. At least, there is no reliable evidence of a significant relationship between mothers working and the current or future delinquency of children.

If the problems that held the center of the stage early in the revolution—the impact on the employment of men, the unsettlement of sex roles in the home, the delinquency of youth—are now receding into history, what are the issues that remain that warrant public attention and action? Some of the more important will be considered here briefly.

One of the characteristics of every society is the failure of institutions to adjust to the new circumstances and conditions that a revolution brings in its wake. There are many important changes and adjustments that are overdue if our society is to take greater advantage of the potential and developed skill of its women. First, our educational and training systems require adjustment. For instance, girls still shy away from mathematics and the sciences in favor of foreign languages and the arts to an extent that has no justification in terms of what we know about the distribution of aptitude or about the needs of the marketplace. Of even greater importance is the inadequacy of guidance and counseling in the home, school, and community with respect to the educational and occupational planning. Most young women still do not realize that they will spend most of their adult years at work, and they do not know how to prepare themselves for the work opportunities they will confront. Few are sophisticated about the different ways to balance career and home. On all these fronts, our society is deficient. We have permitted old models and stereotypes to remain entrenched in the face of a vastly altered reality.

Most colleges and universities continue to favor men over women in their admissions policies and in granting financial aid. Educational institutions continue to ignore the fact that many women will have to interrupt their education in their early twenties, but will seek to complete it later. If the institutions were to recognize their problem they would have to make major adjustments. Almost no imagination has been shown with regard to maintaining the skill and interest of the many women who have to interrupt their education or their careers.

Much career development, especially at the higher levels, takes place outside of colleges and universities. These other institutions, likewise, are negligent. For example, it is rare indeed for administrators of medical residency programs to realize that married women would find it beneficial if they did not have to work the year through. And only the most alert corporation has recognized the advantages of a part-time training program as a way of attracting able women back into employment. Most employers are disinclined to make their in-service and extramural educational and training opportunities available to women for fear that their investment will be lost because so many women withdraw from the labor market. This reasoning ignores the fact that many women might well return shortly, as well as the fact that a large number of men also quit.

With respect to utilization, employers give unequivocal evidence that they prefer stupid men to smart women. They are usually unwilling to make even modest adjustments in hours, vacations, and other scheduling to attract able women. Admittedly it is easier to run a large organization according to a single set of rules. But women are not men and one set of rules is seldom adequate for all men and never for both men and women.

THREE POLICY AREAS

A revolution that alters in fundamental respects the relation of one sex to the world of work will inevitably impinge on a great many social institutions and mechanisms. We will touch briefly on three areas where the opportunities that the revolution has opened up remain to be more fully exploited.

Family as a Unit of Employment. Economists have long postulated that the individual earns income, but the family is the strategic consumption unit. Now, however, we are witnessing a trend which is making the family the effective unit of employment. One director of a large division in an eastern university is fully aware of this, since he is unable to hire desirable staff members unless he can first assure them that he has a job lined up for their wives. Few employers have recognized the extent to which a job transfer or job change for a man increasingly requires a satisfactory situation for his working wife. The implications of this new type of constraint on labor mobility warrants more systematic exploration.

Child Care Centers. For the past several decades the American people have dragged their heels in establishing and expanding good child care facilities, thus evidencing their uncertainty about the desirability of mothers of young children working. But we have seen that despite this cautionary attitude more and more young mothers are in fact working. Recently, the Congress has become concerned with the possible adverse effect of a shortage of suitable child care facilities on the work potential of mothers who are on the Aid-to-Dependent Children rolls. Concerned by the mounting relief rolls of women with children, but without husbands, Congress is seeking to promote the employability of many of these women. While its primary concern is to reduce relief expenditures, it is also concerned about the short-comings of a system which enables many women to live without working. This much is clear. Many of these women would prefer to work, especially if their children were looked after by competent staff. Since Congress has started devoting its attention to the problems of the poor and since certain organizations, such as hospitals and trade unions (Amalgamated Clothing Workers), are beginning to be concerned about working mothers, we may be entering a period of accelerated development of child care centers. If we do, the forecasters had better restudy their earlier calculations because the labor force participation rates of young women are likely to move up more sharply than has been anticipated.

Unions and Wages. A third area of importance involves the unionization and wage levels of low paying service jobs, a high proportion of which have been filled by women. Since more and more women are entering, re-entering, and remaining in the labor force, the quality of the jobs available to them becomes a matter of greater interest and concern. The willingness of state legislators to bring more and more previously exempted jobs under labor standards, the increasing success that trade unions have begun to experience in organizing hospital workers, the upward drift of wages for unskilled service jobs, all bespeak new, if belated, adjustments to the more permanent effects of the revolution in womanpower.

CONCLUSION

It has been the strength of economics that it can reduce the economic activities of men and nations to a few symbols which can be manipulated to yield important insights about the efficiency and equity with which resources are allocated and rewards distributed. But it has been a weakness of economics that it is little concerned with studying and evaluating the changes in the institutional framework which set the parameters of the market and influence the ways in which the supply and demand for various resources are altered. There has been no important study of womanpower since the National Manpower Council's effort of more than a decade ago. Here is proof, if proof is needed, of the continuing predilection of economists to select problems that fit their models rather than to develop approaches that can help to interpret and evaluate the dynamic changes in the economic life of peoples and nations. And the revolution in womanpower is a dynamic change regardless of what else it may turn out to be.

ENVIRONMENTAL QUALITY ══════

THE OFFICE LANDSCAPE: A "SYSTEMS" CONCEPT

Hans J. Lorenzen
Dieter Jaeger

Office landscape systems were developed by the Quickborner Team and implemented for the first time in Germany in 1960. Today, after many years of experience gathered in a great number of such installations, this new concept is an overwhelming success. This is readily confirmed by every company which has experienced the many advantages offered by this office system.

While much criticism has been leveled at the system, we find, in most instances, that these critics have never even seen this office system in operation. It is hardly necessary to stress that such opinions, devoid of knowledge and based on hearsay, carry little weight.

What are office landscape systems and what is their aim? To begin with, we stress that each and every one of them evolved from a complex planning approach in which systems analysts, architects, and interior designers plan, as a team, the optimum layout and work environment for an organization. Team, as understood in this context, is the simultaneous working together of various specialists with the possibility of instantaneous face-to-

From Hans J. Lorenzen and Dieter Jaeger, "The Office Landscape: A "Systems" Concept," Contract Magazine (January 1968). Reprinted by permission.

face communication before ideas freeze in any specialist's mind to the undue limitation of another team member's problem-solving ability.

Each specialist has to learn to understand the "special language" and special viewpoint of his team members and must be willing and able to explain his own proposals, accept criticism prompted by a different perspective, and be ready to re-work his own contribution, so as to minimize the objections of the other specialists, while still reaching his own objective.

Team work does not mean that a number of people work "nicely" together; rather, it means challenging and stimulating each other constantly to arrive at new and better solutions. Only through this kind of planning effort can the great number of different aspects be integrated in the complex problem of planning an office building and office layout. The Quickborner Team is the catalyst and organizer for this kind of complex interdisciplinary planning.

When office landscape systems are challenged by the "design approach" to office planning, and especially, the "broad freedom of contemporary American space planning," we ask: Doesn't the innovation of the Office Landscape concept give the designer even more freedom and opportunity within his own area of responsibility?

It is, however, accepted today by most "space planners" (a term often used for designers who specialize in offices) that this actually is not enough and that "buildings must be planned from the inside out." From where we—as management consultants—sit, this is little more than lip service. It is understandably so, and this observation should not

275

be construed as criticism since the background, the experience, and the vocational emphasis is very different from our own.

Be this as it may, we have today a consensus on the need to get the most of any investment in a new office building and all operating expenses connected with it. Designing beautiful facades, impressive entrance halls, and luxurious executive suites is not enough. The Quickborner Team's system has often been chastised by our critics for having "fixed rules" and "over-simplified panaceas," all of which then lead to the "catchy, but suspicious term: Office Landscape." The term "Office Landscape" is, in fact, catchy—but it focuses only on the visually perceptible result of a very complex planning approach. Whoever can coin a better name may still win a prize.

The "rigid rules" so harshly criticized are nothing but principles grown out of experience, which enable the "inhabitants" of the Office Landscape to maintain and use this highly flexible and efficient system to maximum advantage. Unfortunately, in conventional office planning, such "operating rules" are lacking. Maybe, this is the reason why the original design concept often finds itself almost buried by the operational activities in such office space after a small passage of time.

IMPROVING OFFICE EFFICIENCY

The Quickborner Team's professed aim is to plan office buildings which not only meet fully the requirements of office procedures, but also environmental and "work-needs" of the office personnel—not only for today, but for the entire life span of the building. We do this by drawing, in a systematic way, on all applicable knowledge available. There exists no single technique which can or should be applied. Each office building planned by the Quickborner Team—and the system which is "built into it"—differs from all other previous solutions. This is neces-

sarily so because each is tailor-made for the client. Perhaps for those who simply visit imitated copies of these solutions, the truth of this observation is not yet clear. The companies which are using this system, however, recognize it readily and bear witness to it.

The most decisive effect to be achieved by such office planning is the improvement in office efficiency. We are not just thinking here of routine work, but even more of decision making processes. Traditional "space planners and designers" are insufficiently equipped to cope with this task. Traditional management consultants, on the other hand, have failed to realize that their knowledge is highly essential if optimum solutions are to be achieved in this field. The Quickborner Team, as management consultant, was successful in filling this gap. We realized that the office building is, in effect, management's most important tool.

Our consulting work in Sweden, Belgium, Holland, Germany, and the U.S.A. as well, enables us to compare administrative practices from an objective point of view. In our experiences, generally speaking, managerial functions, the administrative practices, and corporate rituals are all quite similar in the majority of companies in these countries. They smack more of the 19th century than of the 20th. In fact, from our world-wide experience, we assert the number of firms that perform their administrative activities along lines of modern management concepts is indeed small. The scientific knowledge—developed mostly in the U.S.A.—that is published and available unfortunately is very rarely applied.

THE CYBERNETICAL VIEW OF OFFICE WORK

In planning office buildings, the architectural and design approach is well known and practiced with very few exceptions. This approach puts the main emphasis on design aspects and involves the different specialists subsequently in the planning process.

Terms like "we intend to reflect the corporate image in this building," "we are building a landmark," "we will produce a careful blend of woodland screening and rolling lawns," dominate this planning approach. The planning methods of the Quickborner Team differ considerably from conventional office planning. It puts its main emphasis on the cybernetics of organization—on the information processes which have to be carried out in the business organization, which can be regarded as an information processing center. The space to house the elements of this information processing system—people and office machines—is provided in an office building and the effective functioning of the organization is decisively determined by the type of office building and/or office layout used.

The office building is the main tool for our administrative work and decision making process. As of today, it is more costly and affects more people than even the computer. The cybernetical methods with which business organizations are analyzed identify these information processes as paper flow and processes of oral communication (personal visits and telephone calls). All these processes are "linking functions," which gives rise to the question: why are the majority of office buildings today built to separate personnel by placing them in different stories of high-rise buildings, as well as isolating them by means of walls in a multitude of individual rooms or cubicles?

HIERARCHY VERSUS FUNCTIONS

Obviously, the organization chart of a company has decisively influenced building planning. As such the designer is always convinced that his work has a truly "functional basis."

In general, communication is triggered by the following conditions:

1. Basic information for decision making processes must be communicated to all members of the organization.

2. The decision making process must be influenced.

3. Decisions must be communicated to external organizations.

4. The results of the decision making process must be put into practice.

5. The paper flow process must be organized.

6. Mistakes and disruptions must be eliminated.

Anyone using an organization chart, which illustrates the divisive more than the unifying character of the organization, as basis for an office layout, is completely on the wrong track.

The lines of frequent communications seldom follow the lines of command in an organization chart. Although the planned structure provides for a flow of information between superior and subordinate, the daily activities mentioned require frequent and instant communication between positions of equal and/or unequal rank within the work group or department, as well as across group or departmental borders.

The hidden processes of information processing must be made visible.

When studying the flow of information into a company, two distinct types of information are apparent. There is precisely defined information, which enters the system on paper—orders from customers—and which is processed according to a fixed rule. And there is a great deal of information which is not precisely defined and where there are no fixed rules for handling it. The processing of such varied information input must be analyzed separately to insure that the spatial arrangement of working places will make possible the most efficient information processing for each type.

These processes take place primarily between people. The growing use of computers shows that the exchange of information between man and machines will, however, be of continually increasing importance in the future.

Information flow in a company corresponds to material flow in a factory or in a warehouse. These processes demand that the paths of transport be as short as possible, that transit time be held to a minimum, that there be a minimum of working stations for the loading and unloading of material, and that the material be easily accessible. All such demands are just as valid for information flow.

THE OFFICE BUILDING—A TOOL

The office building should make possible the optimal cooperation of the system's elements (man and machines). By doing this the office building becomes a decisive tool for the organization. The productivity of the organization is affected by spreading personnel over many stories of a building, by having many individual rooms and offices. On the other hand, by bringing personnel together in one undivided space, more efficiency can be achieved.

The speed with which the goals are met, the relationship of the employees to each other, the preparation of information for decisions, as well as the way in which the business is managed, are all decisively influenced by the office space layout of the building.

The office building should be a tool which not only meets the needs of today, but also all changes as the organizational structure and operating processes change, without requiring construction changes in a building.

COMMUNICATION ANALYSIS

The Quickborner Team developed methods of analysis of paper flow and oral communications. The latter, often neglected, is a vital factor in the evaluation of the space program. For organizations with more than approximately 600 people, computers are used as a planning tool, especially in the field of optimization.

The spatial arrangement has to follow the lines of communications, not the lines of subordination, thus breaking up the organizational units. Coordination does not mean subordination.

PAPER FLOW ANALYSIS

Layout of individual work places requires further analysis. The line of communication between individual work places is strongly determined by paper flow. A paper flow analysis should encompass the following areas.

a. Total input of written information into the organization.

b. Most frequent types of documents.

c. Distribution of documents among the system's groups.

d. Connection of individual work places by exchange of documents.

e. Type of documents that emerge.

Paper flow is characterized by the frequency and quantity of documents processed, by the number of work stations involved, and the total cycle time.

The total cycle time consists of the sum total of:

a. processing time per work station

b. travel time from work station to work station

c. storage time

Paper flow is only effective when it is continuous, without intermittent storage.

To achieve this flow through the office is another basic demand and aim of the cybernetical approach. It may be astonishing to the layman that the storage time in most repetitive work flow is responsible for the slowness with which many transactions are completed.

Two solutions to this problem are:

1. A new, basic concept for the division of labor in offices has to be implemented. The Quickborner Team proved that the far reaching subdivision of labor in factory work, which was adapted to office work, is not the most effective way. (Within the limits of this article we cannot dwell further on this interesting problem.)

2. Work stations should be arranged in such a manner that paper work flows without piling up.

Compared to oral communications, paper flow is quite stable, because the process is planned and rules are established. A change of processing rules, however, can mean that the location of work places have to be changed. The space concept must allow for these changes without any structural alterations. Carrying out such organizational demands in an office building can only be accomplished in large spaces.

OFFICE BUILDINGS—TOOLS FOR TOMORROW

Most existing office buildings, modern as they might appear when judged by their facades, represent administrative practices of the past. The monument of a high-rise building with limited usable space per floor represents historical continuity. Corridors with single rooms in a row reflect the hierarchical structure of an organization and the status of some executives, not the actual functional needs of the company. These characteristics of an office building might have been of some value when getting information was difficult, when the size of administrations was small, when competition was light, and when maintenance of status was more important than efficiency. But this need not be true today.

INTERIOR FLEXIBILITY

The spatial arrangement of a building has a decisive influence on the speed at which business is carried out. It affects the relationship of the employees to each other, and the method of adjusting the organizational system to changes in workflow and procedures.

Office areas should be divided by as few permanent walls as possible. To ease and facilitate communications, all departments and work groups with frequent contact with each other should be located on as few floors as possible, without being separated by fixed walls. For office landscape concepts there have to be planned undivided areas of at least 100 by 100 feet. The use of office space should provide the same conditions of lighting, air conditioning, and acoustics. A floor system for electricity and telephone supply in a grid of 5 by 5 feet allows work places to be located at any position. The arrangement of columns should not divide and hinder workplaces laid out according to functional and sociological requirements.

Office landscape systems were developed by the Quickborner Team to establish flexibility and to avoid expenditures of hundreds of thousands of dollars continuously spent for structural changes today. During one consulting job, it was discovered that one company had changed 50 percent of all walls within 5 years.

Today, we are confronted with an overflow of information and with new administrative methods and techniques. Growth in business requires more and more personnel. Recent research indicates that the office working force in the U.S.A. is growing at the rate of 850,000 per year. An office building, housing a very complex system consisting of individuals and machines, has to last for the next 30 to 50 years.

A major planning step involves asking the question: How do we provide space for the future and to what extent? Analyses of projected increase of personnel and of business growth determine the amount of office space needed in the future. The building has to be planned in such a way that it can be expanded in economic steps and still remain an operational unit. There is also the possibility, mostly used in the U.S.A., of building a larger building and leasing part of it to other companies on short and long term basis.

More and more companies move to the suburbs not only because of lower taxes, but also because there is a lack of available horizontal space in the city and expansion of a building becomes a problem.

ASPECTS OF THE WORK ENVIRONMENT

The work environment is determined by the technical fixtures and fittings, the interior decoration, and the arrangement of movable furniture. Technical fixtures and fittings here mean: heating and air conditioning, artificial lighting, acoustical materials. These should provide visual and acoustical privacy. Also, the work environment should be sufficiently stimulating.

The following conditions must be strictly observed:

1. Wall-to-wall carpeting throughout.
2. Good sound absorption on both ceiling and walls.
3. The proper positioning of sound absorbing partitions.

It also must be kept in mind that all fairly large ceiling, wall, and window areas, unless acoustically treated, are noise reflecting.

Audible and visual elements in the office environment are of the greatest importance. All the disturbing noises caused by people and machines must so merge into the general noise level that individual sounds are no longer disturbing beyond 13 to 16 feet. This can be achieved, however, when a variety of sounds occur in the room and a minimum of 80 people work there. This will result in a uniformly low noise level of 50 decibels.

As desks are no longer arranged along the windows there must be sufficient non-glare, artificial lighting for every person in the office. Windows are necessary merely to maintain contact with the exterior environment. Colors and furniture arrangement must create a certain intimacy for people who spend more time at the office working together than at home. It enables them to get through the working day without too great a falling off in efficiency and helps them to successfully do work that is often boring. Thus the layout of office landscapes need be neither disturbing nor rigid. Subjective spaces created by partitions and planters provide privacy and also provide a private environment for the creative office worker.

When we point out that communication and paper flow must be a basis for office planning, we again emphasize that this aspect can be too narrow, just as the design approach alone can be too narrow. We are dealing primarily with human beings. The attitudes of personnel toward each other, toward the work they perform, toward the office environment, as well as toward the layout of individual work places and groups, have a decisive influence on performance. The term "subjective space" was credited by the Quickborner Team to describe the main difference between conventional open office layout and the office landscape concept we developed.

Subjective spaces are the basic units of an office landscape. They may comprise individual work places as well as work groups. We must abandon the idea that the arrangement of an office must show visible order to the outsider.

We believe that it is not right to apply the "architectural approach," which is that only of a spectator, to office planning. The office layout has to satisfy the user and not the spectator who comes to visit.

In the office landscape, the desire for a pleasant environment is as legitimate as the need for a highly efficient layout. The layout has to solve the problem of such an environment, as well as provide an environment which supports the need for "group belonging" and thus support "group performance." As much as we are concerned with the productivity of individuals, we also have to recognize their need for relaxation.

Every employee needs several breaks throughout the day. Sitting at his desk all day long, the employee cannot relax properly since he is constantly exposed to visitors and telephone calls. If the employee does not get necessary work breaks, he will spend a great deal of time on so called "hidden pauses," doing either nothing at all or pretending to be busy. Special lounge areas are thus planned for employees. Refreshments and snacks are provided in these areas, together with a change in environment.

WORK PLACE EQUIPMENT AND SPACE REQUIREMENTS

Detailed investigations of the needs of each work place determine future space requirements. There is a decisive relationship between office equipment, speed in which office functions are performed, and the amount of space which is needed. Investigations in offices show that there are an average of from 15 to 18 feet of files per person.

At this point, we differ from the conventional approach by not providing equipment and space for that type of storage. We question the necessity of the material. The volume of paper used is excessive for efficiency at the individual work places and requires too large a portion of valuable space.

There are certain factors leading to this:

1. The type of equipment used provides excessive file capacity at most work places.
2. There is no established system to provide continuous flow of obsolete material to a central archive or for regular destruction. In most cases, the "cleanout" of files is just an annual event.

3. Active and inactive material is mixed within the same file.
4. Duplicate information is filed by different groups.

We, as consultants, consider it our task to identify and solve such problems with new systems and methods before we begin to plan space.

NEW FURNITURE CONCEPTS

The acoustical conditions are better in an office landscape than in small, conventional offices with sound diffused, low, and uniform, so that it does not disturb work in the office, but forms a rather pleasant acoustical background.

New furniture programs were developed in cooperation with designers, limiting storage capacity to the necessary amount for active files and providing flexibility for arrangement and use. Access to active information is speeded up and facilitated.

New filing systems allow a continuous flow of inactive files into archives and retrieval of needed information within minutes when the files become active again.

This represents one example of various factors that can be improved to save space and ease operations.

BUILDING PLANNING—A CHANCE FOR COMPREHENSIVE IMPROVEMENT

Even though we, ourselves, emphasize the systems concept, great efforts have been made to improve environmental conditions for *all employees*. This, while also facilitating information flow and decision making, also insures overall flexibility. New cybernetical, psychological, and technical factors are taken into account.

As a result not only better office buildings were designed, but also improvements in the organizational system were implemented. The latter is of paramount importance, because it makes no sense to put an obsolete system into a new building. In one case, an analysis of workflow and office procedures revealed that 200 employees could be released with proper reorganization.

In planning new office space, we should not neglect this chance to change systems for the better and to consciously aim for as many "fringe benefits" as possible under a new office system.

ADVANTAGES OF THE OFFICE LANDSCAPE SYSTEM

The following is a summary of advantages achieved in office installations planned with the complex planning approach of the Quickborner Team.

Functional Advantages: It is possible to build a system of highly efficient work flow, consisting of continuous flow of documents and efficient information processing. Unnecessary formalities are reduced and communication is improved. This, in turn, accelerates the exchange of information. General service functions, such as internal mail distribution centers, copying centers, typing pools, etc., are situated closer to work areas and are, thus, more accessible.

There is an optimum of orderliness at each desk and throughout the entire office.

Communication lines within the office are considerably shortened.

Special lounge areas are available for breaks, which can be taken freely at any time. Such breaks are thus taken consciously and are less time consuming and, consequently, more effective.

Sociological Advantages: The office landscape office increases the personal feeling of involvement in the work of an organization. Seeing the work and performance of others is stimulating and reduces over-intense, negative group thinking.

Intrigues are reduced. Better, more businesslike contact results between superiors and other office workers.

Punctuality and self-discipline are encouraged.

Economical Advantages: Areas available for work places and work groups can be varied. Work places, work groups, and departments can be arranged easily and rapidly.

Because traffic lanes and movable partitions can be changed, the administrative structure is not determined rigidly in advance.

Construction expansion of the building is possible. This is of the utmost importance, because the growth of a business cannot be forecast precisely for long periods of time.

Building costs and running costs are lower than those of comparable conventional buildings.

The furniture used is less costly than conventional furniture. The space utilization is improved by 10-15 percent. There are no future costs for interior building alterations, other than rearrangement.

INDUSTRY'S ROLE IN MENTAL HEALTH

Pat Greathouse

Disclaiming any particular competence as an expert in the professional and technical aspects of mental health, I approach the subject from my vantage point as an officer of the UAW, wishing to share the knowledge I have acquired as a representative of the union in collective-bargaining activities over a long period of time. What I bring is the knowledge and conviction growing out of my concern with the many problems which workers face, day to day and over their lifetimes. In the mental health field, professional attention is increasingly being directed toward problems with which our union has been concerned for several decades. Thus I feel quite comfortable in maintaining that our interest in our members' mental health is not essentially of recent origin. In many significant ways, it is as old as the organized labor movement itself and part of the union's long-standing effort to gain for workers their just share in the advantages of an advanced industrial society. Our objective has been and will continue to be the preservation of the worker's sense of dignity and feeling of worth—a major goal of the mental-health movement, as well.

During the early history of the UAW, we moved to reach this objective by establishing the right of the union to represent workers in negotiating with employers on hours of work, wages, and other employment conditions. Necessarily, our efforts for the better part of 20 years were concentrated upon building a floor of protection, providing a

From Pat Greathouse, "Industry's Role in Mental Health," Journal of Occupational Medicine 9, 227–231 (1967). Reprinted by permission.

reasonable standard of living, and safeguarding life and limb in the plant. These we believe to be the foundations of personal security and a very real basis for mental health.

"Mental health," like many other social movements, has become a slogan rather than a clearly defined set of objectives. I'm not altogether sure what professionals mean when they talk about promoting mental health. I know the situations about which *we* have become more and more concerned. All too frequently when I work with our membership I am shocked by an obvious lack of mental health.

I see men becoming upset on the job, taking out their anger on machines, on others, and on themselves. They seem unable to deal with the normal frustration of little things going wrong. I hear of men who develop such deep worries that suicide seems to be their only escape. When I am walking through a plant I feel the tense atmosphere and hear of fights with foremen, fights among workers, and other incidents of men losing control. At committee meetings, I miss a familiar face and learn that still another man is suffering with a physical sickness from which he is recovering more slowly than he should.

There are two major parts of these problems, which must be tackled. One is to determine what conditions at work, at home, and in our communities combine to produce signs of ill health, and to move as rapidly as we can to correct them. Secondly, we must make effective treatment available for those who have suffered all too long. My friends in the mental health field describe these areas as the promotion of mental health, and the prevention and treatment of mental illness.

Ours is a society which has achieved an unprecedented rate of productivity. The advanced state of our technological development has stimulated the growth of even more complex manufacturing processes. With the coming of advanced automated manufacturing, we have seen the emergence of huge industrial giants and an ever-increasing dominance of machines over man.

The worker on today's assembly line has little real sense of useful production. More frequently than not, he performs his task knowing little of what precedes him, and frequently cannot point to the small part he has played in the production of the final product. How can a man have a sense of personal achievement and worth if he knows that for every dollar he earns, the company is making a dollar or more of profit?

Is it surprising then, that a study of automobile workers in 13 Detroit area plants reveals that the lowest level of mental health can be found among low or semiskilled workers performing repetitive tasks on a mechanically paced assembly line? We see little in such a work situation which would contribute to a feeling of self-esteem, to overall satisfaction with the work, or to high personal morale. While social research is providing us with some supporting evidence, we in the industrial-union movement have called attention to these matters for many years. The quest for increasing productivity through the application of ever more technically specialized, automated production must be tempered with a concern for the needs of the worker who makes all production possible. Instead of asking that man adjust to the machine, we must find ways for the machine to serve man better.

Several months ago, I attended a conference in Great Britain which dealt with the social and economic consequences of automation. It was encouraging for me to learn that some industrial management circles in England were recognizing the effects of increasing technological specialization, and accepting management responsibility for dealing with the problem. They have taken time to involve the worker in an awareness of the role he plays in producing the end product and thus his importance in the total society. In some instances this involved a rotation of work responsibility over a period of time which permitted a worker to experience the entire process of production; where this was not possible, occasional periods of orientation to the entire manufacturing process were offered. This was accompanied by a dialogue between top management and the worker in which there was an effort to convey the fact of his importance in spite of the seeming insignificance of his particular skill and contribution to the whole.

These specific activities may be most effective in application to smaller units of production, or may in the long run prove to be of limited overall usefulness. What seems to be most significant, however, is the fact that in these instances, management has recognized the problem and has taken responsibility for doing something about it. If we are to deal successfully with the social problems of an advanced industrial society, management must demonstrate more initiative in determining the conditions that prevent mental breakdown. They must become concerned, so that training of personnel can be geared to the maintenance of a worker's sense of usefulness and purpose in spite of automation. We must be prepared to invest as much in research and development in the human sciences for direct application in industry as we do in studies of physical stress and strain in machines. We would like to see management computers applied to the problems of the social and human consequences of technological change. I find it hard to believe that techniques that now analyze the effect of the hundreds of thousands of components in automobile tuning, cannot be applied to the more important job os designing work conditions that are better suited to the needs of men.

We now have the resources and the technical ability to build the kind of society we want. It is our choice to make. I look forward to a society which is measured not by a count of the units of production, not by consumer spending, not by the volume of consumer credit, but by the extent to which a man is both motivated and enabled to live a full and wholesome life. If this is to be our goal, then the persuaders of the advertising business must soften their pitch and allow for a more balanced choice among alternative uses for our wages. The rut of installment buying and overextended credit is not the road to mental health.

Of far greater importance, however, is the challenge of applying the knowledge we now have to the creation of more wholesome environments for men to work in. I think we know that when doors are removed from toilet stalls and closed-circuit television cameras installed, a man's sense of dignity and self-esteem is grossly insulted. I think we know that it is important to a man's state of mental health that he be able to get time off the job when he needs it to deal with problems at home. We know better—but management persists in treating these problems only as economic issues.

We must begin to reassert the importance of men over machines in all aspects of industrial planning. When relocation is being considered, we must insist that it is *men* who have family and community ties that may be broken—*not machines*. A machine does not care where it is located—we need to be more concerned about the men who operate it.

Management has a greater responsibility for environmental planning. Decisions to relocate plants affect the very life of communities. Industry must show a greater responsibility in working with community planners—in both physical and social aspects. It is no longer enough to hire an industrial development firm to take the rap for them. With our increasing population and rapid expansion of new cities, we have an unprecedented opportunity to use our skills for the benefit of men—and not of profits.

We say that it is time for industry to call a halt to its screaming criticism of "planning." We all recognize the fantastic skill with which it plans production. Now we insist that it is

time to use these skills and resources to plan more for the social and emotional needs of people and less for the portfolios of investors.

If there is need for modifying the production process itself to serve the needs of men better, then a second area needing attention is the entire structure of authority and supervision in the industry. In this regard, we need less research and more application of the knowledge we have already acquired, which will result in treatment which is both more rational and more humane. There have been some very promising beginnings in promoting human relations in industry and, unfortunately, some disappointing conclusions. We fully support programs which are honestly directed towards the improvement of relationships among men who work together. But if the effectiveness of these same programs is measured by an increased rate of production, then they become one more insult to the dignity of the workers at whom they are directed. There is ample evidence that we have mastered the techniques of managing human relations towards the end of increasing profits. It is now time for management to apply these same skills to improving conditions of work, and thereby provide some form of personal satisfaction to replace partially the satisfaction felt when the thing manufactured was truly the worker's own creation. With our increasing rate of productivity, it is quite possible to direct some of these professional resources toward making human relations a bit more human and a bit less industrial.

Thus far I have kept within the first category of mental health problems—that of removing the conditions which produce ill health. If we are successful in re-establishing our concern for men over machines, future generations may enjoy a better state of mental health. But there is an immediate concern that we have too long postponed, that of making effective treatment available to those who need it. Through the negotiation of our contracts we have, since the early 50's, progressively provided our membership with means for obtaining quality medical care, through programs of prepayment, group-practice plans, and increased standards of medical services.

Supported by a growing national concern for improving mental health services, and prodded by the growing evidence that workers and their families were experiencing as high a rate of mental illness as other groups in the population, and at the same time having access to fewer treatment resources, we set out to deal directly with the problem. Recent studies establish that workers receive less psychiatric care outside hospitals; that the care they receive is generally of lower quality; that they are generally unfamiliar with and suspicious of psychiatric treatment; that treatment, if available, is primarily designed to deal with problems of the middle class, so that workers and their families are frequently psychiatric drop-outs. We also grew aware of the fact that the high cost of quality psychiatric services, combined with the elements of strangeness and suspicion, resulted in a high rate of long-term hospitalization for a large share of our worker families.

Having faced some of these problems in the early 50's in regard to the provision of medical care, we determined that the first step in providing treatment services for those of our members in need might best come through an extension of our already existing prepaid health benefits. Apparently the mystery of mental health cloaks the insurance industry as well as the layman, for as we began to explore the extension of our medical care contracts to include provisions for the treatment of mental illness, we faced a wall of resistance.

On the one hand, it was maintained that mental health care was an uninsurable benefit. The evidence presented to us to support this argument was very thin. Mental health care had never before been insured on this scale; therefore there was no comparable experience on which to draw. Even though several large firms had developed psychiatric benefit plans under major-medical coverage, we were told that this was not comparable because of the relatively small size of the program and the limited number of plant locations. Utilization rates could not be established; hence mental health care was uninsurable. Furthermore, when these positive experiences were ignored and a few rather well-selected instances were drawn upon, in which insurance programs covered a professional or academic population, evidence was cited that the introduction of this type of benefit would result in large-scale abuse and high rates of overutilization.

On the other hand, we were presented with evidence from the social sciences which conclusively demonstrated a high degree of resistance on the part of industrial workers to outpatient programs of mental health care. The insurance industry and the automotive manufacturers maintained that once the benefit was introduced, long-standing resistance and reluctance would melt and workers and their families would flood existing resources and bankrupt the plan. We believe that neither of these two extremes will prove to be accurate. We hold, however, that the provision of a prepayment plan for mental health care, along with already existing provisions for medical care, will result in an increased utilization of high quality outpatient resources which up to this time have been beyond the financial reach of our working-class population. But we fully expect that there will continue to be resistance and that we will need to assist the mental health professionals in adapting their treatment to the needs of this population.

In preparation for the collective bargaining in 1964 which resulted in our adding provisions for mental health care, we had the support, cooperation, and assistance of leading mental health professionals, including the American Psychiatric Association. As a result of these joint efforts, we believe that the benefits we negotiated are particularly suited for our population.

I was convinced, from 20 years of experience with our members, that a major-medical plan calling for coinsurance and deductibles was not enough. These types of plans only place hurdles in the path of early treatment. Added to the blue-collar worker's known resistance to early psychiatric care—one deterrent to treatment—the threat of a drain on scarce financial resources only acts as another, economic, deterrent to treatment. This impediment has no place in a comprehensive, high-quality health program.

Since September 1966, approximately 3 million UAW members and their families, as well as retirees, have been covered by extended mental health care benefits. Included in this program are: (1) forty-five days of in-hospital care for nervous or mental conditions, including physicians' services during this period; (2) a maximum benefit of $400 per patient per calendar year for out-of-hospital care, including visits for therapy in a doctor's office, treatment for ambulatory patients in approved outpatient or day-care programs, visits to the doctor's office or outpatient clinic by members of the patient's family for counseling services, group psychotherapy, and psychological testing by a psychologist when prescribed by a physician.

The patients share in some costs of outpatient treatment but not of inpatient care. To encourage early referral and minimize the economic barrier to care, there are no charges for the first 5 visits in outpatient therapy, and the patient pays 15% for the second 5 visits, 30% for the third 5 visits, and 45% for the balance of visits. He pays 15% of the costs of one series of psychological testing.

In developing these programs, we are working with our own members so they may better understand and use the services. We also are working with the interested professions so that they may assist in organizing and making the services available. These

benefits were developed to deal with problems known to exist among our members. Our primary objective is to promote early case-finding and referral for early and effective treatment. Thus, for the first time in a major prepaid program, the first outpatient visits are covered without cost to the patient. Group practice plans, where available, will be encouraged to integrate these new benefits into already existing medical-care programs. Our objective is to support the growing move to eliminate the harmful distinctions between physical and mental illness.

We believe that this addition to the health-care programs now available to a large segment of the American industrial-worker population occurs at a most opportune time. We have strongly supported the development of more effective mental health services through the development of community mental health centers. We strongly supported both state and federal legislation which will make possible a redirection and expansion of publicly supported mental health services. We believe that this is a sound beginning. We know that our program is far from ideal and that there is a great need for research which will help us and the community as a whole to make improvements in mental health programs. We look forward to the results of the 2-year study presently being undertaken by the American Psychiatric Association and the Michigan Health and Social Security Research Institute, an organization recently initiated by the UAW. Our efforts in this regard can be furthered by industrial management which is cooperative, supportive, and willing to undertake joint programs of education, interpretation, and support to make these benefits fully operative and to provide for the working population as high a quality of psychiatric service as has been reserved, until now, for those who could pay the high cost.

My position then, is quite clear. I believe that provisions for the treatment of psychiatric illness are as much the responsibility of management as are provisions for the treatment of physical illness. I would go one step further and stress the importance of these services being equally available and, wherever possible, integrated with comprehensive, high-quality medical-care services. Less than 20 years ago the principle of management responsibility in the area of health care was established in NLRB rulings which held that matters of health were essentially forms of wages and conditions of employment and hence were subject to collective bargaining. Building upon this ruling, we have, through the process of collective bargaining, negotiated broad and comprehensive benefits for our membership. In the areas of mental health, however, we seek more than reluctant agreement to contracts which provide dollars to pay for treatment. We are calling upon management to accept the responsibility which is rightfully theirs: To cooperate in making these programs work, and in ensuring less need for treatment in the future through a heightened effort to alter the environment in which men work. If this must be evaluated in economic terms, then it is a cost we must be prepared to bear if we are to continue to grow without sacrificing our dignity and individual worth.

The labor movement will continue to work toward the objective of gaining for the worker full participation in the society of which he is a part. This we believe to be the fullest realization of mental health and it is toward this end that management must become more responsive. Only when there is a willingness to accept this responsibility and to apply a full measure of imagination and creative effort, can we begin to realize the full potential of the good society which America is striving to achieve.

COUNTER-PRODUCTIVE BEHAVIORS

THE UNSATISFACTORY PERFORMER: SALVAGE OR DISCHARGE?

Lawrence L. Steinmetz

Every industry, every profession, and every skill area has its share of individuals who fail to meet the requirements of their jobs, even though it is almost impossible to define unsatisfactory performance precisely. More important than the definition of unsatisfactory performance, however, is the question of what to do about it. Transfer, demotion, promotion, and discipline are all avenues open to the supervisor, but they sidestep the problem more often than they solve it. For that reason, most managers simply get rid of the troublesome employee; he is either fired or "dehired." As commonly used, however, both of these techniques have their drawbacks. Firing, unless it is done expertly, may precipitate a scene, usually evokes guilt feelings on both sides, and can even victimize the wrong person at the wrong time. The only plus factor in the irrevocable discharge is that it is clear-cut, forceful, and final action.

THE DEHIRING TECHNIQUE

In contrast to firing, the indirect method of dehiring "encourages" the employee by sup-

From Lawrence L. Steinmetz, "The Unsatisfactory Performer: Salvage or Discharge?" Personnel 45 (3), 46–54 (1968). Reprinted by permission of the American Management Association.

posedly subtle (but often transparent) actions to quit his job. Most managers who choose the dehiring route do so because in theory it has these advantages: (1) The company and the manager are not exposed to any scene that might erupt if the man were fired outright; (2) the manager can avoid facing up to the fact that someone made a mistake in hiring the man; (3) the organization doesn't have to worry about the bad public relations that it fears would follow if it became known for anything less than 100 per cent secure employment; (4) it permits the manager to comply with company policy (thus helping him to protect his own job); and (5), since it is seen as a way to be considerate of the man's feelings and give him leeway in casting about for another job, the company and manager are spared the conscience pangs that may come from peremptorily showing the man the door.

All these points in favor of gradual dehiring are cancelled out, of course, if the man is so lacking in perception, so naive, or so deficient in motivation or self-esteem that he is impervious to gentle hints that the company no longer needs him. In any case, there are three fundamental objections to the dehiring technique: First, the manager does not control the situation; he relies on the *hope* that the man who is being dehired will get the message, so it is a managerial decision that must be implemented by the unsatisfactory performer rather than by the manager himself. Second, it is usually least effective with the people who present the most serious problems. Because they are conspicuously poor performers, they are usually easily spotted as potential problems by prospective employers and so are less likely to be offered jobs that would persuade them to leave. Third, this easing-out method may be considered unethical because it relies on cunning, duplicity, and even "morale sabotage" rather than on aboveboard initiative.

Since firing may be distasteful and dehiring may fail, the manager may prefer to try the alternative of salvaging unsatisfactory performers. Of course, if the man's personal problem is beyond repairing by means available within the company, his boss should think twice about this course. For example, a man who has become a chronic alcoholic or has serious mental infirmity probably cannot be salvaged as a productive worker without the aid of psychiatric counseling or other long-term treatment; supervisory efforts are simply too limited to be of real help to this person, and it would be presumptuous on the part of management to undertake the salvage task.

WHO SHOULD BE SALVAGED?

If, on the other hand, the manager does decide to try to get a man's performance back to par, he will first have had to analyze the the problem from several angles, not all of them related to the immediate situation or person involved.

Length of Service. One of the first considerations is the employee's length of service with the company. To the employee, length of service means that he has found an employer he is satisfied with and vice versa; this employee interpretation doesn't cut any ice when it is a question of retaining an unsatisfactory performer, but most companies put some weight on length of service, not only because they think they owe something to a long-service employee, but also because of the impact his discharge may have on other employees. They recognize that, even though the company cannot logically consider length of service as a compensable factor, most employees do.

Furthermore, the fact that the unsatisfactory performer has been around for a long time implies that the company may have shown poor judgment in hiring him in the first place and is reluctant to admit a mistake, or that it has kept the man on only because of inertia.

Performance Record. Closely connected with length of service is the employee's prior performance record. This record has little or nothing to do with evaluation of current performance, but the salvage potential of a man who has a good or excellent prior performance record, but whose work has suddenly fallen off, is encouraging. Such a performance drop usually indicates an unusual, often temporary, disturbance, and the man can probably regain his former performance level with the aid of counseling if the cause of falloff can be discovered (or, given a little time, he may regain it on his own). The real problem employee is the person who gradually slows down over the years, under the pressure of a combination of difficulties that become built in.

Skills Involved and the Labor Market. From a practical point of view, the boss must appraise the skills that the unsatisfactory performer is supposed to have to do his job and the demand for them in the current labor market. If the market in the area is very tight and/or his skills are in short supply, the question of whether to salvage the unsatisfactory performer may be academic; if the man cannot be easily replaced or cannot be replaced at all and, however inadequately, is providing a vital skill, the manager had better try to salvage him. However, it might be wise for the manager to look around for a replacement in the future, particularly if the man appears to be an incorrigible periodic backslider.

Absenteeism Record. A man's absenteeism record usually reflects the law of maldistribution that finds only a very few employees accounting for the preponderance of all absences on the job. One study, for example, found that as few as 10 per cent of the employees of a given firm accounted for as much as 45 per cent of all the absences. If the employee in question belongs to the absentee minority, he is probably a poor salvage risk, because statistics show that any employee who develops a poor absentee or work record at one time in his career is very unlikely to ever have a good absentee or work record.

Attitudes and Personality. A man's attitude and personality are considered all-important by some managers when they are deciding whether to salvage a poor performer. Unfortunately, personality is a matter of how one is received by others, rather than a matter of fact, and the subjective element also enters into evaluations of attitudes. Unfair as it may seem, a person who is considered by his supervisor to have a "bad" attitude or "poor" personality is probably not a good candidate for a salvage operation; if the man does not get along well with his boss, it is unlikely that he will be an effective employee no matter how well he tries to do his job. When two disputants are irreconcilable, one probably should leave, and in this case it's the subordinate.

Legal Job Security Devices. Sometimes there is little choice about attempting to salvage the unsatisfactory performer. If the employee has tenure, if he can take up a dismissal with a grievance committee, or if there are any other kinds of job security devices he can turn to, and if he is not the kind to go peaceably, the manager will probably have to try to improve the man's performance. It might be added that this situation is one of the few in which the practice of dehiring is justified: If the man cannot be fired outright and shows little promise of changing, a dehiring campaign is all that is left.

Level in the Organization. Another compelling circumstance is the level that the

unsatisfactory performer has attained in the organizational hierarchy. Some companies will not permit the overt discharge of an employee at the higher levels of management, lest such action damage the company's public image. On the other hand, the intramural image is also a matter of concern, and lower-level supervisors may be forbidden to discharge employees because of the feeling of insecurity that presumably would be generated among the discharged employee's colleagues. In any case, the manager faced with the problem of an unsatisfactory performer should investigate corporate policy before taking any definite action about the employee.

Line Supervision. Many managers fail to recognize that their supervision of the "problem" employee has a lot to do with his performance. They take it for granted that they are good supervisors or, if they feel insecure, they doubt their own effectiveness, but either way they rarely view themselves as a key determinant in the activities of the problem employee. However, the supervisor's superior often has enough perspective to be able to tell whether the employee is getting proper supervision or whether his problem is rooted in other difficulties. Because of the consequences that poor supervision can create for a person on the job, it is a sound idea for the supervisor to consult his superior about the adequacy of the supervision he is giving the unsatisfactory performer. If his boss has any faults to find, perhaps the employee should be transferred, but if a good many employees appear to be problems, serious evaluation of the problem supervisor is in order.

Investment. Many companies are loath to dismiss an employee in whom they have invested a great amount of money, time, and training, not to mention his accumulated benefits. This, of course, has a very practical implication, because it is assumed that a replacement would require the same investment before he could make his full contribution. Still, there is no widsom in throwing good money after bad, and the company must weigh what the employee has cost it against what he may cost it in terms of lost customers, poor morale, inferior products, and so on.

Personal Consequences. Few managers can avoid thinking of what would happen to the unsatisfactory employee if no effort were made to correct his performance. Harsh as it may sound, in theory no company should be expected to "adopt" any employee, so his future if he no longer worked for the company should not be a major consideration in deciding for or against salvage attempts.

Moreover, studies have shown that, contrary to popular belief, most men who are discharged from their jobs are eventually better off financially and also happier as a result. This is something that should be pointed out to any manager who is unduly worried about what will happen to a man if he is discharged. He should also be reminded that there is an inherent bias in favor of a man whose job is in jeopardy, and the manager should be aware of it in making his decision.

Effect on Other Employees. Managers are inclined to be very concerned about the unsatisfactory performer as an example to other employees, and this concern is justified. Problem employees not only create work problems for other employees but also create morale problems if they are allowed to get away with slovenly or inadequate output. No manager can tolerate a bad example on his payroll, because bad examples tend to be imitated far more frequently than do good examples; the situation demands change, and a managerial choice between the problem employee's discharge or improvement. If, after weighing all these factors, the manager decides that they point to salvage of the employee, the next step, of course, is to implement the salvage procedures. On the other hand, if it is determined that the man must be

discharged, that decision, too, should be acted on promptly.

THE SALVAGE/DISCHARGE DECISION

Making a decision to discharge or salvage an employee is a serious supervisory responsibility, one that calls for the best judgment and the greatest objectivity possible. Here are some principles that should be observed.

The manager should consult and check with people in the organization who are in a position high enough for them to be objective in their advice, and with others close enough to be rightfully concerned and knowledgeable about the circumstances.

The manager should be in a relaxed frame of mind before he makes the decision. He should never make the decision at a time of stress or crisis. Deciding to fire a man simply because a given job was not done, or because he was late for work, or because he wasn't prepared for a staff meeting is the mark of a capricious executive. Such crises may lead to making the decision, but they should never be the occasion of the decision.

The manager should not try to anticipate all the eventualities of the discharge, if that route is elected. This does not mean that the manager should ignore possible consequences of the decision, but it does mean that *all* eventualities, both proximate and remote, cannot be foreseen. The manager should limit himself to probabilities and assume that the results that quickly come to mind are the only probable ones.

The man making the salvage or discharge decision should not hope to be considered right by everyone. About the only time the disciplining boss can expect a hearty "aye" all around is when the employee's unsatisfactory work has been a burden to his coworkers.

IF THE DECISION IS DISCHARGE . . .

If discharge is the final verdict, the manager should not fret unduly about the conduct of the discharge interview. There is little point in thinking of where each man will be sitting, of preliminary small talk, and so forth. Such concerns can only encourage procrastination and are usually a complete waste of time anyway, because events seldom work out according to plan.

Nevertheless, translating the discharge decision into action does require a certain amount of foresight and a genuine desire to carry out a distasteful assignment in the best possible way for everybody concerned. A man faced with such a task should establish an atmosphere designed to promote some feeling of mutual respect (though friendliness may be too much to ask for). Discharging an employee is no license to display temper, or to throw the book at someone; it should be handled only as a corrective measure, with no vindictiveness or malice of any kind.

To accomplish this end, some rules for the supervisor to follow include the following:

In the first place, the act of discharging the employee should come promptly after the decision to discharge. An employee should not be discharged for poor work that has been tolerated for years.

The interview with the employee should be carried out in simple, forthright, and clear language, so there is no possibility that the employee doesn't grasp that he is being discharged. The date of his departure should also be definitely stated.

The supervisor should have all the facts at his fingertips. There is no reason to assume that this information will be used, and there certainly is no reason to feel that it must be used, but it should be available if it is necessary to give the employee evidence supporting the discharge decision.

The discharged employee should be given an opportunity to make explanations and ask questions. This does not mean that the employee has the right to argue about the decision itself, but he should be allowed to have his questions clarified and to discuss his side of the story. This may have a bearing on the kind of reference the supervisor will give to a future employer investigating the man's work record.

The supervisor should always—and literally—maintain a "hands off" policy during the discharge interview and afterward. Feelings may run high when the discharge decision is communicated, and it is entirely too easy for a simple gesture, such as patting a man on the shoulder or offering to shake hands, to be misunderstood and lead to physical entanglement.

The supervisor should make a record of what went on during the discharge discussion and also list points that were not covered. The repercussions of a discharge almost always disturb the even pace or keel of the organization. The man who is fired may have projects in the works that need completion; the personnel department will have loose ends that need tying together; a re-evaluation of the process followed in discharging the person may be in order; or the circumstances may have to be reconstructed when another company asks why the man was discharged. This record keeping may end up as useless notes, but it is wise to keep them on hand for about a year, or until it can be assumed that the man has been able to re-establish himself in someone else's employ.

THE SIDE EFFECTS

At the time of discharge there are three personal elements that the boss must take into account, because they are closely involved by the side effects of the decision. These are the man and his family, the boss himself, and the other employees.

The Man and His Family. The impact of the discharge on the man and his family is basically a financial matter and specifically concerns his next job. As a rule, employers take no responsibility for placing people whom they have discharged; about the only help the organization usually gives the man in finding future employment is a not-too-bad reference.

However, there appears to be a growing tendency for companies to assume the obligation of giving the discharged employee more positive help. Many companies provide liberal enough severance pay or set termination dates far enough in the future so the man has plenty of time to look around for another job. Some companies try to broaden the exit interview and make it a genuine counseling conference; others go even further and try to find a suitable job for the departing employee in another company. The attitude here seems to be that "although the man was not doing a good job for us, we know that he performed well at one time, so there is no reason we cannot recommend him to someone who needs an employee at that level."

The Boss Himself. The man who does the firing has to be braced for inevitable criticism. No one likes to be considered a hatchet man, and most bosses would like to feel that they are popular with their employees, but firing an employee who has friends in the organization is obviously not the best route to the top of the popularity list. Still, a certain amount of resentment is almost bound to be the lot of anyone in a powerful position, and the boss faced with the responsibility of discharging an employee had better be resigned to the fact that he may be viewed as an executioner—at least for a time.

The Other Employees. The grapevine is certain to come to life when a person is discharged, and many employees will be fearful that the same thing might happen to them. This reaction may have a beneficial effect on employees who are more highly motivated by the stick than by the carrot, but others may become so insecure that their work is adversely affected.

It is hard to try to foresee the implications and ramifications of discharge within the company, but a good deal depends on the way the news is released to the employees—the timeliness of the news and its accuracy and general tenor. Tact, diplomacy, and good taste are important, and honesty and forthrightness are essential.

It can be assumed that the employees will want to know the details surrounding the discharge and that rumors will be rife in the absence of facts. Morale can be severely damaged or actually improved by the way the news about the discharge is handled. The company should concern itself with erasing, or at least minimizing, anxieties that some employees will undoubtedly develop when they hear that one of their number has been let go. This doesn't require full disclosure to prove that the company was right, but it calls for extra reassurance by supervisors about the job security of those who are doing their work well.

INDUSTRY'S $2-BILLION HEADACHE—THE PROBLEM DRINKER

Richard E. Dutton

"You know the rule, when an employee's drinking begins to interfere with his job, the supervisor is expected to deal with the problem." This statement has been made countless times, but the specific definition or understanding of the phrase "deal with" leaves much to be desired.

According to studies made by the Wisconsin Council on Alcoholism, problem drinking, or early stages of alcoholism, is responsible for more difficulties and disasters than any other medical or social problem, but too few understand the elements of the problem.

In discussing problem drinking we are *not* talking about social drinking. There are over 65 million social drinkers in this country. Four million or more of those social drinkers are problem drinkers (those whose lives are being disrupted by the use of alcohol). One in every 20 drinkers is an alcoholic, and one in every 15 is an excessive, or problem drinker. We shall consider both groups as problem drinkers, with a difference only in degree of dependence upon alcohol.

MANY REASONS FOR CONCERN

There are many reasons why business and industry are concerned about problem drinking. In the first place, more than two million U.S. workers are problem drinkers. These employees cost U.S. industry yearly more than $2 billion and 13 million manhours lost through absenteeism (average: 22 days),

From Richard E. Dutton, "Industry's $2-Billion Headache—The Problem Drinker," Personnel Journal 44 (6), 303–306 (1965). Reprinted by permission.

slowdowns, inefficiency, accidents, loss of trained personnel, wasted materials, and faulty decision. Aside from these costs, companies are interested because of the tremendous human waste and social upheaval which comes from problem drinking.

The business world now appears to recognize four facts about problem drinking:

1. Problem drinking is an illness—not a moral problem.
2. It can be treated.
3. The problem drinker is worth treating.
4. The problem drinker is generally the last to recognize, or accept his problem.[1]

A heavy equipment manufacturing company, one of the industrial pioneers in studying problem drinking, found that people with a drinking problem were absent eight per cent of their working time each year. After the start of a special program aimed at aiding the problem drinker to help himself, the absence rate with this group fell to less than three per cent, which was *lower than the plant average.*

It is during the times when the employee is only half himself that more accidents occur. This is particularly true in heavy industry like steel and equipment manufacturing. It is also shown by scrap and waste losses, low productivity, and high absentee rates in any type of industry.

The evidence shows that the savings in doing something about this problem can be enormous. The heavy equipment manufacturing company previously mentioned reported savings of 10,000 manhours yearly for a group of only 71 men who were given treatment.

THE IMPACT ON THE INDIVIDUAL

According to medical opinion, alcoholism is a progressive condition characterized by

[1] "What to say to an Alcoholic," *Management Review,* p. 34 (January, 1964).

excessive use of alcoholic beverages. A problem drinker is any person who cannot use alcoholic beverages without affecting his obligations to his work, family, friends, and neighbors. He loses control over how much and when he drinks—and becomes physically dependent upon alcohol. The beverage itself, not the companionship of friends, is the thing desired.

The problem drinker may be likened to the diabetic. As the diabetic cannot tolerate sugar physically, so the alcoholic cannot tolerate alcohol emotionally. However, because the individual's will power plays such a dominant role, alcoholism is not considered the same as other illnesses.

It has been said that "alcohol alone will not make an alcoholic." This statement seems reasonable, since observation indicates that the great majority of social drinkers do *not* become alcoholics. However, the steady use of alcohol, together with certain personality traits, is essential for the appearance of alcoholism.

A startling illustration of this combination is the story of an elderly woman with a fine family background, who was quite active in civic and charitable affairs in the New England states. She had been a teetotaler all her life until, at the age of 82, her doctor prescribed a glass of port wine a day as a tonic. She argued strongly against the use of the wine, but the doctor prevailed and she followed his advice. Within a few months, she had begun to drink heavily. Then came a series of arrests and probations for drunkenness and disturbing the peace. About a year from the date of her first drink, she was committed to a private institution.

No emotionally healthy person does anything that will cause himself to suffer, provided he knows that suffering will result from that particular action. Yet, that is exactly what the problem drinker does. He knows from sad experience what will happen if he takes a drink. One drink will be one too many, and any number will not be enough.

Many believe that problem drinkers have a problem only when they are drinking. That is not correct. The alcoholic or problem drinker is "out of step" with everything around him, even when he is sober.

Addiction to the use of alcohol is progressive. The problem drinker does not stay at one level of comsumption—he drinks more and more. The World Health Organization in its second report (Geneva, 1952), cited four phases of alcohol addiction:

1. *Pre-Problem Phase*—Occasional drinking to relieve tension or fatigue. Frequent relief drinking. Slow, increased tolerance in consuming alcohol.

2. *Problem Phase*—Start of "blackouts." Blackouts increase (periods of memory loss). Drinking in secret. Preoccupation with alcohol and drinking.

3. *Crucial Phase*—Loss of control over drinking. Rationalizing of drinking behavior. Drinking pattern changes. Drops friends. Quits jobs. Loses outside interests. Pities self. Neglects proper food. Drinks in morning.

4. *Chronic Phase*—Benders. Impairment of thinking. Drinks hair tonic and other "technical" products. Indefinable fears. Rationalization fails. Mental and physical deterioration.[2]

The Pre-Problem Phase is extremely difficult to identify. Therefore, as a rule it is not until some of the symptoms cited in the Problem Phase or later phases arise that the problem drinker is identified.

THE "PROBLEM" WITH THIS PROBLEM

The person with a drinking problem will conceal it from himself and others as long as he possibly can. When the problem is uncovered, he will seek refuge behind medical or social reasons if at all possible. In this

[2]Lecture by Mark R. Kilp, Executive Director, Wisconsin Council on Alcoholism (1958).

way, he can avoid coming to grips with his problem.

Too often the blanket use of the term "illness," when referring to problem drinking, makes it easy to imply that problem drinking is a disease in the ordinary sense of the word. The difference between the disorders of the problem drinker and the more conventional illnesses is ignored. The key difference is the fact that the victim introduces the cause, alcohol, into his system by his *own* decision. Certainly that is not true in cases of other medical diseases such as arteriosclerosis, polio, tuberculosis, cancer or nerve disorders.

Thus, the person with a drinking problem must admit to himself:

1. That he *does have a problem.*
2. That his problem is different—not just "another illness."
3. That the great majority of his friends are sympathetic and want to help.
4. That he needs and wants aid to get back one of his most valuable possessions—self control.
5. That the real success in overcoming the problem depends upon *complete abstinence* from all forms of alcohol.

The greatest difficulty in problem drinking is that the victim almost never admits that he has a problem. The practice of rationalization becomes so habitual and ingrained, that it prevents this admission. Thus, the problem drinker's big "problem" is consciously believing he has a problem and wanting to solve it.

AIDING THE PROBLEM DRINKER

One of the great problems in dealing with problem drinking is society's attitude toward drinking. In many countries, the use of alcoholic beverages is thought of almost as a folkway, such as bowling or square-dancing. Therefore, in many communities, drinking is socially expected.

In industry, a common fault of a great many supervisors is a tendency to be over-protective toward the problem drinker. This blends into, and aids, the progressive pattern of the illness. Therefore, "it is the supervisor's fault—not the alcoholic's—if department morale suffers because the alcoholic is constantly protected from the consequences of his drinking."[3] A supervisor who takes this approach—pleading, begging and threatening, covering-up, protecting—may well end as a virtual "slave" of his alcoholic subordinate by being exploited. The supervisor is continually hoping that something he may say will force the alcoholic back onto a sober track. However, since the employee's condition is an illness rather than a psychological problem, a rebuke in this instance would be as ineffective as if he had been told to get rid of the arthritis inhibiting his mobility.[4]

At one time in the past, the belief was widespread that the alcoholic had to "reach bottom"—to hit the lowest possible point of degradation—before he could be helped. The theory behind this idea was that until such a point was reached, the victim would not surrender to the fact that he had a serious problem, and only two results were possible: to perish, or to improve.

The fallacy of this theory is that it does not give due credit to the power of human understanding and sheer determination, both in the victim and those who would help him. Today, the philosophy is changing, so that we are inclined to believe that to stand by and let someone "hit bottom" through alcohol is a fearful waste of human resources.

THINGS TO DO

To aid problem drinkers effectively, the following actions will help:

Study informational material about alcoholism. Public libraries, Alcoholics Anony-

---

[3]Donald Robinson and Nadine Robinson, "The Supervisor and the Alcoholic Worker," *Supervisory Management*, p. 13 (February, 1963).

[4]*Ibid.,* pp. 14-15.

mous (AA) offices, medical reports and journals, U.S. Public Health Service literature, State Alcoholism Rehabilitation Services, and newspaper articles will provide data.

Talk to someone—not a relative or friend—about the problem and ask for suggestions. Persons such as a qualified physician, minister or priest, special consultant on alcohol problems (as might be associated with a large hospital or clinic), or leader or member of the local AA chapter, make effective counselors.

Don't condemn or lecture people about alcoholism. Make them feel that you are sympathetic and truly want to help. Your approach must involve facts, not emotions.

Remain as completely objective in your relationships as you can. You will be able to do more if you're not emotionally involved. The people you're trying to help will respect you more—and listen harder—if you can maintain a steady, objective approach.

Remember that alcohol has occupied a large share of the problem drinker's interest and time. Successful rehabilitation depends upon filling the gap left when alcohol is removed. Mental addiction lingers after physical craving ends—so something must occupy his interest and absorb that energy. This "something" can be a new hobby, or more time devoted to an old one, learning a new sport such as golf, bowling, or tennis, or club work, church activities, doing more traveling, and so forth.

In almost all cases of recovery there is a history of one or more returns to drinking during rehabilitation. Try to take the lapses in stride. Increased encouragement is needed more than ever.

The problem drinker is *not exempt* from social pressures and responsibility, and those desiring to aid him should stress that fact in their contacts with him. Any compromise of these responsibilities is not a form of being considerate, but actually a disservice to the victim. Compromise of social responsibility shields the drinker, gives greater justification for his rationalizations, and prolongs the time before he comes to grips with his problem.

MANAGING
THE DRUG USER

Robert J. Firenze
Steven K. Klein

That the problem of drug abuse is restricted to the college campus, and with that vague but all-too-apparent hippie cult is a false impression shared by too many dealing with work forces made up of "mature" individuals. The fact is: The U.S. is a drug-oriented society. We gulp pills to find sleep, pills to wake up, pills to gain or lose weight, pills to tranquilize, and pills to get "high" or "blow the mind." Add to these the multitude of prescribed drugs and the readily available sources of illegitimate drugs and you cannot ignore the fact that drug abuse is now as much a factor requiring the alertness of the safety professional, foremen, supervisors, industrial nurses, and, in fact, everyone responsible for the safety and health of employees as it is to law enforcement and legislative bodies.

To help the safety professional recognize and deal with drug problems when they arise, this article will take a two-fold nitty gritty approach:

1. To show the effect of drugs on human decision-making faculties;

2. To provide the techniques of managing a drug user—particularly in the work environment—so he may be retained, if possible, as a productive member of the work force.

DRUGS AND ACCIDENTS

Before discussing drug-related phenomena, the subject of drugs as a contributor to ac-

From Robert J. Firenze and Steven K. Klein, "Managing the Drug User," National Safety News 103 (2), 48–53 (1971). Reprinted by permission.

cident causation must be considered. It is obvious (see Figure 7.5) that man, in his work process, performs his assignments as part of a man-machine-environment complex. In order for this operating network to function effectively and to achieve its intended purpose, certain processes must take place. The man, as a rational human being, must make decisions, and, as a result of these decisions, he must take risks.

In order to make sound decisions, and thus take calculated risks, man as the risk-acceptor must be:

Familiar with the task requirement;

Aware of his own capabilities relevant to the task;

Cognizant of what he will gain or lose if he succeeds or fails.

Figure 7.5 illustrates the successful task feedback mechanism that man experiences after each successful completion of a task. The "signal" indicates that his actions and reactions have been correct, and that these same actions should be repeated for similar tasks in the future. Preempting all decisions is information—the relevant data that are processed prior to the actual decision-risk episode.

It would seem feasible then that the more complete a man's information may be, the better chance he has to make calculated decisions. For the most part, this is true. However, one factor that interplays with the decision-making process is that of a mechanism called a *stressor*. For practical purposes, a stressor is defined here as "an element that tends to distort or block man's decision-making capacity." Stressors are found in many forms:

1. They can be of psychological origin—caused by an emotional shift within the mind of the decision-maker, such as the emotional crisis a worker undergoes while reliving in his mind an argument he had with his wife prior to leaving for work;

2. They can be of physical origin—produced by factors within the environments,

such as blinding sunlight striking the windshield of a motorist's automobile and causing him to flinch or lose his vision for precious seconds;

3. They can be both physiological and psychological—such as a man physically under the influence of alcohol who has his psychological or mental processes and reactions distorted.

In the case of each stressor situation, one thing is predictable—the man has impaired to the human organism. They contribute to accident causation only insofar as they are able to distort a person's ability to perceive his environment to the extent of forcing incorrect decisions, resulting in unnecessary risks and possibly, accidents.

For discussion purposes here, we are classifying drugs into three main categories—narcotics, hallucinogens, and stimulants. Instead of dwelling much on any particular drug, the sensations experienced within each of the three categories will be detailed. (There

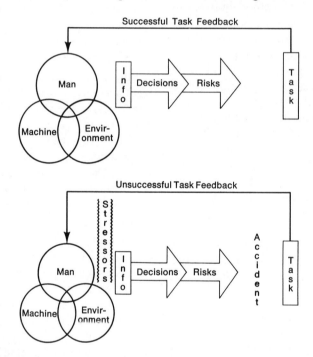

Figure 7.5 Diagrammed are the mechanics of successful task feedback and unsuccessful task feedback. Drugs can become a stressor on the man portion of the man-machine-environment interface, interfere with his reception of information and judgment, and can lead to an accident.

ability to reason and react properly. The stressor itself is for the most part an uncontrollable factor, and no matter how sound a man's information bank is, the stressor can distort and even change an otherwise sound decision into one that is uncalculated and often erroneous—the result of which could be behavior unsafe to himself or to co-workers.

Drugs, therefore, are a particular stressor is an overlap—both physiologically and psychologically—in drug effects, and these are apparent in the discussion.) Most important, there is uniform agreement that a person under the direct mental and physical influence of drugs in these categories has no place in an industrial surrounding. He is a danger to himself and to those around him.

TYPES OF DRUGS

In Table I, which shows the drug hierarchy, three classes of dominant effects are used to categorize the most specific drug effects. (Clinical definitions are not used.) It is not generally true that any particular drug is strictly of one of the three classes—each has specific effects that fall into all three categories. Marijuana, for example, is primarily a mild narcotic (in its effects), but it also stimulates the body's metabolism, and occasionally produces mild hallucinations.

By *narcotic,* we mean here a drug that produces lethargy, drowsiness, euphoria, and stupor while simultaneously relieving pain. Classic examples are the opiates—opium, morphine, and heroin—marijuana, hashish, and even alcohol.

Here we define *hallucinogen* as a drug that produces sights and sounds, together with the physical sensations of objects that are not actually present or by distorting what is actually present.

And by *stimulant,* we mean a drug that increases the body's metabolic rate.

It is in the context of the definitions of these three types of effects of drug influence that drugs are discussed here.

Narcotics

The characteristic effect of the narcotics is that of being "stoned" or "high." These are the terms used to describe a euphoric feeling of omnipotence and ambivalence. When a worker is "stoned" his cares have been lifted away, and he is very much at ease—unless, of course, due to a large dose he becomes frightened of the obvious abnormality in his senses (or feelings). Generally his moods are very intense. If amused, he is very amused, and he laughs very loudly and intensely. Many common and ordinarily unamusing things become amusing to him, so that being high is usually a happy time.

Physically, he has lost considerable coordination. His vision is distorted, so that his sense of perspective is gone (or wholly out of proportion). Things seem flat, two dimensional, and without depth—as though he were looking at a photograph of the world about him. In the street he cannot tell for certain if the approaching headlights are just upon him or many blocks away. Colors are very intense and beautiful. At times his perspective changes to show extreme elongation or width. It may pulsate between these extremes.

Such a person notices a great distortion in time; it passes very slowly. Minutes seem like hours, and hours move into days. Each independent act he performs seems separate and unrelated to any others. This actually amounts to a short-term loss of memory of the immediate past.

He feels as though he is looking at himself living and performing on a stage—each act being separated from each other by unexposed spaces between frames of film.

He is hungry and very intense in his sense of touch.

Sounds take on a new magnitude. Music seems intensely powerful. He hears each instrument, and he is deeply moved by the high and low frequencies. It seems to control him, and makes him want to dance and move with every beat. He feels a part of the music itself—as if it has caught him up and submerged him in it—as if he is swimming in a river of sound. Small insignificant sounds appear very loud and vibrant. They echo.

Occasionally he experiences visual hallucinations of colored flashes of light. Fiery pinwheels, and kaleidoscopic effects, and balls of fire with spectral colors flash along the limits of his vision. He experiences tunnel vision.

These sensations last several hours until he sleeps. He usually sleeps well and awakes refreshed. However, *he is disconnected*—like a picture puzzle lying with all the pieces in place but not yet interlocked. He has an absentmindedness and a loss of purpose. Words are difficult to use in their correct context. It is disturbing to be distracted from whatever he is doing. He is moody.

Such is a composite of the most notable sensations of being "stoned."

Hallucinogens

The most sensational state of mind produced by the newer class of drugs in common usage is that produced by the hallucinogens. The easiest way to describe these effects is by attempting to portray an *LSD trip*. (The sensations presented here hold true, with only minor modification in intensity and length of time, for most of the other hallucinogens—such as mescaline, psilocybine, and STP.)

TABLE I.   DRUG HIERARCHY

(DRUGS CLASSED BY THEIR EFFECT ON USER)

NARCOTICS		HALLUCINOGENS	STIMULANTS
Hard	Sedatives or Depressants	LSD (lysergic acid diethylamide)	Amphetamines (pep pills)
Opium			
Heroin			Dexadrine
Morphine	Phenobarbital	STP	(diet pills)
Soft	Other barbiturates	Mescaline	Methadrine
Marijuana	Darvon	(Peyote)	Benzedrine
Hashish	Thornazine	DMT	Cocaine
Kiev	Alcohol	Psilocybine	
Demerol	(sleeping pills)	(anti-histamines)	
Codeine	(tranquilizers)		
	(anti-histamines)		

Lysergic acid diethylamide (LSD) is usually found in tablet or liquid form. The tablet is ingested by swallowing or by allowing it to dissolve under the tongue. Occasionally, it is powdered and "snorted" (inhaled through the nose). In any event, the site of dissolution—stomach, nasal passages, or mouth—will be the site of considerable sensation later on when the "trip" begins.

Nothing much occurs for about an hour, at which time there's an increase in the body's metabolism. The pulse quickens and the blood pressure rises. The "tripper" feels tense and flushed. Soon his eyes are affected in that the iris pulsates between dilation and contraction several times in the space of a few seconds. As a result, the tripper notices pulsating variation in light intensity. He might put on sun glasses to lessen the discomfort.

His hearing becomes rather acute, and music is amazingly intense. (Sounds seem similar to those described for narcotics.) During the initial phase, many of the sensations are similar to those a person might have if "stoned." The one exception is that the "tripper" is rather hypertensive. This is most likely due to the inner fear of the "trip" to come rather than to any directly drug-related phenomenon.

Soon, it becomes very certain that these early sensations are temporary. The tripper begins to soar far beyond any state of mind that a mild narcotic can produce. He feels as though his mind has fallen through a trap door in reverse, and that it will never cease its upward flight into rapid thoughts and sensations.

He begins to hallucinate visually. It begins along his peripheral vision as brief flashes of light. Red, orange, blue, and green lines flash about at the limits of his vision. Lines appear from horizon to horizon, split into thirds—one extremity being red, the middle blue, and the other extremity green. Rods of multicolored light shoot at him much as things appeared to be thrown at one in the 3-D or stereo movies of the 50's. Soon sheet lightning of red, green, and blue, as well as a myriad of other colors, flashes about him.

The ground beneath his feet seems to be a billowy, misty, cotton-like mass that is interwoven with a multitude of black rods over which he will surely trip and fall, but he doesn't. He seems to be a creature without a body—only a mind. He has transcended the physical and is floating in a world of flashing, rushing colors and eerie sounds. His only link with reality is possibly a distant familiar voice, because none of his other senses registers sensations originating from his actual environment.

At this point the tripper becomes frightened, and paranoia sets in. He is afraid of losing his last touches with reality and of remaining forever in this wonderland. Then, after perhaps several hours in this transcended state he begins to be able to discern some elements in some familiar surroundings—his home for example. But none of these familiar things appear in their usual form. Colors are still intense, lightning flashes. All the hallucinations persist, but, now they are super-imposed over the actual world.

His hands and body are distorted and grotesque. Looking into a mirror his face seems to become plastic, deform, and then melt into a flesh-colored blob of matter.

Walking is amazingly strange. His appendages seem prehensile. He moves by undulation—much as an earthworm or a snake moves. The end of the next block appears very far away, and it is obscured among the color flashes.

Although he seems to walk very far, his destination does not get any closer. Then, in a rush, it is upon him, and then it is past.

Paranoia and a persecution complex surmount him. Everyone seems to be looking at him, laughing at him, and persecuting him. All of his emotions may boil to the surface. He feels violent, sad, angry, happy, excited, anxious, and a hundred other ways at once—many times in contrasting moods.

He introspects. He searches his "soul." His mind—his character—seems to be standing before him, stripped of all the little defenses he has built up around his past actions. His successes and failures, his sins and virtues, all are placed vividly before him in their "true" light. He sees himself as his character really is. He has empathy with other people experiencing extreme emotions of a kind that he has had in the past. He cries extremely hard and long when he recalls sad happenings. He is very happy when he recalls joyful experiences.

His hallucinations take on a different form. Anything in motion possesses a bright, colorful contrail. Quick hand movements leave colorful trails of bright lights. People walking leave colorful geometric patterns. Spinning wheels, fireballs, or geometric forms blast into his closed eyelids. Pyramids are built and destroyed. Rivers of blue flow past with pink pinwheels for a shoreline.

The tripper is physically exhausted from 18 or more hours of this ordeal, but he cannot sleep, because the dreams persist. His arms and legs seem to be in steel-blue traps on a plane of metallic blue, ringed by an orange-colored sky. He is pinned down by galvanized steel cables. He is a *Gulliver in Lilliput*, an *Alice in Wonderland*. He is mentally falling through that trap door again; this time coming down fast. Soon he is flat. He sleeps and awakes refreshed. His mind incredibly clear. However, the spaced-out[1] feeling lingers. He lacks sharp coordination. Some contrails of light linger—perhaps for several days, weeks, or months. Colors are still very beautiful and intense. The trip is over.

Stimulants

The drug-induced effects of the stimulants can best be reduced to the "user's" term of *speeding*.

Although most stimulants, particularly the amphetamines, can be ingested by mouth, the most common method is injection. As the drug is injected directly into the bloodstream, the effects begin rather quickly with the first rushes—flashes of sensation—happening in a matter of seconds or minutes.

The body's metabolism begins to quicken, motions become jerky and aggravated. The person becomes hypertensive. His vision becomes very acute. He wants to dance, run, and move about. Sitting still becomes a chore. He wishes to talk very rapidly. Thoughts come faster than he can examine them. He begins to hallucinate. The hallucinations are

[1]Spaced-out refers to the period of time after the trip when the person is still in varying degrees of disconnection.

quite similar to those produced by LSD, but much more gentle. They are not nearly so all-encompassing. They rush about and flash more quickly, however.

Physically, he feels very strong and well-rested—as though he could run forever. His muscles feel well-toned. Nothing tires him. This feeling of power lasts for a few hours; then he is suddenly quite drained physically and emotionally. All the energy he had has been spent in the hours of rapid movement. He is flat.

His arms and legs are heavy. He cannot focus his attention on any one thought. He begins to quake and sweat even though he is chilled. He desires to take a hot shower and go to bed, but he is too shaky to sleep. He might be sick in his stomach. He feels physically similar to when he has the flu. His body aches. Soon he is able to sleep, and he falls into a restless sleep lasting several hours, during which he may awaken several times. The following day he is physically exhausted.[2]

THE WORK ENVIRONMENT

Whether he be under the influence, "coming down," or "spaced out," such a person should be of concern to management, the safety professional, and to the supervisor in particular.

A worker, immediately upon entering his work environment, becomes part of a system. The organization, in its attempt to control his behavior to a degree to keep him "safe" devises physical control measures, management constraints, rules and regulations, and work procedures, which, if adhered to, would

[2]Editor's Note: While describing biographies of emotional experiences related to drug use, the authors realize they present a composite of many separate experiences and conversations concerning such experiences. However, what is reported here are typical experiences and are not overly dramatized. All are perceptions that the worker within the industrial environment might experience if he is under the influence of drugs.

regulate his behavior in accordance with acceptable (safe) work performance.

But, consider the individual who comes to work either under the influence of drugs or "coming down" from a trip. Consider him as one whose sensory abilities have been impaired. His ability to think, to act, and to react has undergone a profound trauma.

To place this individual at a task (to which he is accustomed), to place him in a situation where other people depend on the predictability of his behavior, and to expect this man to abide by correct work procedures would be naive and, even worse, negligent.

The individual under the influence of drugs, no matter what phase of a trip, undergoes definite physiological and psychological changes. His sensory processes are impaired. His ability to discriminate between sounds and sights diminishes as do the abilities to process information and to see. Realize that the environment that such a person perceives is that which he personally constructs from the information supplied by his senses. Furthermore, the particular elements within that environment result in mental and physical responses to that environment. The influences of drugs might well result in a construction of a false environment or in motor responses wholly unrelated to his actual task. Each of these factors has a profound effect upon his ability to function in that work environment.

If this man cannot see or distinguish colors or sounds—some of which may have been designed as either perceptual or audial cues expressly for the purpose of warning or signaling hazard information, he is exposing himself to hazards without protection.

If he cannot hear correctly, if there is a distortion in his hearing process, if sounds and sights take on new dimensions, again his stability is impaired. Also the very control measures designed to protect the man against hazards become meaningless. His psychological condition would theoretically mask out the very signal that could save him from being injured or even killed.

A good example of such a situation would be the punch press operator whose information-processing activity requires the cues provided by the audible sound of the ram striking the stock. An operator, who is "spaced-out," would find that his bodily skills, manipulative skills, and perceptual skills would be impaired to such an extent that the synchronization between the man/machine interface would provide the accident waiting to happen.

The drug user, then, is seen not as being a hazard to himself, not as a person who is to be overlooked, but as one who has a profound effect upon the entire work atmosphere from the standpoint of injury to personnel, loss or damage to equipment, and damage to the physical facility itself.

MANAGING THE DRUG USER

The most difficult problem related to drug use in the industrial surrounding is not mere recognition but that of managing the drug user within a work situation. To carry out the activities of the management process effectively, it is necessary that the supervisor take appropriate measures to assure that the work of those under his supervision is progressing satisfactorily toward the predetermined objective. Discrepancies, unexpected hindrances, and problems in general will detract from the successful completion of the mission. The capable manager must be quick to recognize such contingencies and to take appropriate counter-measures to bring the situation within acceptable limits of control.

A supervisor's effectiveness in dealing with various problem areas related to employees can be measured largely by his ability to gain an empathy, which allows him to feel their problems to such an extent that he can judge or estimate their behavior patterns and know precisely when corrective actions must be taken. By being able to understand an em-

ployee's feelings, the person in charge is more likely to choose the most desirable corrective path when discrepancies do appear. This fact is particularly true when considering the subject of drugs.

A supervisor must be able to understand explicitly what a person is going through while "under the influence" or "spaced-out" as the result of a drug trip. He must also understand the physiological and emotional shifts on the user's ability to function in the work environment.

It would be highly efficient and uncomplicated if a hard and fast set of rules could be laid down for recognizing and controlling the drug user in the work environment. Unfortunately, this cannot be done at this time. Recently, however, some authors have attempted to set guidelines for recognizing the characteristics of the user. The guidelines often appear in checklist form. At best they are somewhat incomplete. Unfortunately, many are misleading because they are based on traditional ideas related to drug recognition. In addition, the drug user has become increasingly aware of the stereo-typical clues that indicate drug usage. Hence, to counter the situation, the user has become more discreet and cautious of how he goes about using his drugs; he goes to great extremes to eliminate or disguise any noticeable clues of his drug activity. Another reason a checklist is of little use as an indicator or a warning and not as a sure factor of a case of drug abuse is that no two people respond precisely the same way to a particular drug. Because of emotional make-up, size, weight, etc., the effect of a particular drug may vary from person to person. What may be an easily recognizable symptom for one person may not be the same for another.

Probably the best strategy that a supervisor can use when dealing with a suspected drug user is to obtain a thorough understanding of drugs and their effect on a worker's performance, and to let the fact of his having this knowledge be known to his work force.

This is the first step in providing effective control.

Another factor that the supervisor can rely upon in his quest for managing the drug user is that a person using drugs is usually very apprehensive, partially because of the drug's illegality, the associated penalties that go along with using them, and the stigmas that are attached to the drug user himself. The supervisor can play upon this apprehensiveness when he lets it be known that he is capable of recognizing the symptoms and actions of the user. However, he must be very discreet in how he goes about doing this. Confronting the user with symptoms of his condition will put him on the immediate defensive to any questions dealing with the subject.

The key to the whole "management of the drug user" problem is not accusation.[3] It is rather a familiarization with the behavior patterns and symptoms that go along with drug usage and letting employees know that their supervisors are knowledgeable of these indicators and that a user will not be able to go unnoticed.

It is actually difficult to prove that a man is using a particular drug, because no practical testing procedures are available. Unlike the drunk-o-meter device used to test for alcohol, there is no device that can be used by non-medical personnel for determining drug use. (Medical personnel can perform blood and urine tests that will reveal the presence of certain drugs.)

Any direct confrontation, of an accusatory manner, with a person suspected of being under the influence of drugs will put the

suspect person on the defensive. However, a discussion with the suspected drug abuser of some of the symptoms of "tripping" will let that person know his ruse has been detected without having directly accused him.

An unspoken understanding can often serve as a deterrent to the person who is "tripping" on the job or coming to work "spaced-out."

The first encounter that a supervisor has with a person who he feels is using drugs, especially when the supervisor feels that person knows he is aware of the situation, can often be controlled by simply reassigning the employee to a job or task that will not require actions or reactions that could not be handled by a user. Continued encounters can then be handled by sending the employee to the company physician. After alerting the physician, confidentially, to any symptomatic behavior, the physician can confirm whether or not a person is under the influence of drugs and determine whether or not the reason is medical.

The judgment of the physician can then be used to return this person to the job.

[3]There are always legal implications with any accusation. Provisions exist in law that permit medicinal use and dispensing of most drugs listed in the three categories. All an accused has to do is turn up a prescription for the drug, signed by a physician. For this reason the detection of a drug influenced employee must be handled discreetly. Instant dismissal or other severe reproaches, common with alcohol abuse, may backfire with considerable legal embarrassment.

BIBLIOGRAPHY

ALPERT, R., and LEARY, T. "Politics of Consciousness Expansion," *Harvard Review* (Summer, 1963).

AMES, F. "A Clinical and Metabolic Study of Acute Intoxication with Cannabis Sativa, and its Role in Modern Psychoses," *Journal of Mental Science (British Journal of Psychiatry)* **104** (1958).

HUXLEY, SIR JULIAN. *Psychedelic Reader* (New Hyde Park, N.Y.: University Books, 1965).

TART, C. T. "Marijuana Intoxication: Common Experiences," *Nature* **226** (May 23, 1970).

Waller, J. A. "Drugs and Driving," *Concepts* **3** (1), (1969).

WALTON, R. P. *Marijuana—America's New Drug Problem* (New York: Lippincott, 1938).

ZINBERG, N. E., and WEIL, A. T. "A Comparison of Marijuana Users and Non-Users," *Nature* **226** (April 11, 1970).

YOUNG DRUG USERS AND THE "VALUE GAP"

Paul W. Pretzel

Much of the frustration of counselors, teachers, and parents over their inability to communicate with their juniors is due to the false assumption that there exists a basic sense of values that they all hold in common. If there is conflict, then, they feel the solution lies in the correction of the "wrong" value and the reestablishment of the "right" value; or perhaps they feel what is needed is a clarification of how certain behaviors will bring certain results without realizing that no common goals exist.

This false assumption that all members of our culture hold in common similar life goals, similar concepts of good and evil, and similar basic evaluations of behavior, sets the stage for the ultimate frustration that people experience when they finally discover that they really have no common meeting ground. There is no way in which two people can discuss meaningfully the merits of drug use, let alone the broader questions of the planning of one's life, if they are bringing to the discussion different value criteria and measurements. Such a discussion is doomed to frustration and both parties are likely to leave the encounter feeling frustrated, angry and misunderstood, concluding that the other person is unreasonable and closed-minded.

What is needed at such an impasse is to understand what some of the value differences are so that the parties can be conscious that they are operating on different standards. What follows is an outline of some of these value differences between the drug culture and the straight culture.

The first area of value difference is the dichotomy between the values of pleasure and production. Young people using drugs defend their use largely on the basis of the pleasure drugs provide. Holding pleasure as an important value, they frequently criticize the older generation with being so obsessed with work and duty that they have lost the ability to be "turned on" and to accept the multiple pleasures that life has to offer.

The straight culture tends to value productivity over pleasure and is often willing to postpone or even forego pleasure to enhance their own productivity.

The second value dichotomy is that between experience and achievement. Young people experimenting with drugs usually place a high value on experience for its own sake. They search for new feelings, new encounters, new insights, and new experiences through varied patterns of dress, drugs, light shows, and suspect activities. It is an attitude which says that we pass through life but once and that we should taste from many different tables and experience all that there is in life and live it to the fullest. The use of drugs, especially hallucinatory ones, provides experiences of beauty and vividness which the drug culture values highly.

The straight culture devalues this type of life by saying that it is shallow and that it misses what is probably the greatest thrill of all, that of mastery and achievement. The disciplined development of certain skills and achievement provides greater satisfaction, they say, than the alternative of attempting to taste a little bit of everything, but not going into depth with anything.

The third value difference is that of passivity and aggression. The drug culture places a high emphasis on passivity, employing terms like "peace," "love," and "gentleness." It condemns war, violence, brutality, acquisi-

From Paul Pretzel, "Young Drug Users and the Value Gap" (Los Angeles County School Superintendent's Newsletter). Reprinted by permission.

tiveness, and greed. It prefers passivity to power of any kind, and sees itself on a high moral plane with this stand. Drugs are an important part of this value.

The straight culture places equally high value on aggression. It uses terms like "duty," and "honor," and talks about the obligation of every man to fight for what is right. To be a man, as defined by the straight culture, one should be clear-headed and active, defining his worth in terms of what he can accomplish. Competition is a high value and produces progress; passivity is often associated with cowardliness or incompetence.

The fourth value difference has to do with concepts of time. The drug culture places a high value on the present; the straight culture sees more value in both the past and the future. The drug culture says that the only thing that is really real is the present. The past is gone and the future is not yet, and to sacrifice the present moment on the altars of these nonexistent time categories is the epitome of foolishness. All that we hold is the present and we must cherish this.

The straight culture says that we need both to learn from history and to plan the future, even if this means sacrificing much of the meaning of the moment—an unthinkable bargain for the dedicated drug user. The straight culture sees life as an on-going cumulative process, the point of which is to gather wisdom from the past in order that it might be applied to the future and in such a way that life finds its meaning and progress.

It does little good, therefore, for a straight to urge a drug user to think of the chromosome damage or how he will suffer in the years ahead when these time concepts have no more value for the drug user than the sense of immediacy or timelessness have for the straight.

The fifth value dichotomy is that of content and form. The straight culture places high value on the content of issues, but the drug culture is more apt to be concerned about the form or style by which life is being lived. Where the straight culture sees itself as substantive, valuing facts and content and indepth penetration, the drug culture pays more attention to flair, form, style, social maneuverability and performance.

The drug culture thinks of content as dull and compulsive; the straight culture sees style and form as superficial and shallow—and so the two bore each other.

The sixth value dichotomy is between risk and restraint. Adherents of the drug culture place high value on excitement, risk, and adventure; the straight culture prefers restraint, conservatism, and safety. The drug culture faces life with the attitude, "Try it, it might be exciting and fun"; the straight culture retorts "Be careful, you have a lot to lose."

The final difference in values is that between mysticism and intellectualism. The drug culture is mystical, placing high value on feelings and existential experiences. Truth, they say, is known only by submission to religious experience and the higher mystical life is available for all those willing to accept it.

The straight culture wants to intellectualize and it values the ability to think and behave rationally above all. The straight culture is suspicious of superstition and feelings that get out of control; that is, out of control of rational thought.

If one attempts to communicate with those immersed in a basically different value system, he must make a serious effort to understand the other person's values and to recognize the basic assumptions under which both he and the other person are operating. If the effort fails, all subsequent discussion is meaningless.

Any counselor has difficulty working with someone whose values are substantially different from his own. He must continually be aware of his own feelings and work at maintaining a reasonable clinical objectivity.

There are three dangers that the counselor should avoid.

He should, first, avoid overreaction. Recognizing that many students deliberately overstate radical opinions in a dramatic way for the shock effect, the counselor should take this into account as he seeks to understand what the student is telling him. THE COUNSELOR'S RESPONSE CAN ALIENATE THE COUNSELEE. To overreact, to become judgmental or authoritarian, or to exaggerate the dangers of certain kinds of drug usage, can only have the effect of alienating the young person and rendering the counseling ineffective.

The second danger is underreaction. Failing to respond to realistically dangerous situations in the name of open-mindedness or tolerance is destructive permissiveness and usually comes across to the student as insensitivity or a lack of caring.

A third danger is the inappropriate response. An example of this is when the counselor permits himself to be seduced into academic discussions such as the pros and cons of the legalization of marijuana when the student has more immediate personal and pressing concerns.

The appropriate goals in counseling those involved in drug use are usually modest. The counselor should acknowledge the existence of the "value gap" and work not at conversion but at establishing openness and mutual respect.

PART EIGHT

A LOOK AT THE FUTURE

The world is changing. Cultural and societal norms and expectations are in a constant state of flux. Science and technology are opening new dimensions and directions. In such a dynamic environment, there is no place for a static organization. Organizations must change. Organizational change is partly a reaction to a changing environment and partly a precipitator of further environmental change. Just as organizational change bears this relationship to environmental change, so does change in the sub-units of an organization bear the same relationship to change in the total organization.

The personnel function is no exception to this. Change in personnel management is certain; the direction, magnitude and force of such change is to a great extent unpredictable. Yet, even here, projections can be made, hypotheses advanced, even hunches explored.

The two articles in this concluding part of the book contemplate some of the possible forms that such change may take. "The Personnel Function in Tomorrow's Company" delves into what tomorrow's personnel manager might look like and what shifts in personnel emphasis might occur. The author concludes by making some predictions about the nature of the personnel function in organizations of the future.

In the second article the author proposes two models for revamping the personnel function to make it more receptive to changing needs. One is a "maintenance-motivator" model and the other is based on a "personnel segmentation" approach.

THE PERSONNEL FUNCTION IN TOMORROW'S COMPANY

Frank E. Fischer

In the past 30 years technological changes have helped to double the gross national product, and in the next 30 they will more than double it again. In the field of human knowledge, we are told that four times as much is known today as was known 30 years ago and that scientists will learn as much more in the next 15 years as in all of previous history. As for population, we can expect to grow from a country of 200 million people to 226 million by 1975 and 245 million by 1980.

To those engaged in business management generally and in the personnel function particularly these prognostications have a special significance, because all these goods, all this knowledge, all these people will be the concern of a shrinking proportion of the population. The group from which our executives and decision-makers are drawn—the age group from 35 to 55—will have dropped from 47 per cent of the total productive age group to 38 per cent by 1980. Roughly, this means that three managers will be doing the work that four are doing today.

TOMORROW'S MANAGER

To understand what this means for the personnel function, we have to consider first what tomorrow's manager will be like and what kind of work he will be doing. We can be reasonably sure that he will have to know

From Frank E. Fischer, "The Personnel Function in Tomorrow's Company," Personnel 45 (1), 64–71 (1968). Reprinted by permission of the American Management Association.

more and learn more than his counterpart today, and that he will be supervising more sophisticated people than he does today. Professor Harold Leavitt of Carnegie Tech predicts that tomorrow's manager will be more of an intellectual, that he will make more of his decisions on the basis of systematic analysis and less by off-the-cuff methods. There is evidence that this is already happening. Not long ago, the American Telephone & Telegraph Co. studied the records of 17,000 college graduates in the Bell companies and learned that the single most reliable indicator of their success was class standing on graduating from college, and more recently the Prudential Insurance Co. of America came to the same conclusion.

Tomorrow's manager will also be supervising a different kind of workforce. Between 1950 and 1960, the number of professional and technical people employed in business increased 47 per cent, and for the first time white-collar workers in industry exceeded the number of blue-collar workers. This trend is expected to continue. The supervision of primarily professional, technical, and other white-collar employees will require a kind of manager different from the one who is now typical in factory management.

At the same time, despite the best possible preparation for his present job, tomorrow's executive may find himself threatened with obsolescence in mid-career. With "knowledge" compounding at such a rapid rate, no manager can be sure that his skills will continue to be needed or even that his job will exist tomorrow. As MIT's Professor Charles Myers has observed, "It is becoming impossible to learn a skill that will continue for a lifetime." In some companies there is even talk about preparing executives for a second career.

SHIFTS IN PERSONNEL EMPHASIS

Can personnel specialists meet the needs of tomorrow's manager? Their record in responding to new requirements in the past encourages the belief that they can. The personnel function began as an employment and record-keeping function; later, as workers began to organize, it took on the administration of labor agreements. Increasingly, too, it was charged with carrying out programs largely developed by management.

The personnel department then moved in one or more directions: (1) It became the keeper of the corporate conscience, and concerned itself with the morale of the employees; (2) it became "scientific" and introduced systematic techniques for employee selection, salary administration, and other activities connected with personnel; or (3) it began to concoct programs that proved to be more fashionable than useful.

A number of management fads and gimmicks have originated in the personnel department, particularly in the training function. Not long ago, the magic words were "economic education" and "human relations"; later came "brainstorming" and "group dynamics"; and more recently we have been hearing about teaching machines and "human systems development."

THE RECENT RECORD

Aside from busying itself with fads or status-symbol programs, however, the personnel function has shown signs of maturing.

Appraisals are more goal-oriented, and tied in with management development as well as compensation. They are regarded less as a personnel "program" and more as a management tool.

Compensation plans and techniques are becoming less complex, top management involvement is more evident, and the plans are better integrated than before. In the past it was not unusual to find responsibility for a company's compensation program fragmented among three or more departments, but now it is recognized that compensation

is not a matter of discrete programs, and that companies still following that line are probably paying total compensation far beyond what they thought they were paying or need to pay. As a result, it is becoming more common for all elements of the compensation program to report to a single executive.

So-called discretionary bonus plans are giving way to incentive plans based on formulas and distributing funds according to individual performance weighed against planned objectives.

Personnel records and reports are being centralized and put on computers.

Greater attention is being paid to personnel research as an assist in making management decisions.

In divisionalized companies, there is more policy direction by corporate personnel departments but at the same time greater local autonomy in personnel administration.

There is more effort to collaborate with government in personnel matters, such as equal employment opportunity, collective bargaining, wage guidelines, pricing, retraining, and Medicare. For instance, companies are finding that merely pledging to eliminate discrimination or joining the voluntary Equal Employment Opportunity Councils is not enough. Compliance must be positive, and companies are expected to prove good faith by publicizing the fact that appointments are open to minority groups, by recruiting actively from among such groups, and by establishing programs for training them.

The personnel department is beginning to operate internationally, particularly in the areas of compensation and employee benefits.

More attention is being given to the identification of potential managers and to the nurture of talent. As shortages of skills become more acute, recruiting becomes more competitive and companies worry more about how to retain their college trainees and other "elite" groups.

Training is leaving the classroom and returning to the workplace or a simulation of it. A recent reorientation of the training activity at American Airlines illustrates this trend: Aware of the constant changes in the business environment, the training heads at American Airlines believe that it is not enough to pass on managerial wisdom from one generation to another, that managers have to learn how to relate that experience to tomorrow's requirements. Thus, they act on the principles that the organization should be less a traditional school-master and more a provider of resources and experiences; that training is concerned with improvement in both functional skills (such as budgeting or selling) and social skills (such as communications or counseling); that training should both increase individual competence and improve collaboration within and between groups; and that the best way to teach people management processes like planning, organizing, and controlling is to have them plan, organize, and control.

To implement these principles, the company is making use of problem-solving and simulation techniques, such as business games, in-basket exercises, role playing, and team-task methods.

WHAT'S AHEAD?

In addition to these developments, there are signs of other changes, some of which may have a profound effect on the purpose, staffing, status, and organization of the personnel department in the future. Four related changes of particular significance are: (1) the growing profit-orientation of the personnel function; (2) the shift in personnel work from a mechanistic concept to a creative, innovative one; (3) the interest in furthering an organization, rather than just maintaining or servicing it; and (4) the more direct involvement of top management in the development of the human resources of the business. Just what are the implications of these trends?

1. *The personnel function will assume a more important role in the management of the business.* It will do more planning and policy-making in the areas of manpower, organization structure, and compensation, among others. It will have more functional authority, especially in large, complex, and growing organizations. In becoming increasingly oriented toward growth and profits, instead of merely administering personnel activities, it will search out profit-improvement opportunities.

This new awareness will mean that personnel people will view their role in a different light. For example: In selecting people, more weight will be placed on what a candidate has accomplished than on the jobs he has held. In management development, more stress will be placed on identifying company and departmental needs and objectives and training people to help attain them. In compensation, it will be important to relate pay to performance and to its motivational impact, as well as to make sure that rates are competitive. In the area of employee benefits, there will be more consideration of the fact that a large part of expenditures are going to people who are not working in the form of retirement benefits, life insurance payments, medical plans, and the like.

In appraising performance, there will be more emphasis on accomplishments against expectations, and appraisal results will be more closely tied to a man's compensation. In organization planning, there will have to be major emphasis on aligning responsibilities and relationships in the individual company to obtain maximum results with the least manpower, instead of seeking symmetrical or conventional organization patterns or uncritically following principles of organization laid down by others.

In summary, the personnel function will no longer be able to justify itself to top management by citing numbers or listing activities—the number of people interviewed or trained or counseled, the number of reports prepared or of records maintained, the number of job descriptions written, or the rate of employee turnover. Rather, personnel will demonstrate its effectiveness by raising the qualification levels of the employees hired; reducing the turnover among key managerial and professional people; recommending or drafting plans, policies, and programs that are adopted by operating management; and initiating organizational and staffing changes.

2. *The personnel function will become more creative, less mechanistic.* In the future, the disparity between the paper programs and actuality will have to be eliminated. The deficiencies of rigid, packaged "personnel programs" will become increasingly apparent.

Most of us are familiar with companies where "management development programs" have been conducted for years, yet half of their top managers are over 55 years old and there are few successors in sight, and the companies go outside to find people for many higher-level jobs; where management positions are invariably staffed without consulting the head of the personnel department; and where although the companies have performance appraisal programs, half the executives don't even bother to complete the required forms.

In such corporations, most of the top management group have had experience in only one function of the business; there are no inventories of management resources, no plans for management succession, and only a dim notion of future management requirements or how to meet them; participation by top executives in outside management development programs is almost nonexistent; a high proportion of the more promising men recruited on college campuses leave the company within two years; and numerous corporate departments are involved with compensation and employee benefit plans, but no department is responsible for overall policy or coordination in these areas and, for that matter, the compensation plan does not apply to a sizable group of executives in the top levels.

There will be less me-tooism, less concern with imitating industry practice or matching industry averages, and more attention to what's actually required to help the company meet its goals. There will be more concern with ends rather than means, with substance rather than forms, with accomplishments rather than activities. There will be increasing emphasis on what the operating people find workable instead of what is theoretically best or easiest for the personnel department to administer. We already see this trend in the adoption of less complicated job-evaluation plans and in the movement away from automatic merit increases and appraisals based on an employee's activities or traits and toward appraisals based on performance measured against company goals or standards.

3. *The personnel function will be responsible for furthering the organization, not just maintaining it.* Personnel people will devote more time to proposing and promoting changes than to protecting the status quo. Instead of a miscellany of diverse specialties or activities, the personnel department will be regarded as an integrated general management function, responsible for the effective deployment of the firm's human resources, and, as it becomes more oriented to the requirements of the organization, it will view the needs of individuals in the light of their compatibility with those of the organization.

The personnel managers will recognize and encourage sound management practices, fostering concepts like management-by-objectives and team problem-solving approaches. They will seek new ways to awaken the talents that lie dormant in every organization by searching out opportunities and providing training experiences that are challenging and meaningful, rejecting a commitment to human relations as an end in itself.

In planning and developing his company's human resources, the personnel man will have to raise his sights to plan the form of the future organization and of the firm's manpower requirements; to structure and integrate the work; to identify and select management talent; to appraise and reward performance; to provide learning experiences to ensure growth of both the individual and the organization; and to rotate, transfer, and promote people into appropriate positions.

To handle this responsibility, the personnel man will have to be an individual of singular breadth and influence, sensitive equally to the needs and capabilities of people and to the requirements of the business. How many personnel departments or personnel people today perform this role or qualify for it? Apparently, not many. Some companies establish a separate unit within the personnel department to carry out this creative policy-making and program-planning function. In others, a small, high-level staff, responsible for organization planning and development, is created to work directly with the chief executive officer and his key subordinates, while personnel services for supervisory and employee groups are provided by the regular personnel department.

If this trend continues, there is a real possibility that the personnel department will become, in effect, an employee services organization, catering to the needs of lower-level groups and administering the traditional, routine personnel functions. This threat will be averted only if professional personnel people turn their energies to making the organization more effective instead of making it more comfortable or safe; if they start thinking more about making work productive and meaningful than about making it easy.

4. *Top management will become more directly involved in the deployment and development of human resources.* The chief executives of a growing number of companies are spending a good deal of time thinking about the people in the organizations, reviewing management manpower needs and resources, assessing the performance and potential of their executives, and planning their future experiences. Michael Haider, Chairman of Standard Oil of New Jersey, recently wrote:

> In the life of a corporation, today's success is largely a product of three types of executive actions taken yesterday: selecting the right people; placing them in the right jobs; and seeing to it that they were able to grow to meet both their own needs and those of the organization. This activity is not a program in the usual sense, any more than selling or making profits are programs. It has no fixed dimensions, no timetable, no cutoff point.

How seriously he regards this activity, Mr. Haider points out, is indicated by the fact that he assumes the executive development function as his personal responsibility. He, the president and four executive vice-presidents of the company, acting as a committee, met 37 times in 1964 to review the company's human resources. This committee is "involved in a continuing examination of management throughout the Jersey organization. . . . Once a year the chief executive officer of each of the larger affiliates meets with the committee and reviews in depth his company's development activities and its replacement situation, and appraises the performance and potential of all his key management personnel. He goes over his replacement tables, his plans for job rotation assignments, and the specific steps being taken to increase the effectiveness of his organization."

A company in which the chief executive regards the development of its human resources as one of his chief concerns will probably provide the kind of climate in which people are encouraged to grow and to innovate. Those engaged in personnel work are in an excellent position to influence—and to benefit from—that climate.

To exert the proper influence, however, the personnel executive will have to adapt to management's changing expectations of his role. Thus, to sum up, the personnel executive in the future will:

Assume a larger role in profit management.

Concern himself more with ends than with means, with accomplishments rather than activities.

Devote his efforts to building the organization instead of just maintaining it.

Assist top management in the effective deployment and development of the company's human resources.

If the personnel function is going to survive as more than management's maid-of-all-work (to use Professor Paul Pigors' phrase), and if it is to satisfy management's greater demands upon it, there will have to be fundamental changes in its role.

REORGANIZE THE PERSONNEL DEPARTMENT?

Stanley L. Sokolik

Personnel-staff departments of larger firms are usually organized on a function- or task-oriented basis. This pattern seems to have developed as a natural concomitant of the increasing personnel expertise which has come about in the last twenty-five years. Growth in staff specialization has become possible only to make assignments on the basis of more specifically prescribed technical areas (e.g., compensation planning, benefits analysis, technical training, employee publications, college recruitment).

Of course, some of this division of labor also results from the personnel specialists' own efforts to preserve and add to appurtenances of their status. Though an oversimplification, it is not too far wrong to say that personnel specialists have generally equated task specialization with gaining and reinforcing acceptance of their role as the authority in management of their firms' human resources.

However, all has not gone well with personnel departments which have developed on this basis. Their growth and, even more importantly, their particular contribution to the profitable growth of their firms have not kept pace. Symptoms persist to indicate that personnel-staff management is increasingly left at the starting gate in important corporate efforts, if considered at all as anything more than interested onlookers. Surely, in all too many cases, personnel-staff management has failed to earn the direct commitment of top-

management resources—the convincing arguments of some of their most persuasive practitioners notwithstanding. This situation seems appropriately described as a malaise. Four strongly foreboding symptoms stand out:

Work productivity and worker satisfaction continue to languish, and few personnel departments are able to show material gains in either area.

Tasks are being splintered off from the personnel departments' responsibilities and established not only as separate divisions, but often in competition with those who sired them.

The personnel field continues to have difficulties in attracting outstanding men, both from among college students and within management ranks, no matter how exposed some of the potential candidates' "helping" interest is.

Personnel departments are all too seldom in the midst of the creative leadership generated by corporate responsibilities in a changing urban America.

Cries of the bankruptcy of personnel management have been heard for some time. Criticism of the personnel staff's ability to generate effective responses to new and growing problems from within and without the firm is never far from the formal and informal discussions of managers of every stripe (at times, even those who hold management positions within the personnel department). Although not the first to do so, Peter F. Drucker met the question head-on in his book, *The Practice of Management*, concluding that the field (while not bankrupt) was "certainly insolvent, certainly unable to honor, with the ready cash of performance, the promises of managing worker and work it so liberally makes. . . . [Its] assets are frozen."[1]

[1]Peter F. Drucker, *The Practice of Management* (New York: Harper and Brothers, 1954), p. 287.

Thirteen years later, the claims of the creditors do not appear to have been satisfied. Personnel departments have not achieved long-run improvement in work productivity or worker satisfaction, presumably the key reasons for their existence.

To the extent that a malaise exists, corrective action is needed to enable personnel departments to make the unique contribution which can be theirs. A first step—surely a major one—would be giving them a more viable organization structure. Structure must be clearly attuned to purpose. Unless it is, it cannot be expected that personnel specialists will reach out for more creative programs, let alone respond in such a way as to surmount the increasing pressures which beset them today. The consequence of an orderly change now could well be such extreme dysfunctioning that answers will be sought elsewhere—from others who deal with human resources from outside the personnel-staff ranks or from those who would have the enterprise depend far less upon people.

I will present two organizational models which may provide the basis for effectively redesigning personnel departments. The first was recently suggested by Frederick Herzberg, and the second is an outgrowth of my search for a renewal of personnel-staff capacity. Neither is simply achieved, and each

requires major realignment and reorientation in how personnel-staff specialists work together. On the other hand, both are within the grasp of those now in the field.

In the last of his trilogy about job attitudes, Herzberg offers a challenge to even the hardiest and most successful personnel practitioners as he observes, "Present personnel programs, which in effect serve to minimize the natural symptoms of an amputated individual, can lead only to temporary, opiate relief and further the basic psychic pathology."[2]

Herzberg's thrust is direct and piercing as it focuses upon the direction of the historical growth of personnel-staff departments. He finds and questions the almost exclusive concern with the "maintenance" needs of workers (Fig. 8.1). So directed, the personnel specialists end up working at odds with their own best interests. Though they proceed to launch more and more programs as well as intensify or update the old ones, their efforts are largely self-defeating. Little of lasting worth results for the workers and almost nothing for work productivity (as studies by Herzberg and others have verified).

[2]Frederick Herzberg, *Work and the Nature of Man* (Cleveland and New York: World Publishing Company, 1966), p. 170.

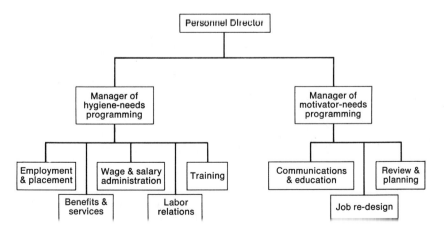

Figure 8.1

Herzberg, moreover, recognizes a structural causality for some of the present state of affairs. He refers to an increasing regard for professionalism among personnel specialists (certainly something not restricted to them) as ironically becoming a "synonym for gathering [for themselves] the harvest of the hygiene factors of status and money."[3] Winning professional status for themselves has thus been seen by many personnel–staff workers as reassurance that their focus upon task specialization in personnel management is proper. Whatever the fears they have about their preoccupation with the hygienic environment of the employee, they are encouraged by the "professional legitimacy" of immersing themselves in the pursuit of refinements of technique, no matter how abstruse or unmotivating these ends become.

To be sure, such concerns with the growth of personnel-staff professionalism are not shared by all. The opinion of many is, to the contrary, most optimistic. They point to the growth in numbers and variety of staff and programming of personnel departments. Such evidence is, of course, undebatable. There are sizable and still-growing personnel staffs in almost every business organization worthy of mention. From the way things look, indeed, the creditors have been staved off. But does such growth signify success?

Some of this growth, it should be remembered, comes directly from growth in the size of many business firms. There is the increased personnel-staff workload brought on by greater payroll-tax complexities and a myriad of government regulations of employment and labor relations practices, not to mention the growing number of mergers with the planning and consequences which they create for personnel-staff specialists. Then, too, there's the persistence of what Dalton McFarland has termed the "trash-can" pattern which has led personnel departments to become a dumping ground for a broad array

[3]*Ibid.,* p. 184.

of functions which have little or nothing to do with the major goals of personnel administration.[4] For those personnel–staff managers who associate organizational stature with size of staff, of course, this may be a personally fortuitous circumstance. Yet the result is often that they then face the added burden of keeping their emphasis (and their superiors') upon their personnel accomplishments.

Splintering off of Personnel Tasks. Sometimes, those who are more optimistic about the personnel-staff contribution will go beyond the organizational limits of the personnel department itself and include other organizational units as relevant to the measure of the full growth in personnel-staff services. When they do, they are really revealing another problem of personnel performance. Three task centers which are clearly part of the personnel process (at least, as I conceived it) are rapidly being splintered off (indeed, if they ever existed as part of the personnel department) and are growing independently of what is known as the personnel-staff function.

I refer here to the growth of staff departments in labor relations, organization planning, and management development. All three of these staff activities—though perhaps reporting to the same senior executive—are more and more being regarded as separate organizational entities. Ironically, too, these are often the "personnel" activities which receive the greatest attention and the most direct involvement of top management. Of course, when this happens, the personnel department loses out. If nothing else, it is blocked in trying to generate a coordinated program of human-resource management. It also finds itself sterile in achieving a strategic

[4]Dalton E. McFarland, *Cooperation and Conflict in Personnel Administration* (New York: American Foundation for Management Research, 1962), p. 49. In contrast to my concern here with internal organization, McFarland's survey focused upon the relationships between the personnel-staff department and those outside of it.

position in corporate planning which would enable it to mount and sustain innovative efforts.

A Helping Posture Without Appeal. The malaise also reveals itself in the lack of appeal which personnel departments hold out for college graduates. Though one would think that a personnel-staff career opportunity would offer a meaningful alternative to the young people who have been turning to the generally recognized "helping professions," the Peace Corps, VISTA, and similar ventures, it does not seem to have worked out that way.

Surely, young people will always have trouble identifying business with a liberal outlook or public service so long as its specialized human-oriented departments are themselves so uninviting. At a time when business in general may be making some headway in attracting more able and creative students, personnel careers are often not among the best, and many who select a "personnel" major in a business school do so for no more deep a consideration that their "liking for people." If the feelings of the college student and graduate offer valid insight into the broader job situation, personnel departments do not appear as the "in" group, offer the greatest challenge, or stand the best chance of rewarding an individual's efforts.

Ineffective Response to Forces From Without. Finally, no matter how much personnel departments are contributing to organizational productivity and development, it's the exception to find them playing a viable and central role in marshalling the organization's capacity to respond creatively to the increased responsibilities thrust upon business firms from without. Indeed, in all too many instances in the past, the answers have been imposed upon—not anticipated by—the personnel department. Civil rights legislation and the summer riots of 1966 and 1967 have truly contributed far more to the renewal of personnel-staff performance than any effort

its practitioners have wrought on their own.

Only recently, Alfonso J. Cervantes, Mayor of St. Louis, wrote:

Either business men will learn new techniques of job simplification, personnel management, and skill development, and take over the leadership of the thrust against chronic unemployment, or it will be necessary to withdraw from the central city and to seal it off as the leprous Pandora's box of American society."[5]

In a recent review of the status of race relations in the business community, Arthur Shostak expresses the fear that the social responsibilities which he sets out for future personnel specialists will not be realized since the challenge which "goes to the very heart of the personnel function" has been left unheeded in the past.[6]

Herzberg's Duality Structure. Only recently has there been a creative suggestion for revamping the internal structure of personnel-staff departments into two major divisions. Though I personally do not know of any business firm which has proceeded to institute the change, it stands a good chance of arresting the existing problems, even of making serious inroads in obliterating many of the causative factors. The suggestion comes from Herzberg as he seeks to provide a more operational base for the celebrated research he and his associates have conducted into worker attitudes. Herzberg advocates that two divisions of personnel-staff activity should be formed to deal separately with the dual needs he has identified as significant to worker attitudes and behavior. One would continue to concentrate on the hygiene or maintenance needs, and the other would be charged with sustaining a creative effort to

[5]Alfonso J. Cervantes, "To Prevent a Chain of Super-Watts," *Harvard Business Review* **XLV** (5), (September-October, 1967).

[6]Arthur Shostak, "Race Relations: Questions and Answers for Personnel Men," *Personnel Administration* **XXVII** (4), 18 (July-August 1964).

satisfy the motivator needs of workers.[7] (See Fig. 1.)

Herzberg's plan is an offshoot of his own research. As the practical import of his investigations, he even advocates paralleling his delineated duality of worker needs with a dual structuring of personnel-staff performance. In short, he says that the best way to meet man's needs is to reflect the dual structure of man's nature (i.e., his maintenance and motivation needs) in the very organization structure of those departments which are responsible for dealing with man's concerns, problems, development, and utilization on behalf of the enterprise. Such an organization structure could be charted as in Figure 1.

Herzberg would have the first of the formal personnel divisions continue to pursue programs concerned with the worker's hygiene-need system. As he sees it, most of the existing personnel-staff activity of business firms today would fall into this division.

The second division would have as its sphere the tasks that have been given far less attention but (as Herzberg's findings evidence) can be far more effective in changing workers' behavior. It would search out and deal creatively with the problems that interfere with workers' psychological growth. Three tasks would predominate in this second division:

The education or, preferably, the re-education of workers and management as to the realism of worker motivation and efforts to this end.

Meaningful job enlargement and other structural changes which provide for greater job autonomy.

"Remedial and therapeutic actions" growing out of periodic reviews of company policies, assumptions, rules and regulations —reviews specifically aimed at uncovering factors which interfere with or do not go far enough in motivating workers.

Some examples of specific objectives for each of these latter sub-units will help to appreciate the contrast with the operation of existing personnel departments. Communications and education with the workers as well as those who manage them would treat directly the effect of work upon them, the realistic prospects of gaining greater satisfaction from work performance, the natural changes in workers' levels of needs as they mature organizationally and personally, and the extreme importance of personal communications. Herzberg holds out much for job enrichment as the major means of realizing worker motivation by providing additional opportunities for recognition of achievement, more challenging job complexity and open-endedness, and more built-in job fluidity.

It is clear that Herzberg has thought out his proposal well. He acknowledges the practical value of manifesting a clear organizational separation of these tasks and takes pains to project realistically possible results. For example, in the wake of changes introduced by the motivator division, he foresees a sharp and dramatic increase in productivity at the creativity level, but an increased number of errors at the operational level. Though he feels that over the long run the creativity output is likely to more than offset the greater errors engendered by the freedom given the individual, he expresses concern that the fear of increased errors at the outset may well block the proposed organizational change. He fears that an agreement to "permit mistakes" might be impossible to achieve.

At the same time, Herzberg stresses the full potential of job environmental factors. Should a firm consequently agree to give the responsibility for the reduction of these errors to lower-level workers, he feels that the way would be opened for additional benefits. It would be giving these workers a motivator

---

[7]Herzberg, *op. cit.,* pp. 171-180. Herzberg provides here a very convincing defense for the kind of reorganization he suggests.

factor, errors would be reduced as they learned to fulfill their new responsibility, and higher management would be released for more challenging endeavors.

Though following Herzberg's suggestion would surely bring about a far greater consideration of motivator-need factors, two questions arise as to how successful his model can be in providing an over-all organizational strategy for a creative, growing personnel-staff role. The first has to do with the persisting differences which exist among workers employed at any one time within a firm, whether they are a matter of fundamental characteristics which pre-exist a worker's employment in a particular job (e.g., sex, age, physical or mental handicap) or are organizationally derived (e.g., status as an operative worker, union-represented worker, scientific worker, manager).

Here, from an internal viewpoint, doubt arises as to whether or not significant individual differences can be productively dealt with to the extent that Herzberg would insist is possible with his broad restructuring. Can motivator answers for such differing workers really be found and implemented when corporate personnel departments need to justify new, far higher-risk undertakings in terms of their global economics?

The second question (and perhaps one more verifiable in practice should a business firm adopt Herzberg's model) lies in this plan's wholly internal orientation. In itself, it seems to offer little likelihood of enhancing the personnel department's capacity to reach out and provide personnel answers to the increasing external pressures *vis-à-vis* a firm's human resources. It really can offer little in the way of providing the organizational impetus necessary to fill the present gaps in the capacity of business firms to deal constructively with the needs imposed by the intense external pressures facing them, both as employers and citizens within a changing, complex urban society.

Personnel Segmentation as the Organizational Strategy. My view of the scene has led to a different design for the internal structure of the personnel-staff department. In essence, it borrows from the concept of "market segmentation,"[8] leading to the establishment of various sub-units within the personnel department—each concentrating somewhat independently upon different segments of the work force on a temporary or continuing basis. The personnel segmentation approach is intended to afford an opportunity for personnel specialists to program their staff assistance (and so to act) in terms of a definable, more homogeneous group of workers.

Decisions to use differentiated practices, tools, and standards for these formally identified subgroups of workers would be steeped in a careful examination of the particular impact of these groups upon overall productivity and worker satisfaction as well as in terms of how they are best dealt with within the specific job culture.

Through what would be tantamount to a continuing reorganization, these structural patterns and specialized staff would evolve to provide and assist in personnel activity specifically directed to segmented groups of workers distinguishable by:

1. The kind of work they do.
2. Their inclusion in a particular employee representational unit.
3. Their job requirements.
4. Social/hereditary factors of the individual worker.
5. A combination of these characteristics.

The expertise of the resulting staff specialists would become more and more a derivative of their own preparation and experience in dealing with all aspects of personnel performance for one or more of the limited

[8] An early, penetrating analysis of this view of marketing strategy can be found in Wendell R. Smith, "Product Differentiation and Market Segmentation as Alternative Marketing Strategies," *Journal of Marketing* **XXI** (1), 3-8 (July, 1956).

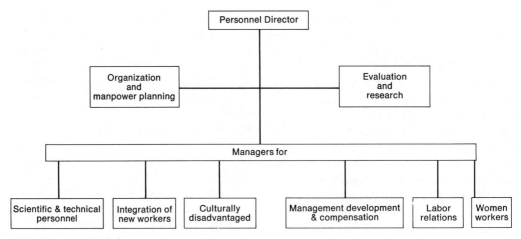

Figure 8.2

segments of workers assigned as their particular responsibility. The traditional functional specialization would no longer exist, except perhaps at the top corporate units of large-scale firms. One form which this organizational change might take is seen in Figure 8.2

This is a matter of no small significance. Can such dual structuring of the personnel-staff serve more than to help in making possible maximum treatment of individual differences of the currently employed? Or can it also provide the kinds of creative approaches necessary to attract and deal with the culturally disadvantaged, women, the physically and mentally handicapped, the increasingly mobile management and scientific workers, and other distinguishable groups on their terms? As time goes on, it may well be found that the kind of personnel performance really needed today can come about only through a carefully designed set of specialized treatments of such significant differences as these, particularly when done in terms which also stand to give effect to a greater and more specialized concern with their motivator needs.

Take, for example, the spread and growing militancy of collective bargaining. Much of the recent development has been all too little connected with problems growing out of the specific employing organization's immediate

employee relationships. Concerned only with an internal orientation, personnel activity (no matter how much it has been able to successfully deal with motivator needs) probably would not be of much help here.

In some instances, it has largely been a matter of the broader labor movement's thrust to regain its economic and liberal dominance or of the competitive maneuvering of various labor leaders. In others, the increasingly troublesome confrontations have stemmed from broader social and economic pressures which have left the unorganized far behind. Teachers, social workers, policemen, firemen, and others are thus turning to power bargaining as their most effective immediate alternative, even though it hasn't been too long ago that these very workers felt that union affiliation would be belittling. This is not to say that a more vigorous personnel effort dealing with motivator needs would not help in meeting the problems of these workers as well. Rather, it raises the question of how much more successful these attempts could be if directed to the motivator needs of these workers seen as union members.

With such a structural model, both hygiene and motivator needs would be effectively met, since the specific elements in the personnel staff's performance would be carefully focused upon dealing with the dynamic nature of more "manageable" segments. There would be greater certainty, too, of a balanced staff effort, purposefully compensating for the all-too-common one-sided view (i.e., hygiene) of present-day personnel management. Similarly, there would be an improvement of other dimensions of its responsibilities, such as meeting temporary personnel dislocations resulting from operating changes and reaching out to help resolve social and individual problems for which creative employment practices can be of meaningful help.

All this would become possible because the activity and results of each subunit would then be more precisely measurable, the need to deal with an amorphous group of workers being a thing of the past. This would be no small gain. Many personnel-staff efforts in the past have had to deal broadly and therefore in a compromising fashion with far more unimportant differences existing within the specific work culture to which they were directed.

One thing should be made clear. Some aspects of this segmentation approach already exist in the organization structure of many personnel departments. The most general, of course, is the separation of the labor-relations functions (as previously indicated, sometimes in the form of a staff department outside the personnel one) which recognizes the desirability of dealing specially with union-represented operative workers. Here, however, the organizational pattern appears to have come about more as a result of the pressures of having to deal separately with an outside group (i.e., the union) rather than from any planned approach on the part of personnel-staff management to deal specifically with this segment.

I am espousing this alternative: a carefully designed structural arrangement for the entire personnel effort which recognizes the existence of a number of distinct segments which merit and can profit from specialized programming and support, no matter how transitory the need. There would then evolve

a continuing interest in reviewing the efficacy of its current design, since the need for and significance of special consideration of particular worker segments would be seen as flowing and ebbing. And, when the particulars changed, there would be a reorganization to suit the new priorities.

Thus, far more organizational changes or at least reassignments of staff would take place, even greater than those made by firms which have vacillated in their resolution of the functional-staff and centralized-decentralized dimensions of their personnel departments. Moreover, the changes would be sought out and expected. A premium, in fact, would be placed upon more effective ways of segmenting the work force so as to serve in a specialized way those segments which appear to benefit the most from specialization.

It should also be recognized that personnel segmentation could lead to some overlapping in personnel-staff activity with more than one sub-unit dealing with a particular worker. For example, if the worker is a woman returning to active employment in a management position after raising a family, she could be the concern of those specializing in the development and utilization of women and of managers, as well as those concerned solely with new employees. However, this is really nothing new. Today, a worker is often confronted by a number of personnel-staff persons (e.g., employment, training, and benefit specialists). With personnel segmentation, however, the various specialists focusing upon a worker's progress would each be viewing him as a particular kind of worker—as older worker, as technician, as physically handicapped. The fragmentation of service which grows out of functionalism would cease to exist.

Here, then, we propose personnel segmentation as an organizational answer to the fact that pre-existing (as well as organizationally derived) differences do exist among workers and do introduce significantly different obstacles and opportunities in achieving effective personnel-staff performance. Personnel segmentation can really succeed only when it recognizes these differences and makes it realistic to deal with them in ways more certain of meeting the internal and external pressures besetting the management of human resources in larger business firms. The traditional organizational pattern of task orientation cannot so succeed, if only because it implies that workers can be managed similarly, no matter what their intrinsic qualities or their organizational roles.

Just as a seller is urged to recognize that his total market is really quite heterogeneous —made up of several or many smaller homogeneous groups of consumers—the major personnel-staff manager would recognize a number of definable subgroups among his firm's employees. He would do so by aligning his staff to specialize in learning about and serving the needs of each of the subgroups. In this way, the different sets of needs (and opportunities for inducing productivity and satisfaction) which each segment represents become more certain of being identified and met.

The personnel manager himself would thereby gain, having the ability to mount effective differentiation of programming and treatment and to reject the "total market" approach which is unsound, no matter how much of an intense interest he sustains in worker differences. With personnel segmentation, moreover, he would find the kinds of profitable opportunities for expansion of specialized personnel programming not only more readily discernible, but with a greater probability of success. Certainly, he would be better able to calculate just how well specific tools and programs would meet the needs of the smaller, more homogeneous groups.

Instead of engaging in wage and salary administration in a way roughly calculated to serve the needs of all workers, personnel segmentation would lead to specialists for particular subgroups of workers, each of whom would perform wage (or salary) administration as one of a range of concerns on behalf of a segment of workers. The risk entailed in "bending" the internal logic of a broad wage and salary administration system to the service of the needs of what are really diverse groups of workers could then be minimized, if not avoided altogether.

Differences between the worker on an assembly line and one who works a drill press, between the salesman and the scientist, between the first-level and the middle manager—all would be recognized for what they are: differences between formally distinguishable segments of workers, each of which is deserving of a different set of logic when it comes to deciding how and what to pay them. Whatever would be lost from a lack of functional specialization on the part of staff specialists performing wage and salary administration as only one of their varied concerns would be more than offset by the value of their deeper insights and relationships with the particular segment of workers assigned them. Functional specialists could also be consulted, either from the ranks of professional consultants or from the corporate personnel unit.

Personnel segmentation could thus achieve selective adaptation in personnel-staff performance with accommodations attuned to effectively deal with the pre-existing and organizationally derived differences between workers. The need to justify particular reorganizations and staff reassignments on the basis of keeping personnel performance in tune with current priorities would force out into the open just what the differences are that are being accorded special consideration and how a firm might best deal with them. There would then be far more likelihood that certain differences which are best met head-on and helped to "melt in" in the broader organizational backdrop would not be left to fester below the surface.

Assigned to deal with Negro workers, for example, a personnel-staff subgroup would be permitted to gain depth of understanding in working through the problems besetting the integration and natural utilization and development of these workers. Assigned to establish and sustain a specialized personnel-staff program with older workers, another subgroup might well design an innovative program of re-training, job re-assignment, counseling, and special recognition, which would stand a better chance of achieving the maximum utilization of this segment. Permitted such opportunity to specialize with older workers, this personnel unit would develop a more thorough understanding of such factors as the learning inadequacies, personal and family anxieties, and socializing patterns of these workers, as well as gain the base for sustaining a meaningful, unthreatening relationship with them.

BENEFITS OF SEGMENTATION

A critical look at personnel segmentation suggests that it offers much promise. Aside from those benefits discussed so far, two others deserve mention. First, effective use of personnel segmentation—just as with market segmentation—would introduce a beneficial dynamism into personnel-staff performance. It would destroy the myth of organizational stability and encourage personnel staff specialists to think periodically about the modification of their structural arrangements so as to facilitate their dealing with those worker segments of greatest import to the current targets of the firm.

If successful, a movement toward new ways of segmenting the work force would result— somewhat as a result of changing pressures and conceptions of what can be done, but also because previously segmented groups will have been successfully dealt with and their differentiating characteristic will no longer be significant (e.g., true integration of the Negro worker or the woman worker). The personnel-staff organization would thus move more and more in the direction of the

greatest need. The specialized programming and treatment of segments of the work force would be dynamically changing, each time moving on to deal with those workers felt to offer the greatest severity of consequences in terms of their problematic situation and those where the potential for achieving a "breakthrough" in personnel-staff performance is predictably the greatest.

At all times, personnel segmentation would hold out the promise of a changing organization structure aimed at the most economic use of staff resources. Too, it would afford greater control over the segments a business purposefully determines to be of greatest consequence to it, as well as to the manner in which these groups are to be managed.

Second, a personnel segmentation approach would tend to place a beneficial stress upon line management, requiring that they act to fill in the gaps and integrate the segmented activity of the personnel specialists. When it becomes a matter of the line manager having to deal with a number of personnel-staff units who seek to view his subordinates in different but integral terms (rather than concentrate upon fulfilling a separate personnel task with them), he is less likely to feel a personal threat that the personnel-staff is doing his job for him. If nothing else, he will be less able to defer to their way of performing the personnel process, since it will be more apparent that the total personnel job cannot possibly be done by a staff which concentrates upon only some of the segmented characteristics existing among his workers. Each line manager will find that all the personnel staff can do is provide him with more certain insights and staff "assists" in managing his workers *qua* worker, no matter how many organizationally segmented differences they individually reflect.

It is as if the salesman finds himself with a customer—needing to uncover which of the various segments represented by him can be most profitably cultivated, calling upon the specific product-service offerings developed for that segment, and then being sure to integrate all that he does with the total marketing effort and (most important of all) with the customer as a profitable customer. If personnel segmentation can be successful in these terms, it is possible to predict that the persisting line-staff conflict in personnel performance may become a thing of the past.

SOME DIFFICULTIES

There will, of course, be difficulties in the way of achieving personnel segmentation as the organization model for personnel-staff departments. As Herzberg emphasizes, much re-education of both line and staff practitioners will be needed. Too, the personnel manager will initially be hard-pressed to stay on top of the new pressures generated by having to deal in a unifying way with the various divisional heads reporting to him. For him, it will be a constant search for the budgetary wherewithal to plan for all the currently recognized segments of the workforce and still look ahead to improved ways of segmentation that do away with existing arrangements in a way which achieves a more dynamic balance of the total personnel-staff effort.

He must also guard against various divisions losing sight of the over-all development of the organization. On one hand, the result could be a wholly selective development and utilization of a particular segment, with little or no positive influence upon the firm's total human resource values (i.e., the marketer's "primary demand"). On the other hand, it could be that one division would so program its activity that it becomes too differentiated and is looked upon as discriminating in favor of one segment of workers to the detriment of others.

Finally, there would exist a need to guard against the kind of myopia which could lead some staff specialists to become so engrossed in working more and more intensively with the segment to which they are currently as-

signed that they would be led to preserve, rather than eliminate, irrelevant and inappropriate differences. This is what has happened in a good many situations where a sub-unit has been set up in the personnel department to deal with women workers. These efforts have led to further and further differentiation of treatment, becoming in "reality" an authentication of stereotyped beliefs about women workers rather than purposeful segmentation. The problems here remain, I might add, even after civil rights and equal-pay legislation specifically aimed at improving the employment conditions of women.

Conclusions. Historically, personnel-staff departments have been dominated by a task orientation derived from their structural arrangements and the pursuit of functional expertise on the part of their specialists. To arrest what is described as a malaise in personnel management and gain a truly decisive corporate role for this staff department, a fundamental reorganization of its operations is in order. The malaise is pinpointed by four general symptoms:

The objectives of personnel management are not being realized in a way which lives up to their promise.

Erstwhile personnel-staff tasks are being assigned outside the personnel department.

The personnel-staff field is continuing to have difficulty in attracting outstanding recruits.

Personnel departments are often being by-passed in the growing efforts of business firms to respond to the challenges of urban America.

CONCLUSIONS

Two broad-base, substantially different models are suggested for reorganizing personnel departments.

First considered was Herzberg's dual

structuring to revamp these departments into two major divisions, one for dealing with the hygiene or maintenance factors had the other for the worker's motivator needs.

My model for segmentation entails grouping personnel-staff activities in accord with their relevancy to selected classes of workers. Various sub-units would be formed on a temporary or continuing basis to concentrate upon providing and administering personnel-staff services and support in terms of roughly homogeneous workers, e.g., new workers, culturally disadvantaged workers, managers, and clerical operative workers. Each case of organization and staffing for a particular segment of workers would require justification on the basis of the potential benefit to the overall effort (e.g., resolution of a persisting problem, comparative advantage from specialized attention and programming). Often, the segmentation of personnel-staff performance would find the specialists working themselves out of one job and going on to restructure their work

to serve another group.

As in the case of any innovative organizational change, there is a need to put these models to the test of actual application. Without a serious attempt to see if they can work in practice, I can only conjecture about their prospects and limitations. Surely, the need for personnel departments to gain the organizational vitality required to meet the challenges which are facing them today is great enough to assume the risk entailed in a radical change. The alternative is almost certain to be further atrophy of personnel departments and more and more difficulty in harnessing a consistent and coordinated long-range effort in the management of a firm's human resources. The risk may be minimized by first adapting the selected model to the particulars of the existing management climate and existing competence of the staff specialists and, for the large-scale firms, experimentally introducing it in only a single divisional personnel department.